# HISTORICAL ROOTS OF THE URBAN CRISIS

CROSSCURRENTS IN AFRICAN AMERICAN HISTORY
VOL. 7
GARLAND REFERENCE LIBRARY OF SOCIAL SCIENCE
VOL. 1148

CROSSCURRENTS IN AFRICAN AMERICAN HISTORY
GRAHAM RUSSELL HODGES AND MARGARET WASHINGTON
*Series Editors*

WRITINGS ON BLACK WOMEN
OF THE DIASPORA
*History, Language, and Identity*
by Lean'tin L. Bracks

THE SLAVES OF LIBERTY
*Freedom in Amite County, Mississippi,
1820–1868*
by Dale Edwyna Smith

BLACK CONSERVATISM
*Essays in Intellectual
and Political History*
edited by Peter Eisenstadt

MOVING ON
*Black Loyalists in the
Afro-Atlantic World*
edited by John W. Puhs

AFRO-VIRGINIAN HISTORY
AND CULTURE
edited by John Saillant

UNYIELDING SPIRITS
*Black Women and Slavery in
Early Canada and Jamaica*
by Maureen G. Elgersman

HISTORICAL ROOTS OF THE
URBAN CRISIS
*African Americans in the
Industrial City, 1900–1950*
edited by Henry Louis Taylor, Jr.,
and Walter Hill

# HISTORICAL ROOTS OF THE URBAN CRISIS
## AFRICAN AMERICANS IN THE INDUSTRIAL CITY, 1900–1950

HENRY LOUIS TAYLOR, JR.
AND
WALTER HILL
*Editors*

GARLAND PUBLISHING, INC.
A MEMBER OF THE TAYLOR & FRANCIS GROUP
NEW YORK AND LONDON
2000

*E
185.86
A3355
2000*

Published in 2000 by
Garland Publishing, Inc.
A member of the Taylor & Francis Group
29 West 35th Street
New York, NY 10001

10   9   8   7   6   5   4   3   2   1

**Library of Congress Cataloging-in-Publication Data**

Historical roots of the urban crisis : Blacks in the industrial city, 1900–1950 /
Henry Louis Taylor, Jr., and Walter Hill, editors.
        p. cm. — (Crosscurrents in African American history ; v. 7) (Garland
    reference library of social science ; vol. 1148)
    Includes bibliographical references and index.
    ISBN 0-8153-2749-8 (alk. paper)
    1. Afro-Americans—Social conditions—To 1964.   2. Afro-Americans—
Economic conditions—20th century.   3. City and town life—United
States—History—20th century.   4. Industrial—Social aspects—United
States—History—20th century.   5. Community development—United
States—History—20th century.   6. Urban policy—United States—History—
20th century.   I. Taylor, Henry Louis.   II. Hill, Walter.   III. Series.
IV. Garland reference library of social science ; v. 1148.

E185.86 .A3355 1999
973'.0496073—dc21                                                     99-034344

Printed on acid-free, 250-year-life paper.
Manufactured in the United States of America

*To Carol and Cinque*

# Contents

# Series Editors' Foreword

The editors are especially pleased to publish *Historical Roots of the Urban Crisis: African Americans in the Industrial City, 1900–1950.* This excellent collection of original essays on the crucial topic of the modern black experience, edited by Henry Louis Taylor, Jr., and Walter Hill, presents work by senior and younger scholars. It depicts the blacks' struggle against racism and segregation in employment and housing, a struggle from which black workers built a potent black community and reached across the barrier of class to identify with middle-class, educated African Americans.

This mixture of analytic and contextual essays offers an array of insights and thoughtful meditations on key questions of the modern urban black experience. Taylor and Hill have collaborated wisely with other scholars to make this book important and timely. Their diligence has made the book broad in scope yet coherent in focus. *Historical Roots of the Urban Crisis* will fascinate anyone concerned about race, the city, and America's significant social experiences. The editors are proud of this collection and hope to publish more quality collections like it in the near future.

Graham Russell Hodges
Margaret Washington

# Acknowledgments

This book grew out of a desire to deepen my understanding of the relationship between the black experience in the industrial city and the contemporary urban crisis. As a historian, urban planner, and social commentator, I believe the current problems facing African Americans cannot be understood fully without deeper insights into their experiences in the industrial city. Yet, as both Kenneth L. Kusmer and Michael Katz have pointed out, sociologists, economists, geographers, and anthropologists dominate much of the current discussion of African Americans in the postindustrial city. The historical perspective is very limited, and relevant information about the past is often distorted or erroneous. Nonetheless, interdisciplinary research on the black urban experience has generated importance insights. As Kusmer points out, now the time has come to construct a *historical framework* that will provide a scaffolding for contemporary studies of the African American urban experience. Such a framework can be helpful not only to social scientists studying the urban crisis but also to planners and policy makers who are formulating and implementing strategies and plans to do something about the crisis.

With this goal in mind, I call my good friend, Walter Hill, to discuss the project with him. The idea was to conduct a study of the historical roots of the urban crisis that linked together the industrial to the postindustrial black urban experience. Walter loved the idea, and we started assembling a research team consisting of both junior and senior scholars. Methodologically, we approached this as a social science history project rather than a "simple" anthology of collected works. We wanted to produce a volume of original essays, researched and written specifically for this project. Walter and I carefully crafted a conceptual framework to guide the research and worked closely with the contributors to ensure that their chapters evolved within the context of this framework. This book is the outcome of that effort.

Many people helped with the production of *Historical Roots of the Urban Crisis: African Americans in the Industrial City, 1900–1950*. Command center for the project was the Center for Urban Studies (CENTER), School of Architecture and Planning, State University of New York at Buffalo. The CENTER sponsored the research project, and many of its staff members and graduate assistants played an important role in its production. Several deserve special mention. Vicky Dula, then Research Coordinator at the CENTER, supervised the development of a working bibliography to guide work on this project. Ms. Dula, with the assistance of Carmille Andrea West, a graduate student in Applied Public Affairs, unearthed hundreds of studies, dissertations, theses, and articles on the black experience in the industrial city. West compiled these works, along with an essay that explains both the methodology and the study's conceptual framework, into a Master's Project entitled *Blacks in the Industrial City: Historical Roots of the Contemporary Urban Problem, 1900–1950—A Working Bibliography* (January 1999).

Frida Ferrer, my administrative assistant, played an important role in keeping us linked to members of the research team and handling many day-to-day issues associated with this project. Timothy Barber compiled and performed the in-house copyedit of the final draft. Nancy Bertraux of Xavier University helped compile data on the college-educated elite and assisted with the conceptualization of this work. Lalit Goel and Jyothi Pantulu conducted extensive research on census data for the study of black residentual patterns in eighteen cities of the period from 1940 to 1950.

Finally, I wish to thank my wife, Carol, and son, Chad-Cinque, for their support and love.

Henry L. Taylor, Jr.
Buffalo, New York

# Preface

HENRY LOUIS TAYLOR, JR., AND WALTER HILL

*Historical Roots of the Urban Crisis: African Americans in the Industrial City, 1900–1950* grew out of a belief that many problems confronting blacks in postindustrial society have their origins in the industrial age. "The African American urban experience since World War II," says historian Kenneth Kusmer, "is a study of continuity as well as change. Its origins and initial direction, its emerging problems and hopeful possibilities, lay to a considerable extent in the era of industrial dominance of the first four decades of the twentieth century."[1] So, then, one key to understanding the predicament of cities, formulating effective policies, and creating initiatives to solve current problems is knowing the historical roots of the urban crisis.

The purpose of *Historical Roots of the Urban Crisis* is to explore the experience of blacks in the industrial city by examining their quest to find a good place to live, build vibrant communities, get jobs, and advance occupationally. To probe these areas, we assembled a team of eight junior and senior scholars to write original essays on select aspects of the industrial city black experience. Team members' research unfolded within a framework created by a fusion of three paradigms. The first paradigm locates the African American experience in the context of city-building and examines black life at specific moments in the industrial city, as well as across time.[2] Conceptually, the focus is on the city building process and how the changing urban environment—due to processes of territorial expansion and land-use and property development—and the forces of economic development combined with the decisions, definitions of problems, and policy formulations of urban leaders to affect the ability of African Americans to find housing, build communities, get jobs, and advance occupationally.[3] In addition, the city-building model places black community building in the context of metropolitan development and views the central city and suburban region as a single urban region, even though it was broken into various municipal areas.[4]

The second paradigm, new African American urban history, portrays blacks as an empowered people actively involved in the struggle to defeat racism, dismantle the race- and sex-segmented labor market, and restructure the race- and class-stratified residential environment. In this approach, emphasis is placed on agency, the role played by workers in the development of black communal life, class conflict, and questions of gender.[5] So the new African American urban history seeks to develop a more comprehensive, textured understanding of classes among African Americans and an understanding of how blacks, despite being fractured along the fault lines of class and gender, worked collectively to build a community.

The third paradigm, new African American labor history, examines workers in the overlapping contexts of work, culture, politics, and community and forms the last component of our conceptual model.[6] This approach emphasizes how black workers fought racism in the labor movement, functioned as members of the African American community, and battled with the college-educated elite and cultural middle class to confront the racist labor movement, shape labor policy, abolish the dual-wage system, and advance occupationally.

*Historical Roots of the Urban Crisis* is divided into two parts and includes a Prologue that introduces the book and an Epilogue that reflects on black life in the industrial city and further exposes the historical roots of the urban crisis. Part I, "Home and Community Building," consists of five chapters and explores the quest of African Americans to find a good place to live and "build community" in a rapidly changing urban environment. Conceptually, Part I examines black residential development and community building within a metropolitan context. During the industrial era, urbanization and suburbanization scattered business, industry, and people across the face of the metropolis and turned the central city and suburb into one big city, despite the municipal boundaries that fragmented it. The industrial city black community, then, consisted of neighborhoods both within the central city and those scattered throughout the suburban hinterland.[7]

The first chapter, "A Unity of Opposites: The College-Educated Elite, Black Workers, and the Community Development Process" by

Henry Louis Taylor, Jr., and Song-Ho Ha, examines the role played by the college-educated elite and cultural middle class in building the black community. Rarely is the college-educated elite viewed as an entity in itself; rather, the study of this group traditionally falls within the ranks of the cultural middle class. In this chapter, Taylor and Ha focus on the college-educated elite as an entity, while simultaneously locating it within the cultural middle class. Taylor and Ha argue that the college-educated elite and the cultural middle class played a significant role in building the black community. Its members were the preachers, teachers, doctors, lawyers, accountants, journalists, writers, scholars, social workers, and entertainers who formed the scaffolding of black institutional life. These important roles notwithstanding, tensions did exist between the college-educated elite and the cultural middle class and the working class, but these differences did not rip apart the black community. This chapter explains why.

Henry Louis Taylor, Jr., continues the exploration of black community building in Chapter 2, when he explores the interplay between black suburbanization and the planning movement. In "Creating the Metropolis in Black and White: Black Suburbanization and the Planning Movement in Cincinnati, 1900–1950," Taylor argues that planners, housing reformers, public officials, and business and civic leaders tried to use land-use regulation and city and regional planning to structure a metropolitan-wide residential environment that was stratified on the basis of housing cost and type, and race and class. However, the process of consciously building the urban metropolis was not simply one of elites imposing their ideas on the rest of society. White elites had one vision of the metropolitan region and the place of African Americans in it, and blacks had another. The ultimate shape and form of the industrial city was a reflection of the outcome of the struggle between these two competing visions.

Chapter 3, "Municipal Harmony: Cultural Pluralism, Public Recreation, and Race Relations," also emphasizes the interplay between public policy and African American community building in Cincinnati. Andrea Tuttle Kornbluh shows that public officials and civic leaders used more than land-use regulations and planning ordinances to shape the residential environment and determine the place of African Americans in it. Concerned about the ever-present danger of racial violence in a congested city, urban leaders sought to create "municipal harmony" between blacks and whites by promoting racial segregation as a strategy for establishing peaceful race relations and building the African American community. This strategy was informed by cultural pluralism, a concept that stressed the possibility of equality among cultures, but emphasized that less-developed cultural groups—such as African Americans—should be residentially segregated in order to develop their own community through programs of self-help and self-determination. Nevertheless, appreciation of the culture of all groups was an essential part of the philosophy of cultural pluralism. In Cincinnati, urban leaders used municipal recreation programs to develop an appreciation of the culture of different groups of citizens, improve race relations, and construct a sense of community. Within this framework, cultural pluralists called for the separation of racial groups in geographic space, while simultaneously celebrating their cultures. African Americans, however, did not passively accept cultural pluralism. Instead, they defined it in a way that reinforced their own notions of community—an ideal that emphasized unity, racial pride, self-help, self-determination, and group advancement. Moreover, at the same time that blacks turned inward to build their own community, they actively participated in the broader effort to build and develop Cincinnati. Over time, however, cultural pluralism gave way to the ideal of integration, and the notion of group advancement gave way to the notion of individual advancement.

African Americans in the industrial city had to fight both the enemy inside the community and outside it. Georgina Hickey, in Chapter 4, "From Auburn Avenue to Buttermilk Bottom: Class and Community Dynamics Among Atlanta's Blacks," argues that Atlanta blacks, while projecting the image of a singular and cohesive community, were fractured along the fault lines of class and gender. In this setting, middle-class African American male leadership consistently muted class divisions and intragroup tensions as a strategy for maintaining racial unity in a hostile environment. From the high ground of intraclass domination, this male leadership continually replaced the interests of African American workers with its own. "What's good for middle-class black men is good for all black people," was its credo. This ideology caused the group to minimize the concerns of black workers and to use a masculine language that marginalized African American women from across the class spectrum.

In Chapter 5, "Blacks in the Suburban and Rural Fringe," Andrew Wiese unpacks the dynamics of black suburbanization and demonstrates why the African American community was a metropolitan one. Weise says the Great Migration of the 1910s and 1920s sparked the first wave of black surbanization. By 1940, about 1.5 million African Americans were living in the suburbs. Outside the South, suburbanites accounted for approximately 15 percent of the metropolitan black population. So while most blacks settled in the central city, a critical mass moved into the suburban region, searching for a good place to live and raise a family. However, in contrast to the well-manicured suburbs of the white middle class, most early black suburbs were unplanned, unregulated, and unpretentious working-class communities.

Part II, "Work and Federal Policy," shifts the focus from African Americans finding good places to live and build communities to the Great Depression and the battle to shape New Deal and federal labor policies. This abrupt shift of emphasis mirrors the unexpected and swift transformation of black life caused by the Great Depression. The collapse of Wall Street suddenly and fundamentally changed reality for African Americans. After 1929, millions of blacks were out of work, farmers and agricultural workers were forced off their land, and black banks and financial institutions failed, losing the life savings of many African Americans in the process. Important and of great significance, the misery and suffering of African Americans is still only a part of the Great Depression story.

The Great Depression also created an opportunity for local, state, and federal leaders not only to find solutions to the problems created by the economic crisis but also to formulate a vision of postwar society, to define socioeconomic problems, to establish new normative patterns of behavior, and to establish a new framework within which black-white relations would operate for years to come. Within this context, the fight over policy issues, especially at the federal level, became a preoccupation for African Americans. Although Part II is concerned primarily with struggles at the national level, it should be stressed that the battle to shape public policy, dismantle the structures of inequality, and formulate a new society took place at both the national and local levels. During the Depression, African Americans instinctively knew they were in a fight not only to survive day-to-day miseries but also to shape the type of new society being spawned by the economic crisis.

The four chapers composing Part II focus primarily on the battle to shape federal policy at the natioanl level. In Chapter 6, "African Americans in the U.S. Economy: Federal Policy and the Transformation of Work, 1915–1945," Liesl Miller Orenic and Joe W. Trotter argue that the forces unleashed during World War I and the 1920s culminated in the growing centralization of the state under the impact of the Great Depression, the New Deal, and World War II. Such changes, they argue, included an increased recognition of organized labor, the deleterious impact of technological change, and unemployment, all of which had a profound influence on the lives of African American workers. In this chapter, Miller Orenic and Trotter provide a critical overview of the issues affecting African American workers during the industrial era by assessing the interplay of race, class, and federal labor policies during the two world wars and the Great Depression. More specifically, they analyze the treatment of federal labor policies in existing scholarship, highlight the experiences of black railroad workers as a case study, and conclude with a call for better and more systematic treatment of federal labor policies in subsequent research on urban black workers and their communities. A central thesis of their chapter is that black workers were not only affected by federal policies but played a major role in shaping them as well.

Henry Louis Taylor, Jr., Vicky Dula, and Song-Ho Ha, in Chapter 7, "The Battle Against Wage Slavery: The National Urban League, the NAACP, and the Struggle over New Deal Policies," examine the struggles of African Americans against the codification of wage slavery. A race- and sex-segmented labor market forced African American workers to take the least desirable jobs, while the best ones went to whites. Even more significant, African Americans were paid less than whites even when they did the same work and had the same qualifications. Ratification of the National Industrial Recovery Act (NIRA) by Congress and the establishment of the National Recovery Administration (NRA) to implement the act triggered a crisis for African Americans. The Wages and Hours provision of the NIRA called for the establishment of a minimum wage that could lead to the equalization of wages between black and white workers. Southern whites rushed forward to make sure this did not happen. They wanted to establish wage differentials as a permanent part of the NIRA. African Americans, however, were fearful that allowing the NRA to maintain a wage differential would lead to the codification of wage slavery. If this happened, differentials might become institutionalized and become the standard by which wages were set for African Americans. Therefore, defeating efforts to codify wage slavery became one of the highest priorities for African Americans. Moreover, the severity of the Great Depression and the dangers of institutionalizing wage slavery caused the National Urban League and the National Association for the Advancement of Colored People to prioritize economic issues and take the lead in the fight against the codification of wage slavery.

In Chapter 8, "Building Bricks without Straw: Robert C. Weaver and Negro Industrial Employment, 1934–1944," Sigmund Shipp reminds us that the fight to shape policy and offer a new vision of the emerging socioeconomic order involved both collective and individual heroics. Robert C. Weaver, an intellectual public figure, was one of the heroes of this struggle. Shipp analyzes the role played by Weaver in shaping New Deal policies and offering an alternative vision of postwar America. Shipp portrays Weaver as a researcher, policy advocate, and administrator who boldly formulated and implemented federal labor policies. Most important, he shares with us Weaver's insight into the problems facing African Americans, his fight to transform hostile agencies and bureaucrats into allies of African Americans, and his bold call for the establishment of full employment as a national policy. This profile of Weaver's activities during the Depression reveals the importance of both research and advocacy in shaping public policy and illustrates how difficult it is to dismantle the structures of inequality.

Eileen Boris, in Chapter 9, "Black Workers, Trade Unions, and Labor Standards: The Wartime FEPC," analyzes the African American struggle for fair employment during War II by untangling two interrelated themes: the place of African American workers in employment policy and labor law, and the relationship of black workers to trade unionism. Central to her story is the Fair Employment Practices Committee (FEPC) and its role in the quest to win the right to work for African Americans. In June 1941, President Franklin D. Roosevelt issued Executive Order 8802, which created the FEPC. The goal of the Fair Employment Practices Committee was to end discrimination in employment related to the war effort. Boris explores the activities of the FEPC to illuminate its limitations and to expose the problems African Americans encountered trying to make race-neutral programs address their needs.

The Epilogue concludes the book by outlining the lessons learned from the black industrial experience and by exposing the historical roots of the urban crisis.

## NOTES

1. Kenneth L. Kusmer, "African Americans in the City since World War II: From the Industrial to the Postindustrial Era," in Kenneth W. Goings and Raymond A. Mohl, eds., *The New African American Urban History* (Thousand Oaks, Calif.: Sage Publications, 1996), p. 320.

2. Theodore Hershberg, "The New Urban History: Toward an Interdisciplinary History of the City," in Theodore Hershberg, ed., *Philadelphia: Work, Space, Family, and Group Experience in the Nineteenth Century*, (Oxford:

Oxford University Press, 1981): pp. 3–35; Theodore Hershberg, Alan N. Burnstein, Eugene P. Ericksen, Stephanie W. Greenberg, and William L. Yancey, "A Tale of Three Cities: Blacks, Immigrants, and Opportunity in Philadelphia, 1850–1880, 1930, 1970," in *Philadelphia,* pp. 461–491; Amos H. Hawley, ed., *Roderick O. McKinsey on Human Ecology* (Chicago and London: The University of Chicago Press, 1968): pp. 3–32; Eric E. Lampard, "American Historians and the Study of Urbanization," *American Historical Review* 67 (Oct. 1961): pp. 49–61; Roy Lubove, "The Urbanization Process: An Approach to Historical Research," *American Institute of Planners* 33 (Jan. 1967): pp. 33–39; Sam Bass Warner, Jr., "If All the World Were Philadelphia: A Scaffolding for Urban History, 1774–1930," *American Historical Review* 74 (Oct. 1968): pp. 26–43; Henry Louis Taylor, Jr., ed., *Race and the City: Work, Community, and Protest in Cincinnati, 1820–1970* (Urbana and Chicago: University of Illinois Press, 1993).

3. A central theme of the city-building model is that building the city is a *conscious* process, which reflects the ideological perspectives of those with the power and authority to impose their views on the rest of society. Our thinking on these issues has been influenced by a range of work that grapples with the social production of urban space. It is rooted in the idea that people have *choices* in how they construct urban settlement patterns and that these choices are dictated by their ideological perspective. In essence, central city and metropolitan growth is not driven by a set of social laws that *predetermine* how settlement patterns will be formed and developed.

Susan S. Fainstein, *The City Builders: Property, Politics, and Planning in London and New York* (Oxford and Cambridge: Blackwell, 1994); David Harvey, *Consciousness and the Urban Experience: Studies in the History and Theory of Capitalist Urbanization* (Baltimore: John Hopkins University Press, 1985); Mark Gottdiener, *The Social Production of Urban Space,* 2nd ed. (Austin: University of Texas, 1994); Mark Goldman, *High Hopes: The Rise and Decline of Buffalo, New York* (Albany: State University of New York Press, 1983); Steven G. Koven, *Ideological Budgeting: The Influence of Political Philosophy on Public Policy* (Westport, Conn.: Praeger, 1988).

4. Gottdiener, *Social Production of Urban Space,* pp. vi–xv; 1–24; Jon C. Teaford, *City and Suburb: The Political Fragmentation of Metropolitan American, 1850–1970* (Baltimore: Johns Hopkins University Press, 1979).

5. Kenneth W. Goings and Raymond A. Mohl, "Toward A New African American Urban History," in Kenneth W. Goings and Raymond A. Mohl, eds., *The New African Americans Urban History* (Thousand Oaks, Calif.: Sage Publications, 1996): pp. 1–16. The chapters in this volume provide examples of various aspects of the new African American urban history. Six works, in particular, sketched the outline of the new African American urban history. Joe William

Trotter, Jr., *Black Milwaukee: The Making of an Industrial Proletariat, 1915–1945* (Urbana and Chicago: University of Illinois Press, 1985) is generally regarded as the work that moved African American urban history in a new direction with insightful analysis of the rise of the black industrial proletariat. Then in 1990, Robin D. G. Kelly, *Hammer and Hoe: Alabama Communists During the Great Depression* (Chapel Hill and London: University of North Carolina Press, 1990) not only took the study of ordinary blacks to a new level but also made popular the study of intraclass conflicts within the African American community. In 1991, Earl Lewis, *In Their Own Interests: Race, Class, and Power in Twentieth-Century Norfolk, Virginia* (Berkeley, Los Angeles and Oxford: University of California Press, 1991) added to the new urban history with his emphasis on understanding the interaction between shifts in social relations and changes at work and at home. The story of blacks during the 20th century, he says, is one of struggling for advancement in the workplace and improvements in the home sphere— primarily defined as the household, the neighborhood, and the black community (pp. 1–7). Then, in 1993, Henry Louis Taylor, Jr. ed., *Race and the City* contributed to the development of the new African American urban history by arguing that the black experience must be understood within the context of a city-building process that places the activities of African Americans in a constantly changing urban setting, where the struggle for occupational advancement and improvements in the home sphere is also a struggle between their vision of the urban metropolis and white elites (pp. xiv–xxiii, 1–28). Also in 1993, Michael B. Katz, ed., *The "Underclass" Debate: Views from History* (Princeton: Princeton University Press, 1993) demonstrated the notion that African American urban history matters in understanding the current crisis of the city. His work provided a powerful testimony to the importance of the need for "history" to inform current public policy debates. See, for example, Michael B. Katz, "The Urban Underclass as a Metaphor of Social Transformation," in *The "Underclass" Debate*, pp. 3–23; Michael B. Katz, "Reframing the 'Underclass' Debate," in *The "Underclass" Debate*, pp. 440–477.

6. In many ways, the new African American labor history is part of the new African American urban history. However, when one reflects on the critique of black labor history in 1969, it seems reasonable to view this literature as separate from the traditional study of black urban life. James A. Gross said that black labor history had "virtually the same faults and virtues" as white labor history. Written from the vantage point of organized labor, black labor history largely ignored unorganized workers, lacked a convincing theoretical framework, and showed little creativity in the location and use of new sources. Most importantly, it failed to produce comprehensive studies that integrated African-American labor history into the larger story of national development. James A. Gross, "His-

torians and the Literature of the Negro Worker," *Labor History* 10 (1969): pp. 536–46, cited in Joe William Trotter, Jr., "African American Workers: New Directors in U.S. Labor Historiography," *Labor History* 35 (Fall 1994): pp. 495–523. Trotter's work offers a comprehensive review on the literature of black labor history, and shows how work on black labor history now provides a dimension that deepens understanding of the African American urban experience.

7. Henry Louis Taylor, Jr., makes this point in Chapter 2, "Creating the Metropolis in Black and White: Black Suburbanization and the Planning Movement in Cincinnati, 1900–1950."

# Historical Roots of the Urban Crisis

# Prologue

## HENRY LOUIS TAYLOR, JR., AND WALTER HILL

The triumph of industrial capitalism transformed African American life and culture between 1900 and 1950. When the 20th century began, blacks were overwhelmingly a southern peasantry with a culture rooted in cotton production.[1] In 1900, more than 90 percent of blacks resided in the South, where about 83 percent lived and worked in rural areas [see Table I.1).[2]

By midcentury, this picture had changed. Then, about 62 percent of African Americans lived in cities, with almost one-third residing outside the South [see Table I.2). Blacks had become an urban people, dominated by the industrial proletariat and white-collar and professional service workers. In just five decades, they had metamorphosed from peasants to urbanites. The purpose of this Prologue is to provide a broad overview of the forces that spawned this social transformation and shaped African American urban life and culture in the industrial era. Such an overview will provide a scaffolding for the chapters that follow.

## THE INDUSTRIAL ERA, 1900-1950: A TIME OF CHANGE

African American urban community-building took place in one of the most complex, volatile, and difficult periods in United States history. The fifty years sandwiched between 1900 and 1950 saw the triumph of industrial capitalism, the transformation of the nation from a rural to an urban society, two world wars, great prosperity, a crippling Depression, growing involvement of the federal government in state and local affairs, recognition of organized labor and the right to collective bargaining, the

*1*

**Table I.1.**   Black Population and Its Growth Rate by Type of
             Residence, 1900–1950

| Year | Total | Growth | Urban | Growth | Rural | Growth |
|------|-------|--------|-------|--------|-------|--------|
| 1900 | 8,833,944 | N/A | 2,004,121 | N/A | 7,329,873 | N/A |
| 1910 | 9,827,763 | 11.25% | 2,689,229 | 34.18% | 7,138,534 | –2.61% |
| 1920 | 10,463,131 | 6.47% | 3,559,473 | 32.36% | 6,903,658 | –3.29% |
| 1930 | 11,891,143 | 13.65% | 5,193,913 | 45.92% | 6,697,230 | –2.99% |
| 1940 | 12,865,518 | 8.19% | 6,253,588 | 20.40% | 6,611,930 | –1.27% |
| 1950 | 15,042,286 | 16.92% | 9,392,608 | 50.20% | 5,649,678 | –14.55% |

*Source*: Bureau of the U.S. Department of Commerce, *Historical Statistics of the United States: Colonial Times to 1970*, Part I (Washington, D.C.: U.S. Government Printing Office, 1975), v. 1, pp. 12–13, Series A, 73–81.

revolution of the money mortgage system, and a reshaping of the urban environment.[3] These economic, social, and political developments radically altered the nation's occupational structure and way of life, and deeply affected African American life and culture. The changes were most visibly reflected in the spatial transformation of cities, the development of a "modern" residential environment, and modifications in the nature of work.

Urban America's face was further reshaped and restructured by the economic shift from commerce to manufacturing and the migration of people from farm to city. The rise of the city was the most conspicuous aspect of these changes. New York grew from less than 1 million inhabitants in 1860 to more than 5.5 million inhabitants in 1920. Chicago, which was a place with less than 100,000 residents in 1860, soared toward the 3 million mark in 1920.[4] Everywhere, urban centers grew. In the older eastern and midwestern cities, in the South, the trans-Mississippi, West, and the Pacific Coast, urban settlements proliferated. From Cincinnati, Cleveland, Louisville, Milwaukee, and Kansas City to Omaha, Denver, Seattle, Atlanta, and Birmingham, people flocked to cities. By 1920, the U.S. census revealed that more than 50 percent of all Americans lived in urban areas.[5]

As thousands of new residents poured into urban areas, cities not only grew, but changed structurally. New methods of transit made possible the territorial expansion of urban areas and led to a transformation of

**Table I.2.** Population of Blacks and Growth Rate by Region, 1900–1950

| Year | Northeast | Growth | North Central | Growth | West | Growth | South | Growth |
|---|---|---|---|---|---|---|---|---|
| 1900 | 8,833,944 | N/A | 2,004,121 | N/A | 7,329,873 | N/A | 7,922,969 | N/A |
| 1900 | 385,020 | N/A | 495,751 | N/A | 30,254 | N/A | | |
| 1910 | 484,176 | 25.75% | 543,498 | 9.63% | 50,662 | 67.46% | 8,749,427 | 10.43% |
| 1920 | 679,234 | 40.29% | 793,075 | 45.92% | 78,591 | 55.13% | 8,912,231 | 1.86% |
| 1930 | 1,146,985 | 68.86% | 1,262,234 | 59.16% | 120,347 | 55.13% | 9,361,577 | 5.04% |
| 1940 | 1,369,875 | 19.43% | 1,420,318 | 12.52% | 170,706 | 41.84% | 9,904,619 | 5.80% |
| 1950 | 2,018,182 | 47.33% | 2,227,876 | 56.86% | 570,821 | 234.39% | 10,225,407 | 3.24% |

*Source: Historical Statistics of the United States: Colonial Times to 1957* (Washington, D.C.: U.S. Government Printing Office, 1961), pp. 11–12, Series A, 95–122.

the city's spatial structure. Transportation lines focused on the city center, driving up land prices, creating downtown shopping districts, and bringing workers to centrally located businesses and factories. Land uses also became fragmented into industrial, commercial, residential, and recreational zones. Simultaneously, new transportation lines opened up the hinterland to settlement, and factories, businesses, and people poured across the suburban countryside.[6]

The factory led the way in this massive development.[7] In 1915, Graham Romeyn Taylor noted that "huge industrial plants are uprooting themselves bodily from the cities. With households, small stores, saloons, lodges, churches, schools clinging to them like living tendrils, they set themselves down ten miles away in the open."[8] Blue-collar and white-collar workers, African Americans and whites, the middle and upper classes all participated in the suburbanization movement.[9] As early as 1920, the rate of suburban population growth exceeded that of the central city.[10] This process of urban growth and residential development fused together the central city and suburb, and transformed them into *one big city,* although municipal boundaries remained.[11] By the end of this period, the automobile, truck, and bus had begun to have an impact, both intensifying some of the earlier patterns of land-use and property development, while simultaneously creating new ones.[12]

The industrial city did not, however, grow in an unconscious, random, and haphazard manner. Rather, city-building was a conscious process, guided through city and regional planning by an urban elite who sought to impose their vision of the metropolis onto the rest of society.[13] These urban leaders believed that the secret to building a modern urban metropolis was the construction of a residential environment that stratified neighborhoods on the basis of home ownership and the detached single-family dwelling, housing cost and type, and class homogeneity.[14] Of these factors, home ownership, more than any other, spawned the class-stratified residential environment and altered the social geography of the industrial city. Home ownership and the detached single-family dwelling unit transformed neighborhoods into defended territories, where residents sought to keep out people and forms of land use that threatened property values. "Protecting" the home investment became an essential component of residential development. In this setting, an "invasion" of neighborhoods by unwanted groups was synonymous to a Declaration of War.[15]

Prior to 1933, home buying was a risky business. Institutions required large down payments, charged high interest rates, and demanded the repayment of loans within a short period of time, typically from two to five years. So when a family used its savings to purchase a house, an enormous economic investment was being made in the dwelling. This investment was risky because rising or falling property values determined the home buyer's fate. Because few people could pay off their mortgage within two to five years, most counted on having it renewed again and again. However, mortgage renewal was not automatic. If a lending company believed that neighborhood conditions were declining and that housing values were depreciating, it might not renew the mortgage, and the home buyer could lose his or her investment. For these reasons, protecting neighborhoods from "invasion" by people who might jeopardize the home investment became a driving force behind residential development after 1920. To help "keep out" unwanted residents, protect owner-dominated neighborhoods, and to promote the idea that home ownership was a "good" investment, city leaders increasingly turned to land-use regulation—zoning laws, building codes, and subdivision regulations—and city planning. This process of commodification transformed the residential development process and made home buying an investment decision in which profit-making was the dominant variable.

This shift from a renter- to an owner-dominated residential environment had been underway since the 1910s. However, it took the Great Depression to trigger the construction of a policy framework that made possible mass home ownership. During this period, the federal government initiated a series of programs that revolutionized the money mortgage system, reshaped the residential housing market, and stimulated the postwar suburbanization of the metropolitan region. Three keys were responsible for this monumental change in the residential structure of the urban metropolis. The first involved institutionalizing the self-amortizing mortgage (which combined interest and principal) into a series of uniform payments over time. Now, instead of having to repay a mortgage in two to five years, the home buyer could pay it off in twenty to thirty years.[16] Second, the Home Owners Loan Corporation, which came into being in 1933, developed a system of classifying neighborhoods by condition and quality of housing.[17] This classification system was used to guide the investment decisions of underwriters. Third, the Federal Housing Administration and the Veterans Administration, made millions of dollars available to prospective home buyers and became the driving forces behind the suburbanization movement of the postwar era. Thus, population growth combined with changes in public policy to commodify the home sphere and transform the industrial city residential-development process.

If population growth spawned dramatic changes in urban life during this period, so too did the emergence of the industrial proletariat and the rise of white-collar workers. In the late 19th and early 20th centuries, manufacturing replaced agriculture and economic growth and development.[18] Concurrently, the industrial proletariat became the single most important occupational class in the United States and a powerful source of change in U.S. society.[19]

Although the industrial proletariat dominated this era, rise of white-collar workers was a significant story that foretold of things to come. In 1936, Dr. Alba Edwards, a statistician for occupations in the Federal Bureau of the Census and head of the bureau's work on occupation statistics, observed that the nation's work force was shifting away from "heavy, arduous, unskilled manual labor" toward more highly skilled work that required education and training.[20] This shift was reflected in three interrelated ways. First, the service sector became the primary generator of jobs and opportunities. In fact, as early as 1920, the service sector began to supplant manufacturing as the engine of job growth in the United States.[21] By midcentury, more than 58 percent of all workers held service jobs, which included occupations in transportation, communications, retail and wholesale trade, professional services, domestic and personal services, and clerical pursuits.[22] Second, education became an increasingly important requirement for accessing the nation's opportunity structure. For example, only 27,410 Americans obtained a college degree in the year 1900. Fifty years later, in 1950, 432,058 people had bachelor's degrees conferred upon graduation. Third, the American opportunity structure was increasingly shaped by white-collar work and professional service, which broadly defined includes not only clerical workers but also those workers in professional service and proprietors, managers, and officials. The industrial city, then, was a complex, volatile, and ever-changing urban environment peopled by residents who were integrated into an increasingly complex class structure. This was the complicated and uncertain urban setting in which African Americans built their communities, searched for jobs and opportunities, and tried to advance occupationally.

## BLACK SETTLEMENT PATTERNS, SOCIAL CLASS, AND COMMUNITY FORMATION

Blacks poured into urban centers between 1900 and 1950 (see Table I.1). Declining opportunities in the rural countryside combined with growing opportunities in the cities to provide an endless stream of migrants to the city. This meant that black urban communities in every region of the country were continually infused with energetic new residents who were filled with enthusiasm and hope (see Table I.2). Thus the industrial city black community was built by an animated, ebullient and optimistic people. The words of Robert Flowers, a black migrant from Alabama who came to Cincinnati in the 1920s, captured the spirit of most African Americans migrants when he said:

> I was excited and overjoyed when I decided to come to Cincinnati. I was under the impression, from what I had heard, that it had better wages and jobs. In other words, you could all around live better. That was my motto when I left Alabama to come here. My motto was that I was coming here to do better, live better, and be truthful with myself. And that's exactly what I set out to do.[23]

The movement of African Americans from the farm to the city led to a social transformation of the black urban community. Prior to 1900, racism and the color line caused most urban blacks to be employed as porters, cooks, waiters, servants, domestics, janitors, and common laborers.[24] Black industrial workers were almost nonexistent and so, too, were black white-collar and professional service workers. Manufacturing jobs were reserved for whites, and strike-breaking was the only way blacks could get into such occupations. So when labor disputes occurred, employers often imported blacks to break strikes and weaken labor organization. Moreover, the small black urban population could not support a large white-collar and professional service class. Accordingly, its numbers remained small.[25]

World War I produced changes in the geographic and occupational distribution of African Americans. It not only accelerated the urbanization of blacks, but offered them a chance to enter the basic industries in large numbers, especially in the North. Tens of thousands of blacks found employment in iron and steel manufacturing, meat-packing, shipbuilding, automobile factories, and other associated industries.[26] Although concentrated in low-paying, hot, dirty, and heavy jobs, this proletarianization of black workers represented a step upward to factory work, from low-level work as farm laborers and sharecroppers, nonfactory common laborers, domestics, and personal servants.[27] The growth and development of the industrial city black community combined with residential segregation to create a demand for schools, churches, banks, newspapers, taverns, hospitals, law offices, and other social and cultural institutions. This demand triggered the growth of a white-collar and professional class rooted in the internal development of the black community.

Urban blacks had their community's class structure radically altered by these socioeconomic developments. Prior to 1900, only an embryonic black class-structure existed. It consisted primarily of unskilled laborers and skilled artisans, along with a handful of professionals and entrepreneurs. Steady migration to the industrial city between 1900 and 1950 led to much greater social and economic differentiation in the black community. While most blacks continued to work as porters, cooks, servants, waiters, and nonfactory common laborers, the black population was swelled by the emergence of black industrial workers and a multifaceted class of white collar/professional service workers. Within this context, class distinctions became more pronounced and intraclass tensions and conflicts grew. Yet the African American community did not sunder. Blacks stressed unity, and throughout the period, confrontation with hostile, virulent racism led to a muting of class differences. Maintaining solidarity and projecting the image of a singular, unified community was a central part of the strategy of fighting against racism.[28] At the same time, however, significant class differences existed between the cultural middle-class and black workers. Later, we sill discuss this in greater detail.

## THE INDUSTRIAL CITY AFRICAN AMERICAN RESIDENTIAL STRUCTURE

The migration of thousands of newcomers to the city radically altered the pre-industrial black residential structure. Before 1900, blacks and whites lived in racially mixed neighborhoods. Although social interaction was limited, blacks and whites nevertheless shared residential space. However, black and white migration to the industrial city combined with innovations in urban transportation to change this residential pattern.[29]

Most scholars argue that the ghetto became the dominant type of residential environment during this period. They suggest that most African Americans lived in a single, geographically compact neighborhood, and they downplay the importance of those residential enclaves located beyond ghetto walls.[30] Recent scholarship, however, suggests that the black residential environment was more complex than this simple picture.[31] To gain insight into the residential structure, we studied black settlement patterns between 1940 and 1950 in eighteen cities: Birmingham, Baltimore, Cincinnati, Cleveland, Detroit, Hartford, Houston, Louisville, Memphis, Milwaukee, Nashville, New Orleans, New York City, Philadelphia, Pittsburgh, San Francisco, St. Louis, and Washington, D.C.[32]

The findings suggests that there were two main types of black residential settlements. The first is the Ghetto model. In this model, the black community consisted of a large ghetto where most blacks lived, and several smaller neighborhoods that were dispersed throughout the central city and metropolitan region. For example, in 1940 about 70 percent of black Cincinnati residents lived in the West Side ghetto, while the remaining blacks lived in roughly ten other neighborhoods, which were scattered across the central city and suburban region.[33] Cities such as Buffalo, Chicago, Dayton, Detroit, Milwaukee, and New York City are also illustrative of this model. Here, the black community is monocentric, and the ghetto serves as its cultural and institutional center. This model of the black residential structure dominated the urban landscape in Northern cities.[34]

The Neighborhood Dispersal model exemplifies the second type of black residential structure. In this model, there were several large neighborhoods located in different parts of the central city and suburban region, and the black community was polycentric, without a discernible center or noteworthy core. While this model is more prominent in Southern cities such as Charleston, Knoxville, Nashville, Louisville, and New Orleans and in the western city of San Francisco, it can also be found in some Northern cities, such as Philadelphia.[35]

In both models, outside the ghetto and major neighborhoods were a number of microresidential clusters scattered throughout the central city and suburban region. For example, in the eighteen cities we studied, including Detroit, Baltimore, Memphis, Nashville, and Birmingham, many census tracts contained 14, 35, 45, 56, 61, and 100 blacks. This suggests that the settlement pattern of industrial city blacks consisted of the majority of blacks living in one or more large neighborhoods, with the remainder residing in smaller neighborhoods and microresidential clusters scattered throughout the central city and suburban region. So although residential segregation was a defining characteristic of the period, blacks continued to live near whites and—even in areas where blacks were heavily concentrated—a surprising number of whites could still be found. Lastly, although dispersed in geographic space, African Americans were nevertheless linked together by a common culture, set of experiences, and the need to fight against racism.[36]

The industrial city evolved during the epoch of suburban ascendancy.[37] From the 1910s onward, the suburbs grew faster than the central city, although most metropolitan residents continued to reside in the city until after 1960.[38] Decentralization was the driving force behind urban development. People were moving to neighborhoods located on the outer edge of the central city and in the suburban region. Most of those decentralizing were whites, who were starting their long trek out of the central city. Blacks, however, were living urban history in reverse. Although a small, but critical mass of African Americans moved to the outer edge of the central city and into suburban neighborhoods, the great majority moved into the older sections of the central city.[39] Dispersal, then, characterized the white settlement pattern, while concentration and dispersal characterized the black settlement pattern.[40]

The differing settlement patterns between blacks and whites represented a gradual but significant shift in the social geography of cities. Reconstructing the social geography of cities was not a conflict-free process: Several factors converged to make this a volatile and explosive process. Although growing numbers of whites moved into the suburban region from 1920 onward, most continued to live in close proximity to blacks in central city neighborhoods.[41] So whites built a "wall" of housing discrimination to keep blacks out of their neighborhoods, leading to a severe housing shortage in the African American community.[42] However, this wall weakened under the pressure of black population growth until African Americans broke through it and started moving into white residential areas.[43] For instance, between 1930 and 1950, the black population of Detroit grew by 180,440, or by more than 150 percent. Simultaneously, black Cincinnati increased by 30,378 residents, or about 64 percent.[44] In every section of the United States, the black urban community grew.[45] The black cultural middle class led the movement into white neighborhoods. During the 1940s and 1950s, their incomes increased, which gave them the fiscal means to purchase or rent housing in white neighborhoods.[46]

White Americans considered the movement of African Americans into their neighborhoods an "invasion" and "declaration of war." The policies of the Home Owners Loan Corporation (HOLC) and the Federal Housing Administration (FHA) contributed to this viewpoint. The HOLC, as previously mentioned, developed a classification system to guide the investment decision of underwriters. This classification scheme literally fragmented the metropolis into a series of neighborhoods that were *likely* and *less likely* mortgage investment locations. Within this context, black neighborhoods were typically coded red, the lowest HOLC rating, regardless of the conditions in the community. This classification system not only devalued black homes but also the homes of whites living in or near black areas. From a white perspective, then, a black presence in their neighborhoods threatened their home investment.[47] Hence, they wanted to keep African Americans out of their neighborhoods, by any means necessary.

These developments intensified the struggles between blacks and whites over residential space and made racial conflict and violence a recurrent theme in the industrial city. This is a major reason why urban leaders worked so hard to advance municipal harmony through the promotion of cultural pluralism, appreciation of the cultures of other groups, and segregated patterns of living.[48]

## COMMUNITY BUILDING

Black America was not a monolith. It was divided along the fault lines of class and gender. Yet these divisions did not break the iron chains of unity. The interplay among racial hostility, strategies of black community building, and the role of the cultural middle class in community-building kept the black community united, despite many differences. In the industrial city, African Americans faced barriers in terms of where they could live, work, and use institutional, social, cultural, educational, health, and recreational services. So they turned inward and concentrated on building their own community. Within this context, as the black urban community continually expanded in the segregated industrial city, it needed a range of goods and services that white society did not provide. This is where the black cultural middle class, especially the college-educated elite, came in. This class consisted of professional service workers, including preachers, teachers, doctors, lawyers, dentists, nurses, accountants, and the like. The black cultural middle class, then, was a service class, whose existence depended on its ability to provide services to the African American working class.[49]

This service role gave the middle class an elite status in the community and allowed it to play a critical role in building black institutions and organizations. For example, a reorientation of black entrepreneurial activities from a white to a black, mostly working class, clientele led to the development of barbershops, beauty salons, restaurants, dance halls, hotels, newspapers, funeral homes, and other establishments that anchored black communal life. Preachers, teachers, and professors helped build black churches, schools, and colleges, three of the most important institutions in the African American community. Black social workers also played a key role in helping African Americans adjust to the urban environment by delivering critical urban services; lawyers helped African Americans negotiate the tricky terrain of a racist legal system; and nurses, doctors, dentists, and pharmacists brought desperately needed health services to African American workers and other members of the community.[50]

African American entertainers also played a key role in black community development. Black singers sang the blues and musicians played jazz in black bars and nightclubs; actors, actresses, and dancers brought black ethos and pathos to life. Meanwhile writers, historians, and social scientists chronicled the black experience and used their scholarship as a weapon against racism. The cultural middle class often headed black protest organizations, while black intellectuals such as Charles S. Johnson, John P. Davis, and Robert C. Weaver made research an indispensable tool in the effort to shape policy and dismantle the structures of inequality.[51] In addition, the black press facilitated the cross-class and cultural integration of the community and linked it together by reporting on day-to-day happenings inside the African American community.[52] It is important to understand, then, that the ghetto was not simply a place where one lived. It was a community, a refuge, and a retreat from the hostilities, indignities, and weariness of interacting in the racist white world. [53]

The struggle to secure services and fight racism formed a social glue of mutual need that held African Americans together despite divisions along class and gender lines. The middle class, much to its chagrin, offered no services that white society needed or wanted. So this strata lived in the black community and serviced a mostly black clientele. It should be emphasized, however, that the cultural middle class always attempted to separate themselves from workers in residential space.[54] Black workers, on the other hand, were an integral part of the *national* (that is, black *and* white) economy, but discrimination and racial residential segregation caused them to rely on the services offered by the cultural middle class. This bond of mutuality, operating in the context of a racist and overtly hostile white society, formed the basis for community building and unity within the African American community.[55]

Racial solidarity also had a retrogressive trend. Behind the image of a singular and cohesive community could be found class and gender divisions. Ideology, lifestyle, and the nature of its work set the cultural middle class apart from black workers. The major problem was that middle-class black leadership often placed its interests above the interests of working-class blacks. That strata was guilty of thinking, "What's good for the cultural middle class is also good for the African American working class." This muting of class differences spawned a myth of racial homogeneity and allowed the middle class to continually co-opt and divert black working-class issues.[56]

Even so, in the years between 1900 and 1930, African Americans built vibrant urban communities that were continually infused with hopeful and energetic African American men and women from the countryside. These rural migrants structured institutions and organizations led by the working class and cultural middle class. African Americans also built protest organizations, fought for inclusion in the organized-labor movement, and engaged in endless daily struggles on the bus, streetcars, and at the workplace, while black intellectuals wrote probing analyses of their plight.[57] So when the Great Depression hit blacks with sledgehammer force, as a community, they were ready and prepared to meet the challenges of the new period.

## BLACKS, FEDERAL LABOR POLICY, AND THE NEW DEAL

The Great Depression hurt all Americans, but struck African Americans the hardest.[58] In the segmented labor market, the floor of occupational opportunity for white workers was the ceiling for black workers.[59] Not only this, but blacks were often paid less than whites even when they had the same qualifications and did the same work.[60] Equal pay for equal work did not apply in the segmented labor market. Historically, labor unions tried to keep blacks outside the ranks of organized labor and they helped to maintain the dual labor system.[61] Racism united bosses and white workers when it came to African American workers. So in an environment dominated by racist white workers, employers, and local and state government bureaucrats, African American workers forged a strategy to transform the federal government into an ally. Experience had taught African Americans that federal labor policy matters.[62] Enforcement issues aside, the right policy created circumstances that facilitated their advancement and constructed a venue for filing grievances and demanding the redress of wrongs.

Before the Great Depression, black workers fought to shape labor policies as a strategy for protecting their own interests and making advances. For example, Charles Wesley discussed the impact of federal labor policy on black workers in the shipbuilding industry. During World War I, when the U.S. Shipping Board took charge of the shipping industry, he noted that the number of black workers in the industry increased dramatically, but declined just as dramatically in the postwar years when federal control ended. In addition, African Americans in the railroad industry continually informed the federal government and other organizations—such as the Colored Trainmen of America and the Interstate Order of Colored Locomotive Firemen—that black workers, with their help, could win labor concessions from racist owners and workers. Consequently, believing that advancements could be won when the federal government sided with them, African Americans' struggle to shape federal labor policy and structure progressive linkages with the federal government was a common theme throughout the 1910s and 1920s.[63]

This tradition was carried forward into the Great Depression. As the Great Depression drastically slowed business as usual in the United States, it forced people not only to engage in a fight for day-to-day survival but also to think about the type of society they wanted to build in the post-Depression years. Thus, the Depression was a time when leaders, policymakers, and ordinary citizens fought for their vision of the type of society that should rise from the rubble of economic disaster.[64]

Viewed from this perspective, every New Deal policy was simultaneously a measure to address immediate economic problems and a policy framework to shape the future. Consequently, the battle over shaping federal policy during the New Deal era was also a fight over shaping public policy in the post-Depression/war era. It was a battle for both survival in the present and survival in the future. Take, for example, the fight against the codification of wage differentials. This was not simply a fight for minimum wages, but a struggle to keep the United States from using wage differentials between blacks and whites as the "legal" normative standard for establishing wage levels for African Americans.[65] Southern whites believed their economy was based on such differentials and fought to make wage differentials part of the National Recovery Act. On the national level, the National Association for the Advancement of Colored People (NAACP) and the National Urban League took the lead in this important struggle. This represented a new focal point in the activities of these two organizations. In particular, critics had urged the NAACP to take an active interest in the economic conditions facing blacks or disband.[66] Likewise, the Urban League historically had focused on economic conditions but rarely fought actively on the political front. Now, however, it stepped forward to join the fight against wage differentials.[67]

Joining the NAACP and the National Urban League in this fight was the organizational efforts of a new group formed solely to lobby Congress and the Roosevelt administration on behalf of blacks. Two Harvard-educated blacks, John P. Davis, a lawyer, and Robert C. Weaver, an economist, founded the Joint Committee on National Recovery in the summer of 1933. The Joint Committee became a federated group and eventually twenty-one organizations affiliated with it.[68] The work of the

Joint Committee was crucial to the defeat of the southern effort to codify wage slavery. Members of the committee attended more than a hundred hearings on NRA codes, examined most government publications, conducted extensive research, pointed out sections that adversely affected blacks, and led the agitation that won Southern support for the cause and convinced the government not to sanction wage differentials.[69] The idea of codifying wage slavery and making wage differentials between blacks and whites the normative standard for establishing the wage paid to African Americans had been defeated.

Another example of the fight to survive in the present while simultaneously shaping the future of the United States was found in the struggle that culminated in the issuance of Executive Order 8802, which created the Fair Employment Practices Committee, and the effort to have the committee continue its operations after the war. The battle against discrimination in employment was central to the struggle of African Americans. Robert C. Weaver put the issue forward bluntly, when he said:

> In place of slavery we have substituted a color occupational system. That system perpetuates the concept of the Negro as an inferior being and establishes institutions to assure his inferior status. It serves to conceal the basic nature of the economic problems and covers them with color situations. Whenever necessary or national policy dictates modifications in the color occupational patterns, the resulting changes are sure to be opposed violently by those who have a real or assumed vested interest in maintaining the color line.[70]

Whites often resorted to simple racism to maintain the color occupational system. Through a discriminatory process of hiring, making job assignments, and promoting employees blacks were restricted to the worst jobs in business and industry. The basic principal was this: clean, light, well-paid jobs for whites and dirty, strenuous, lower-paid jobs for blacks. However, the main method of reinforcing the color occupational system was to concentrate black workers in the most obsolete and technologically backward jobs in the labor market. This meant as business and industry modernized, the jobs they held would be eliminated. Technological innovation, then, played a big role in displacing blacks and keeping them perpetually locked in the labor market's basement.

Black scholars and progressive whites were aware of the long-term dangers of technological displacement and realized that African Americans needed the freedom to acquire jobs with growth potential. For example, writing in 1931, Alba Edwards, head of the census of occupations, said, "It seems quite probable that the machine will gradually take over the work now being done by unskilled Negro workers. Should the further mechanization of industry largely displace the Negroes in their present occupations, what will become of them? Evidently, a large proportion of them must advance to higher occupations, take over the unskilled work being done by white workers, or else be without work." Several years later, in 1936, he suggested that the displacement of the black worker might lead to the development of a permanent underclass among African Americans:

> Is there a real danger that in future years there will be large numbers of unemployed Negro workers and that these and their dependents will largely comprise the permanently unemployed class. . . . That a century after a war was fought largely to free the Negro slaves, the descendants of the slave owners, along with white persons, will be working to support on a permanent dole larger numbers of the descendants of the former slaves?[71]

The task of the FEPC was to tear down the walls of employment discrimination so that blacks could "advance to high occupations" and avoid becoming members of a "permanently unemployed class." Although never given the coercive powers to be effective, the FEPC did spur militancy among black workers and make employment discrimination a cause célèbre among African Americans. Likewise, the fight for full employment represented a major effort to dismantle the segmented labor market and to keep blacks from becoming part of a permanent underclass. Robert Weaver and others, for example, knew that the twin dangers of racism and the mechanization of industry could lead to the permanent displacement of black workers.[72] The struggle for "full employment" was designed to avoid this possibility. The idea was to make the federal government responsible for generating public sector jobs when private sector ones were not available. This effort failed. When the bill finally cleared the House, it was but a frail shadow of the policy Weaver had supported. The battle against employment discrimination and the fight for full employment had been lost.

As the U.S. economy intensified its shift from an industrial to a service base, blacks remained extremely vulnerable to the economic shift. Consequently, when World War II ended, and the postwar economic restructuring commenced, blacks were in deep trouble. In retrospect, then, the 1968 report in the *Monthly Labor Review* should not be surprising:

Negroes have faced a more serious unemployment problem than white workers throughout the postwar period; the jobless rate for Negro workers has remained about twice that of white men and women since the early 1950s. This ratio persists at each level of educational attainment, with the differential even greater among workers with more schooling than among those with a minimal level of education.

## NOTES

1. Lawrence W. Levine, *Black Culture and Black Consciousness: Afro-American Folk Thought from Slavery to Freedom* (Oxford: Oxford University Press, 1977). See, for example, the section on the rise of secular music, pp. 190–297.

2. Raymond A. Mohl, "Part II: The Industrial City, Introduction," in Raymond A. Mohl, ed., *The Making of Urban America* (Wilmington, Del.: Scholarly Resources Books, 1984), p. 71.

3. Steve Fraser and Gary Gerstle, *The Rise and Fall of the New Deal Order, 1930-1980* (Princeton: Princeton University Press, 1989), provides a good overview of the philosophical and political issues driving the policy battles of the New Deal and show how these ways of defining and interpreting reality transitioned into the postindustrial era (pp. ix–xxv).

4. Raymond A. Mohl, "Part II: Introduction," in Raymond A. Mohl, ed., *The Making of Urban America* (Wilmington, Del.: Scholarly Resources Books, 1988), p. 71.

5. Mohl, "Part II: Introduction," p. 71.

6. Mohl, "Part II: Introduction," p. 73.

7. Richard Harris, *Unplanned Suburbs: Toronto's American Tragedy, 1900 to 1950* (Baltimore and London: Johns Hopkins University Press, 1996), pp. 51–85.

8. A number of contemporaries noted that newer industries did not remain at, or near, the city center. The most influential of these was Graham Taylor. His overview, published in a series of articles for the *Survey* and then *Satellite Cities*, argued that industrial decentralization could be traced back to the 1880s. Graham R. Taylor, *Satellite Cities: A Study of Industrial Suburbs* (New York and London: D. Appleton and Company, 1915), p. 1. See also Harris, *Unplanned Suburbs*, p. 50–53. Harris has done the most detailed work on documenting the role of the industrial decentralization as the driving force behind suburbanization.

9. Andrew Wiese, "The Other Suburbanites: African American Suburbanization in the North before 1950," *The Journal of American History* 4 (March 1999): 1495–1524.

10. Jon C. Teaford, *City and Suburb: The Political Fragmentation of Metropolitan America, 1850–1970* (Baltimore and London: The Johns Hopkins University Press, 1979), pp. 76–104.

11. Chapter 3, Henry Louis Taylor, Jr., "Creating the Metropolis in Black and White: Black Suburbanization and the Planning Movement in Cincinnati, 1900 to 1950."

12. Mohl, "Part II: Introduction," p. 73.

13. Richard E. Fogleson, *Planning the Capitalist City: The Colonial Era to the 1920s* (Princeton: Princeton University Press, 1986), pp. 3–27, 199–232; Patricia Burgess, *Planning for the Private Interests: Land Use Controls and Residential Patterns in Columbus, Ohio, 1900–1970* (Columbus: Ohio State University Press, 1994), pp. 1–10, 29–58, 59–101; Mansel G. Blackford, *The Lost Dream: Businessmen and City Planning on the Pacific Coast, 1890-1920* (Columbus: Ohio State University Press, 1993), pp. 1–11, 151–159; Robert B. Fairbanks, *Making Better Citizens: Housing Reform and the Community Development Strategy in Cincinnati, 1890–1960* (Urbana and Chicago: University of Illinois Press, 1988). pp. 1–11, 151–178.

14. Henry Louis Taylor, Jr., "City Building, Public Policy, the Rise of the Industrial City, and Black Ghetto-Slum Formation in Cincinnati, 1850–1940," in Henry Louis Taylor, Jr., *Race and the City: Work, Community, and Protest in Cincinnati, 1820–1970* (Urbana and Chicago: University of Illinois Press, 1993), pp. 156–192; Thomas J. Sugrue, *The Origins of the Urban Crisis: Race and Inequality in Postwar Detroit* (Princeton: Princeton University Press, 1996), pp. 179–207, 209–229.

15. Sugrue, *Origins of the Urban Crisis,* pp. 231–258; Taylor, *Race and the City,* pp. 167–178.

16. Douglas S. Massey and Nancy A. Denton, *American Apartheid: Segregation and the Making of the Underclass* (Cambridge and London: Harvard University Press, 1993), pp. 51–52.

17. Massey and Denton, *American Apartheid,* pp. 52–53.

18. Jeremy Atack and Peter Passell, *A New Economic View of American History: From Colonial Times to 1940,* 2nd ed. (New York: W.W. Norton and Company, 1994), pp. 457–492; Alba M. Edwards, "Composition of the Nation's Labor Force," *Annals of the American Academy of Political and Social Science,* 184 (March 1936): 10–20.

19. David Montgomery, *The Fall of the House of Labor* (Cambridge: Cambridge University Press, 1987), pp. 370–410; Lizbeth Cohen, *Making a New Deal: Industrial Workers in Chicago, 1919–1939* (Cambridge: Cambridge University Press, 1990), pp. 291–360; Joe William Trotter, Jr., *Black Milwaukee: The*

*Making of an Industrial Proletariat, 1915–1945* (Urbana and Chicago: University of Chicago Press, 1985), pp. 196–241.

20. Edwards, "Composition of the Nation's Labor Force," p. 20; Edwards, "The White-Collar Workers," *Monthly Labor Review* 38(3) (March 1934): pp. 501–505. Edwards stressed the problems of classifying white-collar workers. In his 1934 article, he primarily emphasized clerical and support workers. However, in his 1936 article he talked more openly about the issues involved in classifying white-collar workers. Within this framework, he makes two points. First, he says that the trend is plainly away from production and toward distribution and service. Within a *distribution and service category* he included "pursuits" in transportation, communication, and trade; service pursuits; clerical pursuits; public service; professional service; and domestic and personal service. Moreover, to give a better sense of the meaning of these changes, he then talked about the labor force in terms of occupations that form *large social-economic groups.* The distribution/service group was a broad category that included professional persons; proprietors, managers, and officials; and clerks and kindred workers (pp. 13–15). While it is easy to quibble with Edwards over his classification, the point he seeks to make cannot be refuted. During the first half of the 20th century, manufacturing triggered the explosive growth of white-collar occupations, occupations that eventually surpassed jobs in manufacturing. In other words, although the 1900 to 1950 period carried the manufacturing stamp, the period's "hidden story" was about the dramatic increase in white-collar occupations and the growing influence of the middle class.

21. Jeremy Atack and Peter Passell, *A New Economic View of American History: From Colonial Times to 1940* (New York and London: W.W. Norton and Company, 1994, 2d ed.), pp. 457–458. Also during the period, the tremendous growth of the labor force prompted the Census Bureau to change the way it operated. Most important, the Bureau changed the title of the census report on the workforce from *Occupations* to *The Labor Force.* The Bureau was interested in describing the makeup of the United States labor force, not how people, as individuals, were employed. Muryo Anderson Conk, *The United States Census and Labor Force Change: A History of Occupation Statistics, 1870–1940,* (Ann Arbor, Mich.: UMI Research Press, 1978), p. 24.

22. Alba M. Edwards, "Composition of the Nation's Labor Force," *Annals of the American Academy of Political and Social Science*, 184 (March 1936): 10–20. Edwards was a Ph.D. and statistician for occupations in the Federal Bureau of Census, Washington, D.C. Significantly, he headed the Census Bureau's work on occupation statistics. More than any person in the nation, Edwards understood the dynamics of occupational change during the first half of the 20th century.

23. Henry Louis Taylor, Jr., *From Ghetto to Suburb: City Building and the Formation of a Black Town*, Center for Urban Studies, SUNY at Buffalo, p. 139.

24. Robert C. Weaver, *Negro Labor: A National Problem* (New York: Harcourt, Brace and Company, 1946) p. 6.

25. Trotter, *Black Milwaukee,* p. 28–33; Nancy Bertraux, "Structural Economic Change and Occupational Decline Among Black Workers in Nineteenth-Century Cincinnati," in Henry Louis Taylor, Jr., ed., *Race and the City: Work, Community, and Protest in Cincinnati, 1820–1970* (Urbana and Chicago: University of Illinois Press, 1993), pp. 126–155; Kenneth L. Kusmer, *A Ghetto Takes Shape: Black Cleveland, 1870–1930* (Urbana and Chicago: University of Illinois Press, 1976), pp. 65–90, 91–112; Bureau of the Census, *Negro in the United States* (Washington, D.C.: U.S. Department of Commerce, 1914), pp. 32–35.

26. Robert C. Weaver, *Negro Labor: A National Problem* (New York: Harcourt, Brace and Company, 1946), pp. 3–15; Joe William Trotter, Jr., *Black Milwaukee: The Making of an Industrial Proletariat, 1915–45* (Urbana and Chicago: University of Illinois Press, 1985), pp. 3–36. Kenneth L. Kusmer, *A Ghetto Takes Shape: Black Cleveland, 1870–1930* (Urbana and Chicago: University of Illinois Press, 1976), pp. 65–90, 91–112; Bureau of the Census, *Negro in the United States* (Washington, D.C.: Department of Commerce, 1914), pp. 190–205.

27. Trotter, *Black Milwaukee*, p. xii.

28. St. Clair Drake and Horace Cayton, *Black Metropolis: A Study of Negro Life in a Northern City* (Harcourt, Brace and Company, 1945), pp. 723–730.

29. Henry Louis Taylor, Jr., and Vicky Dula, "The Black Residential Experience and Community Building in Antebellum Cincinnati," in Henry Louis Taylor, Jr., ed., *Race and the City: Work, Community, and Protest in Cincinnati, 1820–1970* (Urbana and Chicago: University of Illinois Press, 1993), pp. 96–125.

30. Allen H. Spear, *Black Chicago: The Making of a Negro Ghetto, 1890 to 1920* (Chicago and London: University of Chicago Press, 1967), pp. 11–27; William H. Wilson, *Hamilton Park: A Planned Black Community in Dallas* (Baltimore and London: The Johns Hopkins University Press, 1998). Wilson argues that Hamilton Park, which is located in metropolitan Dallas, is not part of the Dallas community. Implicit in this viewpoint is that Black Dallas is a spatially contiguous, territorially based community and that neighborhoods beyond the ghetto walls are not part of Black Dallas (pp. 1–9); Kenneth L. Kusmer, *A Black Ghetto Takes Shape: Black Cleveland, 1870–1930* (Urbana, Chicago, and London: University of Illinois Press, 1976), pp. 157–173.

31. Earl Lewis, *In Their Own Interests: Race, Class, and Power in Twentieth-Century Norfolk, Virginia* (Berkeley: University of California Press, 1991), pp. 8–28; Christopher Silver and John V. Moeser, *The Separate City: Black Com-*

*munities in the Urban South 1940–1968* (Lexington: University of Kentucky Press, 1995), pp. 1–14; Thomas J. Sugrue, *The Origins of the Urban Crisis: Race and Inequality in Postwar Detroit* (Princeton: Princeton University Press, 1996), pp. 181–207

32. The data on the residential structure of neighborhoods is part of a larger project on the structure of black neighborhoods in the industrial city. The data are in both hard and electronic versions and are found in The Industrial City Project File, Center for Urban Studies, at Buffalo. We have gathered information for each census tract, which allows us not only to examine the clustering pattern but also to examine the economic profile of cluster of tracts. See, for example, U.S. Bureau of the Census, *Population and Housing, Statistics for Pittsburgh, Pa.* (Washington, D.C.: U.S. Government Printing Office, 1942), pp. 4–7, 159–188. The data have been assembled into a database called *The Industrial City Black Neighborhood File,* which is located at the University at Buffalo Center for Urban Studies. Hereafter, data related to this file will be cited as *The Industrial City Black Neighborhood File.* Also, extremely important for gaining insight into this issue is the work of T. J. Woofter. His study shows dot maps for sixteen cities between 1920–1925: Buffalo, Chicago, Dayton, Gary, Indianapolis, New York City, Philadelphia, Charleston, Knoxville, Lexington, Lynchburg, Memphis, New Orleans, Richmond, and Winston-Salem. T. J. Woofter, *Negro Problems in Cities* (Doubleday, Doran and Company, 1928; reprint. New York: Negro University sities Press, 1969), pp. 37–77.

33. Chapter 2, Henry Louis Taylor, Jr., "Creating the Metropolis in Black and White: Black Suburbanization and the Planning Movement in Cincinnati, 1900–1950."

34. The Industrial City Black Neighborhood File.

35. The Industrial City Black Neighborhood File.

36. Chapter 2, Taylor, "Creating the Metropolis in Black and White: Black Suburbanization and the Planning Movement in Cincinnati, 1900 to 1950," and Chapter 5, Andrew Wiese, "Blacks in the Suburban and Rural Fringe." See also Quintard Taylor, *The Forging of a Black Community: Seattle's Central District from 1870 through the Civil Rights Era* (Seattle and London: University of Washington Press, 1994), pp. 135–156.

37. Jon C. Teaford, *City and Suburb: The Political Fragmentation of Metropolitan America, 1850–1970* (Baltimore and London: The Johns Hopkins University Press, 1979), pp. 76–104.

38. Kenneth Fox, *Metropolitan America: Urban Life and Urban Policy in the United States, 1940–1980* (Jackson: University Press of Mississippi, 1986), pp. 79–136; Dennis E. Gale, *Understanding Urban Unrest: From Reverend King to Rodney King* (Thousand Oaks, Calif.: SAGE Publications, 1996), pp. 86–111.

39. Olivier Zunz, *The Changing Face of Inequality: Urbanization, Industrial Development, and Immigrants in Detroit, 1880–1920* (Chicago and London: University of Chicago Press), pp. 372–398, 373; Andrew Wiese, "The Other Suburbanites: African American Suburbanization in the North before 1950," *The Journal of American History* 85 (March 1999): 1495–1524.

40. The Industrial City Black Neighborhood File.

41. Chapter 2, Henry Louis Taylor, Jr., "Creating the Metropolis in Black and White."

42. Thomas J. Sugrue, *The Origins of the Urban Crisis: Race and Inequality in Postwar Detroit* (Princeton: Princeton University Press, 1996), pp. 180–207, 208–229, 231–258.

43. Chapter 1, Henry Louis Taylor, Jr., and Song-Ho Ha, "A Unity of Opposites."

44. The Industrial City Black Neighborhood File.

45. Taylor, *The Forging of a Black Community*, p. 2; Joe William Trotter, Jr., *River Jordan: African American Urban Life in the Ohio Valley* (Lexington: University of Kentucky Press, 1998), p. 97; Christopher Silver and John V. Moeser, *The Separate City: Black Communities in the Urban South, 1940–1968* (Lexington: University of Kentucky Press, 1995), p. 25.

46. Sugrue, *The Origins of the Urban Crisis*, pp. 180–207; 208–229; 231–258.

47. Moreover, the FHA and the VHA, by making millions of dollars available to home buyers on a discriminatory basis, became the driving force behind the race-based movement of the postwar era.

48. Chapter 3, Andrea Kornbluh, "Municipal Harmony: Cultural Pluralism, Public Recreation, and Race Relations."

49. Stephanie J. Shaw, *What a Woman Ought to Be and to Do: Black Professional Women Workers During the Jim Crow Era* (Chicago and London: University of Chicago Press, 1996), pp. 109–163; Charles S. Johnson, *The Negro College Graduate* (New York: Negro Universities Press, 1969; originally published by University of North Carolina Press, 1938), pp. 92–130; W. E. B. DuBois, *The College-Bred Negro American* (Atlanta: Atlanta University Press, 1910), pp. 26–34, 65–70.

50. Chapter 1, Taylor and Ha, "A Unity of Opposites."

51. Chapter 6, Liesl Miller and Joe W. Trotter, "African Americans in the U.S. Economy: Federal Policy and the Transformation of Work, 1915–1945"; Chapter 7, Henry Louis Taylor, Jr., Vicky Dula, and Song-Ho Ha, "The Battle Against Wage Slavery: The National Urban League, the NAACP, and the Struggle over New Deal Policies"; Chapter 8, Sigmund Shipp, "Building Bricks With-

out Straw: Robert C. Weaver and Negro Industrial Employment, 1934–1944";
and Chapter 9, Eileen Boris, "Black Workers, Trade Unions, and Labor Standards: The Wartime FEPC."

52. See, for example, Henry Lewis Suggs, *P. B. Young Newspaperman:
Race, Politics, and Journalism in the New South, 1910–62* (Charlottesville: University Press of Virginia, 1988), p. x.

53. Chapter 1, Taylor and Ha, "A Unity of Opposites." See also Taylor, *The
Forging of a Black Community*, pp. 135–156

54. Sugrue, *The Origins of the Urban Crisis*, pp.181–207; Thomas W.
Hanchett offers a different perspective in his study on urban life in a Southern
city: "Interestingly, this neighborhood of 'tone and character' did not exclude unskilled blue-collar individuals. The tendency of the wealthy to separate themselves from poorer citizens was not nearly as evident in black Charlotte as in
white Charlotte in this era." Hanchett, *Sorting Out the New South City: Race,
Class, and Urban Developing in Charlotte, 1875–1975* (Durham: University of
North Carolina Press, 1998), pp. 116-144; William H. Wilson, on the other hand,
says that the cultural values of blacks were more important than economic status
in determining who was middle class. Black homeowners of the era tended to
have middle-class values that united them, regardless of their income or class status. William H. Wilson, *Hamilton Park: A Planned Black Community in Dallas*
(Baltimore and London: Johns Hopkins University Press, 1998), pp. 1–9.

55. E. Franklin Frazier, *Black Bourgeoisie* (New York: The Free Press,
1957), pp. 43–59; 43; Charles S. Johnson, *The Negro College Graduate* (New
York: Negro Universities Press, 1969; originally published in 1938, University of
Carolina Press), pp. 92–130; Carter G. Woodson, *The Negro Professional Man
and the Community with Special Emphasis on the Physician and the Lawyer*
(New York: Negro Universities Press, 1964; originally published by the Association for the Study of Negro Life and History, 1934), pp. 29–42.

56. Chapter 4, Georgina Hickey, "From Auburn Avenue to Buttermilk Bottom: Class and Community Dynamics Among Atlanta's Blacks."

57. Robin D. G. Kelley, *Race Rebels: Culture, Politics, and the Black Working
Class* (New York: The Free Press, 1994), pp. 55–75; 77–100; Robin D. G. Kelley,
*Hammer and Hoe: Alabama Communists During the Great Depression* (Chapel
Hill and London: University of North Carolina Press, 1990), pp. 92–116; David
Levering Lewis, *When Harlem Was in Vogue* (New York and Oxford: Oxford Uni-
versity Press, 1981), pp. 89–118; Anthony M. Platt, *E. Franklin Frazier Reconsid-
ered* (New Brunswick and London: Rutgers University Press, 1991), pp. 145–155;
213–221; Jacqueline Goggin, *Carter G. Woodson: A Life in Black History* (Baton
Rouge and London: Louisiana State University Press, 1993), pp. 140–179.

58. Eugene Kinckle Jones, "A New Deal for the Negro," *Opportunity*: Vol. XI, April 1933, pp. 105–108; William H. Harris, *The Harder We Run: Black Workers Since the Civil War* (New York and Oxford: Oxford University Press, 1982), pp. 95-122.

59. Alan Dawley and Joe William Trotter, Jr., "Race and Class," *Labor History* 35 (Fall 1994): 486–494; William H. Harris, *The Harder We Run: Black Workers Since the Civil War* (New York and Oxford: Oxford University Press, 1982), pp. 95–122..

60. Allan A. Banks, Jr., "Wage Differentials and the Negro under the N.R.A.," M.A. thesis, Economics; Howard University, 1938; Robert C. Weaver, "Wage Differentials Based on Race," *Opportunity* 12(May, 1934):141-44 in Phillip S. Foner and Ronald L. Lewis, eds., *The Black Worker: A Documentary History from Colonial Times to the Present,* vol. VI (Philadelphia: Temple University Press, 1981), pp. 97–102.

61. Joe William Trotter, Jr., *Black Milwaukee: The Making of an Industrial Proletariat, 1915–1945* (Urbana and Chicago: University of Illinois Press,1985), pp. 39–79; Joe William Trotter, Jr., "African-American Workers: New Directions in U.S. Labor Historiography," *Labor History* 35 (Fall 1994): 495–523.

62. Chapter 6, Liesl Miller Orenic and Joe W. Trotter, "African Americans in the U.S. Economy: Federal Policy and the Transformation of Work, 1915–1945."

63. Chapter 6, Miller Orenic and Trotter, "African Americans in the U.S. Economy."

64. Chapter 8, Sigmund Shipp, "Building Bricks without Straw: Robert C. Weaver and Negro Industrial Employment, 1934–1944," Chapter 9, Eileen Boris, "Black Workers, Trade Unions, and Labor Standards: The Wartime FEPC"; Harvard Sitkoff, *A New Deal for Blacks: The Emergence of Civil Rights as a National Issue: The Depression Decade* (Oxford: Oxford University Press, 1978), pp. 298–335.

65. Chapter 7, Henry Louis Taylor, Jr., Vicky Dula, and Song-Ho Ha, "The Battle Against Wage Slavery: The National Urban League, the NAACP, and the Struggle over New Deal Policies."

66. Harris, *The Harder We Run*, p. 109.

67. Harris, *The Harder We Run*, p. 109; Chapter 7, Henry Louis Taylor, Jr., Vicky Dula, and Song-Ho Ha, "The Battle Against Wage Slavery: The National Urban League, the NAACP, and the Struggle over New Deal Policies."

68. Harris, *The Harder We Run*, p. 109; Chapter 7, Taylor et al., "The Battle Against Wage Slavery: The National Urban League, the NAACP, and the Struggle over New Deal Policies"; Chapter 8, Shipp, "Building Bricks Without Straw: Robert C. Weaver and Negro Industrial Employment."

69. Chapter 7, Taylor et al., "The Battle Against Wage Slavery: The National Urban League, the NAACP, and the Struggle over New Deal Policies."

70. Robert C. Weaver, *Negro Labor: A National Problem* (New York: Harcourt, Brace and Company, 1946), p. 4.

71. Alba M. Edwards, "The Negro as a Factor in the Nation's Labor Force," *Journal of the American Statistical Association* 3119–196 (1936): 529–540, 540.

72. Chapter 8, Shipp, "Building Bricks without Straw."

# PART I

# Home and Community Building

# CHAPTER 1

# A Unity of Opposites
The Black College-Educated Elite, Black Workers,
and the Community Development Process

## HENRY LOUIS TAYLOR, JR., AND SONG-HO HA

### INTRODUCTION

W. E. B. Du Bois, in a classic essay written in 1903, outlined his vision
of the role the black college educated elite should play in the struggle of
African Americans.[1] When Du Bois wrote his treatise, however imper-
fectly formulated, blacks confronted a very complex situation.[2] It was a
nadir and high point for them; a time of despair and a time of hope. By
1900, African Americans had lost their constitutional rights and were
facing increased violence, exploitation, and the spread of Jim Crow
racism. At the same time, the black proletariat was growing, institutions
were maturing, the middle class was expanding, and a new protest movement was about to spring forth.[3] These conditions combined with the
dramatic transformation of U.S. society to construct the setting in which
a black cultural middle class, dominated by the college-educated elite,
emerged.[4]

This chapter explores the role played by the cultural middle class
and educated elite in black community building and examines the basis
for middle-class conflict with black workers. The African American
community was not a monolith. It was divided mainly along class, income, and gender lines.[5] Yet these divisions were not antagonistic ones
that split the community apart. So, while these fissures created conflict
and tension, they did not sunder the African American community. Black
rebels, the Negro bourgeoisie, unskilled and semi-skilled laborers, domestics, the labor aristocracy, and varied religious denominations were
unified, despite their obvious differences. [6] In short, this chapter seeks to

gain insight into the reasons why these differences did not fracture the black community.

The college-educated elite was the driving force behind the development of a black cultural middle class.[7] Yet, surprisingly little is known about this stratum. Most scholars lump the black college educated elite together with other members of the *cultural middle class*.[8] However, the cultural middle class was a diverse group, composed of different strata, and the college-educated elite was the most dominating group within the class. This stratum is unique in that blacks with college degrees were found among all strata comprising of the cultural middle class. However, the rarity of a college education among blacks separated those African Americans with college degrees from other members of the middle class, and made them a group unto themselves.[9]

The term *cultural middle class* was coined by William H. Wilson in his study of *Hamilton Park: A Planned Black Community in Dallas*.[10] Historians of the African American experience have recognized the existence of a black middle class, but have not agreed on its composition, its size, the chronology of its development, or its importance to American society. However, there is consensus that economic factors alone are not sufficient in defining it. Wilson used the term *cultural middle class* to emphasize values, such as dedication to family and work, rather than income or occupation in defining the black middle class.[11] In our definition, however, the term is employed simply to emphasize the differences between the black and white middle class.

## BLACK COMMUNITY FORMATION
## IN THE INDUSTRIAL CITY

*Community* is one of those shadowy terms that demand careful definition. In 1955, George A. Hillery, Jr., found no fewer than ninety-four meanings to the concept.[12] Yet, despite the variations, most definitions of community imply something both geographical and sociopsychological and stress the following themes: proximity and propinquity, territoriality, social interaction, consciousness of kind, socialization, and shared values and institutions.[13]

A number of scholars have emphasized the geographical dimension in their definition. Thomas Bender suggests most definitions of the term focus on community as an aggregate of people who share a common interest in a particular locality. Territorial-based social organizations and social activity thus define a community.[14] Roland L. Warren stresses the interplay between territorial and sociopsychological dimensions of community, with special emphasis on the place of institutions in community formation.[15] The historian James Borchert and the sociologist Gerald D. Suttles define community as a form of activity that occurs within a common geographical area that permits and, we might add, encourages social interaction.[16]

Other scholars have argued that community can exist beyond the boundaries of a common territorial base. Bender indicates that community can also be defined as a network of social relations marked by mutuality and emotional bonds.[17] This network, says Kai T. Erikson, is the essence of community, and it may or may not be coterminous with a specific, contiguous territory.[18] Martin Buber writes, "a real community need not consist of people who are perpetually together; but it must consist of people who, precisely because they are comrades, have mutual access to one another and are ready for one another."[19] Stressing the significance of sociopsychological aspects of community, Robert A. Nisbet says that community "draws its psychological strength from levels of motivation deeper than those of mere volition or interest. . . . Community is a fusion of feeling and thought, of tradition and commitment, of membership and volition."[20] To these scholars, the existence of social networks, shared traditions, values, beliefs, and the psychological bonds of communal life makes it possible for a community to exist, even when people live in different locations.

Most recently, however, the historian William H. Wilson argued that the term community has been stretched "to cover virtually all human associations, even among people scattered over the globe whose connection to with one another is solely electronic," and that it is particularly problematic when used to describe the African American community:

> While it is true that blacks were forced into a common mold in the sense that most members of the white majority denied them their full humanity, they did not all live in the same place in any of the cities under examination. It is also true that African-American voters overwhelmingly favor *liberal* measures and black candidates who are legitimized by major party or other significant endorsements. Otherwise, though, African Americans are divided by income, class, status, religion, and a kaleidoscope of individual preferences and experiences, as are other Americans. The blacks of Dallas, therefore, do not form a community in any meaningful sense of the word. Hamilton Park is a black community, but it is not, nor are its residents, part of a larger group bound only by the city limits of Dallas and defined solely by race.[21]

The question of community, then, seems to be wedded to the extent to which people can be melded together into a singular, cohesive group—even if spatially dispersed—by a set of common experiences and shared traditions, rituals, beliefs and values, organizations, and institutions.

The black experience in the industrial city heightened racial consciousness and caused blacks to think and act as a people with a common history and destiny, despite being fractured along class and gender lines, and spatially dispersed. In this socioeconomic environment, black community building was shaped by a powerful set of external and internal forces that transformed African Americans into a people who built an urban community, with a highly complex, interactive, and multileveled organizational and institutional structure.

White racism, violence, and hostility were key external factors shaping black community formation in the industrial city, and competition over residential space was its main source.[22]

The racial subordination of African Americans affected all aspects of their lives between 1900 and 1950. The colorline was everywhere and places of social interaction were tension-filled venues that could erupt into racial confrontation and violence.[23] However, the two sites of greatest contention were the workplace and the neighborhood. The rise of home ownership turned neighborhoods into *defended territories* and battlegrounds between blacks and whites in the 1910s and 1920s.[24] Then, during the depression and war years, a housing shortage and black population growth combined with the policies of the federal Home Owners Loan Corporation to create a volatile and explosive situation in the nation's cities.[25]

Throughout the period, blacks lived in close proximity to whites, despite continual efforts to segregate them in residential space. Within this context, between 1930 and 1950, the black urban population erupted. Nationally, the black urban population increased from about 5,194,000 to 9,393,000, an increase of 81 percent.[26] In fact, everywhere, the black urban population grew. For example, the African American population in the Ohio Valley cities of Pittsburgh, Cincinnati, Louisville, and Evansville increased substantially. Blacks in Cincinnati increased by 64 percent, Pittsburgh by 50 percent, Evansville by 25 percent, and Louisville by 22 percent.[27] Christopher Silver and John V. Moeser report that the black populations of Memphis, Atlanta, and Richmond also increased during the period.[28] Black population growth and the chronic black housing shortage thus caused African Americans to move into adjacent white neighborhoods.[29]

Concurrently, during the depression, the federal government launched a series of programs designed to make home ownership more accessible. Initiated in 1933, the Home Owners' Loan Corporation (HOLC) was the first of these programs, and it served as a model for later efforts. [30] The HOLC introduced two measures that changed the residential housing market. First, it introduced the use of long-term, self-amortizing mortgages with uniform payments. This revolutionized the money mortgage system and made mass home ownership possible. Second, it established a rating system to guide the investment decisions of underwriters. [31]

The HOLC ratings system involved classifying neighborhoods according to four categories, with the lowest category coded with the color red. People wanting to buy houses in this and the next-lowest category almost never received loans. Most mortgages went to purchase homes in the top two categories, the highest of which included areas that were "new, homogenous, and in demand in good times and bad," while the second constituted "areas that had reached their peak, but were still desirable and could be expected to remain stable."

The HOLC classification system, and its theoretical underpinnings, was adopted by the real estate industry, banks, underwriting companies, and the scholarly community. Arthur M. Weimer and Homer Hoyt, for example, in their 1948 book, *Principles of Urban Real Estate,* contended that neighborhood stability could be maintained only "if the people living in an area are not threatened by the infiltration of people of another racial or national type."[32] The migration of such groups into a neighborhood, they wrote, "frequently stimulates the out-migration of previous residents in the area."[33]

Most whites probably did not know about these scholarly studies or how underwriters classified neighborhoods, but they did know that a black presence in their neighborhoods threatened further home investments. In the industrial city, the house and neighborhood became commodities in which investors stood to make or lose money. Who lived in a particular neighborhood became as much an economic question as a social one. Consequently, whites believed they had every right to protect their neighborhoods from a black invasion by any means necessary. So, then, in the industrial city, white economic interests became inextricably linked with long-standing racist ideas in matters of residential space issues. The result transformed industrial city neighborhoods into a racial battleground.[34]

The Detroit case is indicative of the period. Between 1930 and 1950, black Detroit grew by 180,440 residents, or by more than 150 percent. In the Motor City, like most places, there was a chronic housing shortage among blacks.[35] In Detroit (and many other cities), despite the efforts of white civic society and public policy initiatives to segregate the races, blacks and whites still lived near each other. Consequently, because of the housing shortage, when the black population grew, African Americans had no choice but to move into white neighborhoods.[36]

Detroit's working class neighborhoods stood in the direct path of black community growth. So when black Detroit expanded, its population spilled over into neighborhoods such as Ruitan Park, De Witt-Clinton, States-Lawn near Northwest, and Fenkell-Linwood. It was in neighborhoods such as these, where whites were incapable of moving or unable to move, that tensions ran high and violence was most likely to occur. To whites, the movement of blacks into their neighborhoods was an "invasion" and the "moral equivalent of war."[37] The black influx into white neighborhoods combined with the HOLC policies to create an alarmingly explosive situation. Not surprisingly, in Detroit violent attacks against blacks occurred in just about every racially changing neighborhood in the city during the postwar years.[38]

What happened in Detroit was typical of what happened in other cities around the nation. Indeed, following the 1943 race riot in Detroit, cities across the country rushed to form race relations or intergroup relations committees, such as the Mayor's Friendly Relations Committee in Cincinnati, to reduce interracial tension, hostility, and the danger of violence.[39] Periodic outbreaks of violence and hostility took place throughout the industrial era, but not all blacks were victims of white rage. Even so, all African Americans felt unsafe and threatened. They knew that by accidentally crossing the color line, or by being in the wrong place at the wrong time, they could be murdered, beaten, terrorized, intimidated, or insulted. For example, the bloody Chicago riot of 1919 was triggered by the murder of a black teenager whose raft had floated too close to a "white" beach on the city's South Side.[40] In the 1940s whites attacked Mexicans and African Americans in Los Angeles and Chicago, just for wearing zoot suits. Similarly, hate strikes shut down workplaces in Chicago, Baltimore, and Philadelphia, and countless minor clashes between blacks and whites occurred on the overcrowded streets, parks, streetcars, and buses of virtually every major city in the United States.[41]

Segregation and discrimination joined with violence and hostility as external forces shaping black community building. In the industrial era, continual efforts were made to separate blacks from whites in virtually every aspect of life, although it was accomplished differently in various parts of the nation. For example, in the South, de jure segregation was the norm, while in the North de facto segregation carried the day. However, no matter what segregating process was followed, everywhere, especially between 1900 and 1930, the color line was drawn tighter and tighter.[42]

In the face of racial hostility and discrimination, blacks focused on building and developing their communities. But community building was not simply a reaction to racism. Blacks enjoyed congregating together, and *community* helped them individually and collectively secure housing, find work, meet needs, protest, and fight for advancement. Within this context, African Americans built a multilevel institutional and organizational structure. The cultural middle class played a key role in the community building process. This class comprised blacks holding white-collar jobs in professional service: entrepreneurs, preachers, teachers, lawyers, doctors, nurses, social workers, accountants, pharmacists, and clerical and kindred workers. The cultural middle class was a service class and this enabled them to play an important role in the community development process.[43]

Black entrepreneurs played a big role in community building by establishing barber shops, beauty salons, hotels, rooming houses, grocery stores, restaurants, funeral homes, dance halls, newspapers, and pool rooms. Some businesses, like newspapers, were also important cultural institutions that helped knit the black community together.[44]

The cultural middle class played a key role in building other community institutions as well. They were the black community's teachers, preachers, doctors, lawyers, social workers, nurses, pharmacists, and entertainers. Schools and churches were central to the community building process, and they were both headed by the cultural middle class. Likewise, the emerging civil rights movement was driven by black lawyers, who led the legal struggles of the industrial city era, while social workers dominated the Urban League.[45]

Members of the cultural middle class were also the writers, historians, and social scientists who chronicled the black experience. They were the actors, actresses, and dancers who brought black pathos and ethos to life, and they were the singers and musicians who sang the blues and played jazz in the black bars and nightclubs. The point is that the cultural middle class played a decisive role in constructing the organizational and institutional framework that undergirded the community building process.[46]

## THE COLLEGE-EDUCATED ELITE

The cultural middle class was dominated by the college-educated elite. This stratum became increasingly important during the rise of the industrial city. In 1900, three years before Du Bois published "The Talented Tenth," roughly 156 blacks graduated from college. Then, over the next fifty years the number of blacks graduating from college rose dramatically each year, so that in 1950, 13,108 African Americans had their degrees conferred. This phenomenal growth, however, was uneven. For example, in 1910 only 510 blacks graduated from college, and in 1920 only 1,009. But during the roaring Twenties, the situation changed. This was a watershed decade in black higher education. From 1930 onward, the number of blacks graduating from college each year grew dramatically. For example, 2,177 blacks had degrees conferred in 1930; 5,707 in 1940; and 13,108 in 1950 (Table 1.1).

Beginning in the 1920s, African Americans launched a movement to popularize higher education. For example, Alpha Phi Alpha fraternity instituted a nationwide "Go to High School—Go to College" movement. It sponsored meetings in school auditoriums, on campuses, and within churches and YMCAs throughout the nation.[47] *The Crisis* magazine, the official journal of the National Association for the Advancement of Colored People (NAACP), annually published the names of college graduates. And many other organizations and groups joined the effort by engaging in activities that promoted black acquisition of a high school diploma and college degree. Many of black America's leading thinkers, writers, artists, educators, and activists received their college training

**Table 1.1**   Bachelor Degrees Conferred by Year by Black Institutions, 1900–1950

| Year | Total | Male | Female |
|------|-------|------|--------|
| 1900 | 156 | 134 | 22 |
| 1910 | 510 | 233 | 277 |
| 1920 | 1,009 | 818 | 191 |
| 1930 | 2,177 | 1,200 | 977 |
| 1940 | 5,707 | 2,463 | 3,244 |
| 1950 | 13,108 | 6,467 | 6,641 |

*Source:* Jessie Carney Smith and Carrell Peterson Horton, eds., *Historical Statistics of Black America: Agriculture to Labor and Employment* (New York: Gale Research, 1995), p. 619, Table 717.

during the 1920s, including Gwendolyn Bennett, Horace Mann Bond, Arna Bontempts, Ralph Bunche, Countee Cullen, Aaron Douglas, Charles Drew, E. Franklin Frazier, Abram L. Harris, Langston Hughes, Charles H. Houston, Benjamin Quarles, Ira Reid, and Roy Wilkins.[48] These prominent African Americans helped to promote the value of education among blacks and reinforced the notion that higher education mattered.

The rise of college-trained blacks took place when higher education was becoming increasingly important in U.S. society. In 1900, for example, 27,410 Americans had their degrees conferred and in 1950, 432,000 students graduated. But blacks received only about 3 percent of those college degrees in 1950[49] (Table 1.2).

So college educated blacks were an elite, whose status stemmed from the reality that few blacks managed to get a college education during the industrial era, which made a college degree highly coveted. St. Clair Drake and Horace Cayton argue that a distinctive feature of black culture was that more value was placed on education than occupation. Thus blacks with college degrees, even if they were Pullman porters or waiters, were afforded high status.[50] This happened because most blacks never finished high school. For example, as late as 1950, the median years of school completed for nonwhites 25 years old and older was 6.4.[51] "With a very narrow occupational spread," Drake and Cayton said, "education is used to mark off social divisions *within* [emphasis theirs] the same general occupational level."

The high status enjoyed by the college-educated elite was reinforced by the role they played in community and institutional building.[52] When

**Table 1.2.** Bachelor Degrees Conferred by Year by All Institutions, 1900–1950

| Year | Total | Male | Female |
|------|-------|------|--------|
| 1900 | 27,410 | 22,173 | 5,237 |
| 1910 | 37,199 | 28,762 | 8,437 |
| 1920 | 48,622 | 31,980 | 16,642 |
| 1930 | 122,484 | 73,615 | 48,869 |
| 1940 | 186,500 | 109,546 | 76,954 |
| 1950 | 432,058 | 328,841 | 103,217 |

*Source*: *Historical Statistics of the United States, Colonial Times to 1957* (Washington, D.C.: U.S. Government Printing Office, 1961), pp. 211–212, Series H 327–338.

Du Bois published "The Talented Tenth" in 1903, he was defining the commitment to service that black college graduates owed the black community and explaining the decisive role they should play in community development.[53] At the dawn of the 20th century, Du Bois observed that black college graduates were concentrated in professions that were critical to the development of the black community: teachers, ministers, physicians, and lawyers.[54] Because of their strategic location within the community, Du Bois felt these professionals should be more than mere workers.[55] They must be "leaders of thought and missionaries of culture among their people. No others can do this work and the Negro colleges must train men for it."[56] So Du Bois challenged black colleges to provide their students with a thorough understanding of the masses of blacks and to imbue them with a willingness to work and make personal sacrifices. From Du Bois' perspective, black teachers, preachers, doctors, and lawyers were not just professionals, but an elite, who should be devoted to leading and serving the people.[57]

Racism and the color line limited black opportunities throughout the industrial era, causing most black college graduates to remain concentrated in a handful of occupations. As late as 1950, most black college graduates were working in only nine occupational categories: preachers, teachers, college professors, lawyers, social workers, physicians, dentists, and pharmacists, with a sprinkling employed as journalists, librarians, and entertainers (Table 1.3). So, then, although the black occupational structure had diversified since Du Bois published "The Talented Tenth" in 1903, most African Americans were still working in only a handful of professional positions. Even so, throughout the industrial era, white-collar black professionals continued to hold occupations critical to black community development. Thus while the black cultural middle-class was a nonessential group to white America, they were significant players in building black America. [58]

Gender played a role in the distribution of opportunities within the narrowly crafted black occupational structure as well (Table 1.3). Although women college graduates outnumbered men, they were typically locked out of the highest paying or most prestigious professional positions. For example, in 1950, women constituted 51 percent of black college graduates and 58 percent of professional, technical, and kindred workers.[59] Yet 65 percent of black female professionals were concentrated in teaching, while only 1 percent of them worked as physicians and surgeons, lawyers and judges, and clergywomen combined.

Even in teaching, where women were concentrated most heavily, work was divided along gender lines. On this point, Charles S. Johnson,

**Table 1.3.**   Blacks in Selected Professional and Semiprofessional
Service in 1950

| Occupation | Total | Male | Female |
|---|---|---|---|
| Total | 174,840 | 72,750 | 102,090 |
| Clergymen | 18,630 | 17,880 | 750 |
| College presidents, professors, and instructors | 3,810 | 2,430 | 1,380 |
| Dentists | 1,680 | 1,620 | 60 |
| Lawyers and judges | 1,470 | 1,380 | 90 |
| Librarians | 1,770 | 330 | 1,440 |
| Pharmacists | 1,380 | 1,110 | 270 |
| Physicians and surgeons | 3,660 | 3,360 | 300 |
| Social and welfare workers | 5,220 | 1,470 | 3,750 |
| Teachers (including county agents) | 84,840 | 18,150 | 66,690 |
| Other professional and semiprofessional workers | 137,220 | 25,020 | 27,360 |

*Source:* Table 3 in Department of Commerce, Bureau of the Census, *United States Census of Population: 1950, Special Reports, Occupations by Industry* (Washington, D.C.: U.S.Government Printing Office, 1954), p. 1B29.

in his 1936 study of black professionals, found that "one in every 15 high school principals is a woman; one in every five elementary school principals, and one out of the 21 college presidents is a woman." On the other hand, he says, "83 percent of the librarians and assistant librarians are women, while 70 percent of the social workers, 71 percent of the elementary, and 63 percent of the high school teachers are women."[60] There is little reason to believe that these figures had changed significantly by 1950.

Gender questions notwithstanding the strategic location of the black college-educated elite made them key participants in the community building process. Here it should be stressed that the black college-educated elite were service workers. Teachers and professors taught in black elementary schools, high schools, and colleges. Their job was to deliver educational services to the African American population. Black physicians played a major role in promoting public health among blacks and providing them with health care both in private offices and in the Negro wings of hospitals. Dentists and pharmacists were also key players in the effort to safeguard the health of African Americans.

Likewise, lawyers and social workers played increasingly important roles in black life and culture. Lawyers not only helped blacks navigate the legal landscape, but played a decisive role in the litigation phase of the civil rights movement.[61] Meanwhile, social workers were key staffers in the NAACP, and those like James Hathaway Robinson in Cincinnati were the driving force behind the delivery of social services to African Americans in the industrial city. [62]

This college-educated elite, because of its educational attainment and communicative skills, often produced the most visible and well-known leaders of the black community. For example, David McBride and Monroe H. Little, in a study of the black elite during the 1930s, selected a sample of 240 men and 30 women from *Who's Who in Colored America* from the 1930–1932 and 1938–1940 editions. They found that 90 percent of this group were college graduates, and of the 170 individuals in the sample with occupational information, 65 percent held jobs in just four occupational categories: medicine, education, clergy, and law. The point is the black college-educated elite held white-collar, professional positions, and they were responsible for delivering a range of indispensable services to the black community, especially the working class.[63]

## THE UNITY OF OPPOSITIONS: WORK, PLACE, AND CLASS DIVISIONS

Black professionals' existence depended on the services they provided to African American workers. Consequently, black teachers, preachers, social workers, doctors, dentists, pharmacists, and lawyers typically lived and worked in a mostly black setting, or labored in a segregated environment—such as an all-black classroom in a white school, or in the Negro wing of a public hospital—in white-dominated areas.[64] Moreover, when they did interact with whites, it was generally with the most educated and liberal members of the race, and typically it took place in an amiable setting, such as discussing race problems with white leaders or conversing with other white professionals over issues of mutual concern.[65] This is not to imply that black professionals lived a cushy life. They did not. All blacks endured insults, threats, and violence, especially when they moved into contested neighborhoods.[66] Yet the day-to-day racial experience of black professionals and workers differed, and understanding this difference is crucial to gaining insight into the sources of class division among blacks. Both work and place shaped the experiences of black professional and workers and both contributed to class divisions within the black community.

So while black professionals delivered services to the black community and were dependent on their black clientele for survival, black workers were economically linked to the mainstream economy. As members of the labor reserve and low-wage army of workers, they played a vital role in the nation's economy.[67] Black workers labored in the hard, dirty, and dangerous jobs that no one else wanted. They were the unskilled and semiskilled laborers in the factories, on the trains and waterfront, and in a variety of low-wage jobs. They also worked in the homes of whites as domestics or waited on them in restaurants, hotels, and trains. Black workers labored in the white world and often found themselves in direct competition with other whites for jobs and opportunities in the mainstream economy.[68]

On a daily basis, they left the insulated world of the black ghetto and either walked, drove their automobiles, or rode buses and streetcars to places of employment. This journey to work took them out of the friendly confines of the black ghetto and carried them into the hostile, sometimes violent, and always uncertain world of white-dominated society. On the buses and trains, and in the workplaces, black workers daily faced open racism, encountered insults, were forced to wear the mask of docility, and endured the reality of being an oppressed people in a racist, class-stratified society.[69] The struggles to and from work, and the struggles on the job, endeared the ghetto to the working class. To them, the ghetto was not just a place where they lived, but a refuge and a haven from the stress of life in white society. This is what Drake and Cayton had in mind, when they said, "[when] work is over, the pressure of the white world is lifted. Within Bronzeville Negroes are at home. They find rest from white folks as well as from labor, and they make the most of it. In their homes, in lodge rooms and club houses, pool parlors and taverns, cabarets and movies, they can temporarily shake off the incubus of the white world."[70]

Differences in the location of the workplace and the type of work performed meant that African American workers and the middle class, especially the college-educated elite, had different types of experiences with whites. Other aspects of life separated the middle class from the working class. The black residential structure was segregated on the basis of class. In the ghetto, the middle-class and higher-paid workers claimed the best housing and neighborhood conditions.[71] Also, they were often the first African Americans to move into transitional neighborhoods.[72] Moreover, the housing shortage among blacks in the 1940s, combined with middle-class growth, opened up new housing opportunities for the well-to-do, and this further deepened residential class segregation among blacks.[73]

The nature of work, its location in physical space, residential class segregation in the ghetto, and lifestyle differences created vastly different experiences for African American workers and the college-educated elite and cultural middle class. These experiential differences formed the basis for class tension and conflict in the African American community. Yet class conflict and tension did not sunder the black community during the industrial era. Three reasons explain why. The first was mutual need. The cultural middle class was a service class that provided African American workers with essential goods and services. Black workers were their clients. Likewise, workers needed the services delivered by the middle class. Mutual need, then, formed the social glue that held the middle class and workers together, despite class and gender differences.

Secondly, during the industrial era, the ideals of self-help, racial pride, and racial solidarity were social principles that knitted the black community together.[74] This black version of cultural pluralism fashioned the ideological framework in which African American life and culture evolved.[75] Finally, African Americans across the class spectrum lived in a racist white society, in which they needed to project an image of a singular, cohesive people to the outside world. The job ceiling, black ghetto, petty discriminations, open hostility, racial violence, and unpleasant memories (past and present) were part of black reality. Skin color set blacks, as a people, apart from whites and made racial loyalty the litmus test of black heroes and role models. "Negroes must learn to stick together" was the most persistent theme in the black community. St. Clair Drake and Horace Cayton put it this way:

> Although Negroes of all class levels stress individual initiative as a factor in "racial advancement" they are keenly aware that as a separate-subordinate group in American life, the dice are loaded against the individual. Everybody knows that "no matter how high a Negro gets he's still just a Negro." Race consciousness breeds a demand for "racial solidarity," just as Negroes contemplate their existence as a minority in a white world which spurns them, they see their ultimate hope in presenting some type of United Front against the world.[76]

Collectively, these factors held the African American community together, although it was divided along class and gender lines. But this was a double-edged sword. High status and education made the middle class the most visible leaders within the African American community. Consequently, the muting of differences made it possible for the middle class to project their interests as the interests of the African American people. Over time, this would prove problematic.[77]

## NOTES

1. W. E. B. Du Bois, "The Talented Tenth," in Henry Louis Gates, Jr., and Cornel West, ed., *The Future of the Race* (New York: Alfred A. Knopf, 1996), pp. 132–157; originally published in *The Negro Problem*, 1903.

2. Almost 50 years following publication of the "Talented Tenth," Du Bois, in a memorial address delivered at the Nineteenth Grande Boulè Conclave, clarified some of the views outlined in his earlier essay. He stressed that for the talented tenth to fulfill their destiny as race leaders, they must be willing to acquire thorough understanding of the "mass of Negroes and their problems," and they would have to be willing to work hard, be willing to make personal sacrifice, and dedicate themselves to the liberation of the masses. In this sense, Du Bois argued that the talented tenth would not be an aristocratic class, set apart from the masses, but race rebels who would lead their struggle. W. E. B. Du Bois, "The Talented Tenth Memorial Address," in Gates and West, *Future of the Race*, pp. 159–177. Cornel West, in a provocative essay, argues that "Du Bois—owing to his Puritan New England origins and Enlightenment values—found it difficult not to view common black folk as some degraded other or alien—no matter how hard he resisted." Thus, West says, despite many of its correct formulations, Du Bois's classic essay must be revised before it can serve as a genuine guide to action among African Americans. Gates and West, *Future of the Race*, p. 59.

3. Joe W. Trotter, Jr., *River Jordan: African American Urban Life in the Ohio Valley* (Lexington: University of Kentucky Press, 1998), pp. 55–92, 95–150.

4. Jeremy Atack and Peter Passell, *A New Economic View of American History* (New York: W.W. Norton and Company), pp. 457–492.

5. Robin D. G. Kelley, *Race Rebels: Culture, Politics, and the Black Working Class* (New York: The Free Press), pp. 1–13, 17–54.

6. Allan H. Spear, *Black Chicago: The Making of a Negro Ghetto, 1890–1920* (Chicago: University of Chicago Press, 1967), pp. 91–110, 111–126; Kenneth L. Kusmer, *A Ghetto Takes Shape: Black Cleveland, 1870–1930* (Urbana: University of Illinois Press, 1976), pp. 91–112, 158–173.

7. In this study, to be a member of the college-educated elite, a person must have a bachelor's degree.

8. See, for example, Joe William Trotter, Jr., *Coal, Class, and Color: Blacks in Southern West Virginia, 1915–32* (Urbana: University of Illinois Press, 1990), pp. 39–59; Kusmer, *A Ghetto Takes Shape*, pp. 91–112; Robin D. G. Kelley,

*Hammer and Hoe: Alabama Communists During the Great Depression* (Chapel Hill and London: University of North Carolina Press, 1990), pp. 1–10.

9. St. Clair Drake and Horace R. Cayton, *Black Metropolis: A Study of Negro Life in a Northern City* (New York: Harcourt, Brace and Company, 1945), pp. 515–516.

10. William H. Wilson, *Hamilton Park: A Planned Black Community in Dallas* (Baltimore and London: Johns Hopkins University Press, 1998), p. 3.

11. Wilson, *Hamilton Park*, p. 3; Alan L. Keys, *Masters of the Dream: The Strength and Betrayal of Black America* (New York: William Morrow, 1995), pp. 41–105.

12. George A. Hillery, Jr., "Definitions of Community: Areas of Agreement," *Rural Sociology* 20 (March 1955): 111–23.

13. Henry Louis Taylor, Jr., and Vicky Dula, "The Black Residential Experience and Community Formation in Cincinnati," in Henry Louis Taylor, Jr., ed., *Race and the City: Work, Community, and Protest in Cincinnati, 1820–1970* (Urbana and Chicago: University of Illinois Press, 1993), p. 96.

14. Thomas Bender, *The Community and Social Change in America* (New Brunswick, N.J.: Rutgers University Press, 1978), p. 6.

15. Roland L. Warren, *The Community in America*, 3d ed. (Chicago: Rand McNally, 1978), p. 37.

16. James Borchert, *Alley Life in Washington: Family, Community, Religion, and Folklife in the City, 1850–1970* (Urbana: University of Illinois Press, 1980), pp. 100–142; Gerald D. Suttles, *The Social Construction of Communities* (Chicago: University of Chicago Press, 1972), pp. 21–43.

17. Bender, *The Community*, p. 8.

18. Kai T. Erikson, *Everything in Its Path: Destruction of Community in the Buffalo Creek Flood* (New York: Simon and Schuster, 1976), cited in Bender, *The Community*, p. 7.

19. Martin Buber, *Paths in Utopia* (London: Routledge and Kegan Paul, 1949), p. 145, cited in Bender, *The Community*, p. 7.

20. Robert A. Nisbet, *The Sociological Tradition* (New York: Basic Books, 1966), pp. 47–48.

21. Wilson, *Hamilton Park*, p. 7.

22. Earl Lewis, *In Their Own Interests: Race, Class, and Power in Twentieth-Century Norfolk, Virginia* (Berkeley: University of California Press, 1991), pp. 26–27; Trotter, *River Jordan*, pp. 73–92; Kusmer, *A Ghetto Takes Shape*, pp. 174–189; Kelley, *Race Rebels*, pp. 55–75; Ronald H. Baylor, *Race and the Shaping of Twentieth Century Atlanta* (Chapel Hill: University of North Carolina Press, 1996), pp. 3–12. Separating blacks and whites in residential space was one of the main objectives of segregation. Although the system was imperfect, it gen-

erated much tension between blacks and whites. Then in the 1920s, '30s, and '40s, as the residential environment was gradually turned into a commodity, neighborhoods became very volatile places.

23. Trotter, *River Jordan*, pp. 73–92; Kelley, *Race Rebel*, pp. 55–75.

24. Henry Louis Taylor, Jr., "City Building, Public Policy, the Rise of the Industrial City, and Black Ghetto-Slum Formation in Cincinnati, 1850–1940," in Taylor, ed., *Race and the City*, pp. 156–192.

25. Wilson, *Hamilton Park*, pp. 10–32.

26. Department of Commerce, *Bureau of the Census; Historical Statistics of the United States: Colonial Times to 1970,* Part I (Washington, D.C.: U.S. Government Printing Office, 1975), v.1, pp. 12–13, Series A 73–81.

27. Trotter, River Jordan, pp. 97, 124.

28. Christopher Silver and John V. Moeser, *The Separate City: Black Communities in the Urban South, 1940–1968* (Lexington: University of Kentucky Press, 1995), pp. 25, 28, 32.

29. Thomas J. Sugrue, *The Origins of the Urban Crisis: Race and Inequality in Postwar Detroit* (Princeton: Princeton University Press, 1996), pp. 311–258.

30. Douglas S. Massey and Nancy A. Denton, *American Apartheid: Segregation and the Making of the Underclass* (Cambridge: Harvard University Press, 1993), p. 51.

31. Massey and Denton, American Apartheid, p. 51.

32. Arthur M. Weimer and Homer Hoyt, *Principles of Urban Real Estate* (New York: Ronald Press, 1948) p. 123, 129, cited in Raymond A. Mohl, "The Second Ghetto and the Infiltration Theory in Urban Real Estate, 1940–1960," in June Manning Thomas and Marsha Ritzdorf, eds., *Urban Planning and the African American Community: In the Shadows* (Thousand Oaks, Calif.: Sage Publications, 1997), pp. 58–74.

33. Raymond A. Mohl, "The Second Ghetto and the Infiltration Theory in Urban Real Estate, 1940–1960," in Thomas and Ritzdorf, eds., *Urban Planning*, pp. 58–74.

34. Taylor, "City Building," pp. 167–178.

35. Sugrue, *Urban Crisis*, pp. 231–258.

36. Thomas Sugrue uses scattergram maps, based on census tracts from the 1940 to 1970 period, to show the growth of Black Detroit. To obtain an even more microscopic view, we mapped the entire population by census tract for the 1940 to 1950 period. This shows the magnitude of black movement into the white neighborhoods, which are literally being engulfed by the African American population. Sugrue, *Urban Crisis*, pp. 181–207, 231–258.

37. Sugrue, *Urban Crisis*, pp. 234–241.

38. Robert A. Burnham, "The Mayor's Friendly Relations Committee: Cultural Pluralism and the Struggle for Black Advancement," in Taylor, ed., *Race and the City,* pp. 258–279.

39. Burnham, "The Mayor's Friendly Relations Committee," pp. 258–279.

40. Spear, *Black Chicago*, pp. 219–222.

41. Kelley, *Race Rebels*, pp. 55–75, 161–181.

42. Kusmer, *A Ghetto Takes Shape*, pp. 53–65; Spear, *Black Chicago*, pp. 29–49; Trotter, *River Jordan*, pp. 73–92, 95–121; Silver and Moeser, *The Separate City*, pp. 1–14, 15–61; Lewis, *In Their Own Interests*, pp. 66–88; James R. Grossman, *Land of Hope: Chicago, Black Southerners, and the Great Migration* (Chicago and London: University of Chicago Press, 1989), pp. 123–160

43. Although the cultural middle class grew in importance, they were never more than a small proportion of the total black workforce. For example, in 1900 professional service workers including clerical and kindred workers composed less than 2 percent of the black workforce. By 1950 only 8 percent of all blacks in the workforce fell into this category (including managers, officials, proprietors, clerical, and kindred workers). Department of Commerce and Labor, Bureau of the Census, *Twelfth Census of the United States: 1900: Special Reports, Supplementary Analysis and Derivative Tables* (Washington, D.C.: U.S. Government Printing Office, 1906), pp. 252–253, Table LXXIX; *United States Census of Population: 1950, Special Reports, Occupation by Industry*, (Washington D.C.: Government Printing Office, 1954), pp. 1B29–1B37, Table 3.

44. Trotter, *River Jordan*, p. 81; Henry Lewis Suggs, *P. B. Young, Newspaperman: Race, Politics, and Journalism in the New South, 1910–62* (Charlottesville: University of Virginia Press, 1988), p. x. Trotter says the black press facilitated the cross-class and cultural integration of the black community. Not only did many black communities, even small ones like Evansville, Indiana, have newspapers, but also some local papers, like the *Pittsburgh Courier*, the *Chicago Defender*, and the *Norfolk Journal and Guide*, had national and regional audiences. Within this framework, historian Henry Lewis Suggs says "the black press in the South functioned as a carrier and preserver of black culture. It was not only an advocate and a crusader, it was a mirror, a chronicle, and an encyclopedia of the black experience." Although he was speaking about southern newspapers, Suggs's view was also true of black papers in other parts of the country.

45. Roger Lane, *William Dorsey's Philadelphia and Ours: On the Past and Future of the Black City in America* (New York: Oxford University Press, 1991). Lane provides a wonderful overview that various strata played in black community development in Philadelphia.

46. David Levering Lewis, *When Harlem Was in Vogue* (New York: Oxford University Press, 1981) provides an overview of black artists and entertainers.

47. Herbert Aptheker, *Afro-American History: The Modern Era* (Secaucus, N.J.: Citadel Press, 1971), p. 184.

48. Aptheker, *Afro-American History*, p. 173–190. Charles S. Johnson, *The Negro College Graduate* (New York: Negro Universities Press, 1938; reprint 1969), p. 22.

49. The number of black college graduates was 13,108 and that of the entire U.S. population was 432,058. In 1950 black population was 15,042,286, and total U.S. population was 151,683,000. The data for the number of college graduates are from Tables 1 and 2, and the data of the population are from Department of Commerce, *Historical Statistics of the United States: Colonial Times to 1957* (Washington, D.C.: U.S. Government Printing Office, 1961), pp. 8–9, Series A22–33 and A59–70.

50. Drake and Cayton, *Black Metropolis*, p. 515.

51. The census bureau had data only for "nonwhites" for years of school completed. However, in 1950 the overwhelming majority of nonwhites (about 15,865,000) were black (15,042,286). Hence, while Figures 6.4 and 7.2 might not accurately reflect the actual median years school completed for African Americans, they do not distort the picture. Department of Commerce, *Historical Statistics of the United States: Colonial Times to 1957*, (Washington D.C.: U.S. Government Printing Office, 1961), p. 8, Series 22–33, p. 9, Series A 59–70, and p. 214, Series H 395–406. The number of black college graduates in 1950 was 13,108. Thus the number of black college graduates per 10,000 blacks was about 8.71 in 1950. Smith and Horton, *op.cit.*, p. 619.

52.

**Table 1.4.** Comparison of Selected Occupations of Black College Graduates in 1900, 1910, and 1932

| Occupations | 1900 | | 1910 | | 1932 | |
|---|---|---|---|---|---|---|
| | Number | Percent of total occupations | Number | Percent of total occupation | Number | Percent of total occupation |
| Teaching | 701 | 53.4% | 407 | 53.8% | 2135 | 40.9% |
| Clergy | 221 | 16.8% | 151 | 20.0% | 161 | 3.1% |
| Medicine | 83 | 6.3% | 53 | 7.0% | 1079 | 20.7% |
| Law | 62 | 4.7% | 29 | 3.8% | 186 | 3.6% |
| Total | 1067 | 81.2% | 640 | 84.6% | 3561 | 68.3% |

*Source:* Charles S. Johnson, *The Negro College Graduate* (New York: Negro Universities Press, 1969, originally published in 1938), p. 120, Table LXIX.

53. Du Bois, "Memorial Address," pp. 160–161.

54. W. E. B. Du Bois, *The College-Bred Negro American* (Atlanta: Atlanta University Press, 1910), p. 66.

55. The reader should be aware of the almost impossibility of a very precise analysis of the time-series analysis of the occupations of the blacks during the time period between 1900–1950. We will explain the sources of difficulties. The first and fundamental problem in the data is that they are approximations only. This is particularly true for the data of the year of 1900. The second source of difficulties is that the statistics before 1940 were "civilian gainful workers 10 years old and over," while the statistics for 1940 and 1950 were for persons 14 years old and over. One way to solve this problem is to analyze the occupation categories not by numbers, but by percentages. But the third and more serious problem in the analysis is that the divisions of the categories of occupations changed over time. The census of 1900 used a scheme, that had been used since 1870 and refined in 1890. Thus, there were five categories of occupations in the census of 1900: "agricultural pursuits," "professional service," "domestic and personal service," "trade and transportation," and "manufacturing and mechanical pursuits." In 1910, the categories of occupations expanded to nine: "agriculture, forestry, and animal husbandry," "extraction of minerals," "manufacturing and mechanical industries," "transportation," "trade," "public service," "professional service," "domestic service," and "clerical occupations." The census of 1920 used the same scheme as 1910. In 1930, there were also some minor changes. The category of "agriculture, forestry, and animal husbandry" in the censuses of 1910 and 1920 was divided into "agriculture" and "forestry and fishing," and the category of "transportation" in the censuses of 1910 and 1920 was changed to "transportation and communication." In 1940, however, a major change was made in the census. The category of "agriculture" was divided in two: "farmers and farm managers" and "farm laborers and foremen." The service sector was divided into four categories: "professional and semiprofessional workers," "domestic service workers," "protective service workers," and "service workers except domestic and protective." The category of "clerical occupations" in the census of 1910 became "clerical, sales, and kindred workers" and included some of the trade and transportation jobs. Finally, four categories of occupations were created from the manufacturing, trade, and transport categories in the census of 1910: "proprietors, managers, and officials, except farm," "craftsmen, foremen, and kindred workers," "operatives and kindred workers," and "laborers, except farm and mine." In 1950, there were again several minor changes to the scheme used in 1940. The category of "professional and semiprofessional workers" was changed to "professional, technical, and kindred workers." The category of "clerical, sales, and kindred workers" in the census of 1940 was divided into categories of

"clerical and kindred workers" and "sales workers." On the other hand, the three categories of "domestic service workers," "protective service workers," and "service workers except domestic and protective" were simplified to two categories : "private household workers" and "service workers, except private household." See David L. Kaplan and M. Claire Casey, *Occupational Trends in the United States 1900 to 1950* (Washington D.C.: U.S. Government Printing Office, 1958), pp. 1–2. For the change of the job categories between 1900 and 1940, see Margo Anderson Conk, *The United States Census and Labor Force Change* (Ann Arbor, Mich., 1978), pp. 21–27.

56. Du Bois, "Memorial Address," p. 160.

57. Du Bois, "Memorial Address, pp. 99–100.

58. David McBride and Monroe H. Little, "The Afro-American Elite, 1930–1940: A Historical and Statistical Profile," in *Phylon* XLII, no. 2 (Summer 1981): p. 115.

59. In 1950, the number of male black college graduates in was 6,467 (49.3%), and that of female black college graduates was 6,641 (50.7%). The number of black male professionals in 1950 was 72,750 (41.61%), and that of female professionals in the same year was 102,090 (58.39%). Smith and Horton, *op.cit.*, p. 619; Department of Commerce, Bureau of the Census, *United States Census of Population: 1950, Special Reports, Occupation by Industry* (Washington, D.C.: U.S. Government Printing Office, 1954), pp. 1B29–1B37, Table 3.

60. Johnson, *The Negro College Graduate*, p.109.

61. Lane, *Dorsey's Philadelphia*, p. 166–196; Genna Rae McNeil, "Charles Hamilton Houston," in John Hope Franklin and August Meier, eds., *Black Leaders of the Twentieth Century* (Urbana: University of Illinois Press, 1982), pp. 221–240.

62. Andrea Tuttle Kornbluh, "James Hathaway Robinson and the Origins of Professional Social Work in the Black Community," in Taylor, ed., *Race and the City*, pp. 209–231.

63. David McBride and Monroe H. Little, "The Afro-American Elite," pp.107, 114–115.

64. Spear, *Black Chicago*, pp. 97, 91–110.

65. Carter G. Woodson, *The Negro Professional Man and the Community* (New York: Negro Universities Press, 1969; originally published in 1934), pp. 81–103.

66. F. James Davis, *Who Is Black? One Nation's Definition* (University Park: Pennsylvania State University Press, 1989), pp. 142–143. Davis brings home what it meant to be black in the industrial city with his compassionate story of the death of Walter White, father of the NAACP.

67. Alba Edwards, "The Negro as a Factor in the Nation's Labor Force," *Journal of the American Statistical Society*, XXXI (1936): 529–540.

68. Lane, *Dorsey's Philadelphia*, pp. 63–97; Robert C. Weaver, *Negro Labor: A National Problem* (New York: Harcourt, Brace and Company, 1946), pp. 3–15, 97–108; Trotter, *Coal, Class, and Color*, pp. 9–38.

69. Kelley, *Race Rebels*, pp. 55–75, 17–34.

70. Drake and Cayton, *Black Metropolis*, p. 516

71. E. Franklin Frazier, "Negro Harlem: An Ecological Study," *The American Journal of Sociology* XLIII (July 1937–May 1938): 72–88; Sugrue, *Urban Crisis*, pp. 181–207; Thomas W. Hanchett, *Sorting Out the New South City: Race, Class, and Urban Development in Charlotte, 1875–1975* (Chapel Hill: University of North Carolina Press, 1998), pp. 115–144.

72. Sugrue, *Urban Crisis*, pp. 181–207, 197–198.

73. Wilson, *Hamilton Park*, pp. 10–32.

74. August Meier, *Negro Thought in America: 1880–1915, Racial Ideologies in the Age of Booker T. Washington* (Ann Arbor: University of Michigan Press, 1968), pp. 26–69, 121–139; Wilson Jeremiah Moses, *The Golden Age of Black Nationalism, 1850–1925* (New York: Oxford University Press, 1978), pp. 197–271; Drake and Cayton, *Black Metropolis*, pp. 379–716.

75. See Chapter 3, Andrea Tuttle Kornbluh, "Municipal Harmony: Cultural Pluralism, Public Recreation, and Race Relations."

76. Drake and Cayton, *Black Metropolis*, p. 723.

77. Georgina Hickey discusses this issue in great detail in Chapter 4, "From Auburn Avenue to Buttermilk Bottom: Class and Community Dynamics among Atlanta's Blacks."

# CHAPTER 2

# Creating the Metropolis in Black and White

## Black Suburbanization and the Planning Movement in Cincinnati, 1900–1950

### HENRY LOUIS TAYLOR, JR.

## INTRODUCTION

The Kerner Commission, in its 1968 report on urban riots, argued that the nation was being divided into two societies, "one largely Negro and poor, located in central cities; the other, predominantly white and afflu- ent, located in the suburbs." The discriminatory policies of the Federal Housing Administration (FHA), which spawned the postwar, race-based suburbanization movement, is generally seen as the main culprit behind the creation of the metropolis in black and white.[1]

The Federal Housing Act of 1934, scholars argue, brought home ownership within reach of millions of Americans by placing the credit of the federal government behind private lending to home buyers. However, the openly racist categories in the FHA's "confidential" city surveys and appraisers manuals channeled most of the loan monies toward whites and away from blacks. By routing loans away from older central city neighborhoods and toward white home buyers moving into the increas- ingly segregated suburban municipalities, the FHA and private lenders parented a race-based suburbanization movement that racially split the metropolis.[2]

Certainly, FHA support for suburban segregation did intensify and accelerate the movement toward a racially divided metropolis after World War II, but in this chapter, I argue that the policies and practices that paved the way for such segregation (1) involved mostly local plan- ners, housing reformers, and civic leaders, not federal bureaucrats, (2) centered around residential land-use issues and changing notions of home ownership, and (3) took place between 1900 and 1950, before the rise of mass suburbanization. Moreover, this process of city planning was more complicated than elite whites crafting policies, passing laws, and engaging in varied practices that allowed them to impose their ideas of "community" onto a malleable working-class population. Rather, the city planning process involved a clash between semiskilled and unskilled black and white workers trying to build homes and communities in the suburban hinterland, and the efforts of white planners, housing reformers, and civic leaders to turn the suburbs into a residential haven for higher-income groups.

The purpose of this chapter is to explore this proposition by examining the settlement patterns of black Cincinnatians and their quest to build communities in metropolitan Cincinnati, and by showing how this process of building black communities conflicted with the efforts of Cincinnati planners, housing reformers, and civic leaders to build a modern industrial metropolis between 1900 and 1950. This chapter is divided into two parts: the first part examines the role of race and class in the rise of metropolitan Cincinnati, and the second part looks at the evolution of the planning movement and explores the clash between black community-building efforts and Cincinnati's planning community.

## ONE BIG CITY—RACE, CLASS, AND THE RISE OF THE INDUSTRIAL METROPOLIS

The scattering of factories across Cincinnati's hilltops and valleys triggered a suburbanization movement that transformed the industrial city into an urban metropolis. The factory led the way.[3] Beginning around 1867 along the Mill Creek Valley and Norwood Trough, as factories uprooted themselves and moved outward, workers followed, taking with them their churches, schools, saloons, lodges, and small shops and stores. Initially, to keep pace with the outmigration, the central city gobbled up the self-contained towns and villages surrounding it. Because of this urban imperialism, central city dominance over the suburban region persisted throughout the late 19th century and the opening decade of the 20th century, even though more and more people moved to the outlying areas.[4]

Cincinnati's highly successful incorporation and consolidation movement waned after 1910, and by 1920, the Age of Urban Imperialism was over. As the central city's boundaries became increasingly fixed, and as companies created ever more jobs in the suburbs, factories and workers poured across the central city line into the hinterland. The suburbs grew much faster than the central city, and the center of population growth and community development shifted to the outlying areas, even though most Hamilton County residents continued to live in the central city. For example, between 1920 and 1950 the central city grew by 102,751 residents (26 percent), while the suburban population jumped by 127,523 (138 percent). Yet by 1950, 70 percent of county residents were still living in the central city. So even though the central city's share of the county's population dwindled over time, it remained much larger than the suburbs throughout the first half of the 20th century. Even so, by "citifying" the rural countryside, the expanding urban frontier turned the central city and suburb into "one big city."[5]

The peopling of the suburban region was a remarkably democratic process. People from across the income, occupational, racial, and ethnic spectrum joined the trek to the suburban outskirts as blue-collar and white-collar workers; skilled, semiskilled, and unskilled workers; and white American-born and immigrant workers, along with black workers, moved from the central city to the outlying areas. Thus during the period from 1900 to 1950, corporate presidents, plant supervisors, school teachers, doctors, lawyers, clerks, insurance agents, accountants, machinists, electricians, metal workers, welders, seamstresses, assemblers, textile workers, janitors, stockmen, guards, waiters, yard workers, and domestic servants made their home in the suburban hinterland.[6]

The blue collar worker dominated the suburban movement.[7] During these times, suburbanization was an emblem of working-class culture, not a symbol of middle-class status or entry into that group. For example, a random survey of 392 suburban residents listed in the 1944 Hamilton County Directory showed that 61 percent of the listed suburbanites were blue-collar workers, including a surprising number of semiskilled and unskilled workers. Those moving to the suburbs settled in the bucolic municipalities of the rich, the white-collar municipalities of the new middle class, the blue-collar municipalities of the workers, and the varied subdivisions located in the unincorporated areas.

The suburbs were a "melting pot" of classes, races, and ethnic groups. The bucolic and white-collar municipalities housed an assortment of workers from across the occupational, race and ethnic universe, and even in the blue-collar suburban municipalities, middle-class and elite families could be found. Moreover, in the prestigious Indian Hills community, skilled and unskilled workers, along with domestic servants, could be found living among the elites.

The interaction of four forces made possible this pattern of population movement and settlement. First, the transportation revolution opened up the suburbs for mass settlement and the relocation of industry. Second, because of a lengthy journey to work, many workers needed to live close to work, which led to the growth of blue-collar communities in the suburbs. Third, the availability of cheap land and the existence of a well-organized, "secondary" housing market made it possible for workers, even those with low incomes, to acquire land and housing in the suburbs. Finally, the existence of a weak system of land-use control in the suburbs meant that any type of subdivision could be established and that any type of house could be built.[8]

## THE CENTRAL CITY

As people moved to the suburban hinterland, powerful centrifugal forces led to a redistribution of the central city population. Cincinnati originally formed in a basin surrounded by sharply rising hills. The Mill Creek Valley on the west and the Deer Creek Valley on the east were the only two entrances into the city. The hilly topography limited outward expansion, making Cincinnati an extremely crowded city.[9] In fact, for decades Cincinnati was one of the nation's most congested cities. However, even after a transportation revolution in the late 19th and early 20th centuries made possible the urbanization of Hamilton County and a spate of annexations expanded the central city's boundaries from 6 square miles to more than 50 square miles, many Cincinnatians continued to reside in "the Basin." For example, when the 20th century began, 180,175 people, or 51 percent of all Cincinnatians, were residing in the Basin, along with a jumble of factories, office buildings, shops, stores, and tenements.[10]

During the ensuing decades, this settlement pattern changed. After 1900, thousands left the Basin for other parts of Cincinnati and the suburban region. Between 1900 and 1950, the Basins population plunged by 30 percent [N = 53,985], and the proportion of all Cincinnatians living in this small place dropped from 51 percent to 25 percent. At the same time, the central city's population outside the Basin surged by 122 percent [N=207,783] and the suburban population leaped by 163 percent [N=136,377]. As people vacated the Basin, those neighborhoods located on the city's periphery grew the fastest, with the communities of Hyde Park, Oakley, Kennedy Heights, Pleasant Ridge, and Avondale leading the way.[11]

Blacks and whites experienced the central city differently. As thousands of whites moved out of the crowded Basin, thousands of blacks moved into it. For example, between 1935 and 1950, as the white Basin population fell by 29 percent [N=27,755], the black Basin population jumped by 39 percent (N=15,955]. Yet at the same time, the influx of most blacks into the Basin was accompanied by a scattering of other blacks across the central city and into the suburban region. By 1930, blacks could be found living in every part of Cincinnati, with about 14 percent [N=7,495] of Black Cincinnati living in the suburbs.[12]

Despite the suburbanization trend among blacks, between 1900 and 1950 the proportion of Hamilton County blacks living in Cincinnati increased from 82 percent to 86 percent. Simultaneously, the proportion of Hamilton County whites living in Cincinnati dropped from 76 percent to 59 percent. "Dispersal," then, characterized the white settlement pattern, while "concentration and dispersal" characterized the black experience. Against this backdrop, those blacks being concentrated were moving into a community that whites were abandoning, while those blacks being dispersed were moving into communities where whites were flocking. These communities, into which dispersing central city blacks were moving, were places with moderate to high rates of rent and home ownership. In fact, surprisingly the majority of dispersing blacks moved into the eastern part of the central city, where the highest rental rates in Cincinnati were found.[13]

Ironically, most dispersing blacks were unskilled workers with low incomes. Wherever Cincinnati's black elite settled, their low-income compatriots soon followed. So the dispersal of low-income blacks typically led to the formation of cross-class communities, where high and low-income blacks lived together. Neither racism nor high rents and rates of home ownership could keep blacks out of white-dominated residential areas. For example, as late as 1935, 14 of Cincinnati's 27 communities, not including the Basin, had at least 100 blacks living in them, including five communities that had 500 or more black residents.[14]

The aforementioned statistics show that blacks could be found living throughout Cincinnati. Even in prestigious communities like Hyde Park, Clifton, and Avondale, blacks managed to find housing they could afford, both rental and owner-occupied. During this epoch, the system of land-use controls, even after the passage of zoning laws and buildings codes, could not keep low-income groups out of high-rent communities. The forces of segregation were not sufficiently powerful to residentially separate blacks from whites. Even in the ghetto, blacks and whites shared residential space. However, outside the Basin, in white-dominated communities, blacks lived in a cluster of homes or formed all-black blocks or streets within the larger community.[15]

Despite ghetto formation and white hostility toward blacks, a remarkable degree of residential mobility existed among low-income blacks between 1900 and 1950, and blacks could be found living in every part of the central city and suburban region. This tendency of low-income black residential settlements to pop up almost anywhere in the metropolitan region, as we shall see, became a growing source of concern to Cincinnati's planning community.

## THE PLANNING MOVEMENT AND
## BLACK SUBURBANIZATION

As people, businesses,and industries scattered across Hamilton County, a planning movement emerged to guide the city building process which evolved out of the social reform movement. It was led by Alfred Bettman, a Harvard-educated corporate lawyer, and Bleecker Marquette, Executive Secretary of the Better Housing League (BHL). Bettman and Marquette stood at the forefront of the planning movement until Bettman's unexpected death in 1945.[16] In the years between 1915 and 1950, the planning movement evolved through two stages of development. The era of city planning dominated the first stage in the planning movement and lasted from 1915 to 1925. From 1926 to 1950, the planning movement shifted its emphasis from city planning to regional planning.[17]

The city planning movement was officially launched in 1915 when the United City Planning Committee was formed by representatives of Cincinnati's major business and civic organizations. On July 10, 1916, the Better Housing League of Cincinnati was founded as a result of the efforts of the Women's City Club; Max Senior, founder of the United Jewish Charities; and Courtenay Dinwiddie, Secretary of the Anti-Tuberculosis League. Marquette was brought to Cincinnati from New York City in 1918 to head the BHL. Under his leadership, the league became the leading advocate of city and regional planning and chief architect of housing reform and residential development in metropolitan Cincinnati.[18]

The city planning movement consisted of a loose federation of Cincinnati's most important civic, social, and business organizations, along with members of city government.[19] This planning community was held together by three fundamental ideas. First, they believed that years of unplanned, unregulated, and chaotic patterns of growth and development had led to serious social and economic problems that now threatened Cincinnati's future. [20] Second, they felt that organized, regulated planning was the only way to "correct" past mistakes, and to ensure that the city's growth and development proceeded in an orderly fashion.[21] Third, they believed that the central city and suburbs, despite political fragmentation, was "one big city."[21] So throughout the period from 1915 to 1950, the planning community thought and acted in metropolitan terms.

Although the planning community viewed the metropolis as "one big city," from 1915 until the adoption of the 1925 Official City Plan, central city planning dominated their agenda. During this period, most Hamilton County residents lived in Cincinnati, and the future of the region was dependent on the central city's development. Thus, during its nascent stage, the planning movement focused on formulating a strategy to guide the central city's growth and development.

Within this context, building a modern residential environment was the planning community's top priority.[22] Here, the idea was to structure a residential setting in which neighborhoods were segregated on the basis of housing cost and type. The owner-occupied, single-family house would anchor this modern residential environment. Home ownership, however, was not for everyone.[23] Home ownership had been a symbol of working-class culture, and even low-income workers often purchased or built their own homes, both in the city and suburb. The planning community wanted to change this. To them, home ownership should be an emblem of middle-class status, a rank afforded only to higher-income groups.[24]

The planning community felt that home ownership was beyond the economic reach of low- to moderate-income workers. The houses these workers could afford to buy, construct, or rent were poorly constructed ones that often deteriorated and blighted neighborhoods.[27] Therefore the planning community believed that when these workers moved into communities with higher-income groups, they undermined the home ownership ideal by blighting neighborhoods, devaluing property, and turning "good" neighborhoods into slums.[27] The planning community therefore wanted to curtail the residential mobility of low-income workers. From the planning community's perspective, enclaves of low-income workers, because of the housing they occupied, represented a "menace to the city."[28]

Thus, in order for the home ownership ideal to take root, neighborhoods dominated by the single-family homes had to be protected from "invasion" by undesirable residents. In its 1921 Annual Report, the Better Housing League said, "It would be a short-sighted policy to encourage the construction of small homes and to foster home ownership, and at the same time fail to take every precaution to see to it that the residential districts are not properly protected." So to promote the idea of home ownership, the planning community used zoning laws, building codes, subdivision regulations, and city planning to guide the residential development process.[29]

These methods of controlling residential land use were codified in the 1925 Official City Plan. The residential zoning scheme, outlined in the plan, called for the development of three types of residential areas: Residential Class A reserved land exclusively for single-family homes, class B permitted both two- and four-family housing units, and Class C allowed for the building of any type of dwelling unit. The central idea undergirding this scheme was the creation of homogeneous neighborhoods by segregating the population on the basis of income and race.[30]

During the 1920s, as the city planning movement gained momentum, Bettman, Marquette, and others became increasingly aware that an exodus of people out of the central city had shifted population growth and residential development to the suburbs. So the planning committee changed its focus. City planning, it argued, was no longer adequate in an epoch of metropolitan development.[31] Now planning had to become regional in scope, and from the mid-1920s onward, regional planning became the planning community's top priority. City planning did continue in Cincinnati, but it now took place within a metropolitan context, as the creation of a regional master plan to guide the growth and development of the entire county became the planning community's prime goal.

Beginning in 1926, Alfred Bettman, along with the United City Planning Commission, led the effort to form an organization that would guide the regional planning movement. In 1929, the Regional Planning Commission of Hamilton County, consisting of the governments of the City of Cincinnati, the County of Hamilton, and 14 suburban municipalities, was established. Nineteen years later, on November 22, 1948, the City Planning Commission adopted the Cincinnati Metropolitan Master Plan and the Official City Plan.[32]

The growth and development of this planning movement formed the contextual setting in which black suburbanization took place. The "invasion" of the suburbs by blacks had a big impact on the planning movement, even though only a small number of blacks actually moved there. Between 1920 and 1950, when the center of population growth in metropolitan Cincinnati shifted to the suburban region, the rate of black suburbanization surpassed the rate of white suburbanization. During this period, the black suburban population grew from 3,668 to 11,887, an increase of 224 percent, while the white suburban population grew by 134 percent [N=119,229].[33]

Industrial geography also shaped the pattern of black suburbanization. Most African Americans migrating to the suburbs moved into the rapidly growing eastern half of Hamilton County, with the majority settling in the Springfield and Sycamore townships, where the center of industrial development was located. But pockets of African Americans could be found living in every other section of the suburbs as well.[34]

While a few blacks moved into existing suburban municipalities, most flocked into the unincorporated sections of Hamilton County, where land-use controls were almost nonexistent. Here a speculator could develop any type of subdivision and a person could build any type of house. Even after adoption of the 1925 Official City Plan and the formation of a Regional Planning Commission, city, county, and suburban leaders still had little control over the regulation of residential land in the unincorporated sections of Hamilton County.[35]

Two issues were of major concern to the planning community. First, much of the county was unincorporated. The future of suburban development, the planning community believed, rested with the residential development of the unincorporated sections of Hamilton County.[36] Second, between 1920 and 1950 the Basin was the center of an intense land-use conversion zone, where hundreds of dwelling units were being demolished to make way for commercial buildings, shops, stores, and a new highway system. The planning community was fearful that the displacement of thousands of African Americans from the Basin might lead to the growth of black suburban enclaves, which in turn might jeopardize their vision of turning the suburbs into a residential haven for higher-income groups.[37]

A close look at the experiences of those blacks settling in the Lockland, Wyoming, and Woodlawn sections of the Springfield and Sycamore townships will provide insight into the concerns of the planning community, and show how these planners, housing reformers, and civic leaders tried to hamper the movement of blacks to the suburban region.

Those blacks, who moved into the Springfield and Sycamore townships and formed the suburban municipality called Lincoln Heights, came to Cincinnati during the World War I era. Michael Mangham, a Georgian and a driving force behind the founding of Lincoln Heights, came to Cincinnati in 1921. When asked why he moved there, Mangham simply said, "I came to Cincinnati to do better." He spoke for a generation of black migrants.[38]

For Mangham and others, "doing better" meant, among other things, finding a good place to live and raise their families. During this era, when blacks had little control over the workplace, developing the "homeplace" became an important way of improving their lives and enhancing their social status.[39] Their goals were the same as many other workers: buying a home of their own, with a yard, garden, and open space, and living in a neighborhood free of crime, vice, and congestion that was located in a setting they could control.[40]

Most, but not all, of the migrants to Lincoln Heights initially settled in the West End of the Basin. This was the worst residential location in metropolitan Cincinnati.[41] The area was characterized by congestion, dilapidation, crime, and omnipresent destruction and construction. Consequently, the founders of Lincoln Heights did not think the West End was a good neighborhood and wanted to get out.

The experiences of Sims Thompson and his wife, Elverna, who also moved to Cincinnati in the 1920s, were typical. Thompson said the "roughness" of the West End, along with the "congestion," made him want to get out. "The West End was so bad," he said. "Fighting was going on all of the time. . . . A guy almost hit me with a brick that he was throwing at someone else." His wife, Elverna, said that her family also disliked the crowded living conditions. "Very seldom did a family have over two rooms, regardless of its size," she said. Sims Thompson and Elverna Thompson were determined to leave the West End.[42]

A convergence of three factors made it possible for working-class blacks like Mike Mangham and Sims Thompson to move to the suburbs, buy land, and build houses of their own. First, city and county leaders had limited control over residential development in the unincorporated sections of Hamilton County. Second, the urbanization process made available vast tracts of cheap rural land for residential development. In this epoch, roving bands of land speculators moved around the country, buying cheap farm land, subdividing it without installing water and sewer lines or paving streets, and then selling the lots to low-income workers.[43] While many planners, housing reformers, and civic leaders viewed the practice as exploitive, for blacks like Mike Mangham and Sims and Elverna Thompson it was the only way they could buy land and build a home.

Third, during the 1900 to 1950 period, a dual housing market existed in metropolitan Cincinnati. A primary housing market met the housing needs of higher-income groups, while a secondary housing market catered to the housing needs of the lower-income workers. The secondary housing market was a surprisingly complex one, consisting of real estate speculators, building material companies, banks, savings and loan companies, and an army of carpenters willing to help low-income workers build their own homes. In this setting, a worker could borrow money, obtain "used" lumber and other building supplies, and then find someone, if needed, to help with the construction of his or her home.[44]

Within this framework, between 1923 and 1929 Lincoln Heights was formed from ten subdivisions that were established by white land speculators, without paved roads, water or sewage lines, or connections to electricity. Even so, blacks flocked to the area. Between 1923 and 1950, the population of Lincoln Heights grew from 57 to 6,610, making it one of the largest black communities in the metropolitan region.[45] Most blacks moving to Lincoln Heights were unskilled industrial workers who found jobs in factories located in the upper Mill Creek Valley.[46] Many were owner-builders, who constructed their own homes or hired a carpenter to help them. Often these workers built their homes piecemeal—one or two rooms at a time.

For example, Odell Boggs, a factory worker, purchased a lot, bought used lumber, and worked on his house in the evening and on the weekends with the help of friends. After completing two rooms, Boggs and his family moved in. Several years later, he hired a carpenter to help him finish the house. A few residents, like Robert Bangs, even lived in a tent while building their homes. Other land owners had their homes built by professional carpenters.[47]

The goal of these black workers was to build a community, not just to construct houses. So they formed clubs and organizations, built churches, started volunteer fire and police departments, had an elementary school constructed, and received Works Progress Administration funds to install sewers and pave some streets. Later, in the early 1940s, believing that they could provide for themselves better services and a more responsive government than the county commissioners, the residents filed for incorporation and in 1944 became an independent municipality.[48]

The emergence of a settlement of low-income blacks in the unincorporated portions of Hamilton County concerned the planning community. They thought Lincoln Heights was a "suburban slum." In 1940, for example, BHL President Standish Meacham called the community "the ugliest collection of nondescript, unsanitary shacks in the country."[49] The planning community believed that settlements like Lincoln Heights were a "menace" that jeopardized their goal of turning the suburbs into a residen-

tial haven for higher-income groups.[50] Thus, a conflict existed between
the planning community's and the black migrant's vision of the suburban
region. They had two opposing ideas about what type of housing and
communities should be allowed to develop in the suburban region.

The first sign of this conflict came in 1927. In that year, the BHL
conducted a study of the subdivisions that composed Lincoln Heights to
familiarize the Hamilton County commissioners with the problem of
suburban slums. In describing the settlement, the Report stated:[51]

> In some subdivisions, a few loads of gravel and cinders have been
> dumped in the streets. There are no curbs, no sidewalks, no sewers, no
> water and no gas. . . . In the 8 (sic) subdivisions, there are 200 lots
> which means homes for at least 2,000 families or a population between
> 7,000 and 10,000 persons. . . . We have old subdivisions, such as
> Steele, Dunbar, Fairfax, and Seketan that have been sore spots for
> years. It is inconceivable that we should continue to allow more poten-
> tial slums to take up good building sites in the county.

In submitting the report to the county commissioners, Bleecker and
Marquette urged them to "find ways and means providing such regulation as will require future subdivisions to provide sewers, water, and
paved roads before lots are offered for sale to the public." He hoped this
would stop the spread of suburban settlements like Lincoln Heights.
From 1927 onward, the planning community waged a tireless campaign
to stop the spread of suburban slums.[52] This campaign operated on three
different but highly interactive levels.

At one level, the planning community sought to formulate regulatory controls that allowed them to guide residential development in the
unincorporated areas. Here they fought for the passage of a county zoning law and for subdivision regulations and building codes that outlawed
unimproved subdivisions and poorly constructed houses. By forcing
speculators to provide sewers, water, paved roads, and other improvements in their subdivisions, and by setting high building standards, the
cost of home ownership, they hoped, would be pushed beyond the economic means of most ordinary and low-income workers.[53]

At another level, the planning community sought to change the class
structure of Lincoln Heights. The planning community knew they could
not displace those blacks currently living in Lincoln Heights.[54] So rather
than contest the residents, the planning community worked to change the
class character of this neighborhood. If a black community had to exist in

the suburbs, they reasoned, it should be a middle-class one. To encourage the migration of higher-income blacks to Lincoln Heights, the planning community initiated two major housing projects. In 1940, the Cincinnati Metropolitan Housing Authority (CMHA) applied for a Defense Housing Project for black industrial workers, which was approved by the Federal Works Agency. Construction was completed on a 350-unit defense housing project called Valley View in 1941. Significantly, the CMHA rented units at Valley View for about $25.24 per month, or $302 yearly, which was almost twice the average rental rate of other public housing projects in metropolitan Cincinnati.[55]

Then in 1944 and 1945 Marianna Matthews, daughter of William A. Proctor and Elizabeth Proctor of the Proctor and Gamble Soap Company, with the assistance of BHL built the Norris Homes project, a subdivision of well-constructed, single-family homes for sale to blacks. This was the first project in Cincinnati where new houses had been built for sale to higher-income blacks. During the 1920s, the planning community felt that blacks could not afford new houses. However, by 1940 this view had changed. Now there was a critical mass of blacks, they believed, who could afford new houses. The Norris Homes project was built for this market.[56]

At the third level, market forces bolstered the planning community's goal of turning the suburb into a haven for higher-income groups. Between 1940 and 1945, 89 percent of all new housing in the suburb was single-family dwellings, while only 30 percent of new housing units in the central city were single-family housing units. Thus, by mid-20th century, single-family dwelling units dominated the suburban region, while multifamily dwellings dominated the central city. Throughout the period from 1900 to 1950, the majority of blacks remained concentrated in low-paying, semiskilled, and unskilled jobs, which made much of new, single-family suburban housing too expensive for them. The creation of a built environment in which single-family houses dominated the suburban region and multiple-family housing dominated the central city fashioned circumstances that steered most low-income residents, black and white, to the central city neighborhoods.[57]

The interplay of these three factors helps to explain why the proportion of blacks living in the central city remained virtually unchanged between 1920 and 1950, while the proportion of whites living in the central city declined significantly. For example, over this period the proportion of Hamilton County blacks living in the central city changed from 89 percent to 87 percent. Over the same time, the proportion of Hamilton

County whites living in the central city dropped from 75 percent to 59 percent.

So the planning community, by consciously pursuing policies designed to push the cost of housing beyond the economic reach of lower-income workers, contributed to the concentration of African Americans in the central city. It was within this framework that the discriminatory policies of the FHA operated to produce two urban societies: one, black and poor, located in the central cities; the other, predominantly white and affluent, located in the suburbs.

## NOTES

1. Douglas S. Massey and Nancy A. Denton, *American Apartheid: Segregation and the Making of the Underclass* (Cambridge and London: Harvard University Press, 1993), pp. 3–4.

2. George Lipsitz, "The Possessive Investment in Whiteness: Racialized Social Democracy and the 'White' Problem in American Studies," *American Quarterly* 47(September 1995): 369–387; Kenneth T. Jackson, *Crabgrass Frontier: The Suburbanization of the United States* (New York and Oxford: Oxford University Press, 1985), pp. 190–218.

3. Graham Romeyn Taylor, *Satellite Cities: A Study of Industrial Suburbs* (New York and London: D. Appleton and Company, 1915), pp. 91–126; Zane L. Miller, *Boss Cox's Cincinnati: Urban Politics in the Progressive Era* (New York: Oxford University Press, 1968), pp. 3–8. When the Technical Advisory Corporation engaged in studies designed to prepare the Cincinnati City Plan of 1925, they created maps that showed the transportation routes and the industrial areas of the central city and suburb. Technical Advisory Corporation, "Industrial Map A of the City of Cincinnati, Showing Facilities in Adjacent Territories," Chamber of Commerce, 1925, Cincinnati Historical Society.

4. Miller, *Boss Cox*, pp. 3–8; 27; 109. For an explanation of why the territorial expansion of Cincinnati faltered after 1920, see Roger Hanson, "A Part of the City: Annexation in Cincinnati, 1920–1940," Fifth National Conference on American Planning History, Chicago, Illinois, November 19, 1993.

5. The census analysis used in this study is based on a detailed study of the population census of Hamilton County for the period between 1850 and 1950. Data on the population of Hamilton County was gathered by race, and where possible, by ethnicity, for the entire period by county, township, and urban places with a population between 2,500 and 10,000 and for the central city. Also, the data were analyzed by wards and, for the later periods, by census tracts. One major problem encountered in the interpretation of the data is that the central

city's boundaries are constantly changing. No effort was made to account for this. The constantly changing boundaries was a reflection of the successful annexation and consolidation campaign. Once this ended, the suburb started to grow much faster than the central city. For the purposes of this chapter, I will not cite all of the census records, but simply refer to them as U.S. Bureau of the Census, 1850 to 1950. I coined the term "one big city" to explain the how the urbanization process created an urban metropolis. Also, it helps to explain why Cincinnati leaders thought and acted in metropolitan terms. Robert B. Fairbanks first made me aware that of this trait of Cincinnati leaders. Fairbanks, *Making Better Citizens: Housing Reform and the Community Development Strategy in Cincinnati, 1890-1960* (Urbana and Chicago: University of Illinois Press, 1988).

6. To gain insight into the class structure, I studied the 1944 Hamilton County Directory, which provided a portrait of the class composition of the suburban region. *Williams Hamilton County Directory*, 1944 (Williams Directory Company).

7. Richard Harris, *Unplanned Suburbs: Toronto's American Tragedy, 1900 to 1950* (Baltimore and London: Johns Hopkins Press, 1996), pp 1–20. Harris argues that the pre–World War II suburbs reflected working-class rather than middle-class culture.

8. Taylor, *Satellite Cities*, 1–26; Harris, *Unplanned Suburbs*, 1-20; Olivier Zunz, *The Changing Face of Inequality: Urbanization, Industrial Development, and Immigrants in Detroit, 1880–1920* (Chicago and London: University of Chicago Press, 1982), pp. 285–325. In most places during the industrial era, the conditions that made suburbanization possible for workers were present.

9. Charles Cist, *Cincinnati in 1850* (Cincinnati: W. H. Moore and Company, 1851), p. 13.

10. U.S. Bureau of the Census, 1850–1950; Miller, *Boss Cox*, pp. 3–6.

11. U.S. Bureau of the Census, 1850–1950; James A. Quinn, Earl Eubank, and Lois E. Elliott, *Population Changes—Cincinnati, Ohio and Adjacent Areas, 1900 to 1950., Research Monograph No. 47* (Columbus: Bureau of Business Research, Ohio State University Press, 1947). This monograph provides a detailed look at population movement in Cincinnati by census tract. It contains a number of excellent maps that show population movement and housing characteristics.

12. U.S. Bureau of the Census, 1850–1950. From 1930 onward, the availability of census tracts make it possible to make a detailed examination of the population movement of blacks, whites, and immigrant groups in Cincinnati and in Hamilton County.

13. Regional Department of Economic Security: Regional Census of Hamilton County, Ohio: Table 18—Summary of Family and Home Data, Cincin-

nati, 1935. University at Cincinnati, Archives and Rare Books, Census Tract Data Bank, S.28.11.19. Scholars have not fully appreciated the complexity of the black residential pattern during this period. The ghetto thesis minimizes the extent of black dispersal and the extent to which blacks and whites shared residential space. Although not a focal point of this study, our findings nevertheless raises questions about the ghetto formation thesis. See, for example, Allen Spear, *Black Chicago: The Making of a Negro Ghetto, 1890 to 1920* (Chicago: University of Chicago, 1967), pp. 11–126. See also the Prologue to this book.

14. During the 1930s, University of Cincinnati sociologists organized the City of Cincinnati into census tracts, defined various sections of the central city, and then created tables in which census tracts corresponded with the Cincinnati communities. Using this and other census data, I compiled my own listing of the communities and the census tracts that corresponded to them. The base figures that I used were compiled by Lois Elliott of the University of Cincinnati, Department of Sociology. In addition, the Inspections Department of the Housing Bureau had its own modifications of the relationship of census tracts to various communities in Cincinnati. I incorporated all these viewpoints, along with detailed study of maps, in determining the relationship of census tracts to Cincinnati communities. I have held these boundaries constant for the entire period. Lois Elliott to Mattie, Cincinnati Court of Common Pleas, April 23, 1946. UC Archives and Rare Books, Better Housing League Papers, S.28.10.17; UC Archives and Rare Books, City Planning Commission, Box 19, Folder: Population, Negro, ON-85-3.

15. James A. Quinn, Earle Euban, and Lois E. Elliott, *Cincinnati: Population Characteristics by Census Tracts, 1930 and 1935* (Bureau of Business Research, Ohio State University, Special Bulletin No. X-52, 1935), Municipal Reference Library, City Hall, Cincinnati. Blacks and whites share residential space. In 1935, in the eight census tracts where over 60 percent of all blacks in metropolitan Cincinnati resided, 44 percent of the population of those tracts were white. And large numbers of whites, both American and foreign-born, lived in each census tract. As late as 1950, even in the ghetto, blacks and whites lived together. This pattern is remarkably similar to the one characterizing the residential pattern in Cincinnati in the 1850s. Henry Louis Taylor, Jr., and Vicky Dula, "The Black Residential Experience and Community Formation in Antebellum Cincinnati," in Henry Louis Taylor, Jr., ed., *Race and the City: Work, Community, and Protest in Cincinnati, 1820–1970* (Urbana and Chicago: University of Illinois Press, 1993), pp. 96–125.

16. Bettman's career is chronicled in a number of places including John Lord O'Brian, *Forward to City and Regional Planning Papers, Vol. 13, Harvard City Planning Studies by Alfred Bettman* (Cambridge: Harvard University Press,

1946), pp. xv-xix; and Laurence Gerkens, "Bettman of Cincinnati," in Donald Krueckeberg, ed., *The American Planner: Biography and Recollections*, (New York: Methuen, 1983), pp. 120–148.

17. City Planning Commission, The Cincinnati Metropolitan Master Plan and The Official City Plan, 1948, pp. 3–5. Actually, the history of planning in Cincinnati dates back to the preparation of the Kessler Plan of Public Parks, which was written in 1907, and outlined an official guide in maintaining and extending Cincinnati's park system.

18. Metropolitan Master Plan, p. 3; Jon C. Dowling, "Creating City Planning As Government Function: Alfred Bettman and the City Planning Commission of Cincinnati" (paper presented at the Fifth National Conference on American Planning History, Chicago, November 19, 1993); Bleecker Marquette, "The History of Housing in Ohio" (paper presented at the Conference of Ohio Housing Authorities, Youngstown, Ohio, June 9, 1939), BHL Papers, UC, Archives and Rare Books; BHL, "Housing Progress in Cincinnati: Second Report," July 21, 1921 4, BHL Papers, UC, Archives and Rare Books.

19. Fairbanks, *Making Better Citizens*, pp. 1–8, 13–24.

20. *BHL, Houses or Homes: First Report of the Cincinnati Better Housing League*, Cincinnati, 1991, p. 23. BHL Papers, UC, Archives and Rare Books.

21. *BHL, Houses or Homes.*

22. This metropolitan perspective is made clear in the opening sentence of the 1925 City Plan. The planners say, "By Cincinnati, we mean metropolitan Cincinnati—that is, the whole surrounding region that is directly tributary to the city." This view of the planning community is derived from an examination of the board members of the various organizations, correspondence from various leaders, and examination of the minutes of organizations. These data show the interlocking nature of the relationships that existed among those involved in the city planning process. Many of these individuals participated in the political reform movement in Cincinnati, and over time, maintained the City Charter Committee as an unofficial political party. Between 1924 and 1938, Murry Seasongood and City Manager Clarence A. Dykstra supported the planning movement, and so too did the City Council. Leaders of the "primary" real estate industry participated and benefited from the movement, but in Cincinnati they did not lead it.

23. The BHL first put forward this idea in its 1921 report: "Any city's greatest asset is its homes. Tenement houses do not provided real homes, no matter how well constructed. They are not the best place for children to live in. . . . We must see to it that the single-family home habit is continued." This viewpoint represented an important shift away from a focus on tenement reform and solving the housing problems of moderate- to low-income workers. BHL, "Housing Progress in Cincinnati," p. 10.

24. The second report of the BHL indicated that home ownership was be-yond the economic reach of "ordinary workers." The report says that since these workers cannot afford new houses, that the best that could be done for them would be to construct houses for those with a higher income with a view to re-lieving the pressure from the top. BHL, "Housing Progress in Cincinnati," p. 9; Minutes, Housing Committee, BHL, December 30, 1921; January 19, 1922; Jan-uary 25, 1922; March 8, 1922. BHL Papers, Box 1, Folder 4, UC, Archives and Rare Books.

25. The planning community never say this directly. However, their contin-ued discussions of the inability of "ordinary" workers and workers with low-in-comes make it clear that new houses is for higher income groups: higher paid workers, the middle and upper classes. Moreover, throughout this period they focus on outlawing the type of housing and neighbors that are being created by workers with moderate to low-incomes. Again, there are repeated references to "bad spots" and "suburban slums" and subdivisions where workers have built their own homes. See Harris, *Unplanned Suburbs*, pp. 86–140.

26. In the 1925 City Plan, the planners say that even the cheapest "homes would have to rent for at least $600 a year to produce a safe investment. It is therefore obvious that the construction of single-family houses can not meet the needs of the mass of colored population and the white low-wage earner. . . . This means that it is not feasible now to give any consideration as a part of the City Plan to providing housing for low-wage earners." The City Planning Commis-sion, The Official City Plan of Cincinnati, Ohio, 1925, p. 51.

27. C. M. Stegner (Commissioner of Buildings), "The Menace of the City." n.d., Stanley Rowe Papers, Box 5, Folder 4, Cincinnati Historical Society.

28. Stegner, "The Menace of the City."

29. The ideas of the relationship between zoning, building codes, and subdi-vision regulations are spelled out in a number of documents. These ideas are most comprehensively presented in the 1925 City Plan. City Plan, pp. 25–38, 39–54.

30. See chapters 2 and 3 in the City Plan. Also, a review of the activities of the City Planning Commission and the Zoning Boards provide ample evidence that city leaders actually used the plan as a guide to the development of the cen-tral city.

31. George B. Ford, Vice-President of the Technical Advisory Corporation to Alfred Bettman. Letter on regional planning in Cincinnati, May 27, 1929, Re-gional Planning Committee, Correspondence, Alfred Bettman Papers, Box 8. UC, Archives and Rare Books; Myron Downs, City Engineer, to Members of the Regional Planning Commission, Memo on "Authority of the Regional Planning Commission," June 27, 1929, Regional Planning Commission, Correspondence,

Alfred Bettman Papers, Box 8. UC, Archives and Rare Books; Metropolitan Master Plan, pp. 3–5.

32. Metropolitan Master Plan, pp. 3–5.

33. U.S. Bureau of the Census, 1850–1950.

34. City Planning Commission, Industrial Areas, June 1946. This book shows the distribution of industry in Cincinnati. See also Harris, *Unplanned Suburbs*. pp. 51–85.

35. Ladislas Segoe to Robert Taft, July 6, 1935. They discuss the problem of lack of regulatory controls in the suburbs. Alfred Bettman Papers, Box 9, S.1.9.2. UC, Archives and Rare Books.

36. Charles Urban indicated in a letter to Myron Downs that the unincorporated areas of the county composed 77 percent of the county and "the majority of its planning problems." Charles Urban to Myron Downs, June 17, 1939. See Map Showing Residential Development in Unincorporated Territory Surrounding Greater Cincinnati, Regional Planning Commission, 1944, Hamilton County Public Library, Clip File, Hamilton County Zoning.

37. Henry Louis Taylor, Jr., "City Building, Public Policy, the Rise of the Industrial City, and Black Ghetto-Slum Formation in Cincinnati, 1850–1940," in Taylor, ed., *Race and the City*, pp. 156–192.

38. Michael J. Mangham, interview by author, Cincinnati, April 1977.

39. This conceptual frame has been developed by Earl Lewis, *In Their Own Interest: Race, Class, and Power in Twentieth-Century Norfolk, Virginia* (Berkeley: University of California Press, 1991).

40. Harris, *Unplanned Suburbs*, 168–232; James Andrew Wiese, "Struggle for the Suburban Dream: African American Suburbanization Since 1916," Ph.D. diss., Department of History, Columbia University, 1993, pp. 47–84.

41. Numerous publications by housing reformers, planners and civic leaders lead little doubt that this was the worst place to live in the metropolitan region. The 1925 City Plan also makes this point. City Plan, Chapters 2 and 3.

42. Sims and Elverna Thompson, interview by author, Cincinnati, April 1977.

43. In Cincinnati, the speculators that sold most of the land to blacks were two whites whose home office was Chicago.

44. A study of Mechanic Lien Books, along with deed and mortgage records, provides an incredible source for gaining insight into the process low-income groups used to buy land and build houses. The Lien books, in particular, are an important source. They point out companies that were suing homeowners for nonpayment on contracts. These suits provide insights into who was constructing homes and lending money to low-income homeowners, as well as information on subcontractors who helped in the construction of homes. Most significant,

these records point out the complexity of the "secondary" housing market and provide substantial evidence that these workers were able to gain access to the resources necessary to buy land and build houses. See Oliver Zunz, *The Changing Face of Inequality: Urbanization, Industrial Development and Immigration in Detroit, 1880–1920* (Chicago: University of Chicago Press, 1982), pp. 130–176.

45. There are no accurate figures on population growth in Lincoln Heights prior to 1950. Yet data taken from the Hamilton County Deed and Mortgage Books, the CMHA 1936 application for a public housing project, a special 1940 census of the population for unincorporated areas, and the 1944 Lincoln Heights incorporation census, along with the 1950 census reports provide a rough profile of population growth in the community.

46. Data on the occupation of workers in Lincoln Heights was derived from a study of the 1944 Hamilton County Directory. I identified the streets on which blacks in Lincoln Heights lived and then on the basis of this information, I obtained information on 643 residents. The data contained information on martial status, occupation, employer, and street address. About 74 percent of these workers were unskilled laborers. Also, most listed their employers as companies located in the Upper Mill Creek Valley, where the Springfield and Sycamore townships were located.

47. Odell Boggs, interview by author, Cincinnati, April 1977.

48. Incorporation Proceedings, Deedbook 2185, pp. 245–259, Hamilton County Courthouse; Village of Lincoln Heights, "The Dedication of Matthews Drive," October 24, 1948; "Let History Be Our Guide," The Lincoln Heights Journal, February 1, 1979; John Harris, Jr., and Bargaret Blackwell Thompson, "The City of Lincoln Heights: A Historical Perspective," 1984, Clip File on Lincoln Heights, Cincinnati Historical Society.

49. *Cincinnati Enquirer*, "Protest is Written to Housing League"; *Cincinnati Post*, "Cites Lockland Property Handicap;" "Asks Negro to be Named to Housing League." The Urban League Papers, Newspaper Clip File, Cincinnati Historical Society. See Addendum A. The blacks in Lincoln Heights protested the statements made by Meacham.

50. Stegner, "Menace."

51. Minutes, BHL Board of Directors, November 15, 1927, BHL Papers, Board Meeting, 1916–1940, Box 5, UC, Archives and Rare Books.

52. Minutes, BHL Board of Directors, November 15, 1927, BHL Papers, Box 5, UC, Archives and Rare Books.

53. There are numerous letters and reports on this issue. The main obstacle to the passage of these regulations were powerful rural interests, who felt threatened by the laws. The following document provides an excellent summary of the

issues: Hamilton County Rural Zoning Commission, Proposed Zoning Resolution: Unincorporated Territory, September 1948.

54. Following Meacham comments about Lincoln Heights being a collection of shacks, the residents formed the Lincoln Heights Protective Association, hired Theodore Berry, a black attorney, and chairman of the Housing Committee of the Cincinnati Community Chest's Division of Negro Welfare, to represent them and then forced Meacham to make a public apology. Berry then asked the Better Housing League to appoint Father John Burgess, a black priest at the St. Simon Mission in Lincoln Heights, to the BHL's Committee that was studying housing regulations in unincorporated areas.

55. Cincinnati Metropolitan Housing Authority, Eighth Annual Report, 1941, pp. 8–9; *Cincinnati Enquirer*, March 27, 1941; Memorandum from C. F. Palmer, Coordinator of Defense Housing to the War Department, October 10, 1941. Records of the Home Finance Agency, National Archives. *Cincinnati Enquirer*. See Addendum A October 16, 1941. Hamilton County Library, Clip File: Cincinnati Housing. The picture shows what appears to be a middle-class family entering an apartment at Valley View.

56. Bleecker Marquette, "Mobilized Public Opinion Needed in Housing Program," One City's Housing, Series of articles reprinted from the *Cincinnati Post,* November 1944. In the article there is a photograph of the construction of the Norris Homes project. The houses depicted in the photograph appear to be well-constructed and attractive homes. The caption under the picture reads, "When the war ends, hundreds of families, white and Negro, will have savings for home purchase. There will be a vast market for well built private enterprise housing of moderate cost, like these homes now being completed in Lincoln Heights."

57. City Planning Commission, Communities: A Study of Community and Neighborhood Development, December 1947, The Metropolitan Master Plan.

# CHAPTER 3

# Municipal Harmony
## Cultural Pluralism, Public Recreation, and Race Relations

ANDREA TUTTLE KORNBLUH

## INTRODUCTION

Municipal Public Recreation programs of the 1920s, 1930s and 1940s functioned as tax-supported organized efforts to improve race relations and construct community in cities and towns across America. On the local level as well as the national, trained experts in community organizing sought to create recognition of the value of the cultures of the diverse groups that American society comprised, with the intent of using that cultural appreciation to argue for the equality of treatment for different groups of citizens. The same basic pattern can be found in Northern cities and Southern cities, Eastern cities and Western cities, as field service organizers from the National Recreation Association (NRA) made their way from coast to coast, lending a uniform national framework to recreation work based on local conditions. This chapter looks at Cincinnati as an example of this paradigm of recreation as race relations work, but a similar story could have been told looking at San Antonio, Orlando, Detroit, or Westchester County, New York.

To understand why public recreation came into existence when it did and why public recreation took the form which it did, it is helpful to position the events of the 1920s, 1930s and 1940s in an international and national as well as local context. In an international perspective, public recreation was born and grew to maturity in an era shaped by two world wars and the rise of totalitarian states. Coordinated national programs of comprehensive public recreation grew directly from the War Camp Community Service Programs, which sought to provide recreational facilities for servicemen and civilians during the First World War. In that war the United States saw its task as making the world safe for democracy. In the interwar years recreation advocates hoped that international sharing of music, songs, dances, and play would highlight the universal features of human life across the globe and in so doing promote lasting peace and freedom. As NRA Secretary Howard Braucher put it in 1932, "One international recreation conference has more value for world peace than ten disarmament conferences."[1]

But peace alone did not provide the necessary condition for human fulfillment. For that, self-determination for nations, as well as smaller groups in society, was required. For advocates of public recreation, democracy provided the necessary context for authentic recreation and participation in recreation provided training for democracy; totalitarian governments provided neither. As NRA Secretary Howard Braucher declared in 1936, "To us, active participation in our government, national, state, and local, or at least the right to so participate, is part of abundant living, a form of recreation if you will. Something is taken away from us," Braucher continued, "we are not longer complete, fully members, if we don't participate. . . ." Self-training for democracy thus constituted a key task of recreation workers. As Braucher declared in 1936, "The recreation movement has a vital part to perform in buttressing democracy. . . . its methods should be those that build democracy." When the United States entered World War II, it was with the goal of preserving self-determination—democracy—in those nations where it still existed, and recreation workers took up the challenge.[2]

Just as recreation advocates saw recreation both shaping and being shaped by the international situation, so too with the question of democracy and self-government within the borders of the United States. During the Second World War, recreation advocates like Braucher cautioned against the dangers of the centralized national recreation programs of Hitler and Mussolini. Centralization would lead to uniformity and the possibility of dangerous totalitarianism. To recreation workers cultural differences provided some of the basic backbone for democracy. Unlike the national programs developed in a hierarchical manner in Italy and Germany, Bracher claimed that in the United States, "Each neighborhood, each community, please God, is different from every other and let us hope that each will remain so." In democratic America, recreation advocates thought their work could best be done by the people in the neighborhood themselves. "We want in America," Braucher concluded, "growth in living that is native to the soil of each locality." In the same way that international programs of recreation could teach peace, harmony, and mutual understanding based on the common aspirations of people seeking recreation, so community-based recreation programs within the United States would both teach democratic skills to participants and provide an umbrella of understanding, holding different self-determining communities together, preventing conflict, and allowing self-rule. Just as the international situation in the years from 1915 to 1945 was fraught with conflict among nations, there was also the reality of cultural and racial conflicts within the United States. Recreation advocates thought that self-determination by neighborhoods and a framework for teaching different geographically based groups to appreciate the contributions of other groups, would lessen conflict between groups.[3]

Community-based music programs formed one important aspect of public recreation programs; the role of music can be seen in the Cincinnati Public Recreation Commission's annual June Music Festival that flourished in the 1930s and 1940s. The festivals presented a combination of locally organized musical performers and nationally recognized musicians. In 1942, for example, the Cincinnati Public Recreation Commission arranged for the bass-baritone Paul Robeson to perform as part of the festival. Robeson sang "Ballad for Americans" at Cincinnati's Crosley Field, home of the Cincinnati Reds, where a local chorus of 200 voices, trained for months by the Recreation Commission's music workers, joined him in song. The Recreation Commission organized more than one thousand festival volunteers, mobilizing the community to guarantee a success. "Seven thousand people of both races were in attendance," Recreation Director Tam Deering reported, "in spite of the rain before and during the performance." Robeson's wartime concert exemplifies the race relations work pursued by the Cincinnati Public Recreation Commission in the 1920s, 1930s and 1940s. This municipal agency, established in 1926, served as a publicly funded laboratory for building democracy and racial tolerance through the promotion of cultural pluralism.[4]

Robeson popularized "Ballad for Americans," a musical review of the history of American pluralism and democracy, on a CBS radio program in 1939. The ballad began with the story of the American Revolution and the "raggedy little group" that believed in liberty. A chorus rendition of the Preamble to the Constitution, led into the 19th century's cowboys and Indians, Lewis and Clark, and the Forty-niners. Abe Lincoln sang "Let My People Go," proclaiming "A man in white skin can never be free while his black brother is in slavery." Throughout the ballad the voice of "Nobody" defended freedom and democracy and identified himself as "everybody who's nobody." According to the ballad, "Nobody" was an engineer, musician, street cleaner, carpenter, teacher, office clerk, farmer, mechanic, housewife, stenographer, factory worker, beauty specialist, bartender, truck driver, seamstress, miner, and ditch digger. In response to the question, "Am I an American?" "Nobody" answered with a catalog of ethnic groups: "I'm just an Irish, Negro, Jewish, Italian, French and English, Spanish, Russian, Chinese, Polish, Scotch, Hungarian, Litvak, Swedish, Finnish, Canadian, Greek and Turk, and Czech and double Czech American." In religion, "Nobody" had been baptized "Baptist, Methodist, Congregationalist, Lutheran, atheist, Roman Catholic, Orthodox Jewish, Presbyterian, Seventh-day Adventist, Mormon, Quaker, Christian Scientist, and lots more!" The final chorus summed up the lessons of American history as the righteous fight for justice for all—lessons intended for those interested in fighting for freedom, racial tolerance, and democracy.[5]

Not content to let the music speak for itself, Robeson and the Public Recreation Commission held a press conference for local journalists, highlighting the racial politics of the musical performance. The *Cincinnati Post* of June 18, 1942, summarized the interview: "Nazi Victory Means Return to Slavery, Robeson Says, Famous Singer Hopes Race Will Gain Better Opportunities After War Against Fascism." The interview took place at the Manse, a black hotel, in a black residential neighborhood (the downtown Cincinnati hotels being segregated in 1942). Robeson spoke of the "ache in his heart" for the "millions of Negroes and others of many races, whose skins are not white, but who, as he said, have been denied the right to live and work and achieve as have white people in their countries." Max Hirsch, chairman of the Public Recreation Commission, and other members of the commission joined Robeson in meeting the press. As the *Post* quoted Robeson, "This is not a war just between nations. It is a war to preserve democracy in its truest sense; to readjust the entire class of nation[s] and all races." Recreation Commission Chairman Hirsch concurred, calling attention to the struggle for democracy in India.[6]

Robeson's appearance, the annual festivals of Negro Music, and the Cincinnati Recreation Commission itself, are evidence of Cincinnati's municipal program for improved race relations in the 1920s, 1930s, and 1940s. Cincinnati was not alone in its creation of a system of public recreation, nor was the city unique among American cities in its choice to use municipal recreation as a tool to educate citizens in racial tolerance, to promote racial equality (not integration,) and to build appreciation of the culture of the various groups that comprised the city. At the heart of this program of race relations lay the concept of cultural pluralism.

## CULTURAL PLURALISM

The variety of cultural pluralism promoted by public recreation experts grew from the ideas promoted by Horace Kallen and Alain LeRoi Locke. Scholars of cultural pluralism trace the origins of the concept back to William James and philosophical relativism. One of James's Harvard students, Horace Kallen, is credited with the invention of the term *cultural pluralism* in 1905. According to Kallen, the concept developed out of discussions about racial prejudice he had with another Harvard student, Alain Locke. The two Americans—one Jewish, the other black— had extensive conversations about cultural differences and discrimination while both were studying at Oxford. "And we had to argue out the question of how the differences made differences," Kallen said in describing his discussions with Locke. Kallen continued, ". . . and in arguing out those questions the formulae, then phrases, developed—'cultural pluralism,' the right to be different." Proponents of cultural pluralism included social scientists, as well as philosophers; the term is associated with such people as Franz Boas, John Dewey, William I. Thomas, Robert Park and Melville J. Herskovits. By the 1920s modern social scientists "interpreted character, morality, and social organization as cultural, rather than racial phenomena." Cultural pluralists like Kallen and Locke insisted on the equality possible among this diversity of cultures.[7]

A philosopher by training, Locke both observed and participated in politics. A supporter of the Niagara Movement (an all-black movement initiated in 1905 by W. E. B. Du Bois and William Monroe Trotter) and a founder (with Kelly Miller) in 1924 of Sanhedrin, a national council to coordinate activity in race relations, Locke attended the 1930 National Interracial Conference in Washington, D.C. Locke wrote numerous articles and essays on discrimination and race relations for a variety of national publications. In *The Negro in America*, a 1933 pamphlet, Locke described the history as well as the current state of race relations in America. According to Locke, black Americans had responded to country's call during the First World War, but "the anticipated rewards of the Negro's patriotic response to the idealism of the 'War to Save Democracy' were not measurably realized. . . . [S]purred by the bitter disillusionments of postwar indifference," Locke wrote, "there came that desperate intensification of the Negro's race consciousness and attempt

at the recovery of group morale through a racialist program of self-help
and self-determination which has been the outstanding development in
Negro life during this generation." With this postwar development "came
the beginnings of independent economic enterprise, a growing disposi-
tion for political action and the recovery of civil rights and political participation." For Locke, genius and creative talent constituted "the pivot
of progress and the foundation of group prestige." In the contemporary
search for an authentic American culture, Locke saw "Negro forms and
tradition enjoying a belated but well-deserved victory. . . . .becoming the
cornerstones of the new American art." This, he predicted, would establish "a new principle of cultural diversity and reciprocity. . . . [providing]
one of the great solvents of racial antagonism and misunderstanding." A.
Gilbert Belles described Locke's approach well: "One of Locke's strategies was to use culture as ammunition in the battles for racial survival
and progress."[8]

American intellectuals of this era eagerly sought to describe and define "American culture." In the 1920s, 1930s, and 1940s, Kallen, Locke,
and others saw American culture as a series of subcultures, a sort of mosaic of distinctive groups, each with their own strengths, all of which together made up the larger American culture. As Locke put it in *The New
Negro* in 1925: "America seeking a new spiritual expansion and artistic
maturity, trying to found an American Literature, a national art, and
national music implies a Negro-American culture seeking the same satis-
factions and objectives. . . . Separate as it may be in color and substance,"
Locke continued, "the culture of the Negro is of a pattern integral with the
times and with its cultural setting." For Locke, and for other promoters of
cultural pluralism, culture included, but was not limited to, cultural prod-
ucts such as music and art. Instead they defined culture expansively, and
anthropologically, as all the elements which comprised a people's "way
of life." The framework of cultural pluralism replaced the 19th-century hierarchical ladder of culture and achievement with a horizontal ranking of
all cultures as at least potentially of equal value. In this new context for
understanding society, a key tool for groups seeking equality became as-
sertions about culture. These included the need to demonstrate that one
did, indeed, belong to a culture that represented the aspirations of a folk or
people, for belonging to such a group provided the route to equality of
treatment. Cultural groups seemed to have, as units, rights that might not
be available to individual members of such groups.[9]

Such a strategy can be seen in Alain Locke's 1925 foreword to *The
New Negro*. Here Locke presents the concept of self-determination as a

political interpretation of cultural pluralism. Calling attention to the contemporary international upsweep of nation formation, Locke placed his work in the context of the growing popularity of self-determination: "Europe seething in a dozen centers with emergent nationalities, Palestine full of a renascent Judaism—these are no more alive with the progressive forces of our era than the quickened centers of the lives of black folk." To demand self-determination, a people had to have a self, and had to be conscious of that self; Locke claimed that the artistic self-expression of the American Negro demonstrated a "new figure on the national canvas and a new force in the foreground of affairs." Perhaps Locke stated his position most clearly in a 1928 pamphlet titled *A Decade of Negro Self-Expression*: ". . . this movement is not separatist in a limiting sense; it is no voluntary counterpart to the segregation reaction of an intolerant dominant majority: Rather it is a minority promotional move—an attempt to capitalize and bring one's own stock to par, and to have a quotable market rating and a recognized market standing."[10]

This new understanding of the role of culture did not remain isolated in the theoretical realm; by the 1920s municipal governments across the country had undertaken two new tax-supported missions—city planning and public recreation—both deeply influenced by these new ideas about the role of culture in American life. Historians have told us a good bit about the role of comprehensive city planning in creating a metropolis comprising diverse, but homogenous, communities; we know much less about programs of public recreation that, with public funds for facilities, programs, and organizers, sought both to organize those individual communities and to build understanding among the diverse groups that composed the larger whole. Public recreation and city planning provide the most dramatic examples of a new urban sensibility in municipal government in the 1920s, but other indications of the new role of culture abound. In the early 20th century, tax-supported institutions such as boards of health and public libraries (both created in the 19th century) developed systems of branch institutions designed to serve particular geographic communities with the understanding that those communities had unique cultural characteristics that shaped the form the service required. In so doing, they created racially segregated communities, but viewed them as equal, or at least potentially equal, components of the larger American culture.[11]

Public recreation, it turns out, provides the most fully developed example of cultural pluralism as a municipal strategy. The development of geographically based communities, the emphasis on democracy and participation, and the role of culture as a weapon in the campaign for equality, all mark public recreation, in Cincinnati and around the country, as a crucial and complex element of urban life in the decades between 1920 and 1950.

## PUBLIC RECREATION

Enthusiasm for comprehensive programs of public-funded municipal recreation swept the country in the 1920s as many Americans came to regard public recreation as a public utility, just like the sewers, the streets, and the water system. In city after city, the public recreation movement followed on the heels of the efforts to establish public parks. Beginning in the middle of the 19th century, many American cities created large public parks, such as Central Park in New York (1853) and Eden Park (1867) in Cincinnati. Progressive Era concern with urban children led to a playground movement, and by the turn of the century, fourteen American cities had made provisions for supervised play facilities. The Playground Association of America, formed in 1906, sponsored the first National Recreation Congress in 1907. The organization became the Playground and Recreation Association of America in 1911 and the National Recreation Association in 1930. Through its monthly journal, pamphlets, publications, and field workers the NRA gave direction to the movement for public recreation. By 1910, 336 cities reported the establishment of organized recreation programs for youth. In 1915 states began to pass home recreation bills, permitting cities to carry on year-round municipal recreation programs under the direction of trained, salaried workers. During World War I, at the request of the War Department, the Playground and Recreation Association formed the War Camp Community Service to organize the recreation resources of communities near military areas, creating a national network of community organizations devoted to recreation; after the war many communities continued these recreation efforts under the name "Community Service." The recreation movement grew throughout the 1920s; by the beginning of the third decade of the 20th century, one-half of the states had passed enabling legislation allowing municipalities to conduct broad public recreation programs and 945 cities reported having established recreation systems.[12]

The post–World War I recreation movement sought to meet the needs of the entire community, year round. Old and young, male and female, black and white, all appeared to need organized publicly funded municipal recreation. Cultural, rather than purely athletic, recreation received new emphasis as drama, music, arts and crafts, communitywide projects, special events, and civic programs all fell under the new, much bigger, umbrella of public recreation. No longer regarded as simply something needed by the underprivileged, public recreation appeared to be a universally necessary complement to the burgeoning business of commercial recreation. This call for universality had particular implications for how cities viewed the diversity among citizens, for assumptions about group characteristics and needs, and for assumptions about relationships among groups, particularly for the field of "race relations."[13]

Advocates of a city charter for Cincinnati had as early as 1914 called for the municipal administration of recreation, but it was several more city charters and a dozen years before the creation of the new municipal responsibility. The ordinance creating the public recreation commission, adopted by Cincinnati City Council on May 26, 1926, stipulated that the new commission consist of five members: one member of the Board of Education, one member of the Board of Park Commissioners, and three citizens appointed by the mayor. Four of the first five commissioners had been active supporters of the recently successful Cincinnati Charter reform movement. The first members of the Commission reflected some of the diversity of Cincinnati; they differed in religion, gender, and occupation, but no black members were appointed. It is not especially surprising that the first Cincinnati Recreation Commission did not include a black representative in 1926; the first Afro-American city councilman was not elected until 1931.[14]

The newly created commission choose Will R. Reeves, who had headed Community Service for the past half-dozen years, as the Director of Recreation. However, he had no money to run the commission since the ordinance creating the commission had not provided for operating funds. Thus the first issue for the newly established commission became the organization of a campaign for the passage of a tax levy for recreation purposes. At their second meeting, July 15, 1926, the commission members discussed the need to involve different groups of citizens in the recreation effort. The commissioners decided, for example, to "call on the Archbishop of Cincinnati, to secure his consent to place the phrase 'approved by the archbishop of the Diocese' on all mail relating to the tax levy sent to Catholic organizations." To promote the levy the commission organized a city-wide citizens' committee chaired by Walter S. Schmidt, the first president of the Recreation Commission, and a Catholic.[15]

From the beginning the commission also sought involvement and votes supporting the recreation levy from the Afro-American community. In addition to the city wide tax levy committee, the Recreation Commission decided to "appoint a committee of the outstanding colored people of the city to work for passage of the tax levy among the colored population of Cincinnati." Schmidt volunteered the use of his office for the first meeting of this committee. The Recreation Commission established a Colored Citizens Committee and chose Dr. William T. Nelson, a leader in the Afro-American community with special expertise in recreational issues, to head it. A graduate of Howard University and Medical College, Nelson practiced medicine in Cincinnati's largest black neighborhood, the West End. He pioneered the movement to establish a YMCA for local black men and boys in the West End. When the Ninth Street branch of the YMCA opened in 1915, Nelson served on its first Committee of Management. Nelson was elected to the Board of Directors of the Metropolitan YMCA in 1920, becoming the first Afro-American to hold such a position. The Cincinnati YMCA sent Nelson as its representative to the constitutional convention of the YMCA at Chicago in 1923, and the following year the National Council of the YMCA elected him a vice president of that organization's highest leadership body. Schmidt and Nelson proved able leaders, and the citizens voted to approve the levy; funds were thus made available for the Recreation Commission, which began to offer programs on February 1, 1927.[16] The organizational structure of the Public Recreation Commission reflected its view on race relations, which could be characterized as separate but equal. The five commissioners headed the organizational structure, directly beneath them came the director of recreation. Four supervisors reported directly to the director, handling the areas of community activities; playgrounds, playstreets, and after-school periods; music; and "Negro recreation." Under this organizational framework, recreational work for white Cincinnatians was topically organized, but all categories of Afro-American activity were centrally organized under the Supervisor of Colored Work.[17]

## CINCINNATI'S COLORED RECREATION WORK

The Cincinnati Public Recreation Commission hired Olympic broad-jump champion De Hart Hubbard as the first Supervisor of Colored Work. Hubbard, born in Cincinnati and a graduate of the city's leading public academic high school and the University of Michigan, won a gold medal for his record-setting jump at the 1924 Paris Olympics. In 1927, when he joined the Cincinnati Recreation Department, Hubbard held the world's record for the broad jump. But Hubbard's job consisted of more than serving as a role-model star athlete. Like other recreation staff members, he was hired both to promote recreation and to organize the community.[18]

Hubbard began his work in 1927 by making a survey of the recreational facilities available to black Cincinnatians. Hubbard's was not the first such study; as early as 1913 Helen Trounstine, in a survey for the Cincinnati Juvenile Protective Association, reported that black children faced extremely limited recreational opportunities. A few years later, James Hathaway Robinson, a Yale-educated African American sociologist and local social worker, studied Cincinnati's black citizens for the Negro Civic Welfare Association and recommended the creation of a new agency "devoted to community music and recreation" for the black community. Prompted by Robinson's continued calls for new programs, Cincinnati Community Service created a Department of Negro Recreation in 1922; programs included athletic events, community sings, and a citywide "Colored Orchestra."[19]

In spite of the work of Cincinnati Community Service, the privately funded predecessor to the Public Recreation Commission, Hubbard found the recreational opportunities available to Cincinnati's black citizens badly organized. To improve the situation he arranged for the Colored Department of the Recreation Commission to take over the recreational activities run by the Cincinnati Board of Education, the Negro Civic Welfare Association, and Cincinnati Community Service. He also established a plan of coordinated work with the YMCA and the YWCA that served the black community. In his survey report, Hubbard cataloged the public recreational facilities and athletic activities available. Under Hubbard's leadership the Recreation Department provided play directors for playgrounds in black neighborhoods. The play directors organized inter- and intramural playground leagues, as well as handicraft and musical activities and participation in citywide recreation events. Recreation staff organized summer play periods in suburban black communities and summer playstreets in the city's largest black community, the West End. The Department of Colored Work also ran indoor recreation centers at the two black public schools, conducting evening classes in gym, swimming, indoor sports, dramatics, choral, and cultural activities for men and women.[20]

In its first year the Recreation Commission took seriously the necessity for providing adequate recreational space for the black community, designating the development of a "Colored Playfield and Playground in

West End" as a major project of the commission. The commission also announced plans to create a major "colored Playfield-Playground" in Walnut Hills, another neighborhood with significant numbers of African-American residents. The playground, the Recreation Commission noted, was "badly needed in this location where the area immediately to the west and north has become practically all colored in the last ten years." The following year, 1928, the commission spent $147,000.00 for part of the area planned for the new playfield-playground in the West End. "When developed, improved and properly supervised," the Recreation Commission reported, "this great recreational center, which will be second to none in the United States, should go far toward improving the general health and social conditions in a district that has been long neglected."[21] According to De Hart Hubbard, "an idea of the importance and scope of the work of the Department of Colored Work" could be seen in the recreation participation rate of black Cincinnatians. Estimating Cincinnati's Afro-American population at 35,000, Hubbard's statistics demonstrated that some 258,164 people had attended or participated in the activities of the Department of Colored Work in 1928. The Afro-American community had evidenced plenty of interest in recreational activities, but Hubbard worried that lack of finances and facilities would deter the continued expansion of the work. To better organize the community, Hubbard's department began working with the Negro Civic Welfare Association, a Community Chest–sponsored group that sought to coordinate social services available to the African American community, to organize a Recreational Council of leading citizens in 1929. The year before, the city's Director of Recreation called for the creation of a Public Recreation Council "composed of "interested and influential private citizens" who would volunteer their time and interest to "help promote all activities and to maintain the necessary standards of conduct and practice . . . [and] to interpret the plans and programs of the public board to the citizens and the wishes of the citizens back to the public board." That body being all white, Hubbard created a black community council parallel to the council developed by Reeves. Hubbard's new group would, he said, "act in an advisory capacity in helping promote recreation among the Colored people." With the aid of such a council, he predicted, "all classes and groups of people will be reached, and the program really become all-inclusive. . . . It is our belief," he concluded, "that this Council will be able to so help this department that Cincinnati, as soon as the facilities and additional leadership are available, will have a Department of Colored Work that will equal any in the United States."

Acting on the advice of the Negro Civic Welfare Committee, the Recreation Commission appointed such a group of "prominent Negroes to act as members of the Recreation Council on Negro work" in 1930.[22]

The particular kind of pluralism practiced by the recreation department did not escape notice. In June 1928, for example, the commission discussed a letter from Mayor Murray Seasongood, who had written the commission "stating it was understood that this Commission was discriminating against Negroes in athletic events." The commission asked Reeves, the Recreation Director, to reply to the mayor and to explain that "the policy of this commission in connection with activities under its supervision is to provide equal opportunities and facilities for all Cincinnati citizens without regard to race or color, but that it is impossible for any public administrating group to force white teams or groups to compete against colored teams or groups." When a black citizen wrote the commission complaining that the McKinley Park pool was "closed to other citizens of his race," the commission replied "that every citizen has a legal right to use recreational facilities."[23] After several years on the job, and several years of stressing the extraordinary recreational needs of the black community, Hubbard recommended to the commissioners that they request the National Recreation Association to send staff to Cincinnati to conduct a recreational survey of the recreation situation in the black community. Hubbard also wanted the help of national recreation workers in an organizing effort among local citizens. "There is," Hubbard said, "an awakening recreation consciousness among the leaders of the Colored people and the coming of a National worker will have much more stimulating and beneficial effect than could be achieved by any local agency."[24]

## ATTWELL, COLORED RECREATION, AND THE NATIONAL RECREATION ASSOCIATION

Hubbard's chance for such national assistance came in March 1932, when Cincinnati hosted the annual National Conference of Colored Recreation Workers, a meeting of delegates representing twenty-one cities. Ernest Ten Eyck Attwell of the National Recreation Association came to Cincinnati to lead the conference of delegates who represented recreation work in twenty-one cities. After the conclusion of the conference, Attwell remained in Cincinnati to conduct a citywide survey of the recreational activities and needs of the Afro-American community, as Hubbard had requested. Attwell began his survey by meeting with Tam

Deering, the new Director of Recreation, and announcing that he planned to both complete an analysis of recreational facilities, and, as the *Cincinnati Enquirer* reported, "interest Negroes themselves in recreation." The Recreation Commission, the Negro Civic Welfare Association, and National Recreation Association jointly funded the survey.[25]

Attwell was at that time *the* national expert on Afro-American recreation. Closely associated with Booker T. Washington, Attwell spent seventeen years working at Tuskeegee Institute. During World War I he served as assistant to the food administrator for Alabama. Impressed by Attwell, Herbert Hoover called him to Washington to work with the U.S. Food Administration to organize a nationwide campaign among Afro-Americans for food conservation. After the war, the National Recreation Association asked him to join its staff, and in 1920 the NRA made Attwell head of the organization's Bureau of Colored Work. Attwell spent much of his time conducting, or helping communities conduct, recreational surveys that formed the basis for future programs. As a National Recreation Association field secretary he visited cities throughout the country, meeting with lay groups and public officials, and assisting the municipalities in the establishment and the improvement of recreation programs for black Americans. Some indication of the scope of Attwell's work can be seen in the page of annual statistics published by the National Recreation Association in its *Yearbook*. In 1931, for example, "85 communities received personal help in securing more adequate provision of recreation opportunities for Negroes"; in 1932, 28 communities were so served; in 1933, 116 cities "were helped in conducting their recreation activities for Negroes."[26] The report of Attwell's Cincinnati survey, titled *Limited Survey of Recreation Opportunities for Negro Citizens*, offered a comprehensive picture of local Afro-American life. Although Hubbard had surveyed black recreational opportunities, as national recreation leader Attwell helped to focus new attention on the needs of the local black community. Unlike Hubbard, Attwell drew direct comparisons between the recreational opportunities of black and white citizens. Attwell also utilized the local black community in gathering information for his survey. The survey, which totaled one hundred typescript pages, arguably constituted the most extensive survey of Cincinnati's Afro-American community that had been conducted to date. Divided into thirteen sections, the survey included the following topics: "History and Population," "School Attendance and School Population," "Church Organizations Among Negroes," "General Organization," "Fraternal Organizations," "Housing, Health and Hospitalization," " Delinquency," "Business and Industrial," "Welfare and Social Agencies," "Commercial Recreation," "Public Recreation," and "School and Other Public Recreation." The Supreme Life Liberty Insurance Company of Chicago Association provided the survey staff with office space in the West End, and DeHart Hubbard, as well as George Cooper, Lila D. Rickman, and Marian Shivers, served as temporary survey staff.[27]

The survey began with a history of the local Afro-American experience, delineating changing eras of race relations. First, the period from 1800 to 1850, which Attwell characterized as a time of acute racial friction, passage of the "Black laws," and labor competition between Afro-Americans and immigrant whites. For the next fifty years, Attwell reported, "race relations were devoid of open friction," but this changed during the years from 1910 to 1920 as the city's black population increased by 59 percent. Although this sudden increase led to a dramatic increase in "all forms of social problems," Attwell thought the growth of the black population also brought new opportunities. For example, Attwell reported that the city's 31,869 eligible black voters had recently elected Frank A. B. Hall, the first Afro-American city councilman.[28]

Attwell studied the city as a whole, mapping all the areas with black residents and comparing those services available to blacks with the recreational opportunities white citizens enjoyed. Thus his study was based on the assumption that Afro-American residents deserved a fair share of the recreational facilities and a proportional number of staff positions. In short he called for a truly equal, if separate, municipal recreation program. It is important to note that Attwell did not assume that one geographic center for black facilities would meet the needs of all Afro-Americans. He suggested that recreational resources should be spread throughout the metropolitan area in proportion to the number of African-American residents in a given area.

Attwell strongly argued that the dearth of commercial recreation available to Afro-Americans mandated the creation of an extensive municipal recreation program for these citizens. "No part of the city's activities," he wrote, "is more definitely closed to the Negro in Cincinnati than Commercial Recreation." Of the city's sixty moving-picture houses, he lamented, "only five small moving-picture houses are open to the Negro." Although the five legitimate theaters admitted black patrons, Attwell reported that "when large numbers purchase tickets they are sold so that all are seated in one section." The policies of these theaters, Attwell said, "contribute to more race hatreds and unrest than any other single element in community life,— affecting as it does the better element

of colored citizens." Reflecting a general sentiment of recreation workers, he also called for municipal "guidance and supervision" of pool halls
and dance halls.[29]

Promoting neither racial integration nor racial segregation exclusively, Attwell offered a pragmatic approach to race relations. At McKinley Playground, in a neighborhood of both black and white residents,
Attwell suggested: "Because more than half of the attendance is Negro
children and the smaller proportion consists of whites, there appears at
once a strong indication for the need of a biracial staff of playleaders."
With a bi-racial staff, Attwell predicted, there would be "less friction and
more mutual service to both groups. . . . Such a staff," he said, "would be
in a position to test out methods in the use of the facilities with fairness to
both groups." He added that since black and white children went to
school together—"sit together and bathe together"—in this part of town,
the "possibility of joint use of all the facilities seems feasible." In Madis-
onville, where a white neighborhood committee had protested the black
residents' use of the playground and tennis courts, Attwell recommended
opening the playground, the tennis courts, and the ball grounds to both
blacks and whites. "If this can not be accomplished without continuous
friction," he added, "there should be parallel facilities constructed and
placed under the supervision of a colored staff." A dual system with parallel black and white recreation programs would not be economical, Attwell noted, but it would be "the only fair method of sharing to all
citizens tax supported facilities." Attwell demanded the black community receive a proportional share of the public spending going for recreation. Where integrated groups already existed, and experienced little
open conflict, he suggested maintaining a racially integrated recreational
program. Where there was conflict, or already existing segregation, he
called for the creation of equal facilities for the black community. Thus
racial integration was a tactical issue, which could be adjusted as needed
to meet the strategic goal of equality of opportunity.[30]

Finally, in his report Attwell called attention to a major deficiency in
the existing recreation program—the lack of opportunity for "mass expression in a musical way." He reported that although the churches organized groups of volunteer singers for religious purposes, many citizens
were "unchurched" and thus unable to benefit from those programs. Negroes, he reported, were musically gifted and, "as has been demonstrated
by prominent Negro artists," capable of reaching musical excellence. He
called for the organization of a community chorus of black voices, an an-

nual music festival, lessons in instruments such as the harmonica and the "uke," and the establishment of glee clubs at every community center.[31]

## MUSIC, CULTURAL PLURALISM, AND RACE RELATIONS

Attwell's survey aided DeHart Hubbard in organizing the African-American Committee Citizens' Recreation Council, and it also gave him impetus to expand his department's music program. Hubbard had added music and drama to his popular athletic programs in 1930; that year Hubbard arranged for Cincinnatian Artie Matthews to organize and conduct the Recreation Commission's Community Choral Club. Matthews, a ragtime composer and music educator, had established the Cosmopolitan School of Music, a classical conservatory serving Cincinnati's black community, in 1921. "Competent critics," Hubbard reported, acclaimed the Recreation Commission's concerts performed under the direction of Matthews, announcing them to be "of exceptional merit."[32]

Taking up another of Attwell's suggestions, Hubbard's department expanded its musical work and organized a "Festival of Negro Music and Old Fashioned Dancing." The National Recreation Association had been promoting such festivals across the country for years. The Department of Recreation in Columbus, Georgia, began an annual festival of Negro spirituals in 1925. Other cities, such as Memphis; Orlando; Charlotte, North Caraloina; San Antonio; Springfield, Illinois; and Lancaster, Pennsylvania, followed suit as recreation departments organized black citizens to perform spirituals. The appeal of spirituals, according to the journal of the National Recreation Association, derived from the fact that spirituals "offer evidence that the finest folk music of the world is the product of pain and suffering." Enhancing the attraction of the music was the "striking fact about the spirituals that out of more than 600 which have been collected none show resentment, hate, or revenge." Although emphasizing spirituals, recreation workers did not always limit their choices to traditional music. At Houston's Emancipation Park, for example, the Department of Recreation organized a concert performed by black teenagers that combined songs such as "Lift Every Voice and Sing" (the Negro national anthem) with traditional spirituals such as "Nobody Knows the Trouble I've Had," and readings from African American poet Paul Lawrence Dunbar.[33]

Recreation officials clearly took a keen interest in promoting African American music, especially spirituals, across the country, in the

North as well as the South; it is equally important to note, however, that the recreational music movement saw black music as only one part of the nation's folk heritage. Other musical traditions drew the support of recreation experts as well. In Los Angeles, for example, in 1930 the Department of Playground and Recreation cosponsored, with the Mexican Social and Athletic Clubs, the first annual Mexican Fiesta. The purpose of the fiesta was "to promote international good-will by providing an opportunity for the Mexican clubs to interpret Mexican customs and culture to their American neighbors." The Union County, New Jersey, Park Commission offered a series of programs "depicting through music and drama the customs, habits and life history of various nationality groups," highlighting the cultures of Germans and Italians. The musical culture of the Kentucky mountains and the singing games played by children attracted the interest of recreation experts who noted approvingly the cooperative nature of such cultural traditions. Describing such games as "Scip to My Loo" (*sic*) and "Go In and Out the Window," a playground director proclaimed: "They were excellent for the children because they didn't quarrel about who was to be 'it,' and the boys didn't have an opportunity to fight as only Kentucky boys can."[34]

The interest of recreation experts in the music of particular American cultural groups existed alongside an interest in the idea of American culture as a whole—a culture that appeared to be a diverse mosaic of group cultures. Reporting on the National Folk Festival of 1934, the National Recreation Association's journal noted that the festival brought together "Kiowa Indians, New Mexicans, Ozarkians, Appalachians, Carolinians, cowboys, lumberjacks, Negroes and others—to present some of the fading folk arts." To this particular festival folklorist and writer Zora Neale Hurston brought a group from Daytona Beach, Florida. They presented "dances, work rhythms and games [which] included survivals of African origin." A black group from St. Louis presented Negro spirituals and a white group from Nashville presented "white spirituals." The festival, the National Recreation Association noted, had a double purpose. In the midst of the depression it served to entertain people with leisure time on their hands, but more importantly it served as "the beginning of an organization to enshrine in the hearts of Americans native American art while it can still be found."[35]

The Cincinnati Recreation Commission's Festival of Negro Music and Old Fashioned Dancing took place in Eden Park, Cincinnati's equivalent of Central Park, in June 1932. The 1932 festival, Hubbard declared, served as "a splendid beginning of a renaissance of music and dramatics," language that recalls the words of Alain Locke. Cincinnati Festival participants included a chorus of two hundred men and women, a twenty-five member band, two soloists, a male quartet, and eighty dancers. An estimated five thousand spectators viewed the performances. Organized by Citizens' Recreation Council and Hubbard's Department of Colored Recreation, the festival was sponsored by the Commission's Department of Community Music. As such, the festival was an interracial event, drawing on all the resources of the Recreation Commission. Harry Glore, Recreation Commission Music Director, declared that the festival would become "a permanent and regular function in the future which it is hoped will assume gigantic proportions."[36]

In addition to the inauguration of the music and folk dance festival, under the leadership of Artie Matthews, Hubbard's department organized an eighty-member Community Choral Club, which gave five additional concerts in 1932. Music became an organizing tool for Hubbard's department, as he established community choral groups in three black communities. "The possibilities for service through a strong program of artistic and cultural endeavors," Hubbard declared enthusiastically in his annual report that year, "are almost unlimited, especially in view of the fact that there are no limitations on participation because of age, etc., as in more strenuous physical games." The development of Afro-American culture thus seemed to be an excellent way to develop a comprehensive and inclusive community spirit.[37]

The second Festival of Negro Music took place in Eden Park the following year. For that festival the Recreation Commission asked J. Wesley Jones of Chicago, one of the founders of the National Federation of Negro Musicians, to come to Cincinnati to serve as the guest conductor for the musical event. Jones, a church organist and choir director, published a regular music column in the *Chicago Defender*, and served as director of the chorus of the annual Chicagoland Music Festivals. That year four hundred adults were joined by three hundred children in the Cincinnati chorus. Four thousand spectators witnessed what Hubbard hoped would become "one of the outstanding [music events] of the country." The music events of the Department of Colored Work, Hubbard noted, were being "carried on in direct cooperation with Mr. Glore, Supervisor of Music for the Public Recreation Commission." The following year, 1934, E. T. Attwell returned to Cincinnati to survey the indoor recreational facilities, and brought with him George L. Johnson, Organizer of Music for the

National Recreation Association, who conducted an institute on community song leadership and trained a chorus of two hundred and fifty singers for a music festival at the close of the institute.[38]

No record remains of music festivals for 1935, 1936, or 1937, but in 1938 the Cincinnati Negro Folk Song Festival, directed by Dr. Clarence Cameron White of the National Recreation Association, took place. Hubbard described it as "outstanding among special events" that year. White, a field worker for the National Recreation Association, was a leading Afro-American composer. As before, the Department of Community Music cooperated in the organization and promotion of this festival, which was held in the Eden Park bandstand. An audience of four thousand heard the chorus of two hundred and forty voices. "The event was an unqualified artistic success," said Hubbard, and was given "added dignity and distinction by its eminent director." Harry F. Glore, the Supervisor of Community Music and Special Events added that "Dr. White [had] laid the ground work of good will for some very effective work in the future."[39]

Encouraged by the festival's success, the Recreation Commission moved to make the previously ad hoc annual June Festival of Negro Music a permanent organization in 1939. In so doing the commission self-consciously created what was one of the first interracial civic organizations in the city. "Ninety-nine outstanding citizens of all races and creeds, " Hubbard reported, attended a testimonial dinner in honor of Dr. Clarence Cameron White, who returned to Cincinnati to conduct the Festival Chorus in 1939. More than seventy people, black and white, served as members of the festival sponsoring committee. The new permanent organization took as its purpose the task of "stimulating music" among Cincinnati's Afro-Americans. Although the new organization did not explicitly stress its interracial work, clearly the promotion of black culture appeared to present a way for black and white citizens to improve race relations as well.[40]

The festival organization recruited four hundred and two members by the end of its first year, adopted a constitution, chose a board of directors, and set up permanent committees. To fund the festival, the association made plans to increase the number of its active members to one thousand and to sell three thousand tickets. Unlike 1938 and 1939, when festival performers had had only four weeks of rehearsals, in 1940 the chorus began rehearsals in February and in October 1940 began regular weekly rehearsals for the 1941 festival. That year the festival once again proved a success, and in October the Festival Association announced plans to bring the famous Afro-American soloist Paul Robeson as a guest performer for the Fifth Annual Festival of Negro Music.[41]

Robeson's many and varied accomplishments included not only music, but oratory, drama and athletics, as well as academic honors, and they won him international as well as national acclaim. While a student at Rutgers University he won letters in football, baseball, track, and basketball, and, according to the *Enquirer,* "sports writers talked of him as a possible heavy-weight contender." At Rutgers he was Phi Beta Kappa, the school's star debater, winner of the freshman, sophomore, junior and senior oratory prizes, and commencement orator in 1919. He then went to Columbia University to study law, but changed his plans when he was "discovered" in an amateur YMCA dramatic performance at the Harlem branch. Impressed with his abilities, the founders of the Provincetown Playhouse offered Robeson the role of Emperor Jones in Eugene O'Neill's play of the same name and the part of the husband in *All God's Chillun Got Wings*, a drama that attracted controversy since Robeson played opposite a white actress, Mary Blair, who played his wife in the 1924 production. He spent time in Europe performing the *Emperor Jones*, Rogers and Hammerstein's musical *Showboat*, and *Othello*. Throughout the 1930s he and his family made their home in Europe, traveling to the Soviet Union in 1933–1934 as the guest of famed Soviet film director Sergei Eisenstein. In 1939 Robeson returned to the United States and quickly popularized "Ballad for Americans."[42]

## CONCLUSION

The June Festival Association, delighted with the success of Robeson's 1942 appearance (described at the beginning of this essay), planned to bring the soloist back to Cincinnati the following year; that did not happen. Apparently no festival took place in 1943 or 1944, for no record remains for either. The Festival Association did continue to sponsor a Negro chorus, which gave its annual concert at the University of Cincinnati in 1945. Dr. Clarence Cameron White returned to the city to conduct the June Music Festival in Eden Park the following year. Baritone Theodore Batte, featured in 1946, received "ovation after ovation" according to the *Cincinnati Post*. The following year the festival included, in addition to the regular chorus, a children's chorus drawn from the city's public schools. The festival of 1948 took place at the zoo and featured Todd Duncan, who the *Cincinnati Times-Star* described as "a Negro baritone who, by all accounts, ranks alongside the best white artists that have been heard there [at the zoo] or anywhere." Duncan had been chosen by George Gershwin to create the role of Porgy in Gershwin's folk opera, *Porgy and Bess.* Duncan became "the first of his race to sing a white role with a white cast," breaking the color line of the New York City Opera in 1945. The festival chorus accompanying Duncan consisted of more than one hundred and twenty-five singers, largely drawn from the new Lincoln Recreation Center in the West End. The chorus sang such songs as "Listen to the Lambs," "Joshua Fit the Battle of Jericho," and "Were You There." The performances of these songs, declared the *Times-Star*, demonstrated "the emotional sweep of great Negro Spirituals."[43]

Paul Robeson, as it turns out, made several trips to the Queen City in addition to his Recreation Commission–sponsored concert of 1942, but his political message was not always received with such open arms. In the growing anticommunist climate of the 1940s, special agents reported to FBI headquarters that Robeson was "reputed to be" a member of the Communist Party. When Robeson spoke at a 1948 Cincinnati rally sponsored by the Progressive Citizens of America, a left-wing organization for which he served as vice-chairman, the local press quickly lost its enthusiasm for the singer. The following year, the Cincinnati School Board unanimously banned a Robeson appearance at a "civil rights rally" at Stowe Junior High School in the West End. The *Cincinnati Enquirer* backed the ban, noting with approval that School Board policy prohibited use of school buildings for "meetings engendering racial or religious prejudices or for any purpose inimical to our democratic way of life." Robeson, the newspaper declared, threatened democracy. Recreation workers had praised Robeson's spirituals for their lack of "resentment, hate, or revenge." However, the singers link to left wing politics made him undersirable for many Cincinnatians.[44]

As Robeson's reception suggests, all Cincinnatians did not immediately make the transition easily from thinking about race relations in terms of cultural pluralism to using the concept of civil rights. But that shift in thinking about how to handle race relations unfolded on a much larger stage. The international reaction to Nazi genocide helped pave the way for the new interest in universal human rights. As codified in the 1948 United National Universal Declaration of Human Rights, this movement began with the proposition that "all human beings are born free and equal in dignity and rights." Cultural pluralism had suggested that human beings, by virtue of their membership in groups, deserved rights. The post–World War II view placed the emphasis not on group membership, but on the rights of the individual. In this new framework for international relations, civil rights and race relations became standards for the rest of the world to use to measure the United States. Now, as Barry D. Karl has suggested, "Americans had to rebuild their society to serve as a model for democratic hopes throughout the world."[45]

Within the United States the immediate postwar years brought a growing American impatience with the continued existence of racial segregation. In 1947, for example, the civil rights organization CORE (established in 1942) began planning "an ambitious attack on segregation in the armed forces, the YMCA, apartment complexes owned by the Metropolitan Life Insurance Company, and southern transportation." The antisegregation sentiment also reached the Oval Office in the White House. In his January 6, 1947, State of the Union address, President Harry S. Truman announced that he had created the President's Committee on Civil Rights to "study and report on the problem of federally secured civil rights." In a speech to an NAACP rally in front of the Lincoln Memorial on June 29, 1947, Truman described a new role he envisioned for the federal government in defense of civil rights. "Our immediate task," the president said, "is to remove the last remnants of the barriers which stand between millions of our citizens and their birthright." The speech was, one historian has noted, "the first time in the twentieth century [that] an American president publicly discussed the problem of racial discrimination with frankness and humanity."[46]

The report of the President's Committee on Civil Rights, *To Secure These Rights*, broke decisively with the separate but equal approach that had characterized the organization of American social life since the 1920s. Rather than a glorification of pluralism that had formed the basis for race relations in the 1920s, 1930s, and 1940s, this new report offered a critical examination of the state of American civil rights and found serious civil rights violations in all sections of the country. "We need to guarantee the same rights to every person regardless of who he is, where he lives, or what his racial, religious or national origins are," declared the committee. Unlike the approach of the earlier period, which had suggested individual improvement in status was linked to improvement of group status, the civil rights approach demanded people be treated first as individuals, not as members of racial, ethnic, or religious groups.[47]

In the 1920s, 1930s and 1940s the celebration of cultural pluralism suggested the potential equality among different groups of Americans, and defined American culture as a collection of group cultures. In some ways cultural pluralism helped to prepare the way for the eventual drive for racial integration that caught on in the 1950s. But racial integration arrived in Cincinnati, as in other American cities, not under the umbrella of cultural pluralism, but under the banner of individual rights. In that era, characterized by "the revolt against cultural determinism," the concept of individual rights replaced the group equality popularized by cultural pluralism. Rather than orchestrating celebrations of racial integration, as it had with cultural pluralism, the Recreation Commission quietly phased out its Department of Colored Work. The city integrated the commission leadership itself with the 1950 appointment of Charles Hatcher as the first black Recreation Commissioner.

Racial integration altered the role of music in recreation. In June 1951 the Recreation Commission once again organized a June festival chorus, as it had been doing since the 1930s. (Apparently there were no music festivals in 1949 or 1950, for no record remains of them.) For the 1951 festival, however, the Commission replaced the traditional Negro spirituals with classical music, making the 1951 festival a very different kind of cultural event. Throughout the 1930s and 1940s the Recreation Commission had viewed the June Music Festival as a showcase for the special talents of black musical artists and as an acknowledgment of the contributions of Afro-Americans to American music. In the 1950s this changed; no spirituals were performed. The 1951 program, held at the zoo, featured "Mendelssohn's Ninety-Fifth Psalm," and Afro-British composer Samuel Coleridge-Taylor's "Hiawatha's Wedding Feast." This was the first attempt, the *Post* noted, of the chorus to "present musical works of this magnitude." Although the *Post* did not acknowledge it, this was not just a change in magnitude, it was a shift in the philosophy of the festival. Now rather than demonstrating to Cincinnatians the value of Afro-American culture, the festival served as a demonstration that black citizens could compose and perform classical music. The choice of classical music, like Hatcher's appointment to the Recreation Commission, suggested that an African American individual need not be viewed as a representative of group culture, but could be responsible for general recreational concerns or capable of general musical competence.[48]

Alain Locke's 1925 manifesto of cultural pluralism, *The New Negro*, first appeared as a special issue of *Survey Graphic*; in 1947 *Survey Graphic* published a special issue titled "Segregation: Color Pattern from the Past and Our Struggle to Wipe It Out." Once again Locke wrote on race and American culture. Rather than concentrating his efforts on cataloging the contributions of Afro-Americans to American culture, by this time Locke had moved beyond the campaign for "recognition on the score of merit." Now he turned his attention to the goal of social democracy and racial integration. "On political, industrial, social and cultural levels," he concluded, "social action groups are bestirring themselves, increasingly aware that their efforts are converging toward a present-generation crusade to round out American democracy. To bring forth such a democracy progressive forces must come together to 'liquidate segregation.' . . . [S]ocial reason," Locke declared, "not just commonsense expediency, militant democratic convictions not just piecemeal reforms, must be marshaled to the assault."[49]

In the 1920s, 1930s and 1940s, the concept of cultural pluralism, separate but equal, helped to provide municipal recreation officials with a vision of a democratic community, while reifying racial segregation through culturally specific community-based organization. Although public attention focused on the annual music festivals, underlying the festivals lay years of daily community organizing by the Recreation Commission. For more than two decades, thousands of African American residents, adults as well as children, volunteered to participate in the music programs of the commission. The festivals required not only organization and promotion of the events themselves, but also months of practice by the amateur musicians. The music festivals offered a framework for organizing the black community, from community leaders to school children, in pursuit of a common objective. The success of the festivals depended upon the work of the Recreation Commission and on the voluntary participation of thousands of organized people. Certainly one effect of the music program of Hubbard's department was a better-organized black community. For white Cincinnatians the festivals had impact as well. Whether white citizens attended the festivals, served on the interracial committee planning the festivals, or were merely exposed, through the press, to the fact that such festivals took place, white citizens' views of black culture must have been affected by the festivals. After all, the very fact that the Cincinnati Recreation Commission—an official government body—sponsored the musical events suggested that city officials valued black culture.

Perhaps paradoxically, racial integration, with its emphasis on an individual's civil rights, does not seem to have been accompanied by a powerful philosophical framework to guide the next generation of community organization of the Recreation Commission. At the same time, public recreation itself no longer enjoyed the virtually unanimous support it had had since its inception. Symbolically, the Recreation Commission lost its high status in city government in 1949. Since the creation of the Public Recreation Commission, the municipal agency had been housed in City Hall. Now, to provide space for the Waterworks Department, the Public Recreation Commission found itself relegated to an office building a mile from the center of city power. Bitter disputes on the commission and among local politicians about the leadership of the commission and its proper role and organization began to surface in the mid-1940s and continued for years. The Recreation Commission laid off its supervisor of music for "lack of work" in 1952, declaring that "an organizer was needed rather than an accomplished musician." The purpose of public recreation itself became a topic of investigation, as well as how best to organize public recreation. After more than twenty years of organizing communities to prepare for democracy, recreation workers found themselves faced with the prospect of interracial democracy. Cultural pluralism had both prepared the groundwork for racial integration through its emphasis on equality and, through its emphasis on group culture, made real racial integration problematic.[50]

## NOTES

1. My understanding of the discourse on democracy in this era is informed by the work of Barry D. Karl (*The Uneasy State: The United States from 1915–1945*, University of Chicago Press, 1983). Karl suggests that the two world wars "raised the issue of national loyalty and, with it, the need to define a national culture to which loyalty could be given and by which it could be measured" (234). Howard Braucher, "Recreation and the Way to World Peace," *Recreation* (October 1932) 313; *Recreation* and its predecessors, *Playground* and *Playground and Recreation*, were publications of the National Recreaton Association.

2. Howard Braucher, "Recreation Workers and the Preservation and Development of Democracy," *Recreation* 30 (September 1936): 281.

3. Howard Braucher, "Culture or Kultur?" *Recreation* 38 (October 1944): 337–338. Public recreation programs might be seen as one response to managing the rampant conflict among native born Americans, immigrants, and blacks in the 1920s. For an examination of other organizational urban responses to the ethnic and racial tensions of American cities in the 1920s, see Zane L. Miller and Patricia M. Melvin, *The Urbanization of Modern America: A Brief History* (New York: Harcourt Brace Jovanovich Publishers, 1987).

4. The definitive biography of Robeson, Martin Bauml Duberman's *Paul Robeson* (New York: Alfred A. Knopf, 1988), reports the widespread appeal of "Ballad for Americans" during the war, noting that the Republicans opened their

1940 national convention with Ry Middleton performing the hit song (237). *The Annual Report of the Public Recreation Commission* (Cincinnati, Ohio: The Commission, 1942), p. 4.

5. *Time*, November 20, 1939. John Latouche and Earl Robinson, *A Modern Cantata "Ballad for Americans" for Baritone Solo and Mixed Chorus* (New York: Robbins Music Corporation, 1940), pp. 20, 29, 33–35, 36–43.

6. *Cincinnati Post*, June 18, 1942, p. 23.

7. See George Hutchinson, *The Harlem Renaissance in Black and White* (Cambridge: Harvard University Press, 1995), p. 85; Leonard Harris, ed., *The Philosophy of Alain Locke: Harlem Renaissance and Beyond* (Philadelphia: Temple University Press, 1989), pp. 13–15; Peggy Pascoe, "Miscegenation Law, Court Cases, and the Ideologies of 'Race' in Twentieth-Century America," *The Journal of American History* 83, no. 1 (June 1996): 53.

8. A. Gilbert Belles, "The Politics of Alain Locke," in *Alain Locke: Reflections on a Modern Renaissance Man*, Russell J. Linnemann, ed. (Baton Rouge: Louisiana State University Press, 1982), pp. 50–51, 52–54; Alain Locke, *The Negro in America* (Chicago: American Library Association, 1933), pp. 12–23, 47, 50–51.

9. Alain Locke, ed., *The New Negro* (New York: Albert and Charles Boni) 1925; reprint edition, New York: Atheneum, 1983), p. xvi. For a discussion of cultural pluralism, see "The Place of Culture and the Problem of Identity," in Allen Batteau, ed., *Appalachia and America: Autonomy and Regional Dependence* (Lexington: University of Kentucky Press, 1983), pp. 131–133.

10. Locke, *The New Negro*, pp. xv–xvi; Alain Locke, *A Decade of Negro Self Expression* (Charlottesville, Va.: The Ritchie Company, 1928), p. 7.

11. See, for example, Zane L. Miller, "Pluralism, Chicago School Style: Louis With, the Ghetto, the City, and Integration," *Journal of Urban History*, 18. no. 3 (May 1992), 251–279: and Zane L. Miller and E. Bruce Tucker, *Changing Plans for America's Inner Cities: Cincinnati's Over-the-Rhine and Twentieth-Century Urbanism* (Columbus: Ohio State University Press, 1998); Andrea Tuttle Kornbluh, "The Bowl of Promise: Cincinnati Social Welfare Planners, Cultural Pluralism and the Metropolitan Community" Ph.D. diss., Dept. of History, University of Cincinnati, 1988.

12. On the rise of large urban parks in the 19th century, see, for example, Roy Rosenzweig, *The Park and the People: A History of Central Park* (Ithaca, N.Y.: Cornell University Press, 1992) and Cynthia Zaitzevsky, *Fredrick Law Olmstead and the Boston Park System* (Cambridge: Harvard University Press, 1982). For the Cincinnati parks, see Andrea Tuttle Kornbluh, "Parks and People: The Place of the Kessler Park Plan in the History of Parks and Public Recreation," *Queen City Heritage*, 51, no. 1 (Spring 1993): 52–64; Dominick Cavallo,

*Muscles and Morals: Organized Playgrounds and Urban Reform, 1880–1920* (Philadelphia: University of Pennsylvania Press, 1981). The history of the public recreation movement has primarily been told from the perspective of the National Recreation Association. See George D. Butler, *Pioneers in Public Recreation* (Minneapolis, Minn.: Burgess Publishing Company, 1965); Charles E. Doell and Gerald B. Fitzgerald, *A Brief History of Parks and Recreation in the United States* (Chicago: The Athletic Institute, 1954), pp. 58–59, 60, 72. Finally, see *Encyclopedia of the Social Sciences*, MacMillan, 1937 ed., s.v. "Recreation," by Lee F. Hammer.

13. Doell and Fitzgerald, *A Brief History*, p. 72.

14. *The Charter for the City of Cincinnati, Prepared and Proposed by the Charter Commission of the City of Cincinnati, Election Day, Tuesday, July 14, 1914* (Charter Pamphlet Collection, Cincinnati Historical Society), p. 44. This early conception of public recreation defined recreation as a subcategory of Social Welfare and emphasized the policing powers of such a body, rather than the positive programs it might develop. When citizens adopted a new city charter in 1917, it created neither a Department of Social Welfare nor any administrative body on public recreation (see The Council of Cincinnati, *Seventh Supplement to Codification of Ordinances with Other Information, from December 15, 1916 to December 31, 1917*, Cincinnati, 1918). In the election of 1924, voters amended the 1917 city charter, which still made no mention of recreation as a municipal responsibility. See *Ordinances of the City of Cincinnati, Fourteenth Supplement*, 1924; L. B. Blakemore, *Charter and Code of Ordinances of Cincinnati 1928*, p. 23.

The first commission members included the following: Frederick W. Hinkle, a Yale-educated Catholic lawyer active in civic affairs, who also served as a park commissioner. He was also the only commissioner not publicly identified as a Charter Reform supporter (*Cincinnati Times-Star*, December 5, 1950); Phil Ziegler, labor's representative on the commission, edited the publication of the International Brotherhood of Railway and Steamship Clerks and was an intimate friend of Wisconsin radical Robert LaFollette (*Cincinnati Times-Star*, April 22, 1957); *Cincinnati Enquirer*, April 21,1957); John Josiah Emery, graduate of Harvard and Oxford, a Cincinnati businessman, and a philanthropist (*Cincinnati Post*, September 29, 1976; *Cincinnati Enquirer*, September 24, 1976); Walter Seton Schmidt, a graduate of Xavier University, financial backer of the local college's athletic programs, and a Catholic realtor (*Cincinnati Enquirer*, July 17, 1957; *Cincinnati Enquirer*, May 1, 1957); and Emma Wulke Fillmore, a leader in the Parent-Teacher Association and a Cincinnati School Board member and civic activist. See Andrea Tuttle Kornbluh, *Lighting the Way: The Woman's City Club of Cincinnati, 1915–1965* (Cincinnati, Oh.: Woman's City Club, 1986), p. 31 and *Cincinnati Enquirer*, February 29, 1964; Lyle Koehler, *Cincinnati's Black Peo-*

*ples: A Chronology and Bibliography, 1787–1982* (Cincinnati, Ohio: Cincinnati Arts Consortium, 1986), p. 145.

15. "Minutes of the Regular Meeting of the Public Recreation Commission," July 14, 1926, Typescript, The Public Recreation Commission Binder, City of Cincinnati, 1926–27 (Office of the Public Recreation Commission).

16. *Cincinnati Enquirer*, February 17, 1959; *Cincinnati Post*, February 16, 1959; *Cincinnati Post*, November 22, 1947; Wendell Phillips Dabney, *Cincinnati's Colored Citizens: Historical, Sociological and Biographical* (Cincinnati, Oh.: Dabney, 1926; reprint edition, New York: Negro University Press, 1970), pp. 211, 218. For more on black YMCAs, see Nina Magij, *Light in the Darkness: African Americans and the YMCA, 1852-1946* (Lexington: University Press of Kentucky, 1994); *Annual Report of the Public Recreation Commission* (1927), p. 4.

17. "Public Recreation Commission," *Municipal Activities* (City of Cincinnati, 1928), p. 142; "Minutes of the Regular Meeting of the Public Recreation Commission," January 27, 1926.

18. *Cincinnati Enquirer*, December 21, 1969; *Cincinnati Enquirer*, June 24, 1976.

19. Juvenile Protective Association, *Recreation Survey of Cincinnati* (Cincinnati, 1913), pp. 6–7; James H. Robinson, "The Cincinnati Negro Survey Program," *Proceedings of the National Conference on Social Work at the Forty-Sixth Annual Session held in Atlantic City, New Jersey, June 1–8, 1919*, p. 528; Kornbluh, "The Bowl of Promise," pp. 224, 342. Interest in "Negro Recreation" was not limited to Cincinnati—by the late 1920s, scholars around the country, especially sociologists, began to study it. T. J. Woofter's *Negro Problems in the Cities* (Garden City, N.Y.: Doubleday, Doram and Company, 1928) included "Recreation," by Henry McGuinn, with chapters on recreational needs, municipal facilities, organizations, and commercial recreation, pp. 227–282. See also William Henry Jones, *Recreation and Amusement among Negroes in Washington, D.C.: A Sociological Analysis of the Negro in an Urban Environment* (1927; Westport, Conn.: Negro University Press, 1970); Clyde Minor, MA Thesis, "Negro Recreation in Columbus, Ohio," M.A. thesis, Ohio State University, 1926.

20. *Annual Report of the Public Recreation Commission* (1927), pp. 8, 10, 22–23. The Recreation Commission operated six white and two "colored" community centers. Each of these were "self-governing and partially self-supporting." The Recreation Commission paid the salary of the executive secretary for the center and the fee for instructors in music, choral, and orchestral activities, and in drama "when sufficient participation in these activities is enlisted."

21. *Annual Report of the Public Recreation Commission* (1927), pp. 25, 26, 28. "Minutes of the Regular Meeting of the Public Recreation Commission," November 9, 1926; December 17, 1926; May 14, 1927; July 19, 1927; September

27, 1927; October 4, 1927; November 15, 1927; December 13, 1927. "Recreation Commission," *Municipal Activities* (City of Cincinnati, 1928), p. 143. In 1928, the Recreation Commission purchased two additional playfields, one in Oakley costing $27,000.00, the other in Madisonville, costing $24,627.00; both were in white neighborhoods.

22. *Annual Report of the Public Recreation Commission* (1928), pp. 12–13, 36. For more on the Negro Civic Welfare Association, see Andrea Tuttle Kornbluh, "James Hathaway Robinson and the Origins of Professional Social Work in the Black Community," in Henry Louis Taylor, Jr., ed., *Race and the City: Work, Community, Housing, and Protest in Cincinnati, 1820–1970* (Urbana: University of Illinois Press, 1993), pp. 209–231; *Annual Report of the Public Recreation Commission* (1929), p. 50; "Minutes of the Regular Meeting of the Recreation Commission," January 28, 1930.

23. "Minutes of the Regular Meeting of the Recreation Commission," January 28, 1930; July 21, 1931.

24. *Annual Report of the Public Recreation Commission* (1930), pp. 54, 59.

25. *Annual Report of the Public Recreation Commission* (1932), n.p.; "Survey Is Begun on Negro Recreational Facilities in the City—National Leader in Charge," *Cincinnati Enquirer*, March 22, 1932.

26. *The New York Times*, August 7, 1949; Butler, *Public Recreation* pp. 160–161, 162-163; Doell and Fitzgerald, *A Brief History*, p. 100. The first field secretary employed by the National Recreation Association was Lebert H. Weir, hired by the national group in 1920 after his successful work in improving playground programs and facilities in Cincinnati. The general suggestions the National Recreation Association made for communities conducting surveys are described in a 1932 typescript pamphlet, "Suggestions for Making a Community Recreation Survey" (Library, Ohio State University). The pamphlet mentions the need for population surveys by age and sex, but does not mention race. See also Butler, *Public Recreation*, pp. 162–63. Unfortunately, Attwell's reports were not printed in *Recreation*. However, an indication of his work can be found in a list of the organization's accomplishments for 1932, which included as the second of fourteen items, "28 communities received personal help in securing more adequate provision of recreation opportunities for Negroes," (*Recreation* 27, no. 1 (April 1933): 51; *Recreation* 26, no. 1 (April 1932); 109; *Recreation* 27, no. 1 (April 1933): 31; *Recreation* 28, no.1 (April 1934): 51.

27. National Recreation Association Bureau of Colored Work, "Limited Survey of Recreational Opportunities for Negro Citizens, Directed by E. T. Atwill [sic]" (Cincinnati, Ohio: National Recreation Association, 1932), Rare Books Collection, Public Library of Cincinnati and Hamilton County. The beginning of the report notes that it consists of "excerpts from the Complete Report of the Sur-

vey," which has been "reduced in volume for distribution and mimeographing." Members of the survey committee, by section, were as follows: "History and Population," C. R. Davis, T. M. Berry, F. A. B. Hall, Doris Wooten; "School Attendance and School Population," M. M. Rambo, Mary Morning, Ruth B. Crittenden, Kathleen L. Cannady, Marian Shivers; "Church Organization Among Negroes," George Cooper, Rev. W. H. McCallum, J. H. Thorpe, Rev W. A. Page, Rev. B. F. Reed; "Fraternal Organizations," F. A. B. Hall, Michael Robinson, Sanfred Showes, E. R. Jones, Sarah Haddox; "Housing," Dr. W. M. Springer, Morris Walton, Leo Hopkins; "Health and Hospitalization," Dr. R. P. McClain, Estelle R. Davis, Dr. B. F. Cann, Dr. W. M. Springer, Dr. R. E. Clarke, Dr. B. J. Lockley; "Delinquency," Rev. W. A. Jackson, John R. Fox, Wm. Lovelace, M. C. Clarke, Alexine C. Spurlock; "Business and Industrial," M. C. Clarke, T. M. Berry, Adah Chapelle, M. S. Morning, Henry W. Ferguson, C. R. Davis, C. E. Sampson, Jessie Mae Harris; "Welfare and Social Agencies," Verna P. Greene, Wm. Lovelace, Raba Cann; "Commercial Recreation," Estelle R. Davis, Nellie Underwood, Howard Greer; "Public Recreation," DeHart Hubbard, Dr. R. P. McClain, Carleta Hubbard, George Cooper, Henry Wright, Helen Kerr, Ethel Irving, Laura E. Scott, Lillian Dudley, Bert Dudley, Leo Hopkins, Clara Hough Estill, Jean M. Brown; "School and Other Public Recreation, " James Thorpe, Jennie Austin, Sanfred Showes, M. M. Rambo. The insurance company owned a building, the Supreme Life Building, located at 612–614 West Ninth Street. Among the tenants were black physicians R. E. Breedlove, Ray E. Clark, J. H. Wallace, B. J. Lockley, dentist E. H. Green, and African American attorneys A. Lee Beaty, W. B. George Conrad, and Jesse D. Locker; from *Williams' Cincinnati Directory 1933–34* (Cincinnati, Ohio: Williams Directory Company, 1934), p. 2056.

28. National Recreation Association, Bureau of Colored Work, Section 1: pp. 1–4. The separate sections of this report are not consecutively numbered, perhaps reflecting the work of the individual committees assigned to each section. Therefore, references to this study will include both section and page number.

29. National recreation Association, Bureau of Colored Work, Section 11: p. 1. Attwell identified a few recreational institutions that admitted both black and white patrons, but they were not always admitted on an equal basis. Although anyone could visit the Cincinnati Zoo, "all," Attwell wrote without explanation, "are not permitted to enjoy certain privileges." All citizens could, however, attend Redland Field Ball Park.

30. National Recreation Association, Bureau of Colored Work, Section 14: pp. 1, 5.

31. National Recreation Association, Bureau of Colored Work, Section 14: pp. 7, 8. Attwell also suggested that a drama program should be instituted leading to the production of an annual pageant (music and drama programs were already

available as recreation Commission Departments, but served only white Cincinnatians).

32. Annual Report of the Public Recreation Commission (1932), np; *The New Grove Dictionary of American Music*, s.v. "Matthews, Artie"; *The Greenwood Encyclopedia of Black Music: Biographical Dictionary of Afro-American and African Musicians*, s.v. "Matthews, Artie"; *Annual Report of the Public Recreation Commission* (1930), p. 54.

Atwell called the establishment of the council "the outstanding achievement" of his department for the year 1932. The ninety-three member council, he wrote, had in less than one year "become a definite factor in the life of the city" and the group's volunteer efforts had greatly stimulated the work of the Department of Colored Citizens. The officers of the new council included W. N. Lovelace, President; Rose B. Craig, Secretary; Verna P. Greene, Treasurer and Chairman of the Playground Committee; R. P. McClain, Chairman of the Board of Directors and Athletic Committee; M. M. Rambo, Chairman of the Co-ordination Committee; S. R. Showes, Chairman of the Handcraft Committee; Hazel J. Lucas, Chairman of the Dramatics Committee; B. J. Lockley, Chairman of the Civics Committee; and F. A. B. Hall, J. W. Thorpe, and M. C. Clarke, members of the Board of Directors.

33. *The Playground*, 20, no.1 (April 1926): 605; 31, no. 9 (June 1927): 72; 23, no.1 (April 1929): 430; 23, no.1 (April 1929): 210; 24, no.1 (April 1930): 630; 25, no.1 (April 1931): 39; 23, no.1 (April 1929): 234; 21, no.1 (April 1927): 258.

"Lift Every Voice and Sing," written by the black poet and civil rights leader James Weldon Johnson in 1900, had a controversial history. In 1927, for example, the Rev. Dr. Ernest Lyon published a pamphlet titled "A Protest against the title of James Weldon Johnson's anomalous poem" (Kent State micro-35 e185 .537x no. 313), arguing that Negroes in America did not constitute a nation and therefore shouldn't have a national anthem. Abdul Karim Bangura suggests that "Lift Every Voice and Sing" was widely used by African American organizations across the country between 1901 and the late 1920s, but that from 1930 through the early 1950s, "African American colleges discouraged the singing of the song." According to Bandura, this was because the leaders of black educational institutions felt that "the proper avenue for entering the mainstream was assimilation into white culture." See Abdul Karim Bangura, *Political Presuppositions and Implications of the Most Popular African American Hymns* (New York: Nova Science Publishers, 1996), pp. 38–39.

34. *Playground and Recreation* 24, no. 1 (April 1930): 686; *The Playground* 21, no.1 (April 1927): 323.

35. *Recreation* 18, no. 1 (April 1934): 278.

36. *Annual Report of the Public Recreation Commission* (1932), n.p. This joint ownership of the event constituted a new development and an acknowledgment by the Recreation Commission that its African American work could be viewed not only as something to classify by race, but also as something which could fit into the existing departmental categories, such as community music. Like Atwell's survey, this shift seems to have some connection to Tam Deering's vision of how he wanted to run his department, because it does not begin until his arrival and coincides exactly with it.

37. *Annual Report of the Public Recreation Commission* (1932), n.p.

38. *Greenwood Encyclopedia of Black Music: Biographical Dictionary of Afro-American and African Musicians*, s.v. "Jones, J. Wesley"; *Public Recreation Commission Annual Report* (1933), pp. 25, 28. It appears from Hubbard's calling attention to his close cooperation with Glore that this type of working arrangement was still a novelty (*Public Recreation Commission Annual Report* (1934), p. 24). In his report, Hubbard included only two sentences about the music work of his department. "In cooperation with the Department of Music," he said, "much progress has been made in the development of musical groups. Further details are to be found in the report of the Department of Music." Glore, in his report, did not include racial designations to the different programs he summarized. While it is not clear whether there was a Festival of Negro Music in 1934, it is obvious that the two departments continued to work together. That so much cooperation may have been a national policy of the National Recreation Association is suggested by the joint visit of Attwell and Johnson to Cincinnati in 1934.

39. *Annual Report of the Public Recreation Commission* (1938), pp. 34, 40.

40. *Annual Report of the Public Recreation Commission* (1939), p. 40. In an article with a number of factual errors, the *Cincinnati Post* of April 15, 1947 presented a brief history of the festival, which asserted that the first suggestion for the establishment of a permanent June Festival Association came from Dr. J. H. Thurman, secretary of the May Festival.

41. *Annual Report of the Public Recreation Commission* (1940), p. 41; *Cincinnati Enquirer* (June 9, 1942).

42. Virginia Hamilton, *Paul Robeson: The Life and Times of a Free Black Man* (New York: Dell Publishing Company, 1974), pp. 41–51, 73–75.

43. *Annual Report of the Public Recreation Commission* (1944), pp. 5, 14; *Annual Report of the Public Recreation Commission* (1945), pp. 2, 13; Butler, *Public Recreation* p. 166.

44. See "Robeson Group Refused By Board in Request for Stowe School Rally," *Cincinnati Times-Star*, September 12, 1949; "Not Wanted Here," *Cincinnati Enquirer*, September 17, 1949; Duberman, who mentioned the FBI reports,

says that Robeson never joined the Communist Party (*Paul Robeson*, p. 253); *The Playground* 23, no.1 (April 1929): 234.

45. "United Nations Universal Declaration of Human Rights," U.N. Website at http://www.un.org/Overview/rights.html. Karl, *Uneasy State*, p. 235. According to William C. Berman (*The Politics of Civil Rights in the Truman Administration* [Columbus: Ohio State University Press, 1970] pp. 65–66),W. E. B. Du Bois, Milton Konvitz, Earl B. Dickerson, and Rayford Logan in 1947 drafted a petition addressed to the recently organized United Nations, seeking that organization's aid in compelling the American government to take a stronger stand against racial discrimination. The petition, "A Statement on the Denial of Human Rights to Minorities in the Case of Citizens of Negro Descent in the United States of America and an Appeal to the United Nations for Redress, Prepared for the NAACP," received attention in the world press, as did the claim that racial discrimination was widespread in America. However, the United Nations Commission on Human Rights decided against investigating the charges contained in it.

46. August Meier and Elliott Rudwick, *CORE: A Study in the Civil Rights Movement, 1942–1968* (Urbana: University of Illinois Press, 1975), pp. 40–41; Berman, *Politics of Civil Rights*, pp. 58, 62–63.

47. *To Secure These Rights: The Report of the President's Committee on Civil Rights* (Washington, D.C.: U.S. Government Printing Office, 1947). Of course, Gunnar Myrdal's book, *An American Dilemma: The Negro Problem and Modern Democracy* (New York: Harper and Row, 1944); Twentieth Anniversary Edition, 1962) had already been published. The Carnegie Corporation, which had begun discussing such a study in the early 1930s, funded the study and hired Myrdal in 1937. The Swedish social economist Myrdal was hired, according to Frederick P. Keppel of the corporation, because it desired a scholar "who could approach his task with a fresh mind, uninfluenced by traditional attitudes or by earlier conclusions." The corporation wanted to hire someone from a country "with no background or tradition of imperialism which might lessen the confidence of the Negroes in the United States as to the complete impartiality of the study and the validity of its findings." So the corporation looked only at scholars from Switzerland and Scandinavia. "When the Trustees of the Carnegie Corporation asked for the preparation of this report in 1937," said Keppel, "no one (except possibly Adolf Hitler) could have foreseen that it would be made public at a day when the place of the Negro in our American life would be the subject of greatly heightened interest in the United States." Myrdal's book, like the interracial movement of the 1920s, 1930s, and 1940s defined race relations problems as failures to live up to the demands of American democratic ideals. Unlike *To Secure These Rights*, Myrdal used the words *civil rights* only in brief references to existing civil rights laws. Moreover, he took as his basic social unit not the indi-

vidual, as did the President's Committee, but the group. See Myrdal, *American Dilemma*, xlvii-xlx, 1021–1024; *To Secure These Rights*, pp. ix–xi.

48. Zane L. Miller and E. Bruce Tucker, "The Revolt Against Cultural Determinism and the Meaning of Community Action: A View from Cincinnati," *Prospects: An Annual of American Cultural Studies*, 15 (New York: Cambridge University Press, 1990), pp. 413–447; *Cincinnati Enquirer*, May 24, 1950; *The Greenwood Encyclopedia of Black Music: Biographical Dictionary of Afro-American and African Musicians* (1982), s.v. "Coleridge-Taylor, Samuel"; *Cincinnati Post*, June 9, 1951; *Cincinnati Enquirer*, May 24, 1950.

49. Alain Locke, "More than Blasting Brick and Mortar," *Survey Graphic* 36 (January 1947): 87–89.

50. *Cincinnati Post*, April 20, 1949. In 1944, a several-year battle to oust Tam Deering as Recreation Commissioner began. Despite the support of liberal civic groups, Deering proved to be unable to hold on to his position. See Kornbluh, "Bowl of Promise," pp. 385–386.

# CHAPTER 4

# From Auburn Avenue to Buttermilk Bottom

## Class and Community Dynamics among Atlanta's Blacks

GEORGINA HICKEY

One Saturday afternoon in the spring of 1948, an impromptu parade began on Atlanta's Auburn Avenue when crowds gathered to witness the first patrol of Atlanta's new African American police. So many blacks from the community came to get a look at the new officers that "the street was solid with people."[1] Here were the leading African American citizens of the city as well as washerwomen and industrial laborers.[2] Lying just below the festive atmosphere of the day and this outward display of community unity, however, lurked many of the complexities of the city's black community. While all present celebrated the introduction of black police to the city, working-class African Americans had a different interest in the unfolding events than the elite class of blacks who had negotiated with white city officials for the introduction of black officers. African American triumph in this particular battle meant the further entrenchment of a moderate, elite black leadership. And the noted but unnamed working-class and poor African Americans present that day, while proud of the progress made by this leadership, remained wary of police in general, hoping at the very least "that these [officers] wouldn't do them as bad as the white policemen."[3] While the crowd represented much of the social and economic diversity of Atlanta's black community, the events of the day also reveal the frequent muting of class divisions and tensions in the name of racial progress, a common theme in the history of Atlanta's African American community during the first half of the 20th century.

During the first half of the century, African Americans constituted well over a third of the city's population, yet racially motivated violence during the riot of 1906 and Jim Crow legislation severely limited black's influence on Atlanta's white power structure until after the Second World War.[4] The city's white business leaders employed booster language to cast segregation as the key to peaceful race relations, helping to create Atlanta's long-standing reputation as a city "too busy to hate." Leaders from the black community furthered this image by creating the illusion of a singular and cohesive community of African Americans. Under this moderate leadership, the years of segregation and disenfranchisement actually solidified notions of community among Atlanta blacks and supported African American economic development. It is the legacy of these years that laid the foundation for relatively peaceful public integration, the formation of a political coalition of African Americans and middle-class whites, and the ascendancy of blacks to political office in the 1960s and 1970s.

What is missing from this triumphant picture of a cohesive African American community and steady political progress are the complexities of inter- and intraclass relations among Atlanta's blacks. Despite progress within the black community, the mostly male bourgeoisie leadership, fervently acting out of the belief that what was good for the middle class was good for all, often maligned the interests of the African American working class while creating a masculinized language of racial politics that marginalized women of any status.[5] An exploration of the class, gender, and racial dynamics muted by the "better classes" in the name of progress illuminates the roots of the urban housing crisis and growing poverty that also plagued the city in the 1960s and 1970s. The story of Atlanta's African American community between 1900 and 1950, then, reveals both the best of racial progress, as blacks built a strong presence in Atlanta's political structure, as well as exposes the tensions inherent to cross-class coalition-building that the city's blacks would continue to face into the second half of the 20th century.

## TURN OF THE CENTURY

The watershed for black Atlantans came during the fall of 1906, when events significantly altered the racial atmosphere of Atlanta and facilitated a shift in the composition of the city's black elite and the black community's leaders drawn from this class. After a tumultuous gubernatorial campaign in which the disenfranchisement of blacks was a central issue, a series of exaggerated reports of black men attacking white women set off racial tensions in the heart of Atlanta. For three days in September, mobs of whites assaulted blacks and black-owned property, particularly in the downtown area.[6] The 1906 riot aided the institution of public segregation in Atlanta, and the almost complete disenfranchisement of the city's blacks quickly followed. While these trends affected all of Atlanta's African American population, class identity shaped the way in which blacks experienced and responded to the segregation and loss of access to formal politics and, in the case of elites, the composition of the class itself changed.

On the eve of the 20th century, Atlanta's black community was fractured along geographic and class lines. African Americans lived in small enclaves in the northeast, southeast, and northwest sections of the city, interspersed with white streets and neighborhoods. A number even lived "in the rear" of mixed-race neighborhoods, occupying houses on alleys that ran behind larger black and white homes.[7] Residential segregation did exist, but the racialization of housing often changed street by street, even block by block in some cases. Before the 1920s, no one area in the city functioned as the residential and commercial center of the black community, although east side Auburn Avenue, known to African American residents simply as "the avenue," was home to many of the city's elite blacks.[8] Other well-to-do African Americans inhabited the Summerhill district south of downtown and African American intellectuals clustered around the black colleges on Atlanta's west side. Spread throughout numerous small neighborhoods between these areas lived the city's more fluid population of working-class blacks.[9]

The "better classes" of Atlanta's blacks in the pre-riot years functioned within insular social and economic circles. These African Americans benefited from post–Civil War education and had parlayed their skills and business sense into successful shops that catered to white clientele. One daughter of this class, born on Auburn Avenue in 1890, reflected that many of these men "had been . . . eight to ten years old when they came out of slavery, and naturally they had dreams and they wanted everything to be just like they had seen other people have." The better classes of whites in the city appear to have been their model for socializing and style. Kathleen Adams's father, a lawyer, decided "he needed the type of coat that the lawyers in the other race wore," and his Sunday finery did indeed include a Prince Albert coat.[10] Meticulous in their dress and deportment, this class of often light-skinned blacks represented, in the minds of many Atlantans, the best of black achievement after the demise of Reconstruction. Yet one of the most striking characteristic of this group was the distance they maintained between themselves and the poorer members of their race.

At the top of this class were men like Alonzo Herndon, a light-skinned black born into slavery who owned and operated a string of bar-bershops. Herndon's enterprises included the finest shop on Peachtree Street where "nothing but Negro barbers waited on nothing but whites with accurate service and the best Negro barbers you could find."[11] Besides Herndon, other turn-of-the-century black elites included a building contractor, shoemakers, and draymen.[12] The younger men of this class took jobs in the posh hotels and social clubs frequented by the city's whites. As a mark of class status, the wives and daughters of this elite class rarely worked outside the home. Their days were filled with caring for the home and children, punctuated by church functions and numerous social clubs. As Janette Greenwood has recently noted for Charlotte's "better classes," the men and women of Atlanta's black elite functioned in separate spheres, displaying a modified version of what historians of white women have labeled a "cult of domesticity."[13]

Other distinguishing markers of this turn-of-the-century elite were the social spaces they occupied. First Congregational Church, Wheat Street Baptist, and Friendship Baptist claimed the top of black society as their members. The pastors of these churches—H. H. Proctor, A. D. Williams, and E. R. Carter—occupied prestigious positions in the community and were generally held in high regard as "great leaders in Atlanta."[14] The city's wealthiest African Americans also built social clubs that reflected their status in the community. August Meier and David Lewis estimated that this "mulatto aristocracy" of Atlanta supported six or so fashionable organizations.[15] Club members enjoyed socializing, card playing, and dancing in these exclusive enclaves. Particularly in this realm, the black elite paralleled the wealthy whites of the city by establishing the Negro Driving Club and sponsoring debutante balls.

At the heart of Atlanta's black elite community during these years were values designed to cultivate "respect from the white community and influence in their own."[16] High among these values were strict codes for restrained moral and social behavior. Members of this class shunned the enthusiastic worship style prevalent in many working-class black churches and tended to moderate their emotions at Sunday service. Prominent black Atlantans prided themselves on having parents "who had raised their children with morals and behavior and intellectual ability" and living in "very reputable" neighborhoods where the homes were "kept nice."[17] Parents stressed the importance of education and would send their children across town to the grammar and secondary schools of Atlanta University or Atlanta Baptist College (later Morehouse College). Children of the turn-of-the-century black elite were also forbidden from interacting with black working-class children who lived in surrounding areas. As the daughter of a shoemaker recalled, her father "wouldn't let us play with hardly a child in the neighborhood . . . cause he was afraid we'd pick up some nasty habit or say some dirt word."[18] In the end, almost every aspect of elite black life at the turn of the century seemed to reinforce the distance between the working class and the elite.

## THE WORLD OF BLACK WORKERS

The great bulk of Atlanta's African American population did indeed live a very different life from that of the community's elite. Many working-class blacks were new migrants to the city during the first half of the 20th century, when the city's total African American population grew from 35,000 in 1900 to 121,000 by 1950. These working-class African Americans clustered in poor neighborhoods built on cheap valley land—Darktown, Beaver Slide, and Buttermilk Bottom. These residential areas often lacked city services such as lighting, paved streets, and adequate public schools.[19] As a social worker who visited the residents of some of these homes recalled, "They had a communal toilet outside. They brought water in for the tin tubs to bathe in. It was a deplorable sort of thing. There was no privacy in living because most of the time they had to leave the doors open to the hallway."[20] Responding to these conditions, working-class blacks moved frequently, relocating for new jobs, hoping to improve their accommodations in a neighborhood with a better reputation, or just searching for cheaper rent. Consequently, these areas developed reputations among blacks and whites of all classes as transient neighborhoods, housing those "of a lower income or lower standard of moral behavior or patterns of life."[21]

Most Atlanta blacks found jobs as menial laborers or domestic servants during the early decades of the 20th century. African American men worked as "day hands" in the rail- and factory yards of the city, rarely making it onto the trains or inside the mills until World War I. Other black men found employment in the personal service of whites. "Jobs," recalled a black school teacher, "were real hard on men, they were . . . scrubbing and mopping and washing."[22] Black men regularly experienced seasonal layoffs and competed with whites who were "crowding Negroes" in traditionally black jobs such as "porters, ditchers, news-boys, [and] elevator-boys" during economic slumps.[23] Nine of every ten black women who worked for wages found employment as domestics, working as maids, washerwomen, child nurses, or cooks.[24] Maids often roomed in the homes of their employers, a common arrangement until World War II opened industrial jobs to black women on a substantial scale.[25] Before the war, a few black women found access to industrial employment as scrubwomen in factories or pressers in the city's new commercial laundries.[26] Ultimately, the inadequate job opportunities and poor quality of housing kept Atlanta's poorer blacks searching for better opportunities in the realm of both employment and housing.

Many working-class blacks countered the dehumanizing effects of wage work, poor city services, and inadequate housing by developing an "expressive culture" in their leisure hours. Without access to the campus-sponsored activities open to the college community on the west side or the exclusive social clubs of the Auburn Avenue district, working-class blacks often turned to commercial amusements for recreation and socialization. Decatur Street, running east from downtown and only a few blocks south of Auburn Avenue, housed many of these new entertainments. While the street's amusements remained largely unsegregated in the years following the riot, it quickly developed a reputation as home to Atlanta's "underside." The crowded sidewalks and variety of businesses that catered to limited budgets attracted many working-class blacks who sought fun, anonymity, or a bargain.[27] For as many who found amusement in the street's saloons, theaters, and dance halls, however, just as many others, revealing the variety of working-class attitudes toward the offerings of the city, were warned away from it. "Decatur Street used to be rough," recalled one migrant to the city, "My peoples told me when I came to Atlanta, 'Stay off Decatur Street.' And I did just that."[28]

When meager salaries and racial hostilities made these commercial amusements unappealing or unavailable, working-class blacks retreated to their own neighborhoods for relaxation and release, turning segregation from whites into congregation with other African Americans.[29] Rent or house parties were popular outlets, as were neighborhood baseball games. Anne Scarlett Cochran, a city resident in the early 20th century, recalled when few public amusements were open to blacks: "We've gone around in homes. Entertainment was in the homes."[30] Willie Mae Jackson described these "house parties" as "not anything formal, just was a friendly get together [to] eat and drink and dance. Just a bunch of friends would throw a party most anytime."[31] Churches filled both social and religious needs and were one of the few public spaces in which working-class blacks functioned wholly outside the purview of whites. Many poorer African Americans invested much of their leisure time in these religious institutions and, as a result, Atlanta churches grew with the expanding population, increasing from 54 in 1903 to over 200 by 1940.[32] Alice Adams recalled that domestic workers "would get together and go at night. Every church they used to have a service at night and that was the only time you could go."[33] In the streets, homes, and churches of African American neighborhoods, "black working people carved out social space free from the watchful eye of white authority or, in a few cases, the moralizing of the black middle class."[34]

Without the monetary insulation of wealthier blacks, Atlanta's working-class African Americans often experienced the brunt of early-20th-century racial hostility. Their employment usually involved direct contact with white workers and employers, though racialized employment patterns maintained blacks in subordinate positions to the whites they encountered on a daily basis. The need for African American laborers to travel across the city on public transportation also brought many of the black working class into direct and increasingly hostile contact with the city's whites. The 1890s had introduced both streetcars and Jim Crow segregation to Atlanta' public transportation. Blacks paid their fares at the front but were required by law to sit in the back of cars. Segregation of public theaters and other amusements in the city, which were strengthened in the wake of the race riot, also directly affected the working classes of the black community. Poor and working-class African Americans lived with and endured segregation on a daily basis, but this is not to say that they passively accepted it. In often deliberate and quiet ways, African Americans struggled to control their daily lives and relations with others.

During the first half of the 20th century, while elite blacks built strong institutional bases for their reforms, Atlanta's African American working class engaged in less formal, though no less committed, activism of their own. For Atlanta's black working class, public transportation functioned as a "moving theater" in which its members waged everyday struggles against racism.[35] Racial tensions in the workplace often spilled over into conflicts on public transportation. "Sometimes we'd have arguments," recalled one working-class black, "little specks on the bus or streetcar. Some peoples would just get determined—'I'm not going to work all day and stand!' "[36] Through these actions, Atlanta's working-class African Americans created their own sense of respectability, which usually relied on controlling their own dignity, time, and labor. On the surface this activism might have appeared individual or spontaneous, but the larger community supported these individual efforts and they were passed from generation to generation.[37] In cataloging many of the techniques used by domestic workers and laborers, historian Tera Hunter found women refusing to do specific duties, stealing from employers, borrowing clothes and other items, and otherwise asserting their independence.[38] Willie Mae Cartwright, who worked a variety of service jobs in Atlanta, lied to one employer that her cousin was ill so that she would have time off to try out another job that paid higher wages without jeopardizing her original position.[39] Domestic worker Mary Morton wanted to attend church so she refused to work on Sunday, claiming, "I'm poor, but I know how to live."[40] In the end, working-class activism in public spaces and workplaces centered around efforts to establish or maintain autonomy and respectability, difficult goals to attain in the years after the riot as segregation grew firm roots in Atlanta.

## AFTERMATH OF THE 1906 RACE RIOT

While Atlanta's 1906 racial violence created few dramatic shifts in the realm of work or housing for working-class African Americans, the riot did alter the composition of the elite class, as educators and intellectuals, who had been drawn to Atlanta by the six black colleges, moved into the most prominent leadership positions in the city's black community, and displaced the shopkeeping elite on the front lines of "racial progress." In many ways, this new leadership embodied the qualities and ideas of the pre-riot elite. Black "better classes" still expected respect from both races on the basis of social and economic class standing. Dr. G. S. Penn, for example, approached the Atlanta Chamber of Commerce shortly after the riot, asking for protection from the racial hostilities, because, he argued "he was a law-abiding citizen, living in his own house with his family and had constantly used his influence for obedience to law and the elevation of his own race."[41] A distinguishing factor of the new intellectual elite, however, included an intensified focus on improving the status of the race through programs designed to lift the lower rungs of black society out of their suffering and poverty. This racial uplift ideology centered around a language of respectability that stressed improvements in black morality as the key to improving race relations in the city.[42] Summing up the optimism of this class, W. E. B. Du Bois concluded that "social reforms move slowly and yet when Right is reinforced by calm but persistent Progress we somehow all feel that in the end it must triumph."[43]

The ferocity with which white mobs attacked blacks during the 1906 riot discouraged the city's African Americans from organizing along overtly political lines in the ensuing decades. Deeply committed to "the turning of the high toward the lowly," however, several organizations dedicated to racial progress did emerge from this new leadership after the riot.[44] A group of prominent blacks, including W. E. B. Du Bois and George Towns, created the short-lived Equal Rights League to organize blacks to register and vote against the 1908 disenfranchisement bill.[45] More long-lived and representative of the educational elites' tactics, however, was the organization of the Neighborhood Union by Lugenia Burns Hope in the same year. Hope, an educated, light-skinned woman who had been introduced to social uplift in Chicago's Hull House, had come to Atlanta with her husband, educator John Hope, in 1898.[46] While John Hope worked his way up from professor to being the first African American president of Morehouse College, Lugenia Burns Hope set about improving the neighborhoods surrounding the colleges in which the Hopes and other faculty members lived.

The black sections of Atlanta's west side served not only as a center of higher education but also as home to many of the city's poorest blacks. Abutting the colleges, at the bottom of Fair Street, lay Beaver Slide. Describing this notorious neighborhood, one black woman recalled, "They'd shoot crap in the street and if you come along walking, you'd better walk out in the street and not try to go through there."[47] According to a young faculty member who came to Atlanta during these years, "Dr. and Mrs. Hope had bemoaned the fact that here were educational institutions surrounded by a slum, ghetto-type of community and environment."[48] After several years of battling these conditions on her own, in 1908 Lugenia Burns Hope called together several other elite women associated with the black colleges with the intention of forming an organization to improve the area by "build[ing] the sort of ethnic pride that would take delight in constructive citizenship and happy family life."[49]

The Neighborhood Union, as the organization came to be called, focused on lobbying the city for new and additional resources for west side neighborhoods. The union promoted their cause by describing the area's residents as a moral and respectable population worthy of citizenship. In order to create this image, Neighborhood Union organizers sponsored mothers' meetings, free health clinics, recreational activities, "clean-up campaigns," and classes in nursing, home hygiene, sewing, and cooking.[50] Through these programs, Neighborhood Union organizers sought to "elevate the moral, social, intellectual, and spiritual standards of each neighborhood" as a means of both improving the community in which these women lived and earning the cooperation and respect of Atlanta's white community.[51] Programs encouraged cleanliness, efficiency, and morality, which it was hoped would be values that mothers would pass on to their children. The Neighborhood Union emphasized the role of black working-class women as critical to community improvement in African American neighborhoods and even made limited attempts to include these women in infrastructure of the organization. "It is remarkable," noted Louie D. Shivery, the long-time secretary of the Neighborhood Union, "how uneducated Negroes attacked social problems, single-handed, in religion, education, and civic life, and made noteworthy beginnings in solving these social problems of their racial group."[52]

Among Atlanta's post-riot elite, the black working class was seen alternately as the best hope for racial advancement and the most dangerous impediment to black progress. The policies of the Neighborhood Union and the voter registration campaign of the Equal Rights League, for example, tended to emphasize the ways in which a moral working class could change whites' views concerning blacks. While many working-class blacks demonstrated their own version of moral uplift in their daily lives and through their willing and often enthusiastic participation in the uplift projects of the Neighborhood Union, elite blacks often reviled the poorer members of their own race.[53] Perhaps the most notable incidence of this appeared in 1910, when fears of tuberculosis reached a fevered pitch throughout the city. Whites in the city had already labeled black washerwomen as the agents of contagion, accusing the laundresses of bringing disease into white homes. Elite blacks were not immune to similar fears. In the spring of 1910 the black newspaper printed the thoughts of a doctor who included a discussion of "how we are infected by consumptive cooks" in a list of ways in which the disease was spread.[54] Public health was not the only issue in which class tension emerged. Even while organizing a broad coalition of blacks to vote against the disenfranchisement bill of 1908, leaders of the Equal Rights League, in the words of Du Bois biographer David Lewis, found the bill "appalling . . . in its unfairness in treating all classes of African Americans alike."[55]

In trying to raise the moral standards of the community, Neighborhood Union workers were particularly quick to attack women who refused to fit the model of morality promoted in their conceptualization of respectability, motherhood, and neighborhood. The organization did not hesitate to request that the Atlanta City Council and police department remove specific women and families. The Neighborhood Union justified its actions by arguing, "We were not helping our neighbor when we failed to tell the mother of the evil company her daughter was keeping while she was away trying to make a living. Blind tigers, houses of ill repute, dance halls, and loud and disturbing gatherings are among the cases which come before the Union frequently." Members found enthusiastic support for these campaigns in the white community, and reported that "The police department has backed us when we have called on them. They say they are glad to assist us in our efforts to have a clean community."[56] The efforts of the Neighborhood Union were widely endorsed by elites of both races, but especially by blacks. The *Atlanta Independent*, the city's conservative black newspaper, reiterated Neighborhood Union policies, calling on blacks to build up their "home life" and requesting more wholesome recreational facilities from the municipal government.[57]

Embedded in the work and policies of the Neighborhood Union was much of the ideology of this educational elite. Their visions of social order for the black community included a strong sense of mutual cooperation among a community of moral, educated, and law-abiding families. Consequently, the activities of Lugenia Burns Hope were not unique among women of similar background and class standing. Nellie McNain Towns, the wife of Atlanta University professor and NAACP cofounder George Towns, divided her time between work at the Gate City Free Kindergarten, First Congregational Church's outreach programs, and the Phyllis Wheatley branch of the YWCA.[58] Within the established framework of these race leaders' commitment to "self-respect, self-sufficiency, racial pride and solidarity, and a strong sense of noblesse oblige," elite black women promoted their own role as essential and directly challenged the negative images of African American women popularized in mass culture during the early 20th century.[59]

The maternalist arguments advanced by Hope and her cohort of reformers mirrored a national trend during these years in which a club movement grew "out of the organized anxiety of women who have only recently become intelligent enough to recognize their own social condition and strong enough to initiate and apply the forces of reform. . . . It is a movement," Fannie Barrier Williams further explained, "that reaches down into the sub-social condition of an entire race and has become the responsibility and effort of a few competent on behalf of the many incompetent."[60] Creating arguments similar to maternalist ideologies promoted by white women, these "race women" carved out a significant space for themselves in this generation of black leadership as they strove to "regulate the status of the race" and promote moral and social respectability as a strategy of racial justice.[61] Without reservation, these women claimed that, in the face of hardship, "the Negro woman has been the motive power in whatever has been accomplished by the race."[62]

Just as the aftermath of the race riot encouraged a new leadership to develop, the hardening of segregation also marked a sea change in the economic foundations of Atlanta's black community. Many of the black-owned businesses located in downtown Atlanta were burned or looted during the riot. Those that had eluded destruction faced a new and hostile environment in the predominantly white central business district. In order to start over and escape downtown, many black entrepreneurs turned to Auburn Avenue. The eastern end of the street was already established as a solidly African American residential area and provided business owners a black consumer base that desired a new shopping district in the wake of downtown segregation policies.[63] Black entrepreneurs began establishing their businesses on the western end of Auburn Avenue. Here the Atlanta Life Insurance Company, Citizens Trust Company, Mutual Federal Savings & Loan, and numerous smaller enterprises built new offices.

The growing commercial nature of Auburn Avenue accelerated during the 1910s and reached a frenzied pace during the 1920s. A fire in 1917 destroyed many of the homes along Auburn Avenue, encouraging the residential growth of Atlanta's west side and opening the eastern end of Auburn to commercial use.[64] During these years, Auburn Avenue became known as Sweet Auburn, the place "where Negro businesses were springing up and flourishing as a new Atlanta started to grow."[65] It became the undisputed center of black life, supporting the Prince Hall Masonic Temple and a variety of stores, churches, offices, and even nightclubs. Describing the wealth of businesses found on Auburn Avenue, Phoebe Hart recalled that, "they literally crossed the fields of your physical needs, your spiritual needs and your living needs."[66] In 1930, Ella Martin, a representative of the Poro System of Beauty Culture, came to Atlanta, "married in a family that were well known people," and opened her shop on Auburn Avenue. She counted herself fortunate in these events, recalling, "we were proud because that's the only decent place we had to conduct our businesses and to have our fun and our pleasures, our parties and things like that."[67]

Blacks from all walks of life crossed paths on Sweet Auburn and, while members of different classes attended different churches or frequented different meeting halls, an air of "pride and joy" permeated the street.[68] In the afternoons, people "began clearing off the streets. People would go home and take their baths and get back on the streets and go different places like Yates and Milton [drug store] . . . they didn't go out on the street with ordinary clothes on."[69] Particularly for the young people, Auburn Avenue became the social center of the black community. "Auburn Avenue," according to domestic worker Alice Adams, "used to be like white folks' Peachtree. Auburn Avenue would be one of the places that we would dress up and go at night."[70] A barber recalled, "You had to go there for real decent social entertainment . . . and if you didn't take your girl over there back in those days, why you were a cheapskate. The girls . . . wanted to go to Auburn, if you didn't go down and buy anything but an ice cream cone, just take them to Auburn; that was their evening, that was their glory."[71] For working-class blacks, the street became the mecca of black life far removed from the eyes of white employers and the less-reputable integrated amusements to be found on Decatur Street. For black elites, the prospering businesses also offered recreation, but, more importantly, created the economic base that would launch black political activism in the 1930s and 1940s.

As Auburn Avenue rose to prominence during the 1920s, a new class of African American business and professional men joined educational leaders in eclipsing the power of the turn-of-the-century elites. Among this new leadership were individuals like John Wesley Dobbs, a federal postal employee who headed Georgia's Prince Hall Masons; L. D. Milton, who left a teaching appointment to move "into the top circle of people . . . in banking, business, finance, [and] everything" while working his way up to the presidency of Citizen's Trust Bank; newspaper publisher C. A. Scott, and numerous other members of the newly formed Negro Chamber of Commerce.[72] During the 1920s, the pulpits of the African American community's most powerful churches also passed to new leaders: Martin Luther King, Sr., took over for his father-in-law, A. D. Williams, at Ebenezer Baptist, while William Borders assumed the pulpit at Wheat Street Baptist. A change also occurred in the city's black press as the new *Atlanta Daily World* courted readers from the older and more conservative *Atlanta Independent*.[73]

As this new leadership came to preeminence in the black community, it began to shift the parameters of racial uplift. John Wesley Dobbs and his cohort committed themselves to improving the lot of blacks in the city, state, and nation. But instead of emphasizing morality-based visions of respectability and race progress promoted by the educational elite, these leaders introduced overtly political language and goals. Even the cooperative interracial work of Atlanta's black leaders with organizations like the YWCA and the Commission on Interracial Cooperation shifted to political coalition-building. In promoting their own leadership roles, the new business and professional elite in the black community drew on a sense of duty, an understanding of class divisions, and the realization, in the words of Martin Luther King, Sr., that "action was the only course for those of us whose relative financial security permitted a view of the overall situation . . ."[74]

For the most part, the educational elite who had held sway during the years following the riot joined in these changes and successfully maintained their status as "race leaders."[75] Indeed, some in the educational and intellectual circles of Atlanta had predicted the leadership shifts that occurred in Atlanta in the late 1920s and early 1930s. As early as 1899, W. E. B. Du Bois and John Hope, both academics, publicly backed the idea of the accumulation of capital among blacks as a path for improved status of African Americans.[76] The consolidation of the city's six black colleges as Atlanta University Center in 1929 to 1930 ended some of the isolation the college community experienced in the past and helped the educational elite maintain its leadership status during the shift to political organizing.[77] In the years following the riot and the institution of segregation, however, the foundation of the community's elite circles became black-owned businesses catering to an all-black clientele.

Not surprisingly, both the political language of uplift and the lifestyles of the business and professional leaders shared some basic similarities with the ideologies and characteristics of leadership from earlier generations. Like its predecessors, this new elite used monetary wealth to improve its material surroundings. Members built fine homes both on the newly developed west side and near Auburn Avenue on Houston and Boulevard Streets. Members also attended the same elite churches as earlier generations. Businesswoman Ella Martin admitted that for all the good the First Congregational Church did for the black community through its outreach programs, "the poor didn't feel comfortable by attending this particular church."[78] In general, business, professional, and educational leaders continued to hold themselves up as symbols of what hardworking blacks could accomplish. From many of its ideologies emerged the familiar refrain that at least part of racism's evil stemmed from its denial of class status among African Americans. Benjamin Davis, who came to Atlanta to assume the presidency of Morehouse College, railed that under racism "status made no difference." Davis complained that "black doctors, professors, businessmen, ministers," despite their education and high position within the African American community, "all felt the scourge of discrimination and segregation in travel just as did the black butler, maid, cook and janitor."[79] Echoing this sentiment and explaining why classless racism often motivated activism among the elite, Martin Luther King, Sr., recalled, "Negroes who considered themselves well off in terms of social station or economic security had only to go into downtown Atlanta to discover again just how little those things meant in a racist environment."[80]

Despite the many ways in which the post-1930 leadership demonstrated its class affiliation with the new elite, it often publicly denied that it differed in any substantial way from Atlanta's working-class blacks. Before the turn of the century, W. E. B. Du Bois, for example, eloquently argued in *The Philadelphia Negro* that a class hierarchy did exist in the black community. But later, in the 1920s, Du Bois published editorials in *The Crisis* that argued just the opposite—that "well-to-do men . . . have never been physically or mentally separated from the toilers."[81] John Wesley Dobbs reportedly turned down membership in the class-exclusive social clubs of the old elite, arguing they "would make him feel estranged from the masses."[82] Dobbs, according to one of his daughters, felt "a special affinity for underprivileged people because we're from a poor race."[83] At the same time, members of this class remained residentially removed from the rest of the black community, more financially secure, generally lighter in complexion, and better educated.[84] Even Dobbs flaunted his ownership of two automobiles and used his wealth to ensure that his daughters would never work for whites or endure Jim Crow segregation on public transportation.

While Dobbs's ability to shield his daughters from at least some of Atlanta's racism reflected his class standing, it also points to the shifting gender ideologies of the city's newest black elites. New business and professional leaders believed "that black women historically had undergone enough in terms of being abused and battered and cuffed about" and sought to protect them from white men.[85] Dobbs was not alone in keeping his daughters out of domestic work. One of Atlanta's black teachers recalled that her parents "never wanted a girl of theirs to have to work in the home of a white person [because] the white man would take advantage [of them]."[86] Many working-class blacks also struggled to remove the women of their family from domestic work situations where they might be subjected to sexual abuse, but the relative wealth of African Americans like Dobbs made this strategy more feasible in elite circles. Developing in concert with elite desires to remove women from situations in which they might experience mistreatment at the hands of whites was a masculinized interpretation and perception of racism. This new language eclipsed the maternalist arguments of an earlier generation.

Women had held powerful positions in the years after the 1906 riot, helping to cultivate a theory of racial uplift that relied on morality and created organizations that depended heavily on the leadership of women as the traditional guardians of morality. As businessmen, professionals, and ministers came to the fore in the 1930s and 1940s, however, segregation was increasingly viewed by this overwhelmingly male leadership as "a denial of dignity and manhood."[87] Leadership during these later years was a particularly gendered process, where men served as titular heads of prominent organizations and were recognized by the press for their booster activities in formal politics. Many elite black women, however, "sought to represent concerns that centered most consistently, although not exclusively, on their families and communities."[88] As a result, some women's work went unrecognized in the community while others adapted their own views of racial uplift to mesh with these changes, carving out significant roles for themselves despite the heavily gendered ideology of the vocal and overwhelmingly male leadership. Surviving the gender implications of this new ideology, Lugenia Burns Hope distanced herself from the Neighborhood Union and its emphasis on child welfare and focused her efforts on starting NAACP citizenship schools in the city during the 1930s, while the daughter of George and Nellie Towns, Grace Towns Hamilton, took over the leadership reins of Atlanta's Urban League in 1943.[89]

## THE GREAT DEPRESSION AND WAR YEARS

The Great Depression and war years in Atlanta created numerous fissures in black elite leaders' attempts to promote community and political activism. Divisions along class lines appeared frequently when goals for racial advancement differed. During a struggle to equalize black teachers' pay scales with those of white teachers, for example, community opinion splintered, leaving "poor folks thinking the teachers were elite, middle class brats."[90] Relationships and coalitions among individuals of similar class standing also arose. C. A. Scott and John Wesley Dobbs faced off against A. T. Walden of the NAACP over a 1936 voter registration drive. Later, Dobbs broke with Scott when the former, disillusioned over the treatment of blacks under the New Deal, returned to the Republican Party. In order not to lose the faith of either Atlanta's white leaders or working-class African American constituents, black elites often desperately tried to create the image of a united leadership front. Consequently, these intraclass and leadership struggles were frequently hidden or downplayed in the city's newspapers.

Despite their contradictory notions on the issue of class, ideological differences, and masculinized interpretations of racism, the race leaders who emerged during the 1930s helped cement a feeling of community among blacks during the height of racial segregation and economic distress. The language and policies through which they accomplished this involved a renewed focus on formal politics. Elaborating on this point, Ben Mays concluded "if you don't have the ballot you aren't anybody. If you can't elect the officials who govern you, that's tantamount to being a slave. I think the ballot is the most precious thing in the hands of a man in democracy."[91] While social uplift programs still existed in some realms of the black community, and certain organizations, most notably the Urban League, focused on changing the economic condition of poor blacks, admission to formal politics increasingly became the flagship cause of Atlanta's African American leaders. "The ballot in Georgia," according to these leaders, would "mean better race relations" and more political power for the black elite.[92]

Political organizing among Atlanta blacks started in earnest during the 1930s. The state Democratic Party restricted voting in primaries to whites only but disenfranchisement laws left run-off, bond, and special elections open to black voters, and the rising black leadership intended to exploit the power these elections might carry.[93] John Wesley Dobbs created one of the first associations designed to promote the political ascendancy of blacks through voter registration. The Atlanta Civic and Political League, formed in 1936, set a goal of increasing the number of registered black voters in Atlanta from 600 to 10,000.[94] Other efforts included the NAACP citizenship schools, run by Atlanta University professor Clarence Bacote, which focused on the rudiments of voting, politics, and American government.[95] Pastors joined the campaign by promoting political participation from the pulpit. Recalling the role of the clergy, Wheat Street Baptist's Reverend William Borders emphasized that "the preachers would announce, the preachers would encourage . . . the preachers would tell the masses how much good it would do their children . . . the preachers would attend the voter education meetings. The preachers were physically and bodily evident where ever the problem was most acute."[96] The final power in the leaders' arsenal was the *Atlanta Daily World* and publisher C. A. Scott openly dedicated his paper to "educate and inspire people, to make better citizens out of them . . . to over[come] injustice and segregation."[97]

In advancing their claims to leadership, business and professional leaders reinforced their elite positions and marshaled support from the black working-classes by publicly chastising the old elite "whose myopic minds bulge[d] with thoughts of how superior they [were] to others." In emphasizing the new leadership of the city's rising entrepreneurs, *Daily World* editorials berated "the so-called upper-crust, the pseudo sophisticates" for lacking "the primary essential to successful leadership, intimate and equal contact with those to be led." Editor Franklin Marshall Davis argued further that if the upper class "fulfilled their obligations to Afro-American society they would so raise the level of Negro mass thought and action that the race as a whole would be a constant source of pride and joy and would commit little to provoke mockery."[98] Distancing themselves from older generations of the black elite, these new leaders hoped to prove their commitment to improving the community and thereby garner wide support for their political agendas.

The results of these efforts to raise working-class support for voter registration campaigns were ambivalent, at best. While the black working classes of Atlanta left few direct reflections on the political organizing campaigns of the 1930s, registration numbers rose only slowly during these years.[99] While working-class blacks continued to battle for control over their daily lives and their labor during these years, their experiences and definitions of politics, which grew from these experiences, apparently did not overlap with the formal politics trumpeted by elite leaders.[100] A researcher analyzing Atlanta for Gunnar Myrdal's *An American Dilemma* concluded that the "Negro intellingensia" failed "to provide the proper leadership for the masses in matters political."[101] Looking into specific programs designed to promote black participation in formal politics, this researcher also faulted Dobbs in particular for "lacking an understanding of the complex problems besetting the group" and "on no occasion, demonstrat[ing] any real appreciation of the socio-economic forces affecting the Negro."[102]

The second political project embraced by Atlanta's black elite, particularly the educational wing, involved slum clearance and public housing projects. White Atlantan Charles Palmer started this movement by securing federal funds to clear a dilapidated district between downtown and Georgia Tech. John Hope, representing the interests of the black community, soon joined the "slum fighter" in continuing these projects in African American neighborhoods.[103] The first Black area to be cleared was the notorious Beaver Slide district that the Neighborhood Union years earlier had attempted to clean up. University Homes, built on the site of the cleared neighborhood, opened in 1937. Other black neighborhood renewal efforts in black areas followed over the next decade and three more housing projects for African Americans were built in their place in the 1930s and 1940s.

This push by elites for housing reform embodied both the older ideal of moral respectability and the newer political ideal of racial uplift. Black members of the public housing project boards, such as John Hope and L. D. Milton, understood public housing as both a "powerful factor . . . in building up the loyalty of Negroes to the federal government" and a way to "advance steps that the federal government took on the whole problem of housing and education" for blacks.[104] Consequently, these leaders concentrated on gathering a class of moral African Americans to serve as the model for all that housing reform could accomplish. Even the *Atlanta Daily World* echoed these elite impulses, arguing "apartment life will bring in the open the great task before us. There is the opportunity for the social, political and religious worker to tackle in daylight the problems confronting the group."[105] In order to accomplish these goals, board members purposefully chose locations for housing projects that would "attract not poor Negroes, but Negroes with their minds uplifted and wanting to advance themselves and the race generally."[106]

Working-class blacks may have responded with apathy to early elite political organizing but many were openly hostile to housing reform efforts of the 1930s and 1940s. Managers and strict rules were put in place to ensure that public housing would be a suitable "laboratory" for sociological study and political organizing.[107] Many residents, however, successfully circumvented the rules and took in boarders, sold liquor, or found other ways to bend the rules and supplement their incomes.[108] While public housing residents generally spoke fondly of the amenities the apartments offered, it was widely known in the black community that applicants who made it through the rigorous screening process and received public housing were rarely drawn from the community's lowest rungs. According to one middle-class observer, residents of Beaver Slide, which was cleared for the site of University Homes, "just raised their voices and fought to get back in there. If they had the money they could move in. If they didn't have the money, they couldn't move in."[109] Despite the lofty ideals attached to the projects, slum clearance and early public housing only further contributed to the congestion and poor conditions in Atlanta's remaining poor neighborhoods, problems that intensified in the years after World War II.[110]

Despite the rifts and suspicion created by housing reform and the apathetic response to voter registration campaigns, a growth in community spirit occurred during the era of segregation and depression. A few Atlantans insisted that the economic impact of the Great Depression had little effect on blacks, who rarely kept money in banks and often encountered unemployment. For most blacks, however, the severe economic downturn and continuing racial segregation of the 1930s did bring widespread suffering, which in turn fostered a sense of "more togetherness" among African Americans of all classes.[111] It was during these years, after all, that the "greater integration" of the black community, the "organized provision for the service of this colored group" in the words of W. E. B. Du Bois, grew up in the face of the "greater differentiation" from whites caused by segregation.[112] Remembering these years, Julia Washington Bond recalled that while life in Atlanta was completely segregated, "it was a rich life in the black community."[113] The Great Depression reinforced the "strong points" of the community—"togetherness, working out their problems, [and helping] those that was most unfortunate."[114]

Facing unemployment, increasing racial tensions, homelessness, and hunger, Atlanta's blacks did attempt to work together during these years. Approximately half the city's work force suffered without employment between 1930 and 1933, and in this charged atmosphere, some white workers formalized their anger towards black workers and formed the Black Shirts, an organization that attempted to intimidate employers into replacing African American workers with whites.[115] In order to combat these conditions, some working-class blacks joined Atlanta's fledgling Communist Party, but the arrest and prosecution of black radical Angelo Herndon in 1932 deeply wounded organizational efforts.[116] Others turned to associations like the newly formed Atlanta Colored Committee on Unemployment, a federation of local committees. By and large, however, Atlanta's African Americans sought assistance in the face of economic crisis within established and familiar institutions. The Neighborhood Union, NAACP, and the Atlanta Urban League created programs to aid poor blacks in finding jobs, housing, and food. When New Deal programs brought work relief to Atlanta, these organizations, especially the Urban League, stepped in to guarantee that blacks received a share of federal dollars. As numerous national and regional studies have demonstrated, blacks rarely received equal treatment under New Deal programs.[117] The way in which Atlanta's community organizations fought for relief for blacks and provided assistance where they could, however, brought the black leadership into closer relations with many in the working class.

American entrance into World War II broke the economic crisis created by the Great Depression and profoundly affected the trajectory of Atlanta's black community. Production of war goods invigorated and expanded industrial production in Atlanta, creating new jobs for the city's laboring classes. Jobs in war production industries and military pay "helped the colored . . . people out of trouble . . . starting them on up the upward road to taking care of themselves."[118] The Urban League, continuing its crusades to improve conditions under which blacks labored, aided working-class blacks by establishing new training programs and working to ensure that the Bell Aircraft plant would hire African Americans as well as whites. The new jobs and money flowing into the community revived black businesses and assisted many working-class African Americans in moving out of furnished rooms and buying houses on the west side. Reflecting this increased migration to neighborhoods west of downtown, a new retail center for blacks sprang up along Hunter Street (now Martin Luther King, Jr., Boulevard) that rivaled Auburn Avenue.[119]

While bringing economic recovery to Atlanta's blacks, World War II and the postwar years also served to reinforce community ties formed during the Great Depression. Referring to the community, the pastor of Wheat Street Baptist recalled that by the end of the war "Negroes had a black culture of their own. They did their own singing, dancing, shouting, preaching, praying, their own business. They had something they could call their own . . . "[120] The political leaders of the black community, who largely remained associated with Auburn Avenue despite the growth of the west side, were able to harness these positive changes and finally build mass participation for formal political campaigns such as voter registration.[121] In the 1940s, certainly related to the growing economic prosperity brought by the war, the interests of the black working class seemed to overlap substantially with the goals of the business and professional elite. The first test of black political strength and the new registration campaign came in the spring of 1946, when African Americans quietly and successfully elected the only candidate in a special election who had actively campaigned for the African American vote, Helen Mankin.[122]

Mankin's victory, largely due to the black vote in one precinct, buoyed the community and increased support for political organizing. A new organization, the All-Citizens Registration Committee, was established with the goal of registering 25,000 blacks in the city. Relying on the infrastructure of the Atlanta Urban League, the committee canvassed black neighborhoods all over the city for potential voters. These groups' efforts were aided by the U.S. Supreme Court's decision to let stand a lower court ruling that outlawed Georgia's Democratic whites-only primary.[123] With well over 20,000 registered black voters in the city, African American leaders confronted Mayor William Hartsfield with an issue that had long been on the minds of the city's African Americans—black police. Through the fall of 1947 and the winter of 1948, black leaders met with city officials in order to hammer out an agreement under which the city would hire black police to patrol African American neighborhoods.

In the end, city officials agreed to hire eight black officers. They were to receive the same training as the white officers but, in order to minimize racial hostility from the white police and white community, they would work out of the Butler Street YMCA and were forbidden to arrest whites or wear uniforms when not on duty. These restrictions angered some in the black community, leaving "some scars . . . in the aftermath, wounds that would never completely heal."[124] Reflecting the power of the moderate elite leadership, Benjamin Mays, president of Morehouse College and a vocal opponent of the restrictions, finally overcame his objections, and encouraged the selection of "eight exceptionally good men to begin this experiment . . . men who will perform so admirably that all Atlanta will be proud of the adventure and in this way help to eliminate the prejudice that creates the restrictions."[125] The agreement with city and police officials, despite the divisions it had created, was eventually accepted as a general victory for blacks and in later years was remembered as one of the earliest signifiers of the strength blacks had and would achieve in politics.

## CONCLUSION

Atlanta's African American community experienced enormous changes during the first half of the 20th century. Not only did the black population of the city more than triple, but the economic structure of the community, residential patterns, and leadership coalitions also shifted during these fifty years. The brutal attacks on blacks during the 1906 riot sent a clear message to the city's African American population about its role in the industrial city and helped to firmly entrench segregation in public places. By 1950, however, Atlanta's moderate black leadership had emerged as a powerful force in the city, particularly in the political arena, and was in the process of dismantling many of the city's Jim Crow practices with the help of a relatively cohesive black community and sympathetic whites.

Critical to this transition was the creation of community unity out of a highly stratified population. Atlanta's black working class in the 1930s and 1940s realized the need for a strong group of leaders, in the words of Gunnar Myrdal, "to establish contact with the influential people in the white group."[126] While the poorer classes often had conflicts with the black middle class, most expressed great pride and faith in the leadership provided by the business, professional, and educational elite. While the overly moralizing campaigns for African American respectability in the earlier decades of the 20th century had alienated many working-class blacks whose notions of respectability often differed from those of the elite, the economic prosperity and political organizing of the 1940s proved appealing across class lines and provided the crucial foundation on which much of this community cohesiveness would be built. The leaders who emerged in the 1930s and 1940s were generally well-regarded by "the masses they served," particularly for making blacks "realize the power behind the vote."[127] Consequently, many of Atlanta's African Americans adopted the script of progress promoted by the black business elite. When interviewed by Auburn Avenue high school students in the 1970s, many reflected that they remained "glad to be a part of the growth."[128]

Throughout the first half of the 20th century, the strength of a racial community built under the pressures of segregation and racial hostilities did often come from successfully overriding the disagreements and divisions between classes. The elite African American leaders of this era relied on the black working class for both their livelihood and status, needing the strength of working-class numbers behind them in order to negotiate reforms with Atlanta's white power structure. Realizing this, John Wesley Dobbs argued that only "when 10,000 Negroes in Atlanta get registered, the Signal Light of Opportunity . . . [would] automatically turn from red to green" and blacks could finally command the attention of the mayor and City Council.[129] And the signal light for blacks in Atlanta did change in the 1940s. The successful election of Helen Mankin in early 1946 and the massive voter registration campaign later that same year launched blacks solidly into the political power structure of Atlanta. Voting power translated into changes in city politics, leading to the installation of the eight black policemen, the integration of fire-fighters in the 1950s, and, eventually, the election of the city's first black mayor, Maynard Jackson, the grandson of John Wesley Dobbs.

Beneath this tale of progress, however, were complex gender and class divisions with which Atlanta's black community had to struggle. These complexities of segregation-era Atlanta established both the power and many of the problems of urban development and race rela-tions in future years. That Atlanta's entrenched black leadership proved themselves consistently willing to sacrifice the interests of the working class, as was the case in the public housing projects of the 1930s and 1940s, explains the inability or unwillingness of the African American political administrations of the 1970s and 1980s to effectively battle inner city poverty and housing crises. For all of the political gains of the 1940s, little headway was made in the economic realm under this moder-ate black leadership, and this pattern continued into the second half of the 20th century. Ultimately, Atlanta's elite blacks won their successes in both the industrial and postindustrial eras by creating the illusion of a committed and singular community through a moderate, masculinized political language while denying the complex and often divergent inter-ests of Atlanta's African American population. Black success during these years, then, relied as much on overcoming the divisions between African Americans as it did on negotiating with the white power struc-ture. Apparently, the price to be paid for political advancement in the postindustrial city, if the first half of the 20th century holds any lessons, was the entrenchment of moderate, middle-class leaders and the muting of diverse community interests in the name of coalition-building.

## NOTES

1. Elizabeth Kytle, *Willie Mae* (Athens: University of Georgia Press, 1993), p. 217.

2. *Atlanta Journal*, April 4, 1948; *Atlanta Daily World*, April 4, 1948; and Herbert Jenkins, *Keeping the Peace: A Police Chief Looks at His Job* (New York: Harper and Row, 1970), p. 29.

3. Kytle, *Willie Mae*, p. 220.

4. In 1900, the 35,727 blacks in Atlanta represented nearly 40 percent of the total urban population. By 1950, African Americans had dropped to just under 37 percent of the total population, though their numbers had grown to over 120,000. Ronald Bayor, *Race and the Shaping of Twentieth-Century Atlanta* (Chapel Hill: University of North Carolina Press, 1996), p. 7.

5. Despite these tensions, Atlanta's African Americans did function as a community, especially during the height of segregation. As Elsa Barkely Brown has noted, participation is the key to community, not whether members agree or disagree on every issue. Brown, "Negotiating and Transforming the Public Sphere: African American Political Life in the Transition from Slavery to Freedom," *Public Culture* 7 (Fall 1994): 107–146.

6. For general descriptions and analyses of the riot, see David Godshalk, "In the Wake of the Riot: Atlanta's Struggle for Order, 1899–1919", Ph.D. dissertation, Department of History, Yale University, 1992; Gregory Lamont Mixon, "The Atlanta Riot of 1906," Ph.D. dissertation, Department of History, University of Cincinnati, 1989; Joel Williamson, *The Crucible of Race: Black–White Relations in the American South since Emancipation* (New York: Oxford University Press, 1984) 209–223; John Dittmer, *Black Georgia in the Progressive Era, 1900–1920* (Urbana: University of Illinois Press, 1977) 123–140; Charles Crowe, "Racial Massacre in Atlanta, September 22, 1906," *Journal of Negro History* 54 (April 1969): 150–173; and Charles Crowe, "Racial Violence and Social Reform: Origins of the Atlanta Riot of 1906," *Journal of Negro History* 53 (July 1968): 234–256.

7. Gretchen Maclachlan, " 'A Decent Place to Live': The Politics of Working Women's Housing in Atlanta," paper given at the Social Science History Association, Atlanta, Georgia, October, 16, 1994, and Clifford M. Kuhn, Harlon E. Joye, and E. Bernard West, *Living Atlanta: An Oral History of the City, 1914–1948* (Atlanta and Athens: Atlanta Historical Society and University of Georgia Press, 1990), pp. 33–35.

8. Partial transcript of interview with Kathleen Adams, Living Atlanta Collection, Atlanta History Center, Atlanta, Georgia, July 24, 1929.

9. African American class structure was fairly fluid throughout the early 20th century, making it more feasible, in the words of Gunnar Myrdal, "to describe two extremes—the lower and upper classes—and then handle the great amount of variation by describing a middle class between them." While Myrdal's description of the "lower class" gave in to popular stereotypes of an immoral class of people lacking "resourcefulness, self-reliance and sense of individual dignity," his delineation of class remains useful. As Myrdal notes, class in the black community during the early 20th century rarely paralleled the class structure of white America. Many blacks who had made their way into the elite class in black society, for example, would be considered middle class in white circles. Gunnar Myrdal, *An American Dilemma: The Negro Problem and Modern Democracy* (New York: Harper and Row, 1944, 1962), pp. 700–701.

10. Partial transcript of interview with Kathleen Adams, Living Atlanta Collection, Atlanta History Center, Atlanta, Georgia. July 24, 1979.

11. Partial transcript of interview with Horace Sinclair, Living Atlanta Collection, Atlanta History Center. July 18, 1979. Herndon was later able to turn his barbershop profits toward developing a life insurance company for blacks and a million-dollar fortune for himself. Alexa Benson Henderson, *Atlanta Life Insurance Company: Guardian of Black Economic Dignity* (Tuscaloosa: University of Alabama Press, 1990), Chapter 2.

12. August Meier and David Lewis, "History of the Negro Upper Class in Atlanta, Georgia, 1890–1958," *Journal of Negro Education* 28 (Spring 1959): 128–139.

13. Janette Thomas Greenwood, *Bittersweet Legacy: The Black and White "Better Classes" in Charlotte, 1850-1910* (Chapel Hill: University of North Carolina Press, 1994), pp. 85–86. On elite white constructions of the cult of domesticity, see Nancy A. Hewitt, "Beyond the Search for Sisterhood: American Women's History in the 1980s," reprinted in Ellen Carol Du Bois and Vicki L. Ruiz, eds. *Unequal Sisters: A Multicultural Reader in U.S. Women's History*, (New York: Routledge, 1990), pp. 1–14. June 26, 1978.

14. Transcript of interview with Dr. Homer Nash, Sweet Auburn Neighborhood Project: An Oral History, Auburn Avenue Research Library, Atlanta, Georgia. Like these ministers, elite blacks often used only the initials of their first and middle names so that whites would not be able to address them with familiarity. Kevin Gaines, *Uplifting the Race: Black Leadership, Politics, and Culture in the Twentieth Century* (Chapel Hill: University of North Carolina Press, 1996), p. 56.

15. August Meier and David Lewis, "Negro Upper Class," pp. 130–131.

16. Greenwood, IBettersweet Legacy, p. 77. For a discussion of these "civilizationist" trends on the national level see Gaines, *Uplifting the Race*, especially Chapter 1.

17. Partial transcript of anonymous interview, Living Atlanta Collection, Atlanta History Center, September 28, 1978

18. Partial transcript of anonymous interview, Living Atlanta Collection. Atlanta History Center, September 28, 1978.

19. Not surprisingly, municipal services in Atlanta were introduced first in the business district and wealthier neighborhoods, they then spread to the middle class and white working-class sections of the city but virtually none had reached the residential areas of poorer blacks. Black schools were chronically underfunded and overcrowded. Students were taught in double sessions and usually had to share books and even desks. No public secondary education existed for blacks until Booker T. Washington High School opened in 1924. See James Michael Russell, *Atlanta 1847–1890: City Building in the Old South and the New* (Baton Rouge: Louisiana State University Press, 1988), Chapter 7; Ronald

Bayor, *Race and the Shaping,* pp. 9–11; and Karen Ferguson, "The Politics of Inclusion: Black Activism in Atlanta during the Roosevelt Era, 1932–1946," Ph.D. History dissertation, Duke University, 1996, pp. 17–33.

20. Partial transcript of interview with Nellie Blackshear, Living Atlanta Collection, Atlanta History Center. August 2, 1979.

21. Partial transcript of interview with Mrs. L. D. Keith, Living Atlanta Collection, Atlanta History Center. October 11, 1978.

22. Partial transcript of anonymous interview, Living Atlanta Collection, Atlanta History Center. September 28, 1978.

23. John Hope, "The Meaning of Business," Fourth Conference for the Study of the Negro Problem, in W. E. Burghardt Du Bois, ed., *The Negro in Business* (Atlanta University, 1899), p. 56.

24. Joseph A. Pierce, *The Atlanta Negro: A Collection of Data on the Negro Population of Atlanta, Georgia* Washington, D.C. and Atlanta: (American Youth Commission of the American Council on Education and the National Youth Administration for Georgia, 1940), p. 65.

25. Some black women did make inroads to industry during the First World War, but only in a few instances were they able to retain these jobs after the war. See Gretchen Maclachlan, "Women's Work: Atlanta's Industrialization and Urbanization, 1879–1929," Ph.D. dissertation, Institute of Liberal Arts, Emory University, 1992, pp. 95–99.

26. "Occupational Statistics," *Atlanta Economic Review* 28 (Jan–Feb. 1978): 392–393.

27. The allure of Decatur Street did not completely escape the middle classes of either race, some of whom did take occasional trips into what seemed to most of them a rather exotic world. For a description of some of these adventures, see Howard Steve Goodson, " 'South of the North, North of the South': Public Entertainment in Atlanta, 1880–1930," Ph.D. dissertation, HIstory Department, Emory University, 1995.

28. Partial transcript of interview with Alice Adams, Living Atlanta Collection, Atlanta History Center. December 14, 1978.

29. Robin Kelley, *Race Rebels: Culture, Politics, and the Black Working Class* (New York: The Free Press, 1994), p. 44. On segregation versus congregation, see Earl Lewis, *In Their Own Interests: Race, Class and Power in Twentieth Century Norfolk, Virginia* (Berkeley: University of California Press, 1991), pp. 91–92.

30. Cochran quoted in Clifford M. Kuhn, Harlon E. Joye, and E. Bernard West, *Living Atlanta: An Oral History of the City, 1914–1948* (Atlanta and Athens, Ga.: Atlanta Historical Society and University of Georgia Press, 1990), p. 260.

31. Partial transcript of interview with Willie Mae Jackson, Living Atlanta Collection, Atlanta History Center. December 14, 1978.

32. W. E. Burghardt Du Bois, ed., *The Negro Church* (Atlanta: Atlanta University Press, 1903), p. 72.

33. Partial transcript of interview with Alice Adams, Living Atlanta Collection, Atlanta History Center. December 14, 1978.

34. Kelley, *Race Rebels*, p. 36.

35. Robin Kelley, " 'We Are Not What We Seem': Rethinking Black Working-Class Opposition in the Jim Crow South," *Journal of American History* 80 (June 1993): 83.

36. Partial transcript of interview with Alice Adams, Living Atlanta Collection, Atlanta History Center. December 14, 1978.

37. Robin Kelley draws on James Scott's "infrapolitics" to discuss these kinds of "oppositional practices that constitute the foundational politics for all organized mass movements." Kelley, "The Black Poor and the Politics of Opposition in a New South City, 1929–1970," in Michael Katz, ed., *The "Underclass" Debate: Views from History*, (Princeton: Princeton University Press, 1993), p. 295. James C. Scott, *Domination and the Arts of Resistance: Hidden Transcripts* (New Haven: Yale University Press, 1990) pp. 183–4. See also Jacqueline Jones, "Political Implications of Blacks and White Women's Work in the South, 1890–1965," in Patricia Gurin and Louise A. Tilly, eds. *Women, Politics, and Change*. (New York: Russell Sage Foundation, 1990), pp. 111–112; and Georgina Hickey, "Visibility, Politics, and Working-Class Women in Early Twentieth Century Atlanta," Ph.D. History dissertation, University of Michigan, 1995.

38. Tera Hunter, *To Joy My Freedom: Southern Black Women's Lives and Labors after the Civil War* (Cambridge: Harvard University Press, 1997), pp. 60–61, 132–134. Bonnie Thorton Dill has also written about the "worker's determination to make her occupational role personally meaningful and socially acceptable." Dill, " 'Making the Job Good Yourself': Domestic Service and the Construction of Personal Dignity," in Ann Bookman and Sandra Morgen, eds., *Women and the Politics of Empowerment*, (Philadelphia: Temple University Press, 1988), pp. 35–36.

39. Kytle, *Willie Mae*, pp. 118–120.

40. Partial transcript of interview with Mary Morton, Living Atlanta Collection, Atlanta History Center. December 13, 1979.

41. "A Colored Man's Plea," October 4, 1906, Minutes of the Chamber of Commerce, Atlanta, Georgia.

42. In Chapter 7 of *Righteous Discontent: The Women's Movement in the Black Baptist Church, 1880–1920* (Cambridge: Harvard University Press, 1993), Evelyn Brook Higginbotham has extensively and persuasively articulated this

concept of "respectability" and its relationship to racial uplift in her study of black Baptists.

43. W. E. B. Du Bois had arrived as a young faculty member at Atlanta University in 1897. Du Bois, *The Philadelphia Negro: A Social Study* (New York: Benjamin Bloom, reprint 1967; first edition, 1899), p. 393.

44. Du Bois, *The Philadelphia Negro*, p. 392.

45. Sharon Mullins, "The Public Career of Grace Towns Hamilton: A Citizen Too Busy to Hate," Ph.D. English diss., Emory University, 1976, p. 20. On Du Bois's years in Atlanta, see David Levering Lewis, *W. E. B. Du Bois: Biography of a Race, 1868–1919* (New York: Henry Holt and Company, 1993), pp. 211–407.

46. Background on these educators and activists can be found in Ridgely Torrence, *The Story of John Hope* (New York: MacMillan Company, 1948), and Jacqueline Anne Rouse, *Lugenia Burns Hope: Black Southern Reformer* (Athens: University of Georgia Press, 1989).

47. Partial transcript of anonymous interview, Living Atlanta Collection, Atlanta History Center. September 28, 1978.

48. Partial transcript of interview with Hallie Brooks, Living Atlanta Collection, Atlanta History Center. February 27, 1979.

49. "The Neighborhood Union: An Experiment in Community Cooperation," Neighborhood Union, Special Collection, Woodruff Library, Atlanta University Center. On the founding of the Union, see Rouse, *Lugenia Burns Hope*, p. 65; Cynthia Neverdon-Morton, *Afro-American Women of the South and the Advancement of the Race, 1895–1925* (Knoxville: University of Tennessee Press, 1989), p. 145.

50. Louie D. Shivery, "The History of Organized Social Work Among Atlanta Negroes," M.A. thesis, School of Social Work, Atlanta University, 1936.

51. Undated newspaper clipping, *Atlanta Journal*, Neighborhood Union, Special Collections, Woodruff Library, Atlanta University Center.

52. Shivery, "The History of Organized Social Work," p. 23.

53. On the complex class relations in black women's club work see Hickey, "Visibility," Chapter 2, and Victoria Wolcott, "Remaking Respectability: African-American Women and the Politics of Identity in Inter-War Detroit," (Ph.D. History dissertation, 1995, Chapter 2.

54. *The Atlanta Independent*, March 19, 1910.

55. Lewis, *W. E. B. Du Bois*, p. 231.

56. "Work of the Neighborhood Union," *Spelman Messenger*, November 1916.

57. See, for example, "The South Is Our Home," March 19, 1910, and "Editorial," April 2, 1910, *The Atlanta Independent*.

58. Mullins, "Public Career," p. 53. Reaching a similar conclusion, Deborah Gray White argues that black club women established their claim to race leadership vis-à-vis African-American men through the promotion of social and moral order in the black community. White, "The Cost of Club Work, the Price of Black Feminism," in Nancy Hewitt and Suzanne Lebsock, eds., *Visible Women: New Essay on American Activism* (Urbana: University of Illinois Press, 1993), p. 257.

59. Rouse, *Lugenia Burns Hope*, p. 7. Images that black women defended themselves against ranged from the oversexed jezebel to the subservient mammy. Patricia Morton, *Disfigured Images: The Historical Assault on Afro-American Women* (New York: Praeger, 1991), Chapter 3.

60. Fannie Barrier Williams, "The Club Movement Among the Colored Women," *The Voice of the Negro*, (March 1904).

61. Fannie Barrier Williams, "The Club Movement Among the Colored Women," *The Voice of the Negro*, (March 1904). In looking at Richmond, Elsa Barkley Brown argues that similar organizations founded by black women did not represent new authority but rather women's attempt to maintain authority they had in the black community before black men were disenfranchised. Brown, p. 108.

62. Addie Hunton, "Negro Womanhood Defended," *The Voice of the Negro* (July 1904).

63. Dwight Fennel, "A Demographic Study of Black Businesses, 1905–1908, with Respect to the Race Riot of 1906," M.A. thesis, Atlanta University, 1977.

64. A few of the older elite who had lived on or near the residential Auburn Avenue mourned its passing. One resident commented years later, "no longer did Auburn Avenue have the charm that it once had." Describing Auburn before its commercial life, another resident reflected, "everything in that period seemed to have been—the best that I can do, the best that I can give to my race was the ideal. But after the fire we had other people coming in who had not caught the torch . . . they were a little bit lax in their way of doing." Interview with Dr. Flanagan, Sweet Auburn Neighborhood Project. Atlanta, Georgia, Partial transcript of interview with Kathleen Adams, Living Atlanta Collection, Atlanta History Center. On changes in the racial composition on the west side, see Howard L. Preston, *Automobile Age Atlanta: The Making of a Southern Metropolis, 1900–1935* (Athens: University of Georgia Press, 1979), pp. 98–110.

65. Martin Luther King, Sr., with Clayton Riley, *Daddy King: An Autobiography* (New York: William Morrow and Co., 1980), p. 71. The origin of the name "Sweet Auburn" is commonly attributed to John Wesley Dobbs's reference to a poem by Oliver Goldsmith. See Gary Pomerantz, *Where Peachtree Street Meets Sweet Auburn: The Saga of Two Families and the Making of Atlanta* (New York: Scribner, 1996), p. 124.

66. Partial transcript of interview with C. C. and Phoebe Hart, Living Atlanta Collection, Atlanta History Center. July 18, 1979.

67. Partial transcript of interview with Ella Martin, Living Atlanta Collection, Atlanta History Center. July 9, 1979.

68. Partial transcript of interview with Dan Stephens, Living Atlanta Collectio, Atlanta History Center. July 11, 1979.

69. Interview with Roger McKearny, Sweet Auburn Nieghborhood Project. April 24, 1978.

70. Partial transcript of interview with Alice Adams, Living Atlanta Collection, Atlanta History Center. December 14, 1978.

71. Interview with Horace Sinclair, Living Atlanta Collection, Atlanta History Center. July 18, 1979.

72. Interview with Lorimer Douglas Milton, Atlanta Oral History Project of the Atlanta Public Library, Atlanta, Georgia. March 25, 1975.

73. The *Independent* ran as a weekly paper starting in 1903. Its editor, Ben Davis, lived in a fine home in the Summerhill district and was certainly counted among Atlanta's old elite. His paper followed society, club, and church activities; it contained short editorials and advertisements. The *Daily World* started as a weekly in 1928 and became a daily in 1931. The Scott family, which edited this paper, aligned themselves with the new professional and business elite emerging during these years and used the paper to promote political uplift among blacks. Alton Hornsby, Jr., "Georgia," in Henry Lewis Suggs, ed., *The Black Press in the South*, (Westport, Conn: Greenwood Press, 1983), pp. 119–149.

74. King, *Daddy King,* p. 98.

75. On John Hope's transition, see Leroy Davis, "An African American Dilemma: John Hope and Black Leadership in the Early Twentieth Century," *Atlanta History: A Journal of Georgia and the South* 41, no. 1 (Spring 1997): 27–47.

76. The findings of this conference were later published as *The Negro in Business*, W. E. Burghardt Du Bois, ed. (Atlanta: Atlanta University, 1899).

77. Clarence Bacote, *The Story of Atlanta University: A Century of Service, 1865–1965* (Atlanta: Atlanta University, 1969), pp. 257–272.

78. Interview with Ella Martin, Sweet Auburn Neighborhood Project. August 11, 1978.

79. Benjamin Mays, *Born to Rebel: An Autobiography* (Athens: Brown Thrasher Books, The University of Georgia Press, 1971), p. 80.

80. King, *Daddy King*, p. 107.

81. Du Bois, "The Class Struggle," from *The Crisis*, June 1921, and reprinted in David Levering Lewis, ed., *W. E. B. Du Bois: A Reader* (New York: Henry Holt and Co., 1995), pp. 555–556. An intriguing article by Dominic J.

Capeci, Jr., and Jack C. Knight argues that the 1906 riot profoundly reshaped Du Bois's views. The authors contend that the racist violence caused Du Bois to doubt his leadership abilities and the class assumptions he had brought with him to the South and pushed him to finally come to terms with his own blackness. Capeci and Knight, "Reckoning with Violence: W. E. B. Du Bois and the 1906 Atlanta Race Riot," *The Journal of Southern History* 62 (November 1996): 727–766.

82. Interview with Millicent Dobbs Jordan, Sweet Auburn Neighborhood Project, Atlanta, Georgia. August 22, 1978.

83. Interview with Millicent Dobbs Jordan, Sweet Auburn Neighborhood Project, Atlanta, Georgia. August 22, 1978.

84. Meier and Lewis noted that the few darker-skinned male leaders tended to marry women of fairer complexions. This marriage pattern was also one way that the older generation of elites became a part of the newer elite. Up-and-coming men could improve their status in Atlanta's black community by marrying the daughters of the old "mulatto aristocracy." Meier and Lewis, "Negro Upper Class," pp. 134–135.

85. Interview with Millicent Dobbs Jordan, Sweet Auburn Neighborhood Project, Atlanta, Georgia. August 22, 1978.

86. Interview with Ardie Clark Halyard, Black Women Oral History Project, Schlesinger Library, Radcliffe College, Cambridge, Massachusetts. August 24 and 25, 1978..

87. Mays, *Born to Rebel*, p. 98.

88. These women tended to be marginalized by the moderate black leadership of the 1940s because of the challenges their activism raised to that leadership. Kathy L. Nasstrom, "Women, the Civil Rights Movement, and the Politics of Historical Memory in Atlanta, 1946–1973," Ph.D. History dissertation, University of North Carolina, 1993, pp. 2, 33.

89. Elizabeth Lasch Quinn argues that black settlement house workers, such as Hope, were trying to distance themselves from their positions as wives and mothers and instead focus on citizenship rights. A closer look at the evolution of Hope and the Neighborhood Union reveals that it is only in the 1930s that Hope shifts her focus away from maternalist arguments. Elizabeth Lasch Quinn, *Black Neighbors: Race and the Limits of Reform in the American Settlement House Movement, 1880–1945* (Chapel Hill: University of North Carolina Press, 1993), pp. 112–113, 120. On Hamilton, see Lorraine Nelson Spritzer and Jean B. Bergmark, *Grace Towns Hamilton and the Politics of Southern Change* (Athens: University of Georgia, 1997). Chapters 6–7.

90. King, *Daddy King*, p. 106.

91. Partial transcript of interview with Benjamin Mays, Living Atlanta Collection, Atlanta History Center. January 1, 1979.

92. Benjamin Mays, "Is the South Better?" *Pittsburgh Courier*, June 15, 1946.

93. Led by the educational elite, blacks in Atlanta were able to use bond elections to their advantage in gaining desperately needed school improvements in the late 1910s and 1920s. See Kuhn, *Living Atlanta*, p. 138, and John Dittmer, *Black Georgia*, pp. 147–148.

94. Pomerantz, *Peachtree Street*, pp. This formation of this organization created a rift between Dobbs and A. T. Walden. The fallout from this conflict contributed to Walden's removal from the leadership of the local NAACP branch.

95. These citizenship programs drew high praise from the national NAACP. "May–Nov. 1932" folder, Branch Files, Series I, The Records of the National Association for the Advancement of Colored People, Library of Congress.

96. Partial transcript of interview with William Holmes Border, Living Atlanta Collection, Atlanta History Center. January 29, 1978.

97. Partial transcript of interview with C. A. Scott, Living Atlanta Collection, Atlanta History Center. April 16, 1979.

98. Franklin Marshall Davis, "Editorial," *Atlanta Daily World,* December 2, 1931.

99. "Negroes in the City," p. 15, Ralph J. Bunche Papers, Schomburg Center for Research in Black Culture, New York Public Library, New York, New York.

100. On this point Robin Kelley argues, working class "participation in 'mainstream' politics . . . grew out of the very circumstances, experiences, and memories that impelled many to steal from their employer, join a mutual benefit association, or spit in a bus driver's face." Kelley, *Race Rebels*, p. 9.

101. "Negroes in the City," p. 15, Ralph J. Bunche Papers.

102. "Negroes in the City," pp. 20–21, Ralph J. Bunche Papers. In particular, this researcher argued that Dobbs overlooked the economic hardship the poll tax represented for most blacks.

103. Charles F. Palmer, *Diary of a Slum Fighter* (Atlanta: Tupper and Love, 1955), pp. 16–17.

104. Partial transcript of interview with L. D. Milton, Living Atlanta Collection, Atlanta History Center. November 27, 1978.

105. "Apartment Life Comes South," *Atlanta Daily World*, March 3, 1940.

106. Partial transcript of interview with L. D. Milton, Living Atlanta Collection, Atlanta History Center. November 27, 1978. Karen Ferguson argues at length that the needs of the black working class were sacrificed for federal housing reform. She also concludes that the residents of John Hope Homes and

University Homes fulfilled the political aspirations had for them by providing crucial votes in a 1946 election. Ferguson, Chapter 8. "Politics of Inclusion."

107. Partial transcript of interview with Clarence Bacote, Living Atlanta Collection, Atlanta History Center. February 2, 1978.

108. Elizabeth Kytle, *Willie Mae*, p. 192.

109. Partial transcript of interview with L. D. Milton, Living Atlanta Collection, Atlanta History Center. November 27, 1979.

110. Karen Ferguson argues that the housing projects and other New Deal programs in Atlanta allowed the black elite to finally attain the political inclusion they had sought for so long. This political inclusion, however, drew a clear dividing line in the community between "respectable" blacks and those who did not fit the "behavioral code" outlined by black leaders and reinforced with federal dollars. Ferguson, pp. 1–7. "Politics of Inclusion."

111. Interview with Fletcher Coombs, Sweet Auburn Neighborhood Project, Atlanta, Georgia. May 25, 1978.

112. W. E. B. Du Bois, "The Social Evolution of the Black South," reprinted in John H. Bracey, Jr., August Meier, and Elliot Rudwick, eds. *The Rise of the Getto* (Belmont, Calif.: Wadsworth Publishing Company, 1971), pp. 167–168.

113. Interview with Julia Washington Bond, Atlanta Oral History Project of the Atlanta Public Library. March 9, 1976.

114. Interview with Ella Martin, Sweet Auburn Neighborhood Project, Atlanta, Georgia.

115. Harry Hopkins, quoted in Franklin Garrett, *Atlanta and Its Environs: A Chronicle of Its People and Events, Volume II* (Athens: University of Georgia Press, 1954), pp. 916–918. On the Black Shirts, see Kuhn, *Living Atlanta*, pp. 202–205, and John Hammond Moore, "Communists and Fascists in a Southern City: Atlanta, 1930," *The South Atlantic Quarterly* 67 (Summer 1968): 437–454.

116. Angelo Herndon, *Let Me Live* (New York: Random House, 1937), 186–301, and Charles H. Martin, *The Angelo Herndon Case and Southern Justice* (Baton Rouge: Louisiana State University Press, 1976).

117. Patricia Sullivan, *Days of Hope: Race and Democracy in the New Deal Era* (Chapel Hill: University of North Carolina Press, 1996), pp. 43–45; Harvard Sitkoff, "The New Deal and Race Relations," in *Fifty Years Later: The New Deal Evaluated* (New York: McGraw-Hill, 1985), pp. 93–112; Douglas L. Smith, *The New Deal in the Urban South* (Baton Rouge: Louisiana State University Press, 1988), pp. 56–58, 232–235; John Kirby, *Black Americans in the Roosevelt Era: Liberalism and Race* (Knoxville: University of Tennessee Press, 1980), pp. 141–143; and Michael S. Holmes, *The New Deal in Georgia* (Westport, CT: Greenwood Press, 1975), pp. 12–13, 317–320.

118. Interview with Mr. Hollingsworth, Sweet Auburn Neighborhood Project, Atlanta, Georgia. June 6, 1978.

119. While the black development of the west side started after the 1917 fire, the heyday of this area did not come until World War II. See Kuhn, *Living Atlanta*, pp. 40–45.

120. Interview with William Borders, Sweet Auburn Neighborhood Project, Atlanta, Georgia. April 26, 1978.

121. Leaders were aided in this effort by the Supreme Court, which ruled the Democratic white primary unconstitutional, and Ellis Arnall, the new reform-minded governor who lowered the state voting age to eighteen and removed the prohibitive poll tax. Frederick Allen, *Atlanta Rising: The Invention of an International City, 1946–1996* (Atlanta: Longstreet Press, 1996), p. 4.

122. This was the election of Helen Mankin, a white woman who campaigned in a special election to fill the seat left vacant by her husband's death. C. A. Bacote, "The Negro in Atlanta Politics," *Phylon: The Atlanta University Review* 16 (Fourth quarter, 1955): 344–345. Numan Bartley argues that blacks registering and voting was one indicator of the emergence of a "black establishment" in Atlanta. Bartley, *The New South, 1945–1980* (Baton Rouge: Louisiana State University Press, 1995), p. 139.

123. This court case was *Chapman v. King*, 1946.

124. King, *Daddy King*, p. 124.

125. Benjamin Mays, "It Did Happen," *Pittsburgh Courier,* January 10, 1948.

126. Myrdal, *American Dilemma*, p. 721.

127. Interview with William Borders and interview with Mrs. Jefferson, Sweet Auburn Neighborhood Project, Atlanta, Georgia. April 26, 1978 and March 15, 1978, respectively.

128. Interview with Iona McMeen, Sweet Auburn Neighborhood Project, Atlanta, Georgia. June 6, 1978.

129. Dobbs, quoted in Pomerantz, *Peachtree Street*, p. 148.

# CHAPTER 5

# Blacks in the Suburban and Rural Fringe

ANDREW WIESE

Throughout most of the 20th century, the term *suburban* has evoked images of a low-density residential landscape, single family homes, nuclear families, and high rates of home ownership. For many Americans, suburban images such as these remain enduring symbols of the American dream. Yet for most, these images are inseparable from assumptions about race and class. In common parlance, media communication, and academic literature alike, Americans routinely associate suburbs with the white middle class. Even where black families lived in single family houses in a semirural environment and commuted to downtown jobs from the outskirts of town, observers have often found it difficult to conceive of these places as suburbs.[1] Thus it often comes as a surprise to learn that African American suburbanization is a phenomenon with a long history.

In actuality, African Americans have lived in the suburbs for as long as white Americans. As early as the turn of the century, African Americans had established communities in the suburban and rural fringes of American cities, especially in the southern and border states. However, it was the Great Migration of the 1910s and 1920s, during which more than a million African Americans migrated to urban areas, that sparked the first large wave of black suburbanization. Between 1910 and 1940, the black number of suburbanites grew by about 365,000, and by 1940, as many as 1.5 million African Americans lived in census-defined suburban areas. Although these figures paled in comparison with white suburbanization, the suburbs were home to a substantial proportion of African Americans who lived in urbanized areas. Outside the South, suburbs comprised almost one-fifth (19 percent) of the metropolitan area African American population, and suburbanites accounted for approximately 15 percent of metropolitan black population growth between 1910 and 1940. In the South, almost a million African Americans lived in census-defined suburban areas. Many in this number were actually farmers who lived on the outskirts of urban areas, and their number was declining in the face of pressures for displacement as well as urban migration. At the same time, other families were moving to suburbs and keeping urban jobs, but net suburban increases in the South were relatively small. Even so, by 1940 as many as one in five African Americans in metropolitan areas lived in the suburbs.[2]

The numbers alone suggest that early black suburbanization is an important chapter in 20th-century African American history. However the phenomenon is also significant because it sheds light on the larger processes of African American migration and community formation as well as suburbanization itself. The variety of early black suburbs illustrates that black migrants may have exercised a wider range of residential options and preferences than historians of central cities have appreciated. At the same time, similarities among black suburbanites suggest that they—and perhaps southern migrants in general—may have shared values regarding housing, home ownership, and landscape that have been largely ignored by historians. Early black suburbanization is also significant because it had a lasting impact on the racial geography of American cities. Early suburbs formed nuclei for future community growth, especially as African American suburbanization accelerated after 1960. Hence, racial beachheads established before World War II continued to influence patterns of black (and white) settlement through the end of the century. Finally, the diversity of early black suburbs also suggests that African American suburbanites may have followed distinct paths as deindustrialization swept the economy after mid-century. To some extent, this was the case, although economic currents that affected blue-collar families nationwide proved more important than geographical distribution.

## WORKING-CLASS SUBURBS

In contrast to the stereotype of suburbs as residential enclaves of the white middle class, African American suburbs before 1940 were mostly blue-collar communities in which a large number of residents worked as well as lived—especially where suburban industries or domestic service jobs were abundant. On average, early black suburbanites had less education, lower incomes, and fewer skills than African Americans in central cities, and most early black suburbs were visually unlike middle-class white suburbs of the same era.[3] Many early black suburbanites lived in substandard housing: some of it secondhand, and some of it built at low cost by the owners themselves. They often raised vegetable gardens and raised small livestock in the backyard to supplement their incomes. Many black suburbs also lacked basic infrastructure such as paved streets, gas, electricity, sewers, or city water—especially in the South. Surveying a class of southern suburbs in 1930, for instance, historian Carter Woodson noted that "in most of them there are only a few comfortable homes, a small number of stores, a church or two, a school, and a post office. The population is not rich enough to afford taxes to lay out the place properly, pave the streets, and provide proper drainage and sanitation."[4] In contrast to the well-manicured suburbs of the white middle class, most early black suburbs were unplanned, unregulated, and unpretentious working-class communities.

In spite of apparent contrasts with middle-class suburbs, early black suburbanites represented just one piece of a much larger blue-collar suburban world—one in which suburban workers and their families did their best to accommodate low incomes and restricted job opportunities with aspirations for better places to live. In the decades before 1940, geographer Richard Harris has shown, suburbanization by blue-collar workers was widespread in the United States and Canada, and African Americans were no exception to this rule.[5] Moreover, early black suburbanization reflected many of the same influences that underlay the growth of middle-class suburbs. Cheap land, inexpensive transportation (especially widespread automobile ownership), low-cost fuel, and a relative lack of building restrictions attracted workers as well as middle-class commuters to the suburbs before 1940. Although they were much maligned at the time as shacktowns or suburban slums, working-class black suburbs were fully part of the process of American suburban decentralization.

Although employment was one reason that black families moved to suburbs, early black suburbanization also reflected suburbanites' values regarding housing, family, and community life. Some early suburbanites followed family ties to the suburbs. Some moved to suburbs to escape conditions in the central city, and others moved for the opportunity to buy a house and property. For most, suburbanization reflected a combination of motives. For instance, a woman who grew up in Englewood, New Jersey, in the 1930s explained, "my family came here from the South because this area was one of the best for making a living, yet it had a resemblance to country life."[6] In other suburbs, too, African Americans combined desires for open space, gardens, property ownership, and family based communities with the opportunity to earn an urban wage. The suburban landscape they created, therefore, reflected a conjunction of forces: including the geography of black employment and African Americans' efforts to shape their own lives on the margins of the city.

## BLACK SUBURBANIZATION IN THE SOUTH

For almost a century after the Civil War, the vast majority of African Americans lived in the South. Most were farmers, but by the late 19th century, a growing number began moving to the towns and cities of the region. By 1920, 25 percent of southern African Americans lived in urban places, and in the South's largest cities, African Americans were often a third of the population or more.[7] African Americans labored on the docks and in the rail yards and small factories that brought trade to the region. They worked on the street crews and construction teams that built its infrastructure, they provided services to businesses and private citizens, and they lived in every section of southern cities.

Black residential dispersal was especially pronounced on the outskirts of town. Even before the end of slavery, and long before the extension of urban services or public transit to the urban fringe, free black families and urban slaves had inhabited the periphery of southern cities. Removed from daily control by whites, but close enough to the city to hold urban jobs, many African Americans settled in "urban clusters" at the city's suburban frontier. These settlements had limited infrastructure, and they often occupied marginal land—ravines, rail corridors, or flood plains—but they also offered opportunities for families to purchase a plot of land, to create local institutions, and to supplement meager incomes with domestic produce.[8]

After emancipation, the number and variety of these settlements multiplied. As urban migration fed growing black communities, developers opened new subdivisions for African Americans in the suburban fringe, usually where blacks had established a residential foothold of some kind. In Charlotte, North Carolina, for example, a settlement known as Biddleville developed near a freedmen's school after the Civil War. In 1871, the first president of the Biddle School, a Presbyterian minister from New York, bought fifty-five acres of land adjacent to the school, and sold building lots to African Americans. Displaced plantation laborers, as well as prewar residents of Charlotte, bought lots and built houses in the subdivision, and by 1890 Biddleville was home to about 200 black adults, several churches, a black-owned grocery store, and a small cemetery.[9] Although a few residents worked on nearby farms, most walked the two miles to Charlotte for work each day. In other cities, the pattern was similar. Land owners opened building allotments adjacent to a nucleus of black settlement: a school, a workplace, such as a rail yard or factory, or a cluster of old plantation housing. By the turn of the century, most southern cities had a variety of black "urban clusters" scattered among white neighborhoods on the edge of town.[10]

As southern cities grew, some of these black enclaves were absorbed into the central city. Others, Carter Woodson reported, remained "natural suburbs settled by Negroes who transact practically all of their business in the cities."[11] Families who inhabited these communities often worked in the homes of neighboring whites or in suburban industries. Others walked to town for employment and marketing, while a few worked as farm laborers in the neighboring countryside.[12] Although these were not agricultural settlements, they retained a flavor that Woodson described as "decidedly rural." Families supplemented incomes with garden produce and small livestock. City officials rarely extended utilities. Trees and underbrush grew between houses, and streets were uniformly unpaved. As in the modern day Third World, the urban poor in the late-19th and early-20th-century South were as likely to live on the outskirts of town as in the center city.[13]

## DISPLACEMENT AND GROWTH

Within this context of scattered metropolitan residence, two broad processes shaped African American suburbanization in the South after the turn of the century. First, industrial decentralization and white residential suburbanization displaced thousands of African Americans from the suburban fringe. At the same time, black migration and the expansion of employment opportunities for African Americans in the suburbs led to growth in a smaller number of peripheral communities. Over time, the number of black communities in the suburbs declined, but many of those remaining grew in size and population. As a result, the "checkerboard" pattern of African American and white neighborhoods that had characterized southern urban geography at the turn of the century began to give way to racial concentration in increasingly segregated sectors of the metropolis.[14]

Several forces worked to displace African Americans from the periphery of southern cities. First, improved transportation facilitated movement between the suburbs and the central city and pushed up the value of peripheral land. Second, the growing attraction of suburban living to middle- and upper-class whites intensified pressures to develop marginal land for middle-class housing. Meanwhile, the decentralization of southern industries led to pressures for commercial development. As white suburbanites and industrial developers competed for suburban property, they drove prices upward and triggered shifts in land use. Planters and suburban landlords sold property to white developers who evicted black tenants—farmers and urban workers alike. As geographer Rudolf Heberle noted in 1947, "It happens quite frequently that white people infiltrate into suburban areas occupied by Negroes, buying their property or canceling their leases." As a result, Heberle concluded: "the close ecological symbiosis of whites and Negroes . . . gives way to spatial segregation."[15] Even black land owners often lost in the transition. In theory, property owners stood to profit from rising demand regardless of race, but the racial customs of the South stacked the cards against African Americans. According to Carter Woodson, who witnessed the process in the 1920s, "Negroes are generally offered what they originally paid for the site and urged to sell . . . If they refuse, the blackhand society usually sends a Ku Klux notice that they must sell out and move."[16] Displacement was rarely total, but over time, white suburbanites and suburban industries replaced black sharecroppers as well as black communities at the outskirts of town.

In addition to market-based redevelopment in the suburbs, southern whites harnessed the power of government to facilitate black displacement. Through annexation of suburban land, for example, municipal governments extended land-use controls to formerly unregulated areas.[17] New building codes curtailed informal home building, raising the price of a suburban home for working-class and poor families, and sanitary codes often led to the demolition of existing black housing. Meanwhile, zoning accelerated the process of black displacement. Although racial zoning became unconstitutional after 1917, ordinary land-use zoning was effective in reshaping residential patterns.[18] According to city planner Yale Rabin, early zoning ordinances in cities like Charlotte, Charlottesville, Norfolk, Selma, and even smaller cities like Jackson, Tennessee, "zoned only the major black areas for residential use. Separate enclaves . . . were zoned for industrial or commercial uses."[19] As commercial and industrial enterprises expanded or relocated to the outskirts of town, they built in these zones—in or on top of existing black communities. Guided by the hand of municipal government, private redevelopment displaced black suburbanites as well as sharecroppers from the suburban and rural fringe.

Finally, the expansion of the federal government in the 1930s and 1940s gave local officials even more powerful tools to redraw the color line. Slum clearance and urban renewal legislation, for instance, offered white officials the means to eliminate or isolate African American neighborhoods in suburbs as well as central cities. During the 1930s, many southern cities used slum clearance to reshape the racial landscape of the central city. Cities tore down older black neighborhoods and replaced them with public housing, often moving and isolating black residents in the process.[20]

After World War II, rapid white suburbanization and new legislation brought this process to the suburban fringe. Although early slum clearance legislation had required one-for-one replacement of slum housing with public housing, the National Housing Act of 1949 allowed local governments to replace slums with public uses ranging from parks and public buildings to parking lots and even luxury housing. Urban highway building, too, offered city officials a way to eliminate inconvenient black communities. Across the South, cities demolished black neighborhoods both downtown and on the suburban fringe. Highway interchanges, parks, stadiums, and airports rose in their place, and new freeways carved unmistakable racial barriers into the metropolitan landscape.[21]

Events in Atlanta illustrate the process. As late as 1950, remnants of the old checkerboard pattern of peripheral residence persisted, although pressures toward metropolitan segregation were mounting. The *Atlanta Daily World*, the city's black newspaper, wrote in 1951, "there are small Negro settlements on Old Bolton Road, Moore's Mill Road, Northside Drive, Lenox Road and in several other scattered locations," most of them "antedating the growth of adjacent white suburbs." Ominously, they reported that "each of these settlements is surrounded by high value white property . . . [and] some are in the path of obvious white expansion."[22] The editors had good reason to worry. In 1947, the Fulton County Commission had flattened a community of one hundred black families in the fashionable Buckhead section to make room for a city park restricted to whites, and in 1951 alone, whites proposed the demolition of three additional outlying communities. Moreover, planning documents are filled with references to racial barriers, concentration of African Americans in isolated "expansion areas" and redevelopment of much of the rest.[23] As white suburbanites fanned out along trolley lines and auto parkways, and as southern industries spread to the suburbs, peripheral black communities fell before the bulldozer, and the percentage of metropolitan-area blacks living in the suburbs fell throughout the region. Meanwhile, African Americans concentrated in a smaller number of neighborhoods in the central city and the suburban fringe. As a result, levels of residential segregation rose between 1910 and 1960 in every part of the South.[24]

In spite of the forces working to displace peripheral communities, many early suburbs survived and grew. Fed by the migration of rural blacks to cities after the turn of the century, these communities served as nuclei for growth. The suburbanization of factories and middle-class housing also supported this pattern even as it accelerated the displacement of black farmers and black suburbanites throughout much of the urban fringe. The demands of industries and white suburbanites for labor attracted black families and anchored the communities that remained. As black migration proceeded, many developers took advantage of vacant land near older black enclaves and established new subdivisions specifically for African Americans.

The suburbanization of factory labor was one foundation for black suburbanization in the South. This pattern was especially clear in Birmingham, Alabama, the South's most industrialized city. The establishment of steel mills and coal mines at Bessemer, Alabama, just southwest of Birmingham, for example, attracted thousands of black families, making it home to one of the largest suburban black communities in the South. In nearby Fairfield, town planners and officials from the Tennessee Iron and Coal Company initially excluded African American residents, but, as social worker Graham Taylor noted in 1915, African American workers built houses of their own "just over the city line," and they soon moved into the suburb itself. By 1930, African Americans were the majority in Fairfield, and African Americans lived in a dozen satellite communities across the metropolitan area.[25]

Even in less-industrialized cities, industrial suburbanization reinforced African American residence on the metropolitan perimeter. In Alcoa, Tennessee, near Knoxville, for example, the Aluminum Company of America built houses for African American workers and their families in the 1910s, and in Truxton, Virginia, outside Portsmouth, black shipyard workers moved into publicly financed war housing during the First World War.[26] Surveys conducted by the Home Owners Loan Corporation in the late 1930s provide additional evidence of this pattern. Appraisers reported dozens of peripheral black settlements, which were located in "proximity to occupants' employment." Outlying job sites included rail yards, fertilizer factories, steel mills, slaughterhouses, shipyards, bottling plants, cotton compresses, lumber mills, and numerous other unidentified "industrial plants."[27] By 1940, industrial decentralization had anchored a new landscape of black suburbanization throughout much of the South.

African Americans also moved to suburbs that promised employment in domestic or personal service. As middle-class whites moved to southern suburbs after the turn of the century, they took jobs with them, and African American workers followed. Describing Richmond, Virginia, in 1927, sociologist Howard Harlan noted a pattern that held true in most of the South. In Richmond, he wrote, "every high grade white section has a Negro settlement nearby."[28] Further examples are almost ubiquitous. In Dallas, for example, the black community at Oak Cliff provided domestic laborers for white suburbs south of the city. In Knoxville, the black settlement of Lonsdale developed as "a new colony" in the mid-1920s following the development of elite white subdivisions nearby, and in Charlotte, the black enclave of Cherry expanded after white suburbanites began moving to nearby Myers Park.[29] Thus, where it profited them, white southerners made room for African American workers in the suburban fringe, and African American families took advantage of the opportunity to build communities of their own.

Although jobs were a powerful motivation for early black suburbanization, African Americans also moved to suburbs for reasons unrelated to employment. Like other Americans, many black families were attracted to suburbs by the promise of open space, a semirural atmosphere, and the opportunity to purchase a home of their own. In 1932, a panel of experts on "Negro Housing" convened by President Herbert Hoover described a whole class of residential subdivisions in "outlying territories where Negroes are able to buy cheap land and build for themselves homes from whatever materials they can find, often a room or two at a time." These communities were so common that the panel recognized them as one of three types of African American settlements in urban areas. Describing a subdivision near Houston, the committee wrote, "there is another class of people buying out six or eight miles from town. There is an acreage division out there where they sell in one acre tracts . . . The type of people who buy have their work in town and do not make enough to own and run a car, but they hear the cheap prices quoted and jump at it. . . . It is just land out in the country" without gas, water, or paved streets. [30] In these subdivisions, black families often went to extreme lengths to obtain a home of their own. Many accumulated "sweat equity" by building their own houses. Owner-builders extended construction over time, bought materials on credit, and built as their incomes allowed. Some owners did all the building themselves. Others hired skilled builders for the most difficult tasks, and almost all solicited the labor of friends and family. One owner-builder near Nashville described the process as follows:

> "I had a little Christmas savings and we had bought up some good lumber, so I decided to make a little start. I just meant to put up two little rooms and a shed on the back of the lot and then build the house I wanted in the front as I got the money. I went to a lumber yard and outlined everything to them and told them as soon as I got the Christmas savings in November I would pay them if they would let me have the lumber at that time. I got the lumber, and the man I got to frame it up for me said since I had so much lumber it would be cheaper to just build the kind of house I wanted at once, so we started. After I framed it up, the money ran out and I had to let it stand for five or six months before I could get a top on it. When I was working on the house I had a regular job, and I would get up at four o'clock in the morning and work on it until seven, then go home to breakfast and to work; I would come from work and come right back over here and work until dark . . . People would pass by and wonder why I did not finish the house; I thought that was a silly thing for them to ask because they ought to have known that if I had had the money I would have finished it. . . . but I just kept going, and as soon as I would get a little ahead I would get something else to put on it and work a little more."[31]

Although this process contrasted with the housing market characteristic of middle-class suburbs, owner building reflected the aspirations as well as the means of black families for whom the opportunity to own a home outweighed urban conveniences, leisure time, and even proximity to work. Over time, residents built houses, churches, and small stores in much the same fashion. Local authorities usually provided schools but little else. Paved streets, sewers, water, gas, and electricity often arrived years later. In fact, some early suburbanites opposed improvements in order to avoid paying for them. Still, this rustic landscape reflected the essence of American suburbia. Residents lived in single-family houses on small plots of land, often as owner-occupants. They created a landscape that combined elements of urban and rural living. They enjoyed open space, greenery, and a semirural atmosphere, yet they lived within reach of urban jobs and the social attractions of African American communities downtown.[32]

At the opposite end of the spectrum, real estate developers also opened a number of subdivisions for middle-class blacks who sought housing and amenities akin to other middle-class suburbanites. Many of these subdivisions fell within the boundaries of a central city, but even there, most grew on vacant parcels at the edges of urban growth, in the same fashion as other residential suburbs.[33] Therefore they suggest the strength of a middle-class residential ideal among African American elites. Although white racism prevented most middle-class blacks from achieving suburban home ownership in a package that suited them, the tradition of black land ownership and institution-building in the South facilitated the development of brand new housing in residential subdivisions for the black bourgeoisie. In Richmond, Virginia, for example, the black-owned University Realty Company opened a residential subdivision called Frederick Douglass Court in the mid-1920s for middle- and upper-income black families. Located at the edge of town near Virginia Union University and within walking distance of a streetcar line, this sixteen-acre subdivision offered 30-foot by 135-foot building lots for $675 to $825. Buyers could elect to have a contractor build a home (for not less than $1,500), or they could pay University Realty to build one for them. The company offered three models ranging from a six-room, two-story frame house without central heat to a fully equipped, six-room stucco house with built-in refrigerator, sun parlor, and front porch. An early photograph of the development shows a row of two-story houses set back neatly from the street with a small strip of grass out front and a short sidewalk to the front steps. [34]

In Atlanta, a black entrepreneur named Herman Perry bought several hundred acres of peripheral land in the early 1920s and opened a number of bungalow subdivisions for African Americans. Although Perry's fortunes collapsed a few years later, he opened the west side of Atlanta as an area of elite residence for African Americans, and his subdivisions remain attractive neighborhoods in the 1990s, with small homes, curvilinear streets, clipped hedges, and well-used front porches.[35] In Charlotte, North Carolina, to cite an additional example, a white entrepreneur named W. S. Alexander developed the black suburb of Washington Heights in 1913. Alexander advertised Washington Heights as a "beautiful Negro suburb" with "beautiful streets convenient to churches and schools." Black Charlottians apparently agreed. Within a decade, many of Charlotte's black elite had moved into Washington Heights, and many others built houses to rent.[36] Like Douglass Court and Perry's Atlanta subdivisions, Washington

Heights was adjacent to a black college in a section of town attractive to educated and professional blacks. Located at the end of a trolley line, Washington Park may have been the nation's first black streetcar suburb. Although Douglass Court in Richmond and Perry's subdivisions in Atlanta were inside the city limits, the development of these neighborhoods mirrored processes that were taking place in suburbs nationwide: the expansion of residential development into the undeveloped fringe through the subdivision of bare land and the construction of new housing. Except for the race of the buyers, these neighborhoods were indistinguishable from hundreds of middle-class subdivisions constructed in American cities and suburbs before the Great Depression.

Whether they were members of the middle or working classes, African Americans participated in the process of suburbanization across the South. Through their efforts, they created communities and shaped a suburban landscape that reflected older patterns of racial geography, as well as the changing location of black employment during the early 20th century. At the same time, this landscape reflected the efforts of black southerners to shape the neighborhoods in which they lived. Although racism limited black incomes as well as the availability of land and municipal services, African Americans struggled to create better places to live. On this foundation, they built new communities and created alternatives to residence in the urban core.

## BLACK SUBURBANIZATION IN THE NORTH AND WEST

Outside the South, history and geography contributed to a separate pattern of early black suburbanization, although there were many similarities. As in the South, African Americans had lived on the fringes of northern and western cities during the 19th century, especially in areas where slavery had been common or where abolitionism attracted free blacks and fugitive slaves before the Civil War. However, the small number of African Americans outside the South limited communities in both size and number.[37] Black suburban populations began to grow slowly in the late 19th century. As in the South, African American suburbanites were most common in affluent commuter suburbs and industrial satellites. However, it was not until the Great Migration that large numbers of African Americans began moving to suburbs in the North and West.[38]

As in the South, the decentralization of black employment played a key role in early African American suburbanization. As large numbers of migrants left the South, many of the jobs that were available to them were already moving to the suburbs. In cities like Detroit, Chicago, St. Louis, Kansas City, Buffalo, and Philadelphia, for instance, packing houses, auto factories, and steel mills had already relocated to suburbs by 1920.[39] In Maywood, Illinois, outside Chicago, for instance, black steel workers settled among white immigrants during the Great Migration on streets of modest houses just south of the American Can Corporation. In Ecorse, Michigan, near Detroit, Great Lakes Steel attracted African American workers and their families to a sparsely built neighborhood across the railroad tracks from town, and in Lackawanna, New York, adjacent to Buffalo, Bethlehem Steel anchored a black community. In one of the most notable examples of industrial suburbanization, Ford Motors relocated its main facility to a suburban site on the Rouge River west of Detroit after World War I. By 1924, "the Rouge" was the largest factory complex on earth and the largest employer of African Americans in the area. Many of Ford's 10,000 black workers lived in surrounding suburbs such as Inkster, River Rouge, or Ecorse.[40] By the mid-1920s, the pathway to high-paying industrial work in these cities and a dozen others often led directly to the suburbs.

Service jobs, too, attracted African Americans to the suburbs. Hotels, restaurants, caterers, and personal service employment followed white suburbanites, and as black workers moved North, they trailed these jobs to dozens of elite suburbs. Typically, these communities developed in older suburbs where African American families had gained a foothold in the 19th century before modern practices of housing discrimination had fully developed. By 1930, largely white commuter suburbs such as Evanston, Illinois; East Orange, Orange, Englewood, and Montclair, New Jersey; Mount Vernon, White Plains, and New Rochelle, New York; and Pasadena, California, each had 2,000 or more African American residents. Dozens of other suburbs were home to black communities ranging in size from 100 to 1,000.[41] In the largest of these, black families established branches of the NAACP, the Urban League, YMCAs, scout troops, fraternal orders, and numerous small businesses. In fact, by the mid-1920s, one-quarter of the black YMCAs in the United States were located in suburbs—most of them in suburbs dominated by white commuters.[42] In these suburbs, African Americans made their living in service to affluent whites, but they made their lives across town in communities of their own.

Finally, African American migrants to the North and West also settled in inexpensive residential suburbs where home ownership and semirural living were the primary attractions. As the Great Migration unfolded, a significant market for inexpensive lot subdivisions developed among African Americans, and scores of real estate agents responded to the desires of black newcomers for homes and property. By 1928, sociologist T. J. Woofter, Jr., reported that "in every city, small outlying settlements are growing up where land is cheaper, and where Negroes can afford small houses and use street cars or automobiles to reach their working places."[43] In Chicago, St. Louis, Cleveland, Columbus, Cincinnati, New York, Detroit, and Philadelphia (among other places) real estate speculators purchased small tracts of land at the edges of town, subdivided property, and sold building lots to African Americans.[44] Some of these agents were African Americans who encouraged migrants to "join hands with your own people" by buying lots in a black subdivision, but most were whites who sold to all comers. By the mid-1920s, African American newspapers routinely contained advertisements for these subdivisions. Ads appealed to recent migrants with the promise of open space for gardens and small livestock, proximity to decent employment, and the "great opportunity . . . for colored people to own a home."[45] In spite of inauspicious beginnings, many allotments developed into lasting black communities. In the Cincinnati area, for example, black subdivisions in the Mill Creek Valley developed into a community of 4,500 by 1944 when residents incorporated as the suburb of Lincoln Heights. South of Chicago, the black suburb of Robbins, Illinois, shared similar roots and was home to 1,300 in 1940. Most owner-built suburbs were small places with limited commercial activity and primitive services, but levels of home ownership often outstripped even middle-class white suburbs. In Chagrin Falls Park, Ohio, near Cleveland, for instance, 70 percent of African Americans owned their own homes in 1940 compared to just over 50 percent in the nearby white suburb of Chagrin Falls, where many worked as domestic servants. In aggregate, early black suburbs offered opportunity to tens of thousands of African Americans to purchase a home of their own in a quiet place removed from the central city.[46]

By 1940, almost one-fifth of metropolitan-area blacks outside the South lived in suburbs. They were largely members of the working class, confined to blue-collar jobs in domestic service or industrial labor. Indeed, the changing geography of black employment—both male and female—was an important foundation for early black suburbanization. At the same time, many African American suburbs grew where families took advantage of the opportunity to buy property in the suburban fringe in spite of the difficulties this may have posed in getting to work. In a number of early suburbs, proximity to work was secondary to the desire for home ownership. Although these preferences were most notable in owner-built suburbs, they shaped patterns of black community building throughout the suburbs. Regardless of the suburb, rates of home ownership in black suburbs routinely surpassed home ownership in even the most affluent African American neighborhoods in central cities. Moreover, where land was available, do-it-yourself building was also common in industrial and domestic service suburbs. Black families raised large gardens, kept small livestock, and tended backyard fruit trees throughout the suburban fringe, and they built communities rooted in networks of extended family.[47] For many early suburbanites, life in the suburbs was a choice that allowed them to combine older desires and familiar ways of living with new surroundings and new opportunities for employment in northern cities. Like white suburbanites, they worked to create better places to live that were close enough to city or suburban employment to allow residents to hold an urban job, but they created landscapes and patterns of life that reflected the experiences and aspirations that African American migrants had brought with them from the South.

## LEGACIES OF EARLY BLACK SUBURBANIZATION

Among the legacies of early black suburbanization was the foothold it established for future African American suburbanization. After 1960 especially, older black communities became seeds for new growth. Ironically, white racism actually facilitated this process by creating "open" areas near existing black communities where white developers were unwilling to build. White developers often ceded land near older black suburbs for new African American housing. Even where white suburbs ringed older black communities, new black suburbanites tended to settle in adjacent white neighborhoods rather than pioneering in suburbs where there were no black families for miles. By 1970, the persisting influence of early black suburbanization was apparent. In a survey of the twenty-five most rapidly growing African American suburbs of the 1960s, Harold Connolly revealed that more than three-fourths contained or abutted an older black community.[48] Hence the struggles of poorer black families to make homes in the suburbs before World War II drove a wedge of opportunity for more affluent suburbanites who would follow.

Even as a new cohort of middle-class African Americans began to move to suburbs in the 1960s, patterns of older black suburbanization rendered some early suburbanites especially vulnerable to shifts in the national economy. Like poor and working-class African Americans nationwide, early suburbanites fell victim to the decline in low-skilled industrial labor after 1950. Patterns of informal economic activity and self-provisioning in some black suburbs helped cushion the blows of deindustrialization, but where unemployment was high, poverty was never far away.

In the South, black suburbanization in the early 20th century had co-incided with the industrialization of the region through national economic shifts away from traditional manufacturing areas. During the 1910s and 1920s, firms in so-called sick industries, especially textiles and shoe manufacturing, began to relocate from the Northeast to low-wage and weak-union areas of the South. Where black migrants moved to communities dominated by these industries, or by mining or railroads, they faced seasonal employment, low wages, chronic labor strife, and limited opportunities for economic mobility—even before 1940. The South also welcomed more stable economic growth prior to World War II, and although racism limited black access to skilled industrial jobs, African Americans who found employment in steel manufacturing or shipbuilding, for example, rose in status within black communities, sometimes quite noticeably. In 1950, for example, African American incomes in Birmingham, Alabama, were 10 to 15 percent higher than in cities such as Atlanta, Memphis, or New Orleans, and median black incomes in a number of industrial suburbs of Birmingham were higher than in the city itself.[49] Industrialization was a mixed bag for African Americans before 1950; however, at its best it opened the way to new status and new opportunities.

In the North and West, too, work in industrial suburbs laid a foundation for black economic mobility before mid-century. Although the employment profile among African Americans in factory suburbs was overwhelmingly blue collar, black families in these suburbs often earned higher incomes than families in central cities or other suburbs.[50] And in some suburbs, industrial wages were a stepping-stone to the middle class. In River Rouge, Michigan, for instance, where a substantial number of men worked at Ford Motors or Great Lakes Steel, an astonishing 80 percent of black respondents to a survey of 1965 graduates from River Rouge High School (born in 1947) reported having attended some college, and almost as many were working in white-collar jobs. As early as 1940, more than half of African American families in River Rouge owned their own homes.[51] For a generation or two in suburbs like River Rouge, factory labor apparently laid the basis for a stable black community of home owners in which the dream that children would do better than their parents was not out of reach.

For children who followed parents and grandparents into the mills, however, opportunities for mobility were short-lived. In factory suburbs, African Americans comprised an industrial proletariat in the purest form. In suburbs like River Rouge, Michigan, or Maywood and Harvey, Illinois, for instance, 60 to 90 percent of black men worked in factories at the end of World War I. Thirty years later, almost equal numbers toiled in industrial occupations.[52] In contrast, African American women found few opportunities for wage work in these male-dominated local economies, even when they wanted to work.[53] Thus the fortunes of black families in these communities rose or fell with men's employment. In the event that men lost their jobs or the mills shut down, families faced restricted options. Indeed, as the economy began to shift away from heavy manufacturing, African American families in these communities needed the income of an additional earner, and black women were at a disadvantage to find work nearby.

As deindustrialization swept the nation's Manufacturing Belt during the 1970s, industrial suburbs were devastated. The plight of larger industrial satellites like East St. Louis, Illinois, or Camden, New Jersey, is well-known, but smaller suburbs, too, suffered similar symptoms: high unemployment, housing abandonment, homelessness, drug abuse, and soaring crime rates. As steel mills and auto factories cut back in the Motor City, for instance, suburbs such as River Rouge, Hamtramck, Ecorse, Highland Park, and Pontiac lost thousands of jobs. Services declined, schools deteriorated, social problems spread, and local governments collapsed. The city of Hamtramck went broke in 1970, as tax revenues failed to keep up with expenditures. In the 1980s, after a decade of plant closures, Highland Park, River Rouge, and Ecorse all followed suit. By 1984, Highland Park, the suburb where Henry Ford had introduced modern mass production, had the highest murder rate in Greater Detroit.[54] By the late 1980s, these suburbs presented a landscape of cracked streets, empty storefronts, and vacant lots where industrial workers had once made homes.

For black residents of these suburbs, the consequences of deindustrialization were often grim. Jobs evaporated, and for families who had struggled to purchase a home, plant closures rendered their investments a liability. As local economies faltered, housing markets collapsed, and home owners faced the choice of selling into a panic or staying put on a sinking ship. For those who owned their homes outright, lifetimes of equity were often erased in a matter of years, and for families who still had mortgages to pay, foreclosure was a constant specter. Before 1940, black suburbanites had pinned their hopes to manufacturing at a time when American industries supplied the world with manufactured goods, and for a generation or more, suburban factory work laid a foundation for comparatively high incomes, modest rates of home ownership, and upward mobility. By the 1970s, however, that foundation began to crumble.

In suburbs that were less dependent on industrial labor, shifts in the national economy had less immediate consequences. In many black suburbs that began as inexpensive subdivisions, for instance, connections to industrial labor were often tenuous, and early settlers themselves had made choices that limited their potential for economic growth. From the outset, many unregulated subdivisions attracted black migrants who sought to limit their dependence on the market economy through strategies of subsistence that had served African Americans since the Civil War. To cut costs, they had delayed improvements to local infrastructure, doing without paved streets, sewers, and city water.[55] They raised vegetables and small livestock to stretch family incomes. Frequently, they also built houses of their own, expanding them as their needs dictated and savings allowed. Families pooled earnings, took in boarders, and ran small businesses from their homes, in the process transforming shelter into source of income. Before Social Security or private pensions covered most black workers, a clear title to a house and a small piece of land was the only means of long-term security available to many poor families, and through such means, some suburbanites sought to insulate themselves from fluctuations in the industrial economy, especially where their status in it was marginal.

As African American standards of living improved nationally during the 1950s and 1960s, however, expectations for life in an "affluent society" expanded, and strategies of working-class subsistence that had served early suburbanites could not support a standard of living satisfactory to most urban-born African Americans. Pioneer suburbanites may have been content with a lifestyle reminiscent of the rural South, but their children and grandchildren often saw these places as "the boondocks." Consequently, these suburbs attracted few newcomers after the 1950s. Moreover, because many of these suburbs lacked an independent economic base, young workers seeking economic opportunities looked elsewhere. Some of these communities experienced growth in the 1970s and 1980s due to economic expansion in neighboring suburbs, but where that was the case, they often faced pressures for displacement. In most, population dwindled after 1960, leaving an aging population who lived at the margins of poverty, many of them in homes that they owned. [56]

In affluent suburbs where African Americans had built communities, the effects of deindustrialization were even more mixed. While domestic service employment declined dramatically among African American women after mid-century, longstanding patterns of black female employment persisted in these suburbs, and black women continued to be pillars of economic support as they moved into clerical occupations and other "pink collar" fields, as well as a small number in the professions.[57] Because comparatively fewer black men in these communities had relied on industrial employment, declines in this sector had less impact than in the factory suburbs, and by 1970, black employment in these suburbs tended to be more balanced across various sectors of the economy. [58]

In contrast to pattern in industrial suburbs, shifts in the national economy actually benefited some residents in some of these suburbs, and African Americans were able to share in these gains. Well-educated workers (white as well as black) generally fared well in the "postindustrial" economy, and many of them stayed in these older commuter suburbs. Consequently, local services and school funding remained comparatively high. Furthermore, the concentration of white elites often attracted service employment—at both ends of the occupational ladder. Glass office towers, exclusive hotels, expensive restaurants, and high-tech industry often located in or near these suburbs, bringing a variety of new jobs.[59] For unskilled black workers, new job opportunities were limited to categories offering low wages and few benefits, but for African Americans with education or marketable skills, white-collar employment in service industries provided opportunities for advancement. Not surprisingly, older affluent suburbs attracted a growing cadre of middle-class black families during the 1960s, and local African American communities became more diverse and occupationally balanced over time. Finally, early suburbanites who had purchased property in these suburbs often gained as the demand for local housing remained high. In suburbs like Evanston, Illinois, and Mount Vernon, New York, for instance, former domestic servants earned a place in the middle class by renting and selling to more recent arrivals. In both suburbs, the homes of long time black elites often contained an apartment for rent, and the names of early black families could be found on the deeds to multiple properties across town. Compared to industrial satellites or early subdivision suburbs, then, African American communities in domestic service suburbs continued to offer opportunities for African Americans, even as the economy began to shift in the 1960s and 1970s.

As a whole, early African American suburbanization left a mixed legacy of success and disappointment. In the years before World War II, while most African American migrants moved to crowded central city neighborhoods, thousands of others settled in suburbs, many of which offered substantially different residential environments. Drawn by jobs, family ties, open space, or the opportunity to own a home, early black suburbanites adjusted to urban life from the city's edge. The results varied from place to place, but nationwide, suburbs offered black migrants the opportunity to secure relatively steady urban labor, to raise families, to purchase homes, and—for some—to live in an atmosphere reminiscent of the southern countryside.

As the national economy began to restructure after mid-century, early black suburbs experienced change in different ways. Suburbs built on industrial labor were especially hard hit. Likewise, suburbs that had developed as rustic subdivisions suffered the loss of well-paying, low-skilled jobs among residents. At the same time, the physical characteristics of these suburbs also contributed to economic decline as these suburbs failed to attract or retain younger families. Except where vacant land had allowed the construction of newer subdivisions, these suburbs tended to shrink in size as the first generation of black suburbanites passed away. African American communities in early commuter suburbs, on the other hand, experienced uneven growth related to the rise of a service economy. While domestic service employment declined among women and men, low-paid employment in the service sector remained common. On the other hand, new opportunities for well-educated black workers to find work or housing in these suburbs created more diverse black communities over time. Where early suburbanites had purchased homes or emphasized education for their children, these suburbs often provided a ladder into the middle class.

By the late 20th century, many early suburbs had become economically depressed, and some suffered the worst symptoms of the urban crisis. Opportunities for working-class black families to purchase homes in the suburbs, in particular, was largely a thing of the past. However, the efforts of early black suburbanites to create homes and communities carved a foothold for a new generation of middle-class black suburbanites after 1960. In spite of economic decline or efforts to displace them, early suburbanites struggled to find a place in urban America through life in the suburbs. For a time, these places held out the opportunity for migrants to achieve goals such as home ownership, steady employment, and economic upward mobility. Through their own efforts, early suburbanites left lasting imprints on the racial geography of metropolitan America, and they opened a wedge of opportunity for black suburbanites after 1960.

## NOTES

1. See, for example, Harold M. Rose, "The All-Black Town: Suburban Prototype or Rural Slum?" in Harlan Hahn, ed., *People and Politics in Urban Society* (Beverly Hills, Calif.: Sage Publications, 1972), pp. 405–419; and Harold M. Rose, *Black Suburbanization: Access to Improved Quality of Life or Maintenance of the Status Quo?* (Cambridge, Mass.: Ballinger Press, 1976), p. 27.

2. In 1940, the U.S. Census defined suburbs as the "thickly settled" districts adjacent to a central city of 50,000 or more. However, they drew metropolitan boundaries along county lines, including counties adjacent to central cities in which fewer than 25 percent of the population worked in agriculture. They calculated the suburban total by subtracting the central city figure from the total metropolitan population. By this definition, there were 982,000 African Americans in southern suburbs in 1940 (compared to 903,000 in 1910). There were 468,000 black suburbanites in the North, and 32,000 in the West, (compared to 208,000 and 7,000 in 1910) for a total of 1,482,000. For comparison, 4.4 million African Americans lived in central cities. U.S. Bureau of the Census, Census of Population: 1960, *Selected Area Reports: Standard Metropolitan Statistical Areas*, Final Report PC(3)-1D (Washington, D.C.: U.S. Government Printing Office [GPO], 1963), pp. 2–5.

3. Reynolds Farley, "The Changing Distribution of Negroes within Metropolitan Areas: The Emergence of Black Suburbs," *American Journal of Sociology* 75 (January 1970): 333–351. Early black suburbs shared many similarities with working-class white suburbs. Richard Harris, "The Un-planned Blue–Collar Suburb in Its Heyday, 1900–1940," in D. Janelle, ed., *Geographical Snapshots of North America* (New York: Guilford Press, 1992), pp. 94–96; Richard Harris and Matt Sendbuehler, "The Making of a Working-Class Suburb in Hamilton's East End, 1900–1945," *Journal of Urban History* 20, no. 4 (August 1994): 486–511.

4. Carter G. Woodson, *Rural Negro* (Washington, D.C.: Center for Negro Life and History, 1930), p. 119.

5. Richard Harris, "Working Class Home Ownership in the American Metropolis," *Journal of Urban History* 17, no. 1 (November 1990): 46–69; also Harris, "Self-Building in the Urban Housing Market," *Economic Geography* 67, no.

1 (January 1991): 1–21; Harris, *Unplanned Suburbs: Toronto's American Tragedy, 1900–1950* (Baltimore: Johns Hopkins University Press, 1996).

6. Leslie Wilson, "Dark Spaces: An Account of Afro-American Suburbanization," Ph.D. diss., Department of History, City University of New York, 1991; Interview by author with "Alice B.," Paramus, New Jersey, March 5, 1992.

7. T. J. Woofter, *Negro Problems in Cities* (Garden City, N.Y.: Doubleday and Doran Publishers, 1928), p. 28; African Americans by percent of population in 1920: New Orleans (26 percent), Nashville (30), Atlanta (31), Charlotte (32), Durham (35), Memphis (38), Birmingham and Mobile (39), Houston (40), Montgomery (46), Savannah (47). U.S. Bureau of the Census, *U.S. Census of Population: 1920, Volume II, General Report and Analytical Tables*, (Washington, D.C.: U.S. Government Printing Office, 1922).

8. Richard Wade, *Slavery in the City: The South, 1820–1860* (New York: Oxford University Press, 1964); Zane Miller, "Urban Blacks in the South: 1865–1920: The Richmond, Savannah, New Orleans, Louisville and Birmingham Experience," in Leo F. Schnore, ed., *The New Urban History: Quantitative Explorations by American Historians* (Princeton: Princeton University Press, 1975), pp. 184–204.

9. Biddleville was one of five "urban clusters" that ringed Charlotte in the late 19th century. Thomas Hanchett, "Sorting Out the New South City: Race, Class, and Urban Development in charlotte, 1875–1975." (Chapel Hill: The University of North Carolina Press, 1998), pp. 134–138.

10. In Durham, North Carolina, for instance, African Americans lived in eleven separate clusters throughout the city by 1890. In Lexington, Kentucky, and Atlanta, Georgia, black families lived in at least a half dozen clusters on the cities' edges. John Kellogg, "Negro Urban Clusters in the Post Bellum South," *Geographical Review*, 67, no. 3 (July 1971): 287–303; John Kellogg, "The Formation of Black Residential Areas in Lexington, Kentucky, 1865–1885," *Journal of Southern History*, 4, no. 8 (February 1982): 21–52; Howard Sumka, "Racial Segregation in Small North Carolina Cities," *Southeastern Geographer* 17, no. 1, (1977): 59–75.

11. Woodson, *Rural Negro*, p. 120.

12. Hanchett, "Sorting Out." pp. 135–136.

13. Kellogg, "Negro Urban Clusters." Regarding smaller towns in the South, Charles Johnson noted in 1943 that "practically all the Negro neighborhoods are located at the edge of town. There are no white areas beyond them." Charles S. Johnson, *Patterns of Negro Segregation* (New York: Harper and Brothers Publishers, 1943), p. 9.

14. Hanchett; "Sorting Out," pp. 3–8: Dana F. White, "The Black Sides of Atlanta: A Geography of Expansion and Containment, 1870–1970," *Atlanta His-*

*torical Journal* 26, nos. 2–3 (Summer–Fall, 1982): 199–225; Karl and Alma Taeuber, *Negroes in Cities* (Chicago: Aldine Press, 1965): 40–53.

15. Rudolf Heberle, "Social Consequences of the Industrialization of Southern Cities," *Social Forces* 27 1948–49): 35.

16. Woodson, *Rural Negro*, p. 123.

17. During the first half of the century, many southern cities expanded politically as well as physically, annexing thousands of acres of peripheral land. As they did so, they brought former rural and suburban areas under control of municipal government.

18. In spite of the Supreme Court decision in *Buchanan v. Warley* (1917), cities such as Birmingham, New Orleans, Oklahoma City, Miami, and Lakeland, Florida, passed racial zoning ordinances into the 1940s. Birmingham enforced racial zoning from 1926 through 1949. Robert A. Thompson, Hylan Lewis, and Davis McEntire, "Atlanta and Birmingham: A Comparative Study in Negro Housing," in Nathan Glazer and Davis McEntire, eds. *Studies in Housing and Minority Groups*, (Berkeley: University of California Press, 1960), pp. 59–65; Bobby M. Wilson, "Black Housing Opportunities in Birmingham, Alabama," *Southeastern Geographer* 17, no. 1 (May 1977): 49–57; New Orleans passed a racial zoning ordinance in the mid-1920s, though it did not survive a court challenge. Woofter, *Negro Problems*, p. 70; Courts struck down an Oklahoma City ordinance passed in the mid-1930s. Johnson, *Patterns of Negro Segregation*, p. 176.

19. Yale Rabin, "The Roots of Segregation in the Eighties: The Role of Local Government Actions," *Urban Affairs Annual Reviews*, 32 (1987): 208–226.

20. Thompson, Lewis, and McEntire, "Atlanta and Bermingham" pp. 20–21; Charles S. Johnson, *Into the Main Stream: A Survey of the Best Practices in Race Relations in the South* (Chapel Hill: University of North Carolina Press, 1947), pp. 218–226.

21. Ronald Bayor, *Race and the Shaping of Twentieth Century Atlanta* (chapel Hill: University of North Carolina Press, 1996), pp. 61–63; Christopher Silver, "The Ordeal of City Planning in Postwar Richmond, Virginia: A Quest for Greatness," *Journal of Urban History* 10, no. 1 (November 1983): 33–60; Raymond Mohl, "Race and Space in the Modern City: Interstate 95 and the Black Community in Miami," in Arnold Hirsch and Raymond Mohl, eds., *Urban Politics in 20th Century America* (New Brunswick; Rutgers University Press, 1993), pp. 100–158; Howard Preston, *Automobile Age Atlanta: The Making of a Southern Metropolis, 1900–1935* (Athens: University of Georgia Press, 1979), 69–76; Harold Rose, "The All Negro Town: Its Evolution and Function," *Geographical Review* 55 (July 1965): p. 370.

22. "Locating New Housing Sites for Negroes Challenges Planning Body," *Atlanta Daily World*, April 17, 1951, p. 1.

23. "Fulton County and Negro Housing," *Atlanta Daily World*, February 1, 1950; "$110,000 Improvement Drive Approved for Bush Mountain," *World*, February 11, 1950; "Negroes Join Move to Block Housing Project," *World*, July 4, 1950; Bayor, *Race and the Shaping*, pp. 53–92.

24. In 1910, almost 44 percent of metropolitan-area blacks had lived outside a central city, by 1940, that figure had declined to 30.5 percent. By 1960, it was 25 percent. *Census of Population: 1960, Selected Area Reports*; p. 4, for levels of racial segregation, see Karl and Alma Taeuber, *Negroes in Cities* (Chicago: Aldine Press, 1965) 40–44; Hanchett, "Sorting Out" 134–138; White, "Black Sides," pp. 221–222.

25. In Bessemer, the black population grew by more than 5,000 between 1910 and 1930. In 1930, Bessemer's 11,691 African Americans were 56 percent of the local population. In Fairfield, 6,393 African Americans constituted 63 percent of the population by 1930. U.S. Bureau of the Census, *Census of Population: 1930, Volume III, Part 1, Reports by State* (Washington, D.C.: U.S. Government Printing Office, 1932); Graham Taylor, *Satellite Cities: A Study of Industrial Suburbs* (New York: D. Appleton and Company, 1915), p. 251; Thompson, Lewis, and McEntire, "Atlanta and Birmingham," pp. 57–58.

26. After World War I, a black real estate syndicate purchased the development at Truxton and sold homes to middle-class black families. Woofter, *Negro Problems*, pp. 140, 168.

27. Area Description D-7, North Montgomery, Alabama, (Box 97); Area Descriptions, D-2, South Atlanta, D-10, Edgewood, Georgia, D-23, Rockdale Park, Georgia, (Atlanta, Box 91); Area Descriptions D-25, St. Bernard Parish, Louisiana, D-26, Algiers, Louisiana, D-32, Harvey, Louisiana (New Orleans, Box 88); Area Descriptions, D-5, Wahoo district, D-9, Lemmon Avenue Settlement, (Dallas, Box 153), Home Owners Loan Corporation, City Survey Files, Record Group 195, National Archives; also West Nashville, see James Blumstein and Benjamin Walter, eds., *Growing Metropolis: Aspects of Development in Nashville* (Nashville: Vanderbilt University Press, 1975), pp. 65–81.

28. Howard H. Harlan, "Zion Town—A Study in Human Ecology" (Charlottesville, Va.: University of Virginia, Phelps-Stokes Fellowship Papers, number thirteen, 1935), pp. 6–7.

29. Area Description D-2, Security Map of Metropolitan Dallas, Texas, no date [1939?] (Box 153); Area Description D-40, Security Map of Metropolitan New Orleans, Louisiana, February 6, 1939, RG 195, Home Owners Loan Corporation, City Survey Files; Woofter, *Negro Problems*, p. 106; Hanchett, "Sorting Out." 43–44, 164.

30. The President's Commission on Negro Housing, John M. Gries and James Ford, eds., *Negro Housing* (New York: President's Conference on Home Building and Home Ownership, 1932), pp. 13, 98.

31. Gries and Ford, eds., *Negro Housing*, pp. 89–90.

32. For similar patterns among blue-collar whites, see Harris, *Unplanned Suburbs*; and Becky Nicolaides, *My Blue Heaven: Life and Politics in the Working Class Suburbs of Los Angeles, 1920–1965*, book unpublished manuscript, 1997.

33. T. J. Woofter reported a number of "growing suburbs, occupied by Negroes who own their own homes" at the edges of Memphis, Knoxville, Richmond, Winston-Salem, and Louisville. Woofter, *Negro Problems*, pp. 106, 140.

34. Charles Louis Knight, "Negro Housing in Certain Virginia Cities," Phelps-Stokes Fellowship Papers, 8 (Richmond, Va.: William Byrd Press, 1927), pp. 121–123.

35. White, *Black Sides*, p. 218; Timothy J. Crimmins, "Bungalow Suburbs: East and West," *Atlanta Historical Journal* 26, no. 2–3 (Summer–Fall 1982): 88–92.

36. Hanchett, "Sorting Out," Chapter five.

37. Just 10 percent of African Americans lived outside the South in 1900. Daniel M. Johnson and Rex R. Campbell, *Black Migration in America: A Social and Demographic History* (Durham: Duke University Press, 1981), p. 73. In North Amityville, New York, for example, African Americans established an A.M.E. church in 1815. Andrew Wiese, "Racial Cleansing in the Suburbs: Suburban Government, Urban Renewal and Segregation on Long Island, New York, 1945–1960," in Marc Silver and Martin Melkonian, eds., *Contested Terrain: Power, Politics, and Participation in Suburbia* (Westport, Conn.: Greenwood Press, 1995), pp. 61–70; Black communities in Brooklyn, Illinois, east of St. Louis, and Lawnside, New Jersey, also predate the Civil War. Harold Rose, "The All-Negro Town"; the black community of Tennessee Town, in Topeka, and the Quindaro district in Kansas City, Kansas, developed at the edges of town in the wake of exoduster migration in the late 19th century. Nell Irvin Painter, *Exodusters: Black Migration to Kansas after Reconstruction* (New York: Knopf, 1977) 57.

38. In the West, World War II was the catalyst for African American suburbanization. A comparatively small number of African Americans migrated to the West before the War. In 1940, just 32,000 African Americans lived in suburban areas of the West. Census of Population: 1960, *Selected Area Reports*.

39. Andrew Wiese, "Struggle for the Suburban Dream: African American Suburbanization since 1916," Ph.D. diss. Department of History, Columbia University, 1993.

40. These suburbs included Highland Park, Hamtramck, Pontiac, Inkster, Ecorse, and River Rouge, Michigan. Allan Nevins with Frank Hill, *Ford: Expansion and Challenge, 1915–1933* (New York: Scribners, 1957); August Meier and Elliot Rudwick, *Black Detroit and the Rise of the UAW* (New York: Oxford University Press, 1979), pp. 8–15.

41. Harold X. Connolly, "Black Movement to the Suburbs: Suburbs Doubling their Population in the 1960s," *Urban Affairs Quarterly* 9, no. 1 (September 1973): 92.

42. Kevin Barry Leonard, "Paternalism and the Rise of a Black Community in Evanston, Illinois: 1870–1930," M.A. History thesis, Northwestern University, 1982; Wilfred Lewin, "A Study of the Negro Population of Mount Vernon," Civil Works Administration, 1935; Earl F. Cartland, "A Study of the Negroes Living in Pasadena, M.A. History thesis, Whittier College, 1948; Suburban black YMCA's were located in Evanston, Illinois; White Plains, New York; and Montclair, Orange, and Elizabeth, New Jersey. Wilson, "Dark Spaces," Chapter 5.

43. Woofter, *Negro Problems*, p. 106.

44. Andrew Wiese, "Places of Our Own: Suburban Black Towns before 1950," *Journal of Urban History* 19 (May 1993) 30–54; On the West Coast, developers also opened lot subdivisions for black migrants. The African American community in Watts, annexed by Los Angeles in 1926, began as a series of residential subdivisions. South of San Francisco, African Americans settled in a number of residential subdivisions in East Palo Alto in the 1940s. Patricia Rae Adler, "Watts: From Suburb to Black Ghetto," Ph.D. diss., University of Southern California, 1977; Wallace Stegner, "Changes in the Black Ghetto: East Palo Alto," *Saturday Review* 53, (August 1, 1970): 12.

45. "Join hands with your own people," *Amsterdam News*, October 17, 1923; "Great opportunity open for colored people to own a home," from an advertisement for lots in Jamaica, Long Island (Queens). The ad noted that "those especially coming North from the Southland can find comfort by paying very small payments . . . Plenty work with good wages," and finally, "cottages with all kinds of modern improvements where you can have a garden and raise chickens," *Chicago Defender*, July 7, 1917. See also *Cleveland Gazette*, June 14, 1924, "Stop Paying Rent," Lincoln Heights Land Company advertisement (Oakwood, Ohio).

46. U.S. Bureau of the Census, *Census of Population: 1940, Volume II, State Reports*, Illinois, (Washington, D.C.: U.S. Government Printing Office, 1943), Table 28; Henry L. Taylor, Jr., "The Building of a Black Industrial Suburb: The Lincoln Heights, Ohio, Story," Ph.D. diss., State University of New York at Buffalo, 1979; Andrew Weiss, "The Other Suburbanites: African American Suburbanization in the North before 1950, *Journal of American History* 85(4) March 1999, pp. 1495–1524."

47. Andrew Wiese, "The Other Suburbanites," pp. 1495–1524.

48. Connolly, "Black Movement," p. 92.

49. Earl Lewis, *In Their Own Interests: Race, Class, and Power in Twentieth-Century Norfolk, Virginia* (Berkeley: University of California Press, 1991),

pp. 32–38, 47–49; Thompson, Lewis, and McEntire, "Atlanta and Birmingham," 54. Median black incomes in Bessemer ($1,650) and Fairfield, Alabama ($1,926), were higher than in Birmingham ($1,548). U.S. Bureau of the Census, *Census of Population: 1950, Volume II, Characteristics of the Population, Part 2, Alabama* (Washington, D.C.: U.S. Government Printing Office, 1952).

50. Median black incomes in Lackawanna, New York; Ecorse, River Rouge, and Highland Park, Michigan; and Chicago Heights, Harvey, Maywood, Waukegan, and Venice, Illinois, were higher in 1950 than in the central cities they surrounded: Buffalo, Detroit, Chicago, and St. Louis. *U.S. Census of the Population: 1950, Volume III, Census Tracts* (Washington, D.C.: U.S. Government Printing Office, 1952).

51. "Dreams Made River Rouge: River Rouge High, The Class of '65," *Detroit Free Press*, March 15, 1985. The *Free Press* mailed 140 surveys and received 70. Even if the black graduates who responded to the *Free Press* survey followed radically different paths than their classmates, the educational and occupational achievements of respondents alone suggest that factory labor in River Rouge laid a foundation for substantial inter-generational mobility among blacks after World War II. Black home ownership in River Rouge in 1940 was 60 percent. U.S. Bureau of the Census, *Census of Housing: 1940, Volume II, General Characteristics* (Washington, D.C.: U.S. Government Printing Office, 1943).

52. U.S. Bureau of the *Census, Census of Population: 1920, Census Schedules*: River Rouge village, Michigan, reel 800; Maywood City, Illinois, reel 362; Harvey city, Illinois, reel 363. In 1950, black men in these suburbs remained concentrated in blue-collar factory jobs. In Bessemer, Alabama; River Rouge, Highland Park, and Inkster, Michigan; and Lackawanna, New York, more than 40 percent of black men worked as operatives and kindred workers—the job category for semiskilled factory labor. In other industrial suburbs, the proportion of black men working as factory operatives was greater than 30 percent. When added to the number who worked in skilled craft or foreman positions and unskilled labor (service excluded) the proportion of blue-collar workers in these suburbs generally exceeded 75 percent. In suburbs like Braddock, and Duquesne, Pennsylvania; Highland Park, River Rouge, and Ecorse, Michigan; Venice and Chicago Heights, Illinois; and Bessemer and Fairfield, Alabama, more than 80 percent of black men worked in these three job categories. *Census of Population: 1950, Volume II.*

53. Compared with cities or domestic service suburbs, female labor force participation in industrial suburbs was minimal throughout the Great Migration. In 1920, as few as 15 percent of African American women in some industrial suburbs worked for wages. By 1940, female employment in industrial suburbs was higher but still lagging. In Lackawanna, New York, and Ecorse and River

Rouge, Michigan, female employment ranged between 12 and 18 percent. In suburbs such as Waukegan, Joliet, Harvey, and Chicago Heights, Illinois; Hamtramck, Highland Park, and Pontiac, Michigan; and Bayonne and Rahway, New Jersey, rates of female employment ranged from 25 to 40 percent, compared to rates of female employment in central cities ranging from one–third to one–half: Detroit (30 percent), Chicago (35 percent), St. Louis (37 percent), Newark (40 percent), Los Angeles (42 percent), New York (51 percent). *Census of Population: 1940.*

54. "Tough Times Might Be Ahead for More of State's Factory Towns," *Detroit Free Press*, February 8, 1987; "Highland Park Has Top Rate of Major Crime for 1984," *Detroit Free Press*, August 4, 1985, 3a; "How Highland Park Rusted Out in Ten Years," *Detroit News*, September 20, 1976, 3a; "River Rouge: Can It Save Itself?" *Detroit Free Press*, December 2, 1990, management section, 6; "Rescue Plan Ok'd for River Rouge," *Detroit News*, October 19, 1988, 2b; "Steel Town's Debts Come Due," *Detroit Free Press*, February 8, 1987, 1b. For a survey of deindustrialization in the 1970s, see Barry Bluestone and Bennett Harrison, *The De-industrialization of America: Plant Closings, Community Abandonment, and the Dismantling of Basic Industry* (New York: Basic Books, 1982), p. 22.

55. As late as 1960, more than 60 percent of African American households in the black suburb of East Chicago Heights, Illinois, did not have indoor toilets. Farley, "Changing Distribution," p. 340. Similar patterns were common in other owner-built black suburbs. Wiese, "Places of Our Own." Roger Simon, Olivier Zunz, and Richard Harris demonstrate that this pattern was also common among working-class whites (especially immigrants) in newly developing areas in suburbs and at the edges of the central city before 1940. Roger Simon, "Housing and Services in an Immigrant Neighborhood: Milwaukee's 14th War," *Journal of Urban History*, 2, no. 4 (August 1976): 435–458; Olivier Zunz, *The Changing Face of Inequality: Urbanization, Industrial Development, and Immigrants in Detroit, 1880–1920* (Chicago: University of Chicago Press, 1982) pp. 129–161.

56. Rose, "The All-Black Town"; Rose, *Black Suburbanization*. In northwest St. Louis, for example, the black suburb of Kinloch sits under a glide path of the St. Louis International Airport, and although the airport has anchored a growing "edge city," the Airport Authority has purchased and demolished a substantial proportion of the community. For efforts to eliminate the black Hamilton Park subdivision in Dallas, see William H. Wilson, *Hamilton Park: A Planned Black Community in Dallas* (Baltimore: Johns Hopkins University Press, 1997), pp. 162–163.

57. Between 1960 and 1980, the proportion of black women employed in domestic service in the United States declined from 35 percent to 7 percent. In domestic service suburbs like Evanston, Illinois, and Pasadena, California, 63

percent and 51 percent of women worked outside the home in 1970, but domestic service employment had dropped substantially since World War II. In both communities, black clerical workers outnumbered domestic servants. In Evanston, 31 percent of black women worked in clerical fields versus 20 percent in private household service. In Pasadena, 24 percent worked in clerical fields compared to 19 percent in domestic service, and another 25 percent in unspecified service occupations. Kenneth Kusmer, "African Americans in the City since World War Two: From the Industrial to the Post-Industrial Era," *Journal of Urban History* 21, no. 4 (May 1995): 485; U.S. Bureau of the Census, *Census of Population and Housing: 1970, Census Tracts* (Washington, D.C.: U.S. Government Printing Office, 1972).

58. In Evanston, Illinois, in 1950, for example, 21 percent of black men worked as factory operatives, and another 32 percent worked as laborers, craftsmen, or foremen, who may or may not have worked in industrial settings. In Pasadena, California, 14 percent worked as operatives, and 42 percent worked in these other fields. By 1970, the number of blue-collar workers (except service workers) remained about the same in Evanston and Pasadena, but the number of men employed in white–collar fields (professionals, managers, sales workers, and clerical workers) increased to one quarter, up from about 15 percent in 1950, and service workers fell by 6–10 percent points. Census of Population: 1950, volume III; Census of Population and Housing: 1970.

59. In St. Louis County, Missouri, and Westchester and Nassau counties in New York, for instance, new "edge city" development attracted corporate headquarters as well as high-tech manufacturing to areas where thousands of African Americans had lived since World War I. For job growth in these areas see Jon C. Teaford, *Post-Suburbia: Government and Politics in the Edge Cities* (Baltimore: Johns Hopkins University Press, 1996), pp. 87–90, 162–164.

# Work and Federal Policy

CHAPTER 6

# African Americans in the U.S. Economy
## Federal Policy and the Transformation of Work, 1915–1945

### LIESL MILLER ORENIC AND JOE W. TROTTER

## INTRODUCTION[1]

African American labor history is now a thriving field of scholarly inquiry within U. S. and African American history. Research on African American workers has not only expanded over the past twenty-five years, but also incorporated a variety of new temporal, topical, theoretical, and methodological concerns. Our understanding of urban black workers, for example, has moved well beyond the troublesome relationship between blacks and organized white labor to a fuller treatment of African American work, culture, politics, and community.[2] Yet despite the recent proliferation of scholarship, such studies give inadequate attention to the ways that federal labor policies shaped and were in turn influenced by the responses of black workers and their communities during the interworld war years.

Under the impact of the depression and the two world wars, the relationship between black workers and the state underwent significant, even fundamental, change. During World War I, the federal government instituted the Division of Negro Economics within the Department of Labor. As wartime measures, lawmakers also brought key industries like the railroads, coal mines, and commercial ships under tighter control. Although the government relinquished much of its authority during the period of demobilization in the early postwar years, wartime initiatives established a framework for the gradual expansion of the federal role during the 1920s. Changes unleashed during World War I and the 1920s culminated in the growing centrality of the state under the impact of the depression, New Deal, and World War II.[3] Such changes, including increasing recognition of organized labor and the deleterious impact of technological changes and unemployment on workers' lives, also had a profound influence on African American workers.

African Americans were not only recipients of such social transformations, but also participants in shaping the course of federal policy. From the onset of World War I through the end of World War II, black workers fought to transform the federal government from an opponent to an ally in the protection of their own interests. Certainly, these issues demand much more attention. Thus we here offer an initial effort to assess the interplay of race, class, and federal labor policies during the two world wars and the Great Depression. More specifically, we analyze the treatment of federal labor policies in existing scholarship, highlight the experiences of black railroad workers as a case study, and conclude with a call for better and more systematic treatment of federal labor policies in subsequent research on urban black workers and their communities.

## BLACK WORKERS AND FEDERAL LABOR POLICY: SHIFTING HISTORICAL PERSPECTIVES

Scholarship on black workers and the role of federal labor policy has unfolded within the larger context of the old and new African American urban and labor history. The old African American labor history emerged during the early 20th century and persisted through the mid-1960s. Early studies responded to the racial inequities unleashed by the rise of Jim Crow in the South, and, in its de facto form in the North as well. They aimed to counteract the racist attitudes and behavior of white employers, workers, and the popular and academic press as well as the state. As such, they analyzed federal labor policy as both a lever and impediment to the removal of racial barriers in the labor market. In other words, as Francille Rusan Wilson makes clear in her ground-breaking collective biography of the first generation of black labor historians, "The segregated scholars were self-conscious, self-selected, and sometimes contentious colleagues committed to using empirical research to address labor and economic inequalities." Similarly, as the editor of this volume, Henry Louis Taylor, Jr., puts it, "These were not just 'detached' scholars." They were activists, "trying to influence the direction of public policy by shedding light on a critical issue."[4]

In 1927, labor historian Charles Wesley helped to initiate discussion of race and federal policy in his *Negro Labor in the United States,*

*1850–1925.* Writing amidst the rising migration of blacks into the nation's cities, Wesley noted the impact of federal policy in three broad areas: (1) mobilization for World War I, which precipitated labor shortages and encouraged the use of black labor; (2) creation of the short-lived Division of Negro Economics in the Department of Labor, which coordinated federal efforts to recruit black labor for defense industries; (3) and the passage of federal immigration restriction legislation, which sustained the labor shortage and the level of black labor recruitment through the 1920s. Wesley also acknowledged the impact of federal policy on specific industries, particularly the shipbuilding industry. During the war years, when the U.S. Shipping Board took charge of the industry, he noted that the number of black workers in the industry increased dramatically, but declined just as dramatically in the postwar years when federal control ended. Although he did not systematically analyze the impact of federal policy on specific industries, Wesley suggested that the experience of the Shipping Board with black labor "was very satisfactory."[5]

Finally, and perhaps more important than any single assessment of federal labor policy, Wesley treated the race-specific reports of the U.S. Department of Labor as a source of information for generating favorable attitudes toward the use of black workers. Such surveys emphasized the success of black labor in new industries. In the Detroit area, he noted, "A survey [of northern industries] by the Department of Labor in 1923, shows that 273 firms who reported to the Department were employing 60,427 Negroes, of whom 45,470 were unskilled and 14,957 were skilled; that is a little less than 25 per cent were skilled workers. In the Worthington Pump and Machine Works, many Negro workers have been employed for years. In the foundry division, in 1925, 50 percent of the machine moulders were Negroes. Some of them had been advanced from the lowest laboring grades. The entire cupola gang was composed of Negroes."[6] Wesley emphasized occupations of black men, but also documented the growing transition of black women to industrial jobs as well.[7]

Under the impact of the early depression years, Sterling Spero and Abram L. Harris reinforced scholarship on race, federal policy, and black workers. According to Spero and Harris, wartime mobilization and immigration restriction legislation enabled urban industries to tap what they called a black rural "industrial reserve," and accelerated the transformation of rural blacks into a new industrial working class.[8] *The Black Worker,* by Spero and Harris, also offers one of the earliest and most detailed assessments of the impact of federal labor policy on specific groups of black workers in the meatpacking, steel, coal, shipping, and railroad industries. In the meatpacking industry, for example, Spero and Harris advances three major propositions on the role of federal labor policy in the experiences of black workers: (1) that federal arbitration in the meatpacking industry, 1917 through September 1921, reinforced efforts to recruit black members into the meatpacking unions; (2) that the end of federal arbitration in September 1921 undermined the previous gains of black and white meatpackers; (3) and that the removal of state arbitration opened the way for the use of huge numbers of blacks as strikebreakers (in the strike of December 1921) and helped to embitter class and race relations in the city. According to Spero and Harris, "This injection of the race issue [use of black strikebreakers] intensified and embittered the industrial struggle. One Negro was murdered, and two thousand police were sent to the scene of the strike, turning 'Packingtown' into an armed camp . . . The strike lasted nearly two months. It ended on January 31, 1922, in the complete defeat of the workers. The unions were driven from the yards and have never since been able to regain a footing."[9]

*The Black Worker* offered even greater insight into the role of federal policy in shaping the labor experience of black railroad men. The four major railroad brotherhoods—engineers, conductors, firemen, and trainmen—and their lesser counterparts excluded blacks from membership and established discriminatory wage scales and work practices in contracts with owners. Such practices continued unabated until World War I, when the U.S. government took control of the roads. Under the leadership of Robert L. Mays, head of the black Railway Men's International Benevolent and Industrial Association, black workers urged the federal Railroad Administration to eliminate the racial wage differential on the railroads. On May 25, 1918, Director General McAdoo issued general order number 27, which provided that from June 1, 1918, forward, "colored men employed as firemen, trainmen, and switchmen shall be paid the same rates as are paid white men in the same capacities." McAdoo's report to the president emphasized that such an act was a matter of "simple justice."[10]

Spero and Harris concluded that the new federal policy helped to stabilize black labor in the railway industry and exploded certain stereotypes about the black worker as "unsteady." Moreover, the new federal measures proved wrong the predictions of the white brotherhoods: "that if the pay of the two races were equalized the Negro would disappear from the transportation services." On the contrary, Spero and Harris emphasized, labor was scarce and the roads were eager to employ "steady and experienced employees no matter what their color."[11] Closely intertwined with their discussion of black railroad laborers and craftsmen, Spero and Harris also analyzed the experiences of black porters under the impact of federal legislation and administrative policies. We will discuss federal policy and black railroad workers in greater detail below.

In their book *Black Workers and the New Unions* (1939), Horace R. Cayton and George S. Mitchell extended scholarship on black workers and federal policy into the New Deal era. Focusing on patterns of labor and race relations in steel, meatpacking, and railroad craft shops during the Great Depression, Cayton and Mitchell criticized New Deal labor legislation for its failure to protect the rights of African American workers in particular and American workers in general. Despite passage of Section 7a of the National Industrial Recovery Act, which legitimized collective bargaining for American workers, they argued that the federal government allowed steel companies to draft the "steel code" single-handedly. The steel code established twenty-one districts with differential rates of pay and placed African American workers, particularly in the South, at an extreme disadvantage. "The steel differential in northern communities varied from 35¢ an hour in the Eastern, Kansas City, and Los Angeles districts to 40¢ in the Youngstown-Pittsburgh, Chicago, and Detroit-Toledo districts. The North/South differential was much greater; the lowest wage in the North was 35¢ an hour while in the South it was only 25¢. The highest wage in the North was 40¢ an hour while the highest in the South was only 27¢."[12] Although the discriminatory provisions of the codes did not use the language of race, Cayton and Mitchell argued that African Americans were clearly the principle targets. The category of exempted employees, that is, those removed from minimum wage standards, were disproportionately black:

> The provision in the Cotton Textile Code exempting cleaners and outside workers from minimum rates affects a group which in the South is overwhelmingly colored. The Petroleum Code exempts a certain proportion of its workers from the minimum wage. The effect of the provision is to establish a differential against Negro labor. The section provides that in North Carolina, South Carolina, Georgia, Florida, Alabama, Mississippi, Arkansas, Louisiana, Oklahoma, and Texas for refinery and pipeline work, and in Virginia, Kentucky, and Tennessee in addition for market operations "not more than ten percent, constituting common labor only, of the total number of employees in any plant or operation may be paid at not less than 80 per cent of this minimum rate."[13]

While wage differentials had deep roots in past practices, Cayton and Mitchell maintained that the NRA provided formal recognition and federal sanction for a racially divided and unequal work force.[14] The codes not only discriminated against blacks in wages but also undermined their right to collective bargaining. The National Recovery Administration employed approximately 1,000 people, but not a single black above the rank of messenger. Still, by recognizing the right of workers to bargain on their own behalf, the industry codes accepted Section 7a and helped to unleash a new and vigorous union-organizing campaign among workers. Although the impact of New Deal labor legislation would vary from industry to industry and from region to region, African Americans played a key role in the movement that revitalized the AFL and brought the new Congress of Industrial Organizations (CIO) to the fore in the North and South. As Cayton and Mitchell put it, "Negroes were a very important element throughout the entire procedure and were often in a position to determine by their participation whether the company or an outside organization would represent the workers of a plant."[15]

Swedish economist Gunnar Myrdal's famous study, *An American Dilemma* (1944), offered perhaps the most incisive critique of federal labor policies and their impact on African Americans during the depression and early World War II. Myrdal believed that African Americans faced a cruel dilemma as the government turned toward social legislation to improve the conditions of workers. He stressed, for example, how the Fair Labor Standards Act (1938), also known as the Wages and Hours Law, provided for a minimum wage of 25 cents an hour in 1938, 30 cents in 1941, and 40 cents in 1945; and time-and-a-half the usual rate for work over forty hours a week.[16] Myrdal also emphasized the Wages and Hours Law covered only persons employed in interstate commerce or production of goods for interstate commerce and excluded agricultural and domestic workers from its provisions. Nonetheless, because whites, particularly southern whites, stereotyped the lowest-paying, heavy-lifting, hot, and dirty jobs as "Negro jobs," Myrdal suggested that African Americans would lose increasing ground as labor reforms took hold and made such work less demeaning. As he put it:

> The dilemma, as viewed from the Negro angle, is this: on the one hand, Negroes constitute a disproportionately large number of the workers in the nation who work under imperfect safety rules, in unclean and unhealthy shops, for long hours, and for sweatshop wages; on the other hand, it has largely been the availability of such jobs which has given

Negroes any employment at all. As exploitative working conditions are gradually being abolished, this, of course, must benefit Negro workers most, as they have been exploited most—but only if they are allowed to keep their employment. But it has mainly been their willingness to accept low standards which has been their protection. When government steps in to regulate labor conditions and to enforce minimum standards, it takes away nearly all that is left of the old labor monopoly in the "Negro jobs."[17]

Unlike most of the early studies, Myrdal also analyzed the interrelationship between a variety of social welfare and labor policies. Closely related to explicit legislation and policies effecting wages and hours, he assessed work relief, direct relief, categorical assistance, old age and survivors benefits, unemployment compensation, and public housing. He also analyzed the role of the United States Employment Service (USES) and the emergence of the federal Fair Employment Practices Committee (FEPC) in 1941. Although its powers were quite limited, Myrdal believed that the president's new fair employment committee represented the most positive break in the tradition of federal inattention to the needs of black workers. For its part, the USES was well situated to play a key role in expanding and diversifying the employment of blacks, but it failed to play such a role until the onset of World War II. Even after the agency was brought under full federal control in 1942, only the vigorous activities of the FEPC helped to curb its discriminatory activities.[18]

In the early postwar years, economist and public policy analyst Robert Weaver offered a similarly detailed assessment of federal policy and black workers. Although he argued that such programs as the PWA, NRA, and Fair Labor Standards Act "initiated a trend toward weakening the wage differential," he concluded that such developments "offered little encouragement" to African Americans before World War II. Only during World War II, under the growing impact of war emergency and the demands of African Americans themselves would the federal government defend African American rights to equal employment. According to Weaver, labor, management, and government resisted the full use of black labor because "it involved modifications of the occupational color-caste system."[19]

Conversely, African Americans were "convinced that the problem had to be met" and "viewed with alarm the long-run economic implications of tying the Negro to restricted occupational and industrial patterns."[20] Hence, for Weaver, the key turning point in federal labor policy was the March on Washington Movement, which resulted in FDR's Executive Order 8802 and the establishment of the Fair Employment Practices Committee. Although the FEPC would soon become the primary mechanism for improving the position of black workers, Weaver shows how the FEPC built upon previous federal efforts to address racial discrimination. The Minorities Groups and Negro Training and Employment Branches of the War Manpower Commission and WPA preceded the FEPC and for a short period facilitated its efforts. Weaver also demonstrates how the FEPC helped to gradually revamp the policies of the United States Employment Service (USES). Like Myrdal, he noted that until the advent of the FEPC, the USES had routinely accepted applications from employers based upon racial preferences.[21]

Early 20th century studies of black workers and federal policy set the stage for postwar studies on the subject. As suggested from the outset, such studies were by no means uniform in their coverage. Even slight differences in timing produced significant differences in scope, emphasis, and argument. Charles Wesley emphasized key developments of World War I and its early aftermath but offered few details or systematic analysis. Writing just four years later, Spero and Harris offered close analyses of federal policy in the lives of specific groups of African American workers. For their part, Cayton and Mitchell, Myrdal, and Weaver produced their studies during the 1930s and 1940s. They carried the story forward into the depression and World War II. As such, they also addressed the profound changes that accompanied the New Deal and mobilization for another world war. While all in varying degrees pinpointed the impact of the NRA, public works programs, and the Fair Labor Standards Act, Myrdal offered the most comprehensive coverage of these efforts as well as the impact of housing and a variety of direct relief, unemployment, old age, survivors, and other social welfare programs.

The first generation of scholarship was not only marked by diversity of coverage, it was also characterized by adverse but complementary policy recommendations. Although Wesley acknowledged the significance of federal involvement in shaping the transition of African Americans from an agricultural to an urban proletariat, he failed to offer a clearly articulated role for the federal government in his suggestions for improving the status of black workers. Instead he emphasized the role of education, cooperation among workers across racial and sex lines, and the building of black businesses that would employ black workers. Conversely, Spero and Harris emphasized the necessity of the black world changing its outlook on organized labor, building a strong indigenous labor movement, and playing a role in the development of "progressive" governmental labor policies. Still, they placed the burden for social change that cut across racial lines on the vast majority of white workers: "No such alignment could be effected by the will of the outcast minority alone. It must depend upon the will of the controlling majority, and that majority is white."[22]

Cayton and Mitchell suggested the United Hebrew Trades as a model for black labor emancipation. Formed by a group of Jewish intellectuals in 1888, the UHT, Cayton and Mitchell believed, offered a two-pronged approach to organizing black workers: (1) activities designed to improve relations between black and white workers; (2) activities designed to launch "a propaganda agency" to enlist the "aid and sympathy" of both black and white communities.[23] For his part, Myrdal popularized the notion that the problems of African Americans were fundamentally "a problem in the heart" of white Americans. He advanced a broad-based program of social scientific research and education that would enable Americans to see, recognize, and close the gap between their creed of justice and equality and the reality of black labor subordination.[24]

Finally, Robert Weaver advanced the most specific and coherent recommendations for dealing with the question of black employment. First, he advocated an active federal role in planning for "full employment." Specifically, Weaver supported passage of the Murray-Wagner Full Employment Bill, which would give government and private industry joint responsibility for creating full employment. Second, he recommended measures to protect the gains of black war workers, while expanding opportunities for African Americans to enter a wider range of industrial jobs. Third, Weaver called for a close look at the seniority issue, arguing that while simple seniority procedures would protect some black workers, others could benefit from work-sharing rather than seniority procedures. Fourth, he advocated the continuation of the FEPC in the postwar years as "tangible evidence" to blacks that their nation, state, and community "are all prepared to encourage and secure fair employment practices." Such an agency, he believed, would help to prevent the resurgence of prejudiced labor union practices and oversee the continued movement of blacks into new industrial jobs on a nondiscriminatory basis. Weaver's policy recommendations were deeply rooted in his conviction that work was central to the expanding African American struggle for equity. "The Negro is dedicated to fight for the right to work. . . . In the United States, it is work or fight on the color line."[25]

Such studies were not only quite varied in approach, argument, and suggestions for social change but they were also limited as a body. Early 20th century scholars emphasized the impact of labor policies, giving little attention to the possible impact of black attitudes and behavior on shaping such policies. While such studies frequently considered issues from the larger vantage point of the black community, particularly middle-class organizations and leadership, the dynamics of community were the weakest components. Moreover, the way in which black workers and the poor helped to shape the larger institutional and political life of the African American community, much less federal policy, was hardly acknowledged.

Under the influence of the modern civil rights and Black Power movements, a new generation of scholarship on African American urban and working-class history emerged. The new studies built upon key insights of the earlier studies and deepened our understanding of federal labor policies at work, at home, and in the larger community. This broader perspective on federal policy, race, and the black urban worker is embedded in three overlapping bodies of scholarship: what I have described elsewhere as the ghettoization, proletarianization, and recent culture, gender, and class studies.[26] Studies of the rise of the African American urban ghetto emphasize the role of World War I, federal manpower needs, and immigration restriction legislation during the 1920s, while the new proletarian studies stress the interrelationship between black workers and elites in work, culture, institutions, and politics of black urban communities during the two world wars and the Great Depression. For its part, the emerging scholarship on African American women, gender, and labor issues offers increasing insights into the precise ways that working-class black men and women both reflected and influenced the role of federal labor policies. In her book on Atlanta, Tera Hunter convincingly demonstrates how black female domestic workers not only took a hand in the growth of the industrial city (from the postbellum years through World War I) but also developed specific strategies for empowering themselves therein.[27] In a ground-breaking essay on Birmingham, Alabama, during the inter–world war years, Robin D. G. Kelley also advances our understanding of the various ways that the black poor refracted federal policy at the local level. According to Kelley, "The poor took pride in their ability to get through difficult times, but they also insisted on receiving some government or private assistance." When one welfare recipient was told that his check was in the mail, he responded:

"I'm going to send somebody to hell to get me something to eat." Officials issued him a check immediately.[28]

Recent scholarship suggests a solid theoretical and methodological foundation for expanding our treatment of federal policy in future scholarship on black urban communities. Such a study would take into account the major processes in the development of black urban communities, migration, economic discrimination, residential segregation, and especially the dynamic cultural, political, and institutional activities of black workers themselves. In a pioneering essay on black workers and federal labor policy during World War I, historian Earl Lewis and geographer David Organ offer an insightful and detailed look at such policies within a black community framework. Financed by the U.S. Housing Corporation, the all-black town of Truxton, Virginia, represented federal efforts to secure black labor for its military installations, including a naval base, shipyard, and munitions depot, in the Norfolk-Portsmouth area. As Lewis and Organ make clear, however, the creation of Truxton was a complicated process with deep roots in African American history and patterns of inter- and intraracial and class relations. According to Lewis and Organ, Truxton was not merely the creation of the federal officials and an ambitious black middle class, but the work of black workers as well. As they put it, "Black workers who joined in partnership with the government to promote Truxton's completion had both economic and political reasons for participating, ones framed by contemporary aspirations and a critical understanding of their place in the local political economy."[29] The railroad industry reveals additional possibilities for expanding our treatment of federal labor policies and black urban workers.

## BLACK AND WHITE WORKERS, THE RAILROAD INDUSTRY, AND FEDERAL LABOR POLICY BEFORE WORLD WAR I

The interplay of race, class, and federal policy were not new to the railroad industry on the eve of World War I. From the outset of industrialization, federal policy influenced the development of the railroad industry, including its accumulation of capital, the ethnic and racial composition of its work force, and the nature of labor-management relations. The enormous amount of capital necessary for the launching of any rail line brought federal and local governments into the picture from the very beginning. Charters placed everything from construction to prospective services of the railroad companies under regulation. Companies first sold stocks and bonds in both the United States and Europe to private investors. Federal, state, and local legislative bodies invested as well, through direct purchase, tax relief, and land grant schemes. By the early 1870s, state and federal governments had invested about $350 million in the construction of railroad and canal systems, along with millions of acres in land grants.[30]

Struggles among politicians, shippers, farmers, local governments, workers, railroad owners, and the federal government appear throughout the 19th century.[31] As companies lay thousands of miles of track, utilized for both passengers and freight, railroads and government struggled with definitions of public utility and private commerce. Railroad industrialists and the federal government set the stage for other industries on issues of pricing, market share, safety, and labor-management relations. Although the federal government assumed a dual role of investor and regulator, its regulatory function, particularly vis-à-vis worker rights, remained weak well into the 20th century.[32] In 1877, for example, when rail workers responded to wage cuts by shutting down lines and destroying rail yard property, both federal and state governments sent in troops with orders to disperse groups of strikers and protect railroad property. This action on the part of both local and federal governments not only reflected the ties between the railroads and the state but also set the pattern of government intervention in labor disputes for the next several decades. To be sure, while the creation of the Interstate Commerce Commission in 1887 would increase the role of the state in regulating freight rates, such regulations buttressed the interests of industrialists, who now used the federal government to set standards that favored big railroad companies.[33] As the historian Gabriel Kolko put it: "If for some reason the power of various key business interests was endangered, even for causes of their own making, the state was to intervene to preserve the dominant position."[34]

Only slowly did the federal government respond to the interests of workers. Under increasing pressure from organized labor during the 1890s, Congress passed new safety legislation over the opposition of the railroad owners. The new legislation improved working conditions on the rails and slowly acknowledged the interests of workers as well as industrialists. Unfortunately, as we will see, by transforming previously hazardous jobs into relatively safe positions, the institution of new safety measures would undercut the position of black railroad workers, who labored disproportionately in the hazardous jobs.[35]

From the antebellum years through the early 20th century, southern blacks represented an important component of the railroad labor force. Before the Civil War, southern railroad companies became one of the largest employers of slaves in the industrial sector. These companies used slaves to lay track, work on the trains, and serve as maintenance-of-way workers. In the wake of the Civil War and Reconstruction, tens of thousands of rural blacks left fieldwork for railroad jobs farther west. Although white workers and employers largely excluded blacks from the highest-skilled jobs of engineers, switchmen, and conductors, African Americans made up the majority of workers in the yards and on the trains as mechanic's helpers, locomotive firemen, and brakemen.[36]

As white workers organized to improve their position in the industry during the late 19th century, they increasingly undermined the position of black workers. In 1893, as alluded to above, Congress passed the Safety Appliance Act over the opposition of the railroad companies. The new law required all railroads to install power-driven brakes and automatic couplers by 1898. At the same time, mechanization such as the adoption of the automatic stoker, which transformed the task of firemen into cleaner and less labor-intensive work, increased pressure on jobs formerly occupied principally by blacks.[37] As the new regulations and technology took effect, some railroading jobs such as fireman and locomotive engineer became far less perilous and thus more desirable. White railroad workers now coveted these positions and soon launched concerted campaigns to remove blacks from jobs as firemen and locomotive engineers. Spearheading this effort were the "Big Four" railroad brotherhoods: the Brotherhood of Locomotive Engineers, the Order of Railway Conductors, the Brotherhood of Locomotive Firemen, and the Brotherhood of Railroad Brakemen.

For over two generations, these powerful white unions waged a struggle to remove blacks from the rails and/or relegate them to the least desirable positions. From their inception in the 1860s through the 1880s, these unions inserted "white clauses" into their constitutions and excluded African American railroad workers.[38] While some northern railroad men expressed interest in organizing black and white workers together, few blacks found work on northern railroads before the early 20th century.[39] Moreover, the white brotherhoods exhibited little interest in radical injunctions about the potential of black workers as brothers. In response to a letter stating that the only way to secure higher wages was to let blacks into the union, *The Locomotive Firemen's Magazine* replied:

Now, my brother, I think if you would come South and get a glimpse of our typical Southern "coon" or "burr-head" and get one good sniff of the aroma he always carries with him, both winter and summer, but more especially when he is out on an excursion train, cooped up in a passenger coach when the thermometer registers 104 in the shade, you would be in favor of sending him back to Africa, his original home, and never entertain such a thought of trying to organize him.[40]

In the cases of all four railroad brotherhoods, the southern membership most intensely fueled the agenda for the elimination of black workers. The brotherhoods used their collective bargaining to negotiate contracts that included restrictions on the hiring of African Americans on the railroads. Most contracts established wage differentials as well as an agreed upon percentage of African Americans in certain job categories. Under the impact of World War I and its aftermath, African American railroad workers would continue to face highly exploitive and unequal conditions in the industry. Despite the emergence of federal control of the railroads during the war years, the white brotherhoods intensified their efforts to bar African Americans from the higher-skilled and better-paying jobs on the rails. The passage of the Railway Labor Act of 1926 also validated the Big Four and thus their demands.[41] Railroads had to participate in collective bargaining with those organizations representing employees in certain districts. Because the Big Four represented white employees throughout the railroad industry, they negotiated the contracts for all employees and furthered their own race-exclusion agenda. Agreements including racially based hiring practices remained in force until 1941, when the Supreme Court decided the Railway Labor Act inferred a duty of fair representation for black as well as white workers.[42] By then, white workers had increased their hold on the most desirable jobs in the North and South and increasingly relegated blacks to the job of porter.

As the white railroad brotherhoods increased their influence and undercut the position of black workers, African American railroad workers responded by organizing their own unions. They formed the Colored Locomotive Firemen's Association in 1902 and the Railway Men's (International) Benevolent Industrial Association in 1915. The latter soon claimed 15,000 members in 187 locals. Other African American railroad labor organizations such as the Colored Trainmen of America, the Interstate Order of Colored Locomotive Firemen, and the Southern Association of Colored Railway Train-men and Firemen were also formed in the first quarter of the 20th century. Founded in 1912, the Association of

Colored Railway Trainmen and Locomotive Firemen reached a peak membership of 3,500 in 1926. It also gained company recognition, though its contracts systematically placed the earnings of black workers below those of their white counterparts.[43] The association held an agreement with the Virginian Railway for black "car riders" for $6 a day, while on a nearby railroad white brakemen performing the same duties were paid $7.82 a day. Another agreement covering black brakemen and firemen on the Louisiana & Arkansas Railway stipulated weekly wages for these men that were two to three dollars less than those received by white workers doing similar tasks.[44] Although black labor organizations experienced limited success in their efforts to bargain with employers, their unionizing activities suggest how the emergence of the Brotherhood of Sleeping Car Porters and Maids during the mid-1920s was not an entirely new departure in the unionization of black railroad workers.[45]

The emergence of the Brotherhood of Sleeping Car Porters and Maids represented an important shift from a period in which black railroad workers occupied a variety of jobs on the rails to a narrowing of opportunities to the role of porter on cars with and without passengers. The responsibilities of both groups of porters included attending to passengers' needs on the journey as well as helping with baggage and keeping the cars properly cleaned, heated, and ventilated. Before World War I, their duties included those of the headend brakemen, a job which could include turning the brakes on the rail cars nearest the locomotive, clearing snow from the tracks, opening and closing switches, and aiding the fireman.[46] Although jobs as porters with the Pullman Sleeping Car Company required excessively long hours, low wages, and dependence on tips, they nonetheless represented one of the best jobs open to African American men during the era of Jim Crow.[47] Under the leadership of A. Philip Randolph, black porters formed the Brotherhood of Sleeping Car Porters and Maids in 1925 and pushed for recognition by organized white labor as well as the Pullman Company. Only during the mid-1930s, however, with the rise of the New Deal and the emergence of the new mass production unions did black porters gain recognition from white workers and employers.[48]

Historians have given much attention to the activities of the Brotherhood of Sleeping Car Porters and Maids during the 1920s and 1930s. We also have substantial insights into the ways that federal policies militated against the position of black workers. Less apparent, however, are the ways that black workers used federal labor policy as a leverage for advancing their own interests before the onset of the Depression and World

War II. Focusing on the activities of the U.S. Railroad Administration during World War I and its aftermath, the next section not only examines the impact of federal policy on black workers but also illuminates the efforts of African Americans to transform such policies into a vehicle for the improvement of their own position in the railroad industry.

## THE RAILROAD ADMINISTRATION AND AFRICAN AMERICAN WORKERS[49]

In April and May of 1917, the United States government placed the railroad industry under federal control. It divided the country into seven major regions, appointed a "railroad man" head of each region, and suspended antitrust and antipooling laws for the duration of the war. Each railroad was also assigned a federal officer, usually a railroad man as well, to work with its executives. Using selections from the correspondence of the United States Railroad Administration from 1918 to 1935, it is possible to understand some aspects of the relationship between the federal government and black railroad workers during the World War I era. The correspondence between the office of the Director General of the Railroad Administration, members of the Railroad Division of Labor, African American workers, and their attorneys show that workers understood the changes made in wage and job classifications under federal control.

Under the leadership of Robert L. Mays, the African American Railway Men's International Benevolent and Industrial Association took advantage of federal control to protest the railroads' unequal pay scales for black and white workers. On May 25, 1918, Director General William McAdoo issued General Order Number 27.[50] The order stated that from June 1, 1918, forward, under federal control of the railroads, "colored men employed as firemen, trainmen, and switchmen shall be paid the same rates as are paid white men in the same capacities."[51] African American railroad workers remained on the rails, although the attempts by white unions to remove them continued with some success, through violence, strikes, and the cooperation of railroad foremen. Before black railroad workers could fully reap the fruits of equal pay for equal work, however, strikes, racial conflict, and the threat of further work stoppages led to the passage of new federal work rules, effective September 1919. The new rules aimed to restrict the occupational mobility of African American workers, a fact not concealed by the Railroad Administration or the railroad brotherhoods. These new rules stated the following:

1. All men entering the services on and after September 1, 1919 to fill positions of brakemen, flagmen, baggagemen, and switchmen will be subjected to and required to pass uniform examinations and comply with regulations as to standard watches and to know how to read and write.

2. Discipline will be applied uniformly, commensurate with the facts of the case, without distinction to color.

3. When train or yard forces are reduced, the men involved will be displaced in order of their seniority, regardless of color. When a vacancy occurs, or new runs are created, the senior man will have preference in choice of run or vacancy, either as flagman, baggageman, brakeman or switchman; except that Negroes are not to be used as conductors, flagmen, baggagemen or yard conductors.

4. Negroes are not to be used as flagmen except that those now in that service may be retained therein with their seniority rights. White men are not to be used as porters, no porter to have any trainman's rights except where he may have established same by three months of continuous freight service.[52]

The new rules regarding job choice, seniority, and race severely limited the occupational choices of black workers. Before federal control many railroads used porters to perform the duties of head-end brakemen at a porter's wage. Under General Order Number 27, the job classification "porter-brakeman" was created to address this cross-utilization. The wage increase from porter to "porter-brakeman" went from $50–$55 a month to $120 plus overtime. This change ended the job's classification as a "black man's job." Besides higher wages, the improvements for African American railroad workers were impressive. Porters who performed brakemen's duties for a period of three months could also join the general yard and train seniority list. In short, the change opened the previously "black" porter job to whites, without opening up "white" jobs to blacks. Moreover, in some cases individual railroad companies redefined the duties of certain jobs, especially those of porters, so that their wages would not be covered under the new federal scale.[53] African American railroad workers did not take such discrimination sitting down. Numerous letters from black workers to the Railroad Administration, coming from the North as well as the South, protested train porters performing the duties of brakeman and the lack of subsequent compensation through the new wage and classification scales. Throughout the collection of correspondence it appears that black workers were usually

confident of their rights under the new rules and the Railroad Administration. Their letters to railroad administrators cited violations of the new
wage scales that granted them higher wages. In most letters, black workers
cited infractions of specific sections of General Order 27 and its various
supplements. On August 19, 1919, Julius Cole wrote from Columbus,
Mississippi, on behalf of his fellow porters:

> We are very formelior with the supplement No. 16 To General Order
> No. 27 Effective January 1st 1919 and we are not yet receiving the pay
> for passenger service as therein stated and we are asking you for your
> personal reply as to why we haven't yet recieved this rate of pay as pro-
> vided in Article 1. on Supplement No. 16 to General order No. 27 we
> have been waiting pationly for some time in hopes that we would here
> something very soon but it seemest the longer we wait the longer it will
> be now we cant get any satisfaction from our supior all he says is that
> he has never been instructed to reclassifie us, and that the presant scale
> of pay that we are now recieveing is all that he is instructed give us.[54]

In his response to Cole, J. A. Franklin, an assistant director of the
Division of Labor of the Railroad Administration, asked for more information so that he might be able to "handle your case to a conclusion."[55]
In a second letter, Cole identified himself as a member of the Colored Association of Railway Employees and explained that the porters had taken
the situation into their own hands. Certain porters would perform only
the duties of a porter because they were not being compensated for performing a brakeman's duties. In retaliation, some managers apparently
barred the porters from making their usual runs, as suggested in Cole's
second letter to the Railroad Administration:

> We the porters of this this the Southern Railway Company in Missis-
> sippi are hereby Apealing to you for your earliest informations as we
> are now being Discriminated and are now being refuese to be carried
> out on the trains in whitch we are assigned to on account of some of the
> old porters has failed and refused to do work on these passengers trains
> as brakeman with out being paid brakeman pay we have had an con-
> frence with our Suprintendent and his instructions was as followers:
>
>                    Buletin No. 128
>                    Columbus Miss. September 27. 1919

ALL CONCERNED

Passenger porters are not required to perform any of the duties of flag-man or brakeman where it can be avoided. it is not intended that these instructions will relieve the porters of flagging. in case of emergency or when the safety of the train requires them to do so.porters are under the direction of there conductors, and will Obey his instructions.

Signed F. E. Patton
Supt.[56]

Records show that H. P. Daugherty, an assistant director of the Division of Labor of the administration responded to Cole's December letter by asking the federal manager of the Southern Railway in Mississippi to look into the matter. This federal manager, R. W. Taylor, in a letter to Daugherty refuted Cole's claim that porters were barred from the trains and went on to say that Cole was held out of service because "he refused to go out on train when called. He also refused to call stations and assist in handling baggage which is a part of a porter's duties."[57] This was not the last of Julius Cole; he responded to a letter from Daugherty concerning his refusal to call stations and stated that he had a witness who said he (the witness) did not "report any such everdence and you (Daugherty) can get a stastement from the Conductor who's name is J.T. Elliot in whitch I was Employed under and I would thank you if you will handle this to an conclusion."[58]

African American railroad workers not only addressed the unfair treatment they received despite General Order 27 and its supplements, but pointed out their patriotism as reason for the government to step in and enforce the new wage scale. On July 29, 1919, Thomas Redd of Louisville, Kentucky, wrote to the director general of the Railroad Administration. He enclosed a copy of a bulletin from the superintendent of the Illinois Central and Yazoo & Mississippi companies. The bulletin stated that all porters would be relieved of the duties of brakeman. In his letter, Redd stated that this bulletin was in "direct violation of Article No. 6 of General Order No. 27, and section No. 3, of Supplement No. 12, to General Order No. 27, and Article No. 1, of Supplement No. 16, to General Order No. 27." Eloquently, Redd went on to explain:

When the U.S. Government took over the Railroads, it immediately ordered an investigation of wages and working conditions of the

employees found on the railroads and it found the Train Porters had
been treated very unfair, and therefore gave instructions to reclassify
these men and pay them as Brakemen, and it further instructed that the
duties of that class of Train Employees formerly known as Train
Porters, should not be curtailed, but the attached Bulletin Order No. 55
of June 30th, 1919 will show you that their duties have been curtailed
on the Kentucky Division of the Illinois Central R.R. by Mr. T. F. Hill,
Superintendent of said Division, and the pay of these men have been
cut from a living wage of $120.00 per month to the pitiful sum of
$63.00 per month, which amount is insufficient to support themselves
and family under the present high cost of living. These men have liber-
ally subscribed for both Liberty and Victory Loan Bonds of the United
States; but under the present conditions, which have been forced upon
us; we will be compelled to cancel our subscriptions for bonds by
reason of having no means with which to complete our payments
thereon.[59]

J. A. Franklin of the Division of Labor responded to Redd's letter
but offered no relief. Franklin pointedly explained that decisions were
left to the "discretion of the operating officers of the road as they are best
able to determine whether these duties should be performed by porters or
trainmen employed as such and I can offer you no relief." Franklin's
reply angered Redd who later wrote to President Wilson as well as to
railroad officials. In this letter dated, October 29, 1919 (which was for-
warded to and received by the Division of Labor on December 18th),
Redd cites sections of General Order 27 and states that he regrets having
to write again; however, "owing to the weakness and inability of your Division of Labor to cope with the situation in hand . . . we can find no
other means of redress."[60] Redd concluded his long letter by appealing to
Hines's and Wilson's sense of fair play and American character:

It has always been the policy of the United States Government to treat
all its citizens and employees fair, just and right irrespective to race,
creed or color, and we believe it is and will be your aim and purpose to
uphold and perpetuate this time honored policy of your Government,
therefore, we shall not go on further to recite grievances real or imagi-
nary, but it is sufficient that our faith in your sense of justice and fair
dealing will award this petition all the consideration to which it is
justly entitled and in the end our request for a proper adjustment
thereof will be both prompt and cordial. Although the period of Gov-

ernment control is now very brief, we shall expect fair treatment while such control does continue. Thanking you in advance for a thorough consideration of this matter and awaiting your reply, I have the honor to remain,

yours very truly.
*(signed)* Thomas Redd
826 S. 12th St.[61]

Redd's letters are perhaps some of the most demanding of those in the collection of correspondence, but they are not the only ones written to federal officials when black railroad workers felt they were being cheated out of wages or job classifications. Following federal control, black workers continued their struggle to gain redress. From June 1919 to March 1935 Charles J. Brown (also known as Johnson Brown) of Montgomery, Alabama, wrote to various departments of the Railroad Administration and to the American Red Cross, Family Service, and the Veterans Administration regarding back wages while the railroads were under government control.[62] According to a letter from Brown to the Railroad Administration dated August 15, 1927, he had been discharged from the Louisville & Nashville Railroad after the roads reverted back to private ownership for "contenting with the government. and frankly tolde so."[63] Judging from an internal memo dated May 11, 1927, federal officials seemed somewhat intimidated by Brown's persistence: "His (Brown's) claim has been fully investigated and declined by the Director General and Comptroller General of the United States. He is writing under a fictitious name annoying everyone he seems to think of. If he is still employed by the L&N under the name of Johnson Brown his present general manager Mr. T. E. Brooks at Louisville, Ky. might be of some assistance in having this matter terminated."[64]

W. W. Holt of Tifton, Georgia, wrote to President Coolidge as well as to officers of the Railroad Administration. Holt reported that his wage complaint had been under investigation since June 1918 without any satisfactory results. He had rejected a settlement voucher issued by the Georgia Southern & Florida Railway Company for $67.70 for labor during federal control, insisting that the attorney who arranged the agreement did not represent him. The $67.70 offered to Holt and other railroad employees equaled 25 percent of the difference between the porter's pay and the brakeman's pay for the time period in question, in this case, from June 1 to August 1, 1919. In March 1924, A. A. McLaughlin, General

Solicitor, Office of the General Director of the Railroad, informed Holt: "Neither the President, nor the Director General has any right or authority to pay you any amount since the running of the statute of limitations (July 15, 1920), and your repudiation of the agreement made by your attorney in your behalf before the time to sue expired."[65]

Despite their failure to gain a just settlement of their claims, the correspondence shows African American railroad workers taking action on their own behalf to ensure the fair application of General Order No. 27. In their letters to the Railroad Administration, blacks often mentioned fellow employees on whose behalf they also wrote. In some cases it may have been the duty of the local representative of the Colored Association of Railway Employees to compose letters for a group of other workers.[66] In the face of such a large government bureaucracy, especially in light of the racial violence of the summer of 1919, it must have appeared a daunting task for a single employee to inquire about his wages under General Order No. 27. Yet most letters emphasized job discrimination rather than racial harassment or intimidation per se.

African American railroad men frequently employed lawyers to articulate their grievances. In at least one case a lawyer filed claims in spite of the contrary wishes of his clients, who felt that such actions would jeopardize their jobs. In a letter dated February 28, 1922, to the General Solicitor of the Railroad Administration, Frank W. Smith, a Birmingham, Alabama attorney wrote:

> My clients did *not* want me to file suits for them, for fear it would, in some way, jeopardize their jobs; but, I hope that such action on my part will not cause them to lose their jobs, and, I cannot see why it should, as their claims are just claims, and such claims have already been paid to such employees on other railroads, and, I presume, would have been paid by this road, through you, had you received in due time, the report requested. I consider such suits friendly ones and will still hope to make friendly settlements of the same through your office, without a trial, if possible. So, please be kind enough to let me hear from you as soon after you receive the report, as possible. [67]

At the end of the letter, Smith thanked A. A. McLaughlin, the general solicitor, for the "kindly interest you have already shown in this matter for these poor negroes."[68]

Some railroad presidents assumed that most black porters, possibly confused by General Order No. 27, hired lawyers because of the lawyers' solicitation. Clearly, African American railroad workers were capable of writing their own complaints to the Railroad Administration as the letters of Julius Cole, Thomas Redd, and others show. In areas where lawyers were available to African American railroad workers, it is likely that the relationship between clients and lawyers was mutually engaged. Yet the relationship between lawyers and workers was not tension-free. As discussed above, W. W. Holt, a railroad worker from Tifton, Georgia, rejected a settlement with the Georgia Southern & Florida Railway Company because he did not consider the agreement between the lawyer and the railroad in his best interests.[69]

Railroad Administration documents also cover the work of African American women in the rail yards and service depots. African American women found relatively well-paid work in the rail yards in the era of the Great Migration. In some instances these women may have replaced black men who had moved into newly opened industrial jobs elsewhere. Work in the rail yards could be an escape from the predominant arena of black female employment: domestic work. In 1918 a woman explained, "All the colored women like this work and want to keep it. We are making more money at this than any work we can get, and we do not have to work as hard as at housework which requires us to be on duty from six o'clock in the morning until nine or ten at night, with might [*sic*] little time off and at very poor wages . . ."[70]

While the hours and wages of railroad work were preferable to domestic service, the Women's Services Section of the U.S. Railroad Administration reported evidence of racial discrimination. In a company owned laundry in Clifton Forge, Virginia, for example, one investigator noted that although their work environment was reasonably comfortable, with quite modern washing machinery, African American laundresses did not rotate duties and several had no opportunity to sit during their work.[71] During the early postwar years, another report described the experiences of thirty black female railcar cleaners in Memphis. According to the report, the foreman believed it best to have these women under the direction of a white forewoman; they were not permitted to congregate together because they "wasted time" that way. The report also noted that black women improved their compensation under federal control, but the foreman believed that such wages were "too much for a negro."[72] Like the laundresses in Clifton Forge, these women had previously worked ten-hour days, which changed to eight hours under federal control. In 1918, these women earned 15 cents an hour, under General Order No. 27, Addendum to Supplement No. 4, they earned 45 cents an hour.

Unfortunately, while black men continued to fill occupations outside the job of porter and white women received employment in the expanding clerical positions, black women worked primarily in the domestic service sectors of the industry with few opportunities to work elsewhere.[73]

Despite the improved wage scales ushered in by federal regulation of the railroad industry, African American men and women faced difficulties retaining a foothold. The problems that they faced were exacerbated by cyclical swings in the industrial economy. Under the impact of the depression, their difficulties were especially acute. Violence and intimidation intensified as white workers sought to remove their black counterparts from available jobs.[74] As a result of seniority provisions that the Railroad Administration had instituted, some African Americans, including firemen, were able to hold on to their jobs while white workers with lower seniority were laid off. Consequently, white workers launched a three-year reign of terror against black firemen and trainmen. Between 1931 and 1934, ten African American railroad workers were killed, while others faced harassment and injuries from gunshots.[75] Authorities took few steps to bring the perpetrators to justice. A jury acquitted one white railwayman in six minutes. The defendant then sued for false arrest. When law officers arrested another man for the murders of several black railroad workers, they discovered in his pocket a seniority list of black firemen with checks beside the names of those killed thus far. He was also acquitted.[76] In an article in the *Nation,* the journalist Hiton Butler recounted the murder of black trainmen on the job and concluded that: "Dust had been blown from the shotgun, the whip, and the noose, and Ku Klux Klan practices were being resumed in the certainty that dead men not only tell no tales but create vacancies."[77] Despite such violence during the early depression years, African American railroad workers would soon join other blacks in demanding equity in the workplace as well as in their communities.

## CONCLUSION

The correspondence of the U.S. Railroad Administration, supplemented by the existing secondary literature, suggests a dynamic and shifting relationship between federal labor policies and the experiences of black workers. First and most important, favorable federal labor policies emerged only during moments of crisis—during the two world wars and the depression years—coupled with an acceleration of activism by blacks on their own behalf. Second, despite the emergence of policies designed to combat racial inequality in the labor force, including the Bureau of Negro Economics, the Railroad Administration's General Order Number 27, and the Fair Employment Practices Committee, such efforts proved insufficient and ultimately short-lived. In the early aftermath of World Wars I and II, respectively, the Bureau of Negro Economics (along with federal control of the railroads) and the FEPC collapsed and black workers lost important mechanisms for pressing their demands for economic justice. More important, even under the most favorable wartime conditions, African Americans not only had to mobilize their forces to gain the desired legislation, but they also had to continue their agitation to gain compliance with the new and more equitable labor policies. As such, their lives revealed the ongoing interplay of black worker activism and federal labor policy formation and implementation.

As demonstrated by their demands on the federal government during World War I and the 1920s, African Americans sought to transform federal authorities into allies. Under the impact of the Depression and World War II, this effort continued and produced substantial results. A variety of forces helped to transform the role of federal policy in the lives of black workers: the increasing significance of the black vote in salvaging the New Deal coalition; the emergence of the new Congress of Industrial Organizations and its struggle with the conservative American Federation of Labor; and the growing political mobilization of black workers and their communities in the March on Washington Movement. In 1941, these various forces culminated in the emergence of the President's Fair Employment Practices Committee.

The FEPC banned racial discrimination in government employment, defense industries, and training programs receiving federal assistance. Although the agency would expire in the early postwar years, the government soon reinstituted a ban on racial discrimination by firms holding business contracts with the federal government. As important as federal policy would become as a leverage, however, only the increasing political mobilization of African Americans themselves gradually transformed the federal government into a positive force for economic change. Unfortunately such change remained inadequate and fueled the explosion of racial conflict throughout urban America during the 1960s and early 1970s. Again, black workers and their communities demonstrated that they were not merely targets, victims, or recipients of federal decisions but shapers of such decisions in their own behalf.

## NOTES

1. Author's note: This paper is a revised version of a paper coauthored by Joe W. Trotter and Liesl Miller Orenic, and presented by Liesl Miller Orenic to the Conference on the Politics of Social Welfare and the Rationalization of Everyday Life: The United States and Germany During the Interwar Years, Werner Reimers Foundation, Bad Homburg, Germany, February 8–11, 1995.

2. For a recent critique of this scholarship, see Joe W. Trotter, "African-American Workers: New Directions in U.S. Labor Historiography," *Labor History* 35, no. 2 (Fall 1994): 495–523; and "African Americans in the City: The Industrial Era," *Journal of Urban History* 21, no. 4 (May 1995): 438–457.

3. Melvyn Dubofsky, *The State and Labor in Modern America* (Chapel Hill: University of North Carolina Press, 1994); Alan Dawley, *Struggles for Justice: Social Responsibility and the Liberal State* (Cambridge: The Belknap Press of Harvard University Press, 1991).

4. Francille Rusan Wilson, *The Segregated Scholars: Black Social Scientists and the Development of Black Labor Studies, 1895–1950* (In progress, the University Press of Virginia); correspondence from Henry Louis Taylor to Trotter and Miller Orenic, August 1997.

5. Charles H. Wesley, *Negro Labor in the United States, 1850–1925: A Study in American Economic History* (1927; reprt. New York: Russell and Russell, 1967), pp. 282–307, quote, p. 296.

6. Wesley, *Negro Labor*, p. 298.

7. *Ibid.*, p. 302.

8. Sterling D. Spero and Abram L. Harris, *The Black Worker: The Negro and the Labor Movement* (1931; reprinted New York: Atheneum, 1968), pp. 138–139, 145, 149–181.

9. Spero and Harris, *Black Worker*, p. 281.

10. *Ibid.*, p. 295.

11. *Ibid.*

12. Horace R. Clayton and George S. Mitchell, *Black Workers and the New Unions* (Chapel Hill: University of North Carolina Press, 1939), pp. ix–97.

13. Clayton and Mitchell, *Black Workers*, p. 100.

14. *Ibid.*

15. *Ibid.*, pp. 87, 102.

16. Gunnar Myrdal, *An American Dilemma: The Negro Problem and Modern Democracy, Vol. I* (1944; reprinted New York: Pantheon Books, 1962), pp. 397–398.

17. Myrdal, *American Dilemma*, pp. 397–399.

18. *Ibid.*, pp. 212, 400–419.

19. Robert C. Weaver, *Negro Labor: A National Problem* (New York: Harcourt, Brace and World, 1946), pp. 10–27, quotes, pp. 14–15.

20. *Ibid.*

21. Ibid., pp. 123, 136–137, 142–146. In his study of black workers, *The Negro and Organized Labor* (New York: John Wiley and Sons, 1965), economist Ray Marshall also identified the FEPC as a pivotal example of federal involvement with black workers' lives. Although the FEPC's effectiveness was severely restricted by a lack of authority to enforce its will, according to Marshall, its hearings and orders "added weight to a long stream of moral indictments of racial discrimination" that produced state FEPC laws, court decisions, and government contract committees in the postwar years (p. 123).

22. Wesley, *Negro Labor*, pp. 305–306; Spero and Harris, pp. 468–469.

23. Clayton and Mitchell, *Black Workers*, p. 429.

24. Myrdal, *American Dilemma*, pp. xvii–lxix.

25. Weaver, *Negro Labor*, p. 16, 306, quote p. 316.

26. See Trotter, "African American Workers"; August Meier and Elliott Rudwick, *Black History and the Historical Profession, 1915–1980* (Urbana: University of Illinois Press, 1986); Darlene Clark Hine, ed., *The State of Afro-American History: Past, Present, and Future* (Baton Rouge: Louisiana State University Press, 1986).

27. Tera W. Hunter, *"To 'Joy My Freedom": Women Workers' Odyssey of Hope and Struggle in the Post–Civil War Urban South* (Cambridge: Harvard University Press, 1997).

28. Robin D. G. Kelley, "The Politics of Opposition in a New South City, 1929–1970," in Michael B. Katz, *The "Underclass Debate": Views from History* (Princeton: Princeton University Press, 1993), pp. 293–333. In this volume, Eileen Boris' essay addresses similar gender, class, and race dynamics during the struggle for "fair employment" during World War II. See also the essay by Sigmund Shipp, especially his discussion of Robert Weaver's scholarship and activism, in this volume, Chapter 8.

29. Earl Lewis and David Organ, "Housing, Race and Class: The Government's Creation of Truxton, Virginia, A Model Black War Workers' Town," in Jerry Lembcke and Ray Hutchison, ed., *Research in Urban Sociology: Race, Class, and Urban Change* (Greenwich, Conn.: JAI Press, 1989), pp. 53–78. For World War II and the FEPC, see Merl E. Reed, *Seedtime for the Modern Civil Rights Movement: The President's Committee on Fair Employment Practice, 1941–1946* (Baton Rouge: Louisiana State University Press, 1991).

30. Walter Licht, *Working for the Railroad: The Organization of Work in the Nineteenth Century* (Princeton: Princeton University Press, 1983), p. 9; Carter Goodrich, *Government Promotion of American Canals and Railroads,*

*1800–1890* (Westport, Conn.: Greenwood, 1974), as cited by Gabrial Kolko, *Railroads and Regulation, 1877–1916* (Princeton: Princeton University Press, 1965), p. 15.

31. Walter Licht, *Working for the Railroad*, p. 9.

32. Gabriel Kolko, *Railroads and Regulation,* p. 15.

33. Kolko, *Railroads*, Chapters 4 and 5.

34. Kolko, *Railroads*, p. 12.

35 Licht, *Workers*, p. 188.

36. Howard W. Risher, Jr., *The Negro in the Railroad Industry* (Philadelphia: University of Pennsylvania Press, 1971), pp. 12. According to Risher, in 1875, 35,000 African Americans from rural areas of Georgia and South Carolina left for jobs on the railroads in Louisiana, Arkansas, and Texas. Also see Eric Arnesen, "'Like Banquo's Ghost, It Will Not Down': The Race Question and the American Railroad Brotherhoods, 1880–1920," *American Historical Review* 99, no. 5 (December 1994): 1601–1633.

37. Herbert Hill, *Black Labor and the American Legal System: Race, Work, and the Law* (Madison, Wisc.: University of Wisconsin Press, 1985), p. 343.

38. The Brotherhood of Locomotive Engineers, founded in 1863; the Order of Railway Conductors, founded in 1868; the Brotherhood of Locomotive Firemen, founded in 1873; the Brotherhood of Railway Brakemen, founded in 1883, renamed seven years later the Brotherhood of Railway Trainmen; and the Switchmen's Mutual Association, founded in 1886. Philip S. Foner, *Organized Labor and the Black Worker, 1691–1981* (New York: International Publishers, 1982), p. 103; Hill, *Black Labor*, p. 334.

39. Licht, *Working*, p. 223.

40. *Locomotive Firemen's Magazine* 33 (September 1902): 427–435, as quoted in Foner.

41. The Railway Labor Act of 1926 made collective bargaining legal. Its purpose was to avoid interruptions in railroad service and thus, commerce. The act established a National Mediation Board, which certified unions as collective bargaining agents for all classes of workers. It also established the National Railroad Adjustment Board made up of representatives of unions and companies to settle disputes over wages, working conditions, work rules, and so forth. Because black workers were not allowed in the "Big Four," they were not able to participate in the options available to workers through the act. Hill, *Black Labor*, pp. 341–342.

42. Hill, *Black Labor*, pp. 107–108.

43. Risher, *Railroad Industry*, pp. 43–44.

44. *Ibid.*, p. 44.

45. Hill, *Black Labor*, p. 339; Risher, *Railroad Industry*, p. 44.

46. Risher, *Railroad Industry*, p. 39; Licht, *Working*, p. 90.

47. William H. Harris, *The Harder We Run: Black Workers since the Civil War* (New York: Oxford University Press, 1982), p. 78; William H. Harris, *Keeping the Faith: A. Philip Randolph, Milton P. Webster, and the Brotherhood of Sleeping Car Porters, 1925–37* (Urbana: University of Illinois Press, 1977); Jervis Anderson, *A. Philip Randolph: A Biographical Portrait* (Berkeley: University of California Press, 1972).

48. *Ibid.*

49. All correspondence quoted or paraphrased can be found in the microfilm collection, James R. Grossman, ed., *Black Workers in the Era of the Great Migration, 1916–1929* (Frederick, Md.: University Publications of America, 1985). All documents related to the United States Railroad Administration are included on reels six through eleven (8:00594). All quotes, both those of railroad workers and administrators, are presented in their original spelling, capitalization, and punctuation. Any words or names added by the author to avoid confusion appear in italics. Grammatical corrections to the text have been avoided in all instances.

50. U.S. Railroad Administration, *General Order No. 27 with Its Supplements, Addenda, Amendments and Interpretations to June 30, 1919* (Washington, D.C.: U.S. Government Printing Office, 1919).

51. *Ibid.*, p. 26.

52. Quoted in Spero and Harris, *Black Workers*, p. 300.

53. *Ibid.*, pp. 300–303.

54. Julius Cole to J. A. Franklin, August 19, 1919, in File No. E38-11-A, "Application of Supplement No. 12 to General Order No. 27 to Colored Trainmen, 1919–1920," Records of the Division of Labor, United States Railroad Administration, Record Group 14, National Archives and Federal Records Center, Suitland, Maryland.

55. J. A. Franklin to Julius Cole, August 25, 1919, in File No. E38-11-A, "Application of Supplement No. 12 to General Order No. 27 to Colored Trainmen, 1919–1920."

56. Julius Cole to Walker D. Hines, December 6, 1919, in File No. E38-11-A, "Application of Supplement No. 12 to General Order No. 27 to Colored Trainmen, 1919–1920."

57. R. W. Taylor to H. P. Daugherty, December 18, 1919, in File No. E38-11-A, "Application of Supplement No. 12 to General Order No. 27 to Colored Trainmen, 1919–1920."

58. Julius Cole to H. P. Daugherty, January 18, 1920, in File No. E38-11-A, "Application of Supplement No. 12 to General Order No. 27 to Colored Trainmen, 1919–1920."

59. Thomas Redd to Walker D. Hines, July 29, 1919, in File No. E38-11-A, "Application of Supplement No. 12 to General Order No. 27 to Colored Trainmen, 1919–1920."

60. J. A. Franklin to Thomas Redd, September 6, 1919, in File No. E38-11-A, "Application of Supplement No. 12 to General Order No. 27 to Colored Trainmen, 1919–1920."

61. Thomas Redd to President Woodrow Wilson and Walker D. Hines, October 29, 1919, in File No. E38-11-A, "Application of Supplement No. 12 to General Order No. 27 to Colored Trainmen, 1919–1920."

62. Susie Boland, American Red Cross Family Service, to Director General of the Railroads, August 12, 1931; W. C. Black, Veterans Administration, to Chas. J. Brown, February 13, 1931, in Case No. 115-2, Part 3, "Claims of Negro Porters on the Southern Railway and the Louisville and Nashville Railroad for Increased Wages and Back Pay, 1921–1935," Records of the Division of Law, Files of the General Counsel, 1918–1937, United States Railroad Adminstration, Record Group 14, National Archives and Federal Records Center, Suitland, Maryland.

63. Chas. J. Brown to Solicitor of U.S. RR Administration, August 15, 1927, in Case No. 115-2, Part 3, "Claims of Negro Porters on the Southern Railway and the Louisville and Nashville Railroad for Increased Wages and Back Pay, 1921–1935."

64. W. B. Robinson to S. Andrews, May 11, 1927, in Case No. 115-2, Part 3, "Claims of Negro Porters on the Southern Railway and the Louisville and Nashville Railroad for Increased Wages and Back Pay, 1921–1935."

65. A. A. McLaughlin to W. W. Holt, March 11, 1924, in Case No. 115-2, Part 3, "Claims of Negro Porters on the Southern Railway and the Louisville and Nashville Railroad for Increased Wages and Back Pay, 1921–1935."

66. J. A. Franklin to C. M. banks and B. M. Taylor of Houston, TX, May 28, 1919, in File No. E38-11-A, "Application of Supplement No. 12 to General Order No. 27 to Colored Trainmen, 1919–1920."

67. Frank W. Smith to A. A. McLaughlin, February 28, 1922, Case No. 115-2, Part 3, "Claims of Negro Porters on the Southern Railway and the Louisville and Nashville Railroad for Increased Wages and Back Pay, 1921–1935."

68. *Ibid.*

69. Deposition signed by W. W. Holt, Bibb County, GA, April 25, 1922, Case No. 115-2, Part 3, "Claims of Negro Porters on the Southern Railway and the Louisville and Nashville Railroad for Increased Wages and Back Pay, 1921–1935."

70. A woman quoted in Maurine W. Greenwald, *Woman, War, and Work: The Impact of World War I on Women Workers in the United States* (Westport, Conn.: Greenwood Press, 1980) as cited in Jacqueline Jones, *Labor of Love, Labor of Sorrow*, pp. 166–167.

71. Adjustment Re: Rate of Pay, Report by E. R. Hall, January 27, 1920, File No. 81, "Chesapeake and Ohio Railroad, Richmond, Virginia, Laundry,

Kitchen Work, and Freight Office, 1918," Women's Service Section, United States Railroad Administration, Record Group 14, National Archives and Federal Records Center, Suitland, Maryland.

72. Coach Cleaning Yards—Memphis, written by Agent H. R., December 5, 1919, File No. 144, "Louisville and Nashville Railroad, Memphis, Tennessee, Cleaners, 1919," Women's Service Section, United States Railroad Administration, Record Group 14, National Archives and Federal Records Center, Suitland, Maryland.

73. *Ibid.*

74. Hill, *Black Labor*, p. 338.

75. *Ibid.*, p. 343.

76. Horace R. Clayton and George S. Mitchell, *Black Workers and New Unions* (Chapel Hill: University of North Carolina Press, 1939), p. 444 as cited in Hill, *Black Labor*, p. 345.

77. Hilton Butler, "Murder for the Job," *Nation*, July 12, 1933, p. 44 quoted in Philip S. Foner and Ronald L. Lewis, eds., *The Black Worker: A Documentary History from Colonial Times to the Present*, 8 vols. (Philadelphia: Temple University Press, 1981), vol. 6: *The Era of Post-War Prosperity and the Great Depression, 1920–1936*, pp. 307–308.

CHAPTER 7

# The Battle against Wage Slavery
## The National Urban League,
## the NAACP, and the
## Struggle over New Deal Policies

## HENRY LOUIS TAYLOR, JR., VICKY DULA,
## AND SONG-HO HA

The Great Depression hit African Americans with the force of a sledge-hammer. It exaggerated previous economic liabilities and created newer, potentially more dangerous ones as well. "At no time in the history of the Negro since slavery," concluded T. Arnold Hill of the Urban League, "has his economic and social outlook seemed so discouraging."[1] Histori-cally, the location of blacks in the occupational structure defined their economic, social, and political status in the United States. Their role in the economy was to furnish an endless supply of cheap labor and to serve as members of the nation's reserve army of labor.[2] So when slavery ended, a color-conscious occupational system was established to keep blacks chained to the bottom rungs of the occupational ladder and to make them a perpetual source of cheap labor and members of the labor reserve. Robert C. Weaver, the Harvard educated economist, coined the term and defined it this way:

> In the place of slavery we have substituted a color occupational sys-
> tem. That system perpetuates the concept of the Negro as an inferior
> being and establishes institutions to assure his inferior status. It serves
> to conceal the basic nature of economic problems and covers them
> with color situations. Whenever necessity or national policy dictates
> modifications in color occupational patterns, the resulting changes are
> sure to be opposed violently by those who have a real or assumed
> vested interest in maintaining the color line.[3]

The color occupational system locked almost half of the black work-force in the archaic Southern agricultural system throughout the post-bellum era. In urban centers, North and South, this system forced blacks to work mostly as unskilled casual laborers, domestic servants, waiters, bellhops, janitors, delivery boys, and washerwomen and to labor in heavy and dirty industries, such as coal mining, iron and steel factories, foundries, turpentine, tobacco processing, and fertilizer.[4] Moreover, when blacks did make economic advancements, it was generally an up-ward movement into jobs being vacated by whites; typically, blacks ad-vanced upward into occupations found in the most obsolete and technologically backward sectors of the economy. Consequently, when-ever these sectors modernized and became more productive, black work-ers were displaced. For example, technological advances continually caused the displacement of black workers in the railroad industry, in the longshore industry, and in skilled construction work.[5]

Difficult and agonizing as the color occupational system made life for black workers, perhaps nothing was more distressing than differential wages—a term indicating African Americans often were paid less than whites, even when they performed the same work and had the same qual-ifications. For example, the railroad industry paid black and white fire-men and trainmen different wages, even though they did the same work. Black and white school teachers also had different wage scales, despite the fact that their qualifications were the same. During this time, conven-tional wisdom dictated that black workers had a niche in the labor market only because they accepted wages less than those paid to white workers. Therefore any attempt to equalize wages would cause black workers to be displaced by white workers. For example, in 1910, the Brotherhood of Locomotive Firemen and Enginemen, rather than bargaining for equal pay for all potential union members, centered its activities on completely eliminating blacks from certain job classifications.[6]

The Great Depression magnified the economic problems generated by the color occupational system, including the custom of wage differen-tial and the Jim Crow practices of organized labor. By 1933, unemploy-ment was high among blacks and conditions were deplorable in both the city and the countryside.[7] As bad as conditions were, however, the poli-cies of the New Deal threatened to make them even worse. The New Deal created a perilous situation among African Americans by giving white workers the opportunity to structure new unions along racist lines and by giving southern employers a chance to codify wage slavery.[8]

Fighting de facto racism was hard enough, but when it was codified and made part of the legal landscape, fighting racism became even more complex and difficult.

Against this backdrop, efforts to codify the wage differential represented one of the gravest dangers blacks faced during the New Deal era. "No issue affecting Negroes under the recovery program is of more importance than that of wage policy under the NRA (National Recovery Administration)," lamented Weaver in a 1934 article on racial wage differentials.[9] He was referring to the dozens of NRA codes that permitted southern employers to (1) pay their workers a lower minimum wage than was allowed in the rest of the country, and (2) to pay many blacks a minimum wage that was lower than the minimum wage for whites.[10] If these wage differentials became codified, blacks reasoned, wage slavery would become part of the nation's legal fabric.[11]

The worsening economic situation made economic matters the top issue facing blacks during the 1930s.[12] The severity of the crisis forced the National Urban League and the National Association for the Advancement of Colored People (NAACP) to place much greater emphasis on the economic struggle of black workers.[13] While the Urban League and the NAACP worked on a range of economic issues, including the fight against the racist policies of the American Federation of Labor, their most significant contribution to the struggle came in the fight against the codification of wage slavery. This chapter explores the role played by these two organizations in the struggle to keep racial wage differentials from becoming institutionalized, and seeks to shed light on the role played by black intellectuals who were aligned with these organizations.

## THE DEPRESSION AND NEW DEAL

When Franklin D. Roosevelt took office in March 1933, the United States had already struggled through four years of the Great Depression. The number of unemployed had risen to 13 million, while the national income had fallen by more than 50 percent.[14] Within the first one hundred days of the New Deal, Roosevelt pushed through Congress the National Industrial Recovery Act (NIRA) and established the National Recovery Administration (NRA) to implement it. The NIRA called upon employers in each industry to regulate prices by establishing codes of fair competition and to establish minimum wages and maximum hours of work. In addition, the act granted the right of employees to organize into unions and called for the abolition of child labor, the fair pricing of commodities, safety and health standards, collective bargaining rights, and a variety of other measures.[15]

The Wages and Hours provision formed one cornerstone of the act. Its central goals were to (1) increase the buying power of industrial workers by increasing wages, and (2) to attack unemployment by reducing the number of hours people worked. NRA administrators believed that these measures would lead to higher prices, but were confident that wage increases and the increased buying power of workers would offset inflation. Commenting on the Wages and Hours provision of the National Industrial Recovery Act, President Roosevelt said:

> Nobody is going to starve in this country. It seems to me to be equally plain that no business which depends for existence on paying less than living wages to its workers has any right to continue in this country . . . And by living wages, I mean more than a bare subsistence level—I mean—the wages of decent living.[16]

The NIRA, and particularly the Wages and Hours provision, generated much interest within the black community, especially when the economic situation of blacks was taken into account. In 1930, over 60 percent of black workers were concentrated in domestic and personal service and farming.[17] The workers in these two categories were extremely vulnerable because of their weak attachment to the economy. When hard times came, domestics and farm laborers were the first workers to lose their jobs. Moreover, in virtually every industry black workers had the lowest seniority and were concentrated in the lowest-paying, least desirable jobs. So when the stock market crashed, many of these workers were the first fired.[18]

No segment of the African American community was spared. Writing in December 1933, John P. Davis, the Harvard-trained black lawyer, said the Great Depression forced thousands of farm workers off their land, and the black farm owner was the first to lose his farm by foreclosure. Black entrepreneurs suffered too. Their businesses and banks were almost entirely dependent on black patronage. The decline of black purchasing power decimated profits of black businesses, thus causing many to fail.[19] Lack of employment and the loss of savings caused the number of blacks on relief to soar. By 1935, about 30 percent of the African American population was on welfare. Furthermore, in northern cities one out of every two blacks was unable to earn a living. Conditions in the

South were just as bad, as cities such as Atlanta, Birmingham, Charlotte, and Norfolk saw the majority of employable blacks on welfare.[20]

The pressing economic problems of the 1930s forced the NAACP to adopt a more aggressive stance toward economic issues and join the struggle to shape New Deal labor policies.[21] Likewise, the Urban League departed from its "hands-off" policy toward political and legal issues and became involved in the fight to shape labor policy and to help blacks share equitably in programs for relief and economic recovery.[22] As the depression deepened, these vanguard organizations took up the cause of black workers.

## A NEW ERA BEGINS

On June 16, 1933, enactment of the NIRA ushered in a new era in the history of these two organizations. Both examined the significance of the NIRA to African Americans shortly after its adoption. In a July 1933 editorial, that appeared in *Opportunity*, the Urban League hailed the National Industrial Recovery Act as "the most significant piece of legislation enacted since the Civil War." It went on to say that black workers constituted 11 percent of the labor force, but were disproportionately concentrated in unskilled, low-paying jobs. Consequently, a minimum wage and maximum-hours bill, they argued, "will be of immeasurable benefit to the Negro worker, who above all others has borne the cruel weight of prolonged unemployment and its resulting misery and want."[23]

John P. Davis, in an article published in *The Crisis,* said "there was every reason to hope that this new plan would destroy the inequality between white and black labor."[24] Jesse O. Thomas, the Southern Field Secretary of the National Urban League, said the NRA offered the South an opportunity "to be lifted above the starvation level by paying the minimum wage as provided by the several codes to all employees, regardless of race."[25]

W. E. B. Du Bois, editor of *The Crisis*, however, did not believe the wage provision of the NIRA would benefit most black workers. "The law," he said, "will be administered from the point of view of the great employer." Also Du Bois contended that African Americans would not get much help from organized labor. "Men like Frey and Green (the President of the [American Federation of Labor]) are known for their opposition and at best do-nothing policy, with regard to black labor."[26]

The league responded by soberly stating, "If the fate of the Negro worker is left to chance and to the evanescent influences of rhetorical good-will, there is little likelihood that his historic relationship to industry and to the American labor movement will undergo any important change."[27] Consequently, it became apparent to both the league and NAACP that African Americans would have to fight for inclusion in the NRA.

## THE BATTLE AGAINST WAGE SLAVERY

The question of wage differentials between blacks and whites quickly emerged as a major battleground. If the campaign against lynching was the dominant civil rights issue of the 1930s, then the campaign against wage differentials was the dominant economic issue of that decade. A plentiful supply of cheap black labor, many southerners believed, was central to the economic well-being of the South. Without it southern employers did not think the region would have a competitive business environment.[28] So by paying slave wages to African Americans, southern employers could lower the wages for all workers and, following this line of reasoning, make the South competitive on a national scale.[29] The southern wage system, then, was based on wage differentials between blacks and whites.

As previously mentioned, the NIRA's minimum wage provision, equalizing the wages of black and white workers, threatened the South's dual wage system. John P. Davis, for example, said, "The establishment of uniform minimum wages would normally result in the abolition of a system whereby black workers doing the same work as white workers and working longer hours received less pay than they."[30] Southern employers knew this too. As soon as the National Recovery Administration was established, they launched a movement to establish wage differentials. Some even traveled to Washington for the NRA code hearings, where they supported lowering the minimum wage for blacks.

Southern employers said it was traditional to pay blacks less than whites and argued that higher wages for African Americans would disrupt the South's labor market. Moreover, they believed that if black agricultural workers, who normally earned 30 to 60 cents a day (or from $1.50 to $3.00 a week) would become dissatisfied and unmanageable if black industrial workers were earning as much as $10 to $12 per week.[31] Others argued that employers would replace black workers with white ones if they were forced to adopt a uniform minimum wage. For example, in an editorial on July 31, 1933, the *Thomasville* [Georgia] *Times-Enterprise* said:

It is safe to say that no store in town with delivery or porter service will sign any agreement to pay that boy fourteen dollars per week. If he does, the messenger will be some white boy who will do the work satisfactorily . . . When the Negroes get the idea that they are all going to be paid fourteen dollars per week, they are being poorly led, misinformed. They cannot hope to get that and any organization to attempt to put that over will meet with a form of resistance that will prove very unfortunate to many of them . . . [32]

The *Atlanta Constitution* expressed a similar opinion in an August 24, 1933, editorial: "Undoubtedly, the lack of wage differentials, based on the difference in living costs between whites and Negroes, would result in wide increases in Negro unemployment."[33] Judge Max L. McRae, a member of the highway board in Georgia, stated, "There will be no Negroes pushing wheelbarrows and boys driving trucks getting forty cents an hour when the good white men and white women, working in the fields alongside these roads can hardly earn forty cents a day."[34]

Southern politicians also called for wage differentials based on regional differences in the cost of living. Senator Ellison D. "Cotton Ed" Smith of South Carolina said, "South Carolina's living conditions are so kindly that it takes only 50 cents a day for one to live comfortably and reasonably, and up in the New England states it takes a dollar and a half a day." Likewise, blacks, many southerners reasoned, had a lower standard of living than whites. Consequently, their wages did not have to be as high.[35] After all was said and done, the South had drawn a line in the sand. The NRA could work, they believed, if it was based on a wage differential between blacks and whites. "In the application of the minimum wage scale, there must be an exception to the general rule when it comes to Negroes," they posited.[36]

Not since *Plessy v. Ferguson* had blacks been faced with such a serious legal crisis. Wage differentials were a big problem, but they would become a huge issue if codified and made part of the American legal fabric. Eugene Kinkle Jones, executive secretary of the National Urban League, said that blacks must fight to keep the principle of wage differentials from becoming an "established, accepted, approved, legal reality."[37] If this happened, Jones said, wage differentials might become a permanent way of establishing the wage rate for African Americans.[38] "Employers," he argued, "would not be able to resist the temptation to exploit the Negro worker and through him to exploit the white worker.

We would have a continuation of the lower standard of living among Negroes which would in turn have its effect, as in the past, on the standard of living of white workers, especially those residing in the South . . ."[39] Robert Weaver said that racially based wage differentials would "relegate Negroes to a low wage caste and place the federal stamp of approval upon their being in such a position."[40]

The Urban League and the NAACP took the lead in this fight. Moreover, both organizations knew that some African Americans would lose their jobs in the process. In 1933 most black workers were still living in the South, and in that region everyone predicted the mass displacement of black workers if racial wage differentials were abolished or modified. Yet most black leaders believed the effort to codify wage slavery had to be defeated, no matter what the cost. On September 25, 1933, the Urban League issued the following statement:

> The National Urban League is unalterably opposed to differential wage codes directly or indirectly based upon the color of a worker's skin. Every intelligent argument to defeat their establishment should be employed . . . The Urban League Movement must permit no departure from this point of view within its ranks. It should seek every means to destroy the virus which expresses itself in such undemocratic and unsound economic action. It should be vigilant in reporting instances of discrimination to those national and local groups unwilling to countenance the perpetuation of a racial differential in wages.[41]

"If employers are unwilling to pay Negroes wages equal to those paid whites," said T. Arnold Hill, director of the Department of Industrial Relations for the Urban League, "then let them [blacks] be discharged."[42] The displacement of some black workers, according to the Urban League, was a small price to pay for dismantling the dual wage system. In a letter to Weaver, Walter White of the NAACP said he knew some blacks would lose their jobs if a uniform wage scale was adopted, but added, ". . . their individual and collective interests are not as important as that of those of the race as a whole."[43]

The League and NAACP went forward. They carried on a relentless campaign to keep African Americans informed about the NRA and the Wages and Hours provision. They published updates of its implementation, documented abuses, and turned *Opportunity* and *The Crisis* into forums where New Deal issues were discussed by scholars, professionals, members of Roosevelt's Administration, and leaders of organized labor.

Between 1933 and the passage of the Fair Labor Standards Act in 1938, the pages of *Opportunity* and *The Crisis* were filled with numerous articles about wage differentials. African Americans were exposed to the theories and ideas of scholars and practitioners like Charles Weaver; John P. Davis; Abram Harris, the Howard University economist; Ira De A. Reid, research director for the National Urban League; Joseph H. Willis, director of the Wharton School of Finance, University of Pennsylvania; Gustav Peck, executive director of the Labor Advisory Board; William Green, president of the American Federation of Labor; and others.[44]

## DEVELOPING ALLIES

Gaining the support of organized labor was key to the struggle. The Urban League and NAACP tried to convince the AFL that it was in its best interest to support a uniform wage scale. They further argued that a racial wage differential would destroy the organized labor movement by undermining collective bargaining and by depressing the wages of white workers.[45]

The NAACP protested and used persuasive diplomacy as well. For example, it picketed the 1934 AFL convention held in San Francisco and demanded, among other things, that the union adopt a resolution condemning wage differentials for blacks.[46] On October 31, 1934, William Green wrote to Walter White, informing him that the AFL passed a resolution protesting wage differentials for black workers.[47] During the same month, Green said in *Opportunity*:

> There is an immediate problem in many industries with which the advanced groups may cope—the Southern differential which in so many cases means the determination of the industry to depress Negro wages. Opportunity for Negro wage earners lies not in undercutting wages for white workers but in cooperating for the elimination of such a differential.[48]

The AFL's initial opposition to racial wage differentials was not philanthropic. It believed the underconsumption of workers was a principle cause of the depression. Moreover the AFL maintained that national recovery would occur only by finding jobs for the unemployed and increasing the buying power of workers.[49] However, without a uniform wage scale, it would not be possible to successfully counteract the underconsumption of the working class. The African Americans' fight against wage differentials, AFL surmised, was good for organized labor. So eventually the organization supported it.

With the AFL as an ally, the struggle against racial wage differentials was greatly strengthened. The Urban League and NAACP intensified their efforts to win support from the president, his cabinet, and agency heads. They sent telegrams, reports and other messages to the president. These communiqués spelled out specific problems that New Deal policies caused for black workers. For example, on July 7,1933, the NAACP issued a news release saying, "President Franklin D. Roosevelt was warned this week that the proposed industrial code of the cotton textile industry does not benefit the Negro workers in that industry and, in fact specifically omits benefits from the classes of work which have the most Negro employees . . ." It also warned "the minimum wage provision and the hours of labor arenot guaranteed to 'outside crews and cleaners' in the textile code and that those two classes of workers contain many Negroes." It further urged the president, who had the final say in the adoption of the various codes, "to insist on the inclusion of these classes in the benefits of the National Recovery Act."[50] These efforts proved effective and were helped by the fact that southern businessmen and politicians were not able to put forward convincing arguments in favor of a separate wage scale for black workers.

The next strategy was to attend the NRA Code hearings, especially the prehearing conferences, and lobby for eliminating race-based wage differentials. The code hearings created a window of opportunity for southerners to institute separate wage scales for blacks. The hearings were open meetings in which any group affected by a proposed code could speak. However, major issues were usually resolved at prehearing conferences between sponsoring groups of businessmen and labor union representatives, along with a NRA administrator and his advisers, who acted as referees.

This process of code-making stacked the deck against black workers. Since blacks were not represented at the prehearing conferences, race codes could be introduced without opposition. On this point, A. Howard Myers, Labor Advisory Board Director, told a group of Howard University students that the NRA was "fundamentally an effort to work out our economic problems on a democratic basis," but "such a democratic system usually gave the greatest benefits to those who were best organized." Because southern workers were affiliated with strong unions, he said they "gain little . . ."[51]

To attack this problem, the Urban League established 196 Emergency Advisory Councils around the country to handle complaints and give advice.[52] However, these efforts were inadequate. African Americans needed to have representatives at the preconference meetings and code hearings. Unfortunately, neither the Urban League or the NAACP had offices in Washington, D.C., and serious financial problems kept them from carrying on a concentrated lobbying effort.[53] To fill the void, Walter White, George Edmund Haynes of the Race Relations Department of the Federal Council of Churches, John P. Davis, and Charles Weaver formed the Joint Committee on National Recovery in September 1933.

A central goal of the Joint Committee was to identify codes with racial differentials and get them overruled. Davis and Weaver attended more than one hundred hearings and carried on relentless agitation.[54] Their efforts paid off, as the NRA decided not to lower wage and hour standards for black workers.[55]

A major victory had been won. Wage slavery would not be codified. Yet the struggle was not over. Although the NRA refused to establish wage differentials based on race, it did permit minimum wage differentials under thecodes by industries, regions,and size of the community within a region.[56] This practice enabled southerners to establish regional wage differentials that were racially motivated. However, in 1935, before the League and the NAACP could take additional action, the United States Supreme Court declared the NIRA unconstitutional.[57]

Two years later, in 1937, in *West Coast Hotel Co. v. Parrish*, the U.S. Supreme Court reversed its earlier position and upheld the state minimum wage law.[58] Fourteen days later, the Court upheld the National Labor Relations Act, which expanded the definition of interstate commerce so that Congress could regulate industrial and labor relations. These Supreme Court rulings opened the door for the federal government to enact wage and hour legislation. Less than two months after the Supreme Court decision, President Roosevelt sent a message to Congress requesting legislation to establish a Federal Fair Labor Standards Act. He said, "All but the hopelessly reactionary will agree that to conserve our primary resources of manpower, government must have some control over maximum hours, minimum wages, the evil of child labor, and the exploitation of unorganized labor."[59] Secretary of Labor Frances Perkins enthusiastically supported minimum wage legislation and suggested that an industrial approach, similar to the one used under the NRA, be established.[60] This meant that the proposed law would probably use the same regional differences employed in the earlier legislation.

The Urban League and NAACP decided to attack the idea of regional wage differentials.[61] As long as these differentials existed, they believed, black workers would be threatened. In October 1937, the

NAACP protested the enactment of a Fair Labor Standards Bill that allowed regional wage differentials. It argued that such regional wage differentials were, in reality, *racial* wage differentials.[62]

Voicing the sentiments of the NAACP, John L. Lewis (of the CIO) said the passing of regional wage differentials would freeze the below-subsistence wages, hours, and working conditions of most blacks.[63] In an attempt to block passage of the legislation, the NAACP called on African Americans to fight to keep Congress from passing a bill that codified wage slavery.[64] They inundated senators and representatives with letters voicing the concerns of African Americans.[65] Although Congress appeared sensitive to the cause, the League and NAACP were still losing the fight.[66]

Throughout the battle, Congress and many whites were not convinced that regional wage differentials were synonymous with racial white differentials. Meanwhile, southern whites intensified their campaign. They said differences in the cost of living between the South and North justified establishing regional wage differentials. With this, a simple but powerful point had been made: higher wages were required to live in the North than in the South.

In late October, White asked Weaver to develop a more in-depth analysis of the wage differential question. He said members of Congress needed more information to make a decision.[67] Weaver completed his analysis in less than a week. He told White to use a "cost of commodities" rather than a "cost of living" framework. Weaver said the idea that cost of living was higher in the North than in the South was based on the cost of goods that a family actually consumed. This approach, Weaver argued, was based on family income. A more accurate approach would compare the cost of a specific list of goods in one area with the cost of similar or equivalent goods in another region. Consequently, Weaver's approach was not biased by family income.

Using the cost-of-commodities method, Weaver presented convincing evidence that little difference existed between the cost of living in the North and South.[68] The research of other scholars supported Weaver's findings, as the young economist had reframed the debate.

Sensing victory, the NAACP changed its strategy. It decided to attack the issue of regional wage differentials without reference to race. The cost-of-commodities model had given it a new weapon.[69] Now White tried to win racist employers and politicians to his side. The strategy was to convince Southern newspaper editors that regional wage differentials hurt the South's image by implying it could not compete with northern business and industry.

In a letter to Felix Frankfurter, White said, "In asking for concessions of this character, the South is stultifying itself and admitting that it cannot compete in the skill and other attributes with other sections of the country, and that the asking for or acceptance of differentials will serve to keep the South more or less permanently in the rank of sub-normal producers."[70] Southern newspaper editors picked up on the NAACP's viewpoint.[71]

In June 1938, the Fair Labor Standards Act became law.[72] The bill was adopted without regional wage differentials. In its final version, wage minimums would be set on an industry-by-industry basis, and there would be certain circumstances in which requests could be made to set wage differential based on geography.[73] Still, the idea of geographic wage differentials, in principle, had been defeated.

Federal policy mattered during the industrial era, and successful efforts to shape federal policy required a range of activities that including picketing, demonstrating, coalition-building, lobbying cabinet members and agency heads, behind-the-scenes negotiating, agitating, and scholarly researching and writing. It also required transforming hostile opponents into allies. Finally, success depended on the ability of African Americans to find common ground and work collectively to achieve a common objective.

## NOTES

1. Hill quoted in the *New York Times,* April 5, 1931, cited in Harvard Sitkoff, *A New Deal for Blacks: The Emergence of Civil Rights as a National Issue: The Depression Decade* (New York: Oxford University Press, 1978), p. 35.

2. Robert C. Weaver, *Negro Labor: A National Problem* (New York: Harcourt, Brace and World, 1946), pp. 3–15.

3. *Ibid.*, p. 4. William Harris, *The Harder We Run: Black Workers since the Civil War,* p. 45.

4. Robert Weaver, *Negro Labor,* pp. 3–15.

5. Robert C. Weaver, *Negro Labor,* pp. 97–98, 99, 100, 102–105.

6. Herbert Hill, *Black Labor and the American Legal System: Race, Work, and Law* (Madison: University of Wisconsin Press, 1985), pp. 336–337; *Ibid.*, p.103 and Charles S. Johnson, *The Negro College Graduate* (New York: Negro Universities Press, 1969), pp. 143, 150.

7. Sitkoff, *New Deal,* p. 35.

8. Herbert Hill wrote that "In many industries collective bargaining agreements systematized seniority practices in which job assignment, promotion, furlough, and dismissal were based on race. Furthermore, such discriminatory

systems were routinely enforceable through union contracts. In the South this was done explicitly by designating racial lines of job progression; in the North, though a variety of euphemisms and through the operation of departmental seniority." *Black Labor*, p. 23.

9. Weaver, "A Wage Differential Based on Race," *The Crisis* 41, no. 8 (August 1934): 236. Weaver was working as an adviser to Secretary of Interior Harold Ickes at the time he wrote the article.

10. Weaver, "Wage Differential," p. 236.

11. John P. Davis, "N.R.A. Codifies Wage Slavery," *The Crisis* 41 (October 1934): 298–299, 304, cited in Phillip S. Foner and Ronald L. Lewis, eds., *The Black Worker: A Documentary History from Colonial Times to the Present: Volume VI, The Era of Post-War Prosperity and the Great Depression, 1920–1936* (Philadelphia: Temple University Press, 1981), pp. 110–114.

12. For the life of blacks during the Depression, see Raymond Wolters, *Negroes and the Great Depression: The Problem of Economic Recovery* (Westport, Conn.: Greenwood Publishing Corporation, 1970), pp. 1–30; Sitkoff, Harris, *The Harder We Run*, pp. 95–122; Roger Biles, *Memphis in the Great Depression* (Knoxville: University of Tennessee Press, 1986), pp. 88–107; Cheryl Lynn Greenberg, *"Or Does It Explode?": Black Harlem in the Great Depression* (New York: Oxford University Press, 1991), pp. 42–92; Joe William Trotter, Jr., *River Jordan: African American Urban Life in the Ohio Valley* (Lexington: University Press of Kentucky, 1998), pp. 122–141.

13. For the scholarship on the activities of the NAACP and NUL during the Depression, see Sitkoff, *New Deal*, pp. 244–267; Guichard Parris and Lester Brooks, *Blacks in the City: A History of the National Urban League* (Boston: Little, Brown and Company, 1971), pp. 204–275; Nancy J. Weiss, *The National Urban League* (New York: Oxford University Press, 1974), pp. 237–309; Jesse Thomas Moore, Jr., *A Search for Equality* (University Park: Pennsylvania State University Press, 1981), pp. 63–85.

14. Stanley Vittoz, *New Deal Labor Policy and the American Industrial Economy* (Chapel Hill: University of North Carolina Press, 1987), p. 73.

15. U.S. Department of Labor, *Statutes at Large of the United States, from March 1933 to June 1934, Vol. XLVIII, Part I* (Washington, D.C.: U.S. Government Printing Office, 1934); Rudolph A. Oswald, "Fair Labor Standards," in Joseph P. Goldberg et al., eds., *Federal Policies and Worker Status since the Thirties* (Madison: Industrial Relations Research Association, 1976), pp. 107–134.

16. Editorial, *Opportunity II* (July 1933): 199.

17. U.S. Bureau of the Census, *Fifteenth Census of the United States 1930: Population, The Labor Force: United States Summary* (Washington, D.C.: U.S. Government Printing Office, 1931).

18. Robert C. Weaver, "The New Deal and the Negro," *Opportunity* 13, no. 7 (July 1935): 200–201.

19. John Davis, "What Price National Recovery, " *The Crisis* 40, no. 12 (December 1933): 271.

20. Library of Congress, *NAACP Papers*, Record Group 1, Series C, Letter from Eugene Kinckle Jones to Franklin D. Roosevelt, 4 January 1937, pp. 3–4.

21. Wolters, *Negroes and the Great Depression*, pp. 219–227.

22. Weiss, *National Urban League*, p. 267, pp. 276–280.

23. Editorial, "A Critical Period," *Opportunity*, 11, no.7 (July 1933), p. 199.

24. Davis, "National Recovery," p. 271.

25. Jesse Thomas, "Will the New Deal Be a Square Deal for the Negro?" *Opportunity* 11 (October 1933): 308.

26. W. E. B. Du Bois, "The NIRA and the Negro, " *The Crisis* 40, no. 9 (September 1933): 212.

27. Editorial, *Opportunity* 11, no. 7 (July 1933): 199.

28. Wolters, *Negroes and the Great Depression*, p. 98.

29. Jeremy Atack and Peter Passell, *A New Economic View of American History: From Colonial Times to 1950* (New York: W.W. Norton, 1994), pp. 522–553.

30. Davis, "National Recovery," p. 271.

31. Wolters, *Negroes and the Great Depression*, p. 99.

32. Thomas, "A Square Deal for the Negro?," p. 308.

33. *Ibid.*, 309.

34. Editorial, "The Cats Come Out of the Bag," *The Crisis* 41, no. 10 (October 1934): 300.

35. Wolters, *Negroes and the Great Depression*, pp. 99–100.

36. Thomas, "A Square Deal for the Negro?," p. 308.

37. Eugene Kinckle Jones, "The Negro in Industry and in Urban Life," *Opportunity* 12 (May 1934): 143.

38. *Ibid.*

39. *Ibid.*

40. Weaver, "Differential Based on Race," p. 238.

41. Library of Congress, *National Urban League Papers*, Press Release, "The Urban League opposes wage differentials," Record Group 1, Series C, 25 September 1933.

42. Library of Congress, *National Urban League Papers*, Press release, "T. Arnold Hill Attacks Proposed Wage Differentials For Negroes," Record Group 1, Series C, 2 September 1933.

43. Library of Congress, *NAACP Papers*, Record Group 1, Series C, Letter from Walter White to Robert Weaver, 2 November 1937.

44. For example, John P. Davis in his article, "The Maid-Well Garment Case," *The Crisis* 41, no.12 (December 1934): 356, studies the experiences of blacks in Forrest City, Arkansas, in an attempt to understand the problems of displacement among black workers in the garment industry as a result of the NRA industrial codes. In an instance of analyzing governmental policies, an article was written in *The Crisis* announcing that the NAACP was "attempting to get a congressional committee to investigate the general situation of the Negro under all phases of the New Deal program"; In Ira De A. Reid's article, "Black Wages for Black Men," *Opportunity* 12 (March 1934): 73–76, he presents an analysis of the movement for a differential wage for blacks under the Recovery program.

45. Library of Congress, *NAACP Papers*, Record Group 1, Series C, Letter from White to Green, 6 December 1937.

46. Library of Congress, *NAACP Papers*, News release, "NAACP Pickets AFL in San Francisco Convention," Record Group 1, Series C, 5 October 1934.

47. Library of Congress, *NAACP Papers*, Record Group 1, Series C, Letter from William Green to Walter White, 31 October 1934.

48. Green William, "Negro Wage Earners and Trade Unions," *Opportunity* 12 (October 1934): 299.

49. Library of Congress, *NAACP Papers*, Record Group 1, Series C, Letter from Green to White, 30 October 1934.

50. Library of Congress, *NAACP Papers*, News Release, "Industry Codes Must Include Negro Worker, Roosevelt Told," Record Group 1, Series C, 7 July 1933.

51. Wolters, *Negroes and the Great Depression*, pp. 107–108.

52. T. Arnold Hill, "The EAC and the NRA," *Opportunity* 12 (December 1933): 122; Library of Congress, *National Urban League Papers*, Record Group 1, Series C, Wire from the Urban League to the President and General Johnson, 19 August 1933.

53. Wolters, *Negroes and the Great Depression*, p.110.

54. *Ibid.*, pp. 11, 19.

55. National Archives, *Bureau of Employment Security Papers*, Record Group 183, Box 1390, National Recovery Administration Division of Research and Planning, "Report of Effect of N.R.A. Codes upon Negroes," March 1934, p. 7.

56. Wolters, *Negroes and the Great Depression*, pp.124–135.

57. *Schechter Corp. v. U.S.*, 298 U.S. 495 (1935).

58. United States Reports, *Cases Adjudged in the Supreme Court at October Term, 1936*, Vol. 300, (Washington D.C.: : U.S. Government Printing Office, 1932), Manual 16.157.

59. Oswald, "Fair Labor Standards," pp. 112–113.

60. *Ibid.*, p. 113.

61. Library of Congress, *NAACP Papers*, Record Group 1, Box 256, Series C, Telegram, From Walter White to Robert Weaver, 7 October 1937.

62. Library of Congress, *NAACP Papers*, News release, "New Warning Sounded on Wages-Hours Bill." Record Group 1, Box 256, Series C, 15 October 1937.

63. Library of Congress, *NAACP* Papers, News release, "New Warning Sounded on Wages-Hours Bill," Record Group 1, Box 256, Series C, 15 October 1937.

64. Library of Congress, *NAACP Papers*, Press Release, "Negro Voters Warned to Demand Fair Wages-Hours Bill," Record Group 1, Series C, Box 256, 24 September 1937.

65. Library of Congress, *NAACP Papers*, Record Group 1, Series C, Letter from Walter White to 79 Senators and 357 Congressman, 19 October 1937.

66. Library of Congress, *NAACP Papers*, News release, "51 Congressmen Are Watching Wage Bill," Record Group 1, Series C. , 29 October 1937.

67. Library of Congress, *NAACP Papers*, Record Group 1, Series C, Letter from Walter White to Robert Weaver, 28 October 1937.

68. Library of Congress, *NAACP Papers*, Record Group 1, Series C, Letter from Robert Weaver to Walter White, 4 November 1937. Weaver's "cost of commodities" concept represented a significant breakthrough, forcing the NRA officials to abondon the up to this point widely used but flawed "cost of living concept." It is significant to note that Raymond Wolters mistakenly attributes this finding to Walter White rather than to Robert Weaver. See Wolters, *Negroes and the Great Depression*, p. 100. See also Library of Congress, *NAACP Papers*, Record Group 1, Series C, Report, "Cost of Living as a Basis for Determining Regional Wage Rates," December 1937; Library of Congress, *NAACP Papers*, Record Group 1, Series C, Letter from Walter White to Robert Weaver, 5 November 1937; Library of Congress, *NAACP Papers*, Record Group 1, Series C., Letter from Walter White to Felix Frankfurter, 13 November 1937.

69. Library of Congress, *NAACP Papers*, Record Group 1, Series C, Letter from Walter White to Robert C. Weaver, 4 December 1937.

70. Library of Congress, *NAACP Papers*, Record Group 1, Series C, Letter from Walter White to Felix Frankfurter, 13 November 1937.

71. Library of Congress, *NAACP Papers*, Record Group 1, Series C, Letter from Walter White to Felix Frankfurter, 13 November 1937.

72. Public Laws, 75th Congress, 3d Session, Chapter 676, June 25, 1938.

73. Paul H. Douglas and Joseph Hackman, "The Fair Labor Standards Act of 1938," *Political Science Quarterly* 54 (1939): 40.

# CHAPTER 8

# Building Bricks without Straw
## Robert C. Weaver and Negro Industrial Employment, 1934–1944

### SIGMUND SHIPP

Robert C. Weaver's exemplary public service career was marked by an unrelenting struggle to eliminate the tradition of race prejudice that prevented blacks from attaining social and economic equality. This chapter focuses on how this struggle manifested itself during his early federal career in the 1930s and 1940s, when he devoted a considerable amount of time to getting blacks trained and employed. During this point, blacks were at the bottom of the economic ladder. In fact, two contemporary researchers offer significant insights about the condition of black labor. One was chief census statistician Alba Edwards and the other was Robert Weaver himself. In a 1936 article, "The Negro as a Factor in the Nation's Labor Force," Edwards muses soberly over the plight of black workers as the economy in the 1930s was restructuring from a dependency on manual to machine labor. Edwards contended that the status of black labor did not bode well for the future. According to census data, most blacks had poorly paying jobs or were in occupations (chiefly farming) that were on the decline. If the Negro farm owners and tenants can be considered manual workers, then in 1930, more than 95 out of every 100 (95.4 percent) Negro workers were engaged in manual work; and if the 392,897 Negro sharecroppers can be considered unskilled, then, in 1930, 74.1 percent of Negro workers were in unskilled pursuits (e.g., domestic and personal service)[1]. These trends led Edwards to predict future conditions that have come to symbolize the most troubling aspects of modern inner city-life. In his 1936 article about Negro labor, Edwards prophetically wondered if blacks would be displaced as mechanization progressed because they lacked the training to acquire machine-oriented unskilled work or to compete for advanced-level jobs. If jobs were not found as machines took over, he prophesied that there was "a real danger that in future years there will be large numbers of unemployed Negro workers and that these and their dependents will largely comprise [a permanent] unemployed class."[2]

While ostensibly foreboding about the status of black labor, Edwards comes to an optimistic conclusion about future black employment trends. Between 1910 and 1930, census data revealed a rise in the numbers of black professionals, proprietors, managers, clerical, skilled, and semiskilled workers. Edwards thought that this rise would continue and cause a significant change in the "socio-economic distribution of Negro gainful workers."[3] This was a positive indication that blacks would adapt to a future of increased reliance on machines.[4] Edwards's predictions reflect the work he had completed about the growth of the white-collar employment sector in general.[5] He could be hopeful because black employment was rising in occupations in the white-collar sector, where Edwards had predicted tremendous growth.

As with Edwards, Robert Weaver produced research and analysis that examined black employment trends. Similar to Edwards, Weaver was particularly interested in skilled and whitecollar employment opportunities. However, it was the understanding that blacks had few opportunities except for the lowest positions that was apparent in Weaver's interest in the skilled and white-collar sector. Historically, black labor had remained in menial and low-paying occupations:

> From the Civil War through the 1930's, Negroes increasingly were limited in the kind of work they could seek. Under slavery, Negroes in the South had almost a monopoly of skilled jobs. By the 1930's, Negroes were almost restricted to one of three kinds of occupations: (1) personal service (including entertainment), (2) farming, and (3) unskilled labor.[6]

Weaver points out that conditions always conspired to keep blacks at a marginal level of job and economic attainment despite periods of prosperity such as the one that prevailed following World War I:

> At times, it has seemed that the black worker was gaining ground; more often his relative position appeared to be deteriorating. Only in retrospect have we been able to appraise the real situation. It is, therefore, from the vantage point of the Great Depression that one can eval-

uate the economic gains that were thought to have existed in the Gilded Twenties. Looking back, it becomes clear that, despite the mass migration of colored workers from the South and their entrance into industrial employment during World War I, the black worker was only on the fringe of the American economy.[7]

However, it was his unprecedented 1936 survey that brought to light the fallacy about menial employment among blacks. The survey documented, contrary to widely held opinions, the existence nationally of an available pool of black skilled and white-collar workers.

On November 24, 1937, the Office of the Advisor on Negro Affairs in the Department of the Interior released its report, *The Urban Negro Worker in the United States, 1925–26*, to the public. It was the vision of Robert C. Weaver that led to this ground-breaking research. The report had been based on data gathered from a 1936 national survey—*A Survey of the Training and Employment of White-Collar and Skilled Negro Workers*—that was formulated to create a database about black workers in these occupations.[8]

This unprecedented survey was a Civil Works Administration project that the Office of the Advisor on Negro Affairs developed when Weaver's predecessor, Clark H. Foreman, was its director. In December 1935, the Works Progress Administration provided $467,042 in funding to cover survey costs. Administered in eighty-five cities from April 13 to June 30, 1936, the survey elicited information from 335,000 black respondents through personal interviews. In addition to the expertise that Robert C. Weaver contributed to the national survey, Ira De A. Reid, professor of sociology at Atlanta University, served as administrator of the survey and editor of the report. Charles S. Johnson, director of the department of Social Sciences at Fisk University, completed the tabulations, and Preston Valien supervised the research.[9]

Ostensibly, the national survey was designed to offset the lack of information about black workers in skilled and white-collar occupations. The survey revealed that more than half of the respondents (55.3 percent) had white-collar occupations as professionals, clerks, kindred workers, and proprietors and managers of commercial establishments. The remaining respondents (44.7 percent) were engaged in various forms of skilled work.[10] Weaver was acutely aware of the importance of statistical data as a policy tool. By providing this information about black labor, it was hoped that New Deal policy makers would be able to make more intelligent decisions about public policies that would help blacks.

Though complementary, in many ways Weaver's research strategy differed from Edwards's in terms of design and ultimate purpose. First unlike Edwards, Weaver and his colleagues used a broader definition of "white collar." For their purposes, the category included not only clerical workers but also professionals, managers, and business owners. Survey administrators felt compelled to recode Edwards's classification of occupations because it was concluded that such shiftings, while invalidating close comparisons with the Edwards data, would permit a more valid analysis of Negro occupations in terms of skills and status.[11]

Finally, Weaver and Edwards had different motives and purposes. Edwards was trying to predict the future. In contrast, Weaver was trying to deal with a more clear and present danger: inequality and racial discrimination. Consequently, Weaver's activities as Negro Advisor were aimed at the elimination of the color-caste system. He contended that it represented a highly polarized labor market where there were wide differences between "white men's jobs and black men's jobs."[12] Blacks were employed in "hot and heavy" jobs such as those found in the steel and iron industries. It was thought that blacks were only suited for jobs requiring "strong backs and, it was assumed, weak minds." The higher-paid skilled opportunities, the "clean, light, well paid jobs," were the domain of whites.[13] This ingrained code about race and work, Weaver pointed out, was an artifact of slavery that endured because it made job discrimination that was based on color logical and reasonable. "This [color-caste] system is justified by the assumption that the Negro is inferior; it in turn establishes patterns to institutionalize an inferior status."[14] Weaver's career in the New Deal was dedicated to the cause of eliminating this system of unequal treatment, to debunk the myths, and to show their inaccuracies.

The survey of black skilled and white collar-workers fit into this mission. While the survey was designed to respond to the huge loss of jobs that the Great Depression caused throughout black America, this research had a larger purpose. According to Robert L. Gill, author of the article "The Crusading Spirit of Robert C. Weaver," Weaver was responsible for revealing the "[d]ifficulties faced by the federal government in counteracting discrimination, especially in those areas where previously such was almost the rule. In order to help remedy the matter, his department planned and administered in 1936 a national survey."[15] Despite the significance of the survey, it was merely one achievement in a federal career devoted to the removal of the color-caste system. As a public official, Weaver's fight against employment discrimination began with his first appointment in 1933 as Associate Advisor on Negro Affairs in the

Department of the Interior. The battle would be waged on several fronts to validate how employment discrimination was morally wrong and that black workers were a valuable source of labor. It would be Weaver's crusading spirit fortified by cunning and perseverance that would ultimately culminate in increased jobs, training opportunities, and the elevation of the employment status of blacks.

Robert Weaver's crusade for equal opportunity started before he accepted his first federal position. After having finished the work for his Ph.D. in economics from Harvard in September 1933, Weaver and John P. Davis formed the Joint Committee on National Recovery. In a 1973 interview, Weaver described the reason why he and Davis had created the Joint Committee:

> Nobody was appearing at the hearings on the codes under the National Industrial Recovery Act to state the Negro's case, and Negroes were generally excluded because they were excluded from the activities and the occupations which were covered by the codes, such as janitors and unskilled laborers, particularly in the South. We went in and spoke at the hearings.[16]

Their appearance at the hearings created quite a stir. The *New York Times* and *Wall Street Journal* ran articles about the testimony: "All of a sudden people knew who we were . . . You'd thought that Jesus Christ had come back. We had no idea we would get this sort of public recognition," Weaver said in a 1992 interview.[17] Nevertheless, it was the publicity that would bring him to the attention of the nation and that of Clark H. Foreman, who had been appointed as the department's first advisor on Negro Affairs by Harold L. Ickes, Secretary of Interior, in August of 1933. Foreman was a "dollar a year man." The Julius Rosenwald Fund, a philanthropy that provided funding for many black organizations, paid all but a dollar of Foreman's salary to expedite his appointment. The intention was to avoid controversy from segregationist forces who may have objected to using public funds to pay Foreman's salary for a job that dealt with the needs of blacks.[18] While the financial arrangement was logical and appropriate to the times, controversy did erupt; ironically, it came from the black community. The leaders of the NAACP, Walter White and Roy Wilkins, felt that the appointment "symbolized a patronizing approach to race relations."[19] In an interview with Judah L. Grabert, Weaver describes the controversy more fully and how it led to his appointment as the first black Advisor on Negro Affairs:

Although he was a liberal Southerner, [Clark Foreman] was under great attack from blacks because, number one, they didn't want whites in the Rosenwald Fund deciding who would hold the position, and number two, they didn't want a white person holding it. Clark then got in touch with me to ask if I would became the Associate Advisor in Negro Affairs, which I did in November of 1933. Then after about a year [in 1934], he resigned for another job and I become the Advisor. That was how I got involved in the New Deal.[20]

Weaver was hired with the understanding that he would, eventually, become the Advisor. Thus Foreman's departure was a part of a large scheme to keep peace with the black community. During his tenure in the Office of Negro Affairs, Weaver was guided by a clear sense of purpose, a part of which had been evident when he and Davis formed the Joint Committee on National Recovery. He understood the inner workings of the New Deal—its intentions and limitations—relative to black people. In addition, he understood that his special role as a black policymaker brought a specific obligation to ensure that the New Deal policies reflected a commitment to racial equality, especially those designed to spur employment:

You see, the New Deal was not designed to benefit blacks, but the men who were lowest on the totem pole. So I had to recognize that the problem of black Americans was an accentuation of the problems of all Americans. There were extremely high rates of unemployment and they were much higher among blacks than whites, so that the job was the primary issue. What this meant was that if the New Deal was equitably administered, there would be a wider participation of blacks, but not as blacks per se, but as people covered by the program. Therefore, I not only had a function of trying to get close to equal participation in the programs for blacks, but also to maintain their morale so that they would participate. Subsequently, one of my functions was to help get the administration re-elected, but in the beginning that was a secondary interest of mine.[21]

Weaver reached his primary goal—to get New Deal benefits for blacks—in a variety of ways. He and his staff routinely made speeches and wrote articles, "urging blacks to participate" and to make them "feel that they were getting something out of the New Deal."[22] He served as an advisor to the National Recovery Agency, Federal Emergency Relief

Agency, and the Rural Settlement Administration, offering them advice about ways to improve racial relations between workers in the Department of Interior and its affiliates. From time to time, he would handle cases in which blacks had alleged they were being unfairly treated or turned down for jobs.

However, two more significant projects marked Weaver's career with the Department of Interior as a crusader and pioneer. The first was the 1936 national survey of black white collar and skilled workers. As previously mentioned, this represented a landmark effort in demonstrating statistically why the color-caste system had to be removed.

The second significant accomplishment was the creation of what he called the "first affirmative action program in the federal government."[23] This occurred while he concurrently served as Advisor on Negro Affairs and consultant to the Housing Division of the Public Works Administration (PWA) from 1934-1936. His interest in housing issues was linked to his concern about employment issues.

> Once I got into government, I soon decided I wanted to get into the field of housing. I was interested in housing (I started out [at Harvard] in engineering and I was an electrician by trade). I was interested in labor problems, particularly problems of skilled Negroes and unskilled Negroes in the labor unions, and I was also interested in the social and economic aspects of housing; and, obviously, if we were doing housing for low-income families, it meant that Negroes should participate in it.[24]

In terms of participation, Weaver was vigilant about getting black construction workers to help build the PWA's public housing projects. More than one-third of the projects were to be occupied by Negroes. Blacks belonged to the local advisory boards planning these projects, and in some cases black architects had been responsible for the design of the projects. Because of the heavy emphasis on the black community, "[i]t was natural that colored people expected to participate in their construction," Weaver contended.[25]

Unfortunately, it would take more than substantiating the level of black participation to get blacks public housing construction jobs. The construction industry was highly unionized, and unions excluded blacks as members or had them in separate locals, which kept them out of these jobs. To remedy this situation, Weaver worked out an agreement with the Department of Labor to get unions to grant memberships or work permits to blacks so they could get PWA jobs and help build public housing projects.

Other New Deal officials before this time had formulated policies against employment discrimination. In October 1932, Ogden Mills, the Secretary of the Treasury, issued a communiqué to construction engineers stating that discriminatory employment practices would not be tolerated. Almost a year later, on September 21, 1933, Secretary Ickes, as administrator of the PWA, released an order to state engineers prohibiting discrimination based on color or religious affiliation. Unfortunately, according to Weaver, "[n]either order was effective. It was humanly impossible to define discrimination (much less prove it).[26] Moreover, borrowers, contractors, and labor unions could minimally act to respond to allegations of discrimination by hiring only a few skilled Negro workers because "there was no criteria which could be used to indicate when discrimination had been abolished."[27]

Working with William Hastie, who was then the assistant solicitor with the Department of Interior, Weaver did more than push for negotiated and cooperative agreements. To further ensure that blacks received jobs, they designed a prima facie (quota) formula to measure the existence of discrimination. According to Weaver, "The formula said in effect, that unless X percent of the skilled labor payroll, Y percent of the semi-skilled payroll, and Z percent of the unskilled payroll was paid to blacks, its was prima facie evidence that there was discrimination."[28] The definition established a prima facie basis of discrimination when employers failed to pay Negro skilled workers a minimum percentage of the wages that white skilled laborers would receive. The minimum percentage that Weaver and Hastie used as a criterion was based on the data from the most current occupational census with slight variations adjusted to current population movements.[29]

To further ensure compliance with the newly developed criterion, Weaver's staff made monthly site visits to examine construction companies' payrolls to determine if the companies were complying with the agreements to employ black construction workers. This level of vigilance was undertaken to ensure that blacks were not being hired one day and fired the next and that they were receiving jobs as plasterers, cement finishers, bricklayers, and carpenters. These were skilled occupations with the potential for large numbers of already trained blacks to be employed.

According to Weaver, the minimum percentage criteria proved to be "more effective" than what had been done before to combat employment discrimination. The U.S. Housing Authority, which replaced the Housing Division of PWA, adopted the criterion to avoid racial discrimination in construction projects. Weaver became Special Assistant in Charge of Race Relations to Nathan Strauss, Director of the Housing Authority. Weaver served in this capacity from 1938 to 1940.

Weaver's push to end the color-caste system was exceptional. Nonetheless, he did have his critics, both black and white:

> Blacks felt that not enough was being done and criticized me for being without power and then criticized me for not using the power they said I didn't have. Whites, particularly Southern whites, objected to Negroes being in any type of government jobs, certainly in executive positions, which came from my efforts to break down discrimination within public works. Then I was also resented in some parts of government, as was the whole of the PWA, for moving too fast.[30]

Despite the criticism, Weaver remained steadfast and clearly understood the reason for these negative opinions. For example, he placed the responses from his white critics in their proper context: fear and hatred for Weaver's commitment to equal job opportunity. "I was encouraging blacks to get out of the kitchen and to not work for so little money, and of course, I was going to cause riots and that sort of thing."[31]

Weaver was equally as clearheaded about his goals and the impact of his work as federal policymaker during the New Deal. He knew essentially that many of the policies, because they depended on negotiations and cooperative agreements, lacked the needed muscle to make real differences. For example, he had the following to say about his minimum criterion policy: "This mechanism for defining and enforcing nondiscrimination in employment was a significant development, although not a definitive solution of discrimination on public financed construction."[32] In fact, he concludes that, in general, the New Deal had little impact on Negroes in the 1930s. Blacks were continuing to lose the battle to gain "economic security and occupational advancement."[33]

Nonetheless, Weaver would continue his crusade against racial employment even as the nation stood on the brink of a second world conflict. However, as in the era of the New Deal, many of his achievements would lead to ineffective policies, lacking the sanctioning power to enforce compliance. This did not stop Weaver. He would use his cunning and determination to go beyond the policies to bring about employment equality.

It was the Second World War and the federal positions that Weaver held during this period that led to major advancements in removing the color-caste occupational system. However, at the beginning of the war years, conditions in the black community were desperate. More than a million people nationally were jobless, and blacks represented a disproportionate part of this number. The situation was not that much better for blacks who had jobs. Weaver writes "[C]olored workers were generally relegated to unskilled jobs in heavy industries. In building construction, Negroes were gradually returning to participation as skilled mechanics, and in many industries such as machine tool manufacture, aircraft, and, for the most part, ordnance, colored labor was not even considered as a source of potential production workers."[34] Philosophically, Weaver viewed World War II as a propitious moment—a window of opportunity—when the federal government could intercede to remove the color-caste system and elevate the economic status of blacks. Moreover, he contended that the Second World War would produce opportunities that were vastly different than those created during World War I. World War I gave an unprecedented number of blacks their first industrial employment, yet many of these jobs were unskilled, low-paying, and conformed to the color-caste system. Weaver felt that World War II would depart from this employment pattern by giving "many Negroes their first opportunity to demonstrate their ability to perform basic factory operations of skilled, single skilled, and semi-skilled types in a wide range of industries and plants. It also [would permit] some Negroes to work alongside white workers in many individual establishments on the basis of industrial equality."[35] In particular, Weaver singled out aircraft production as an ideal example of World War II's unique potential to upgrade the employment status of blacks by giving them skilled and semiskilled work:

> I was interested in [Negro employment in the aircraft industry] because it was a new industry, it didn't have any racial barriers. The second thing was that it was a semi-white collar production job. It wasn't like working in the steel mill or some of the other industries, and everybody had to be trained. So that the black trainee would start out more or less on an equal footing.[35]

However, to achieve the goal where black workers would be considered as capable as their white counterparts, training was essential. This was particularly true for the World War II defense program, as Weaver pointed out:

The importance of training cannot be overemphasized. Until there is a supply of qualified Negro labor prepared to do the type of jobs which war industries require, little can be done to tap the labor potential of our Negro citizens. Until there is such a supply of Negro workers, there is little hope of securing the serious consideration of real absorption of Negro labor in the war effort.[36]

The absence of skilled black workers was largely a consequence of racial discrimination. Blacks had been excluded from skilled jobs in certain basic industries, prevented from joining trade unions and from participating in vocational educational programs. Weaver understood that war production employment and training had to be included as phases in the struggle to get rid of the color-caste system.

On July 12, 1940, Weaver received his first wartime appointment. Assigned to the National Defense Advisory Commission (NDAC), Weaver served as administrative assistant to Sidney Hillman in the NDAC's Labor Division. Weaver was responsible for formulating policies to integrate blacks into the employment and training phases of the wartime buildup.

True to his eagerness to create training opportunities, he successfully got the U.S. Office of Education (USOE), the agency responsible for defense-training programs, to break with its practice of racial discrimination. On August 15, 1940, the USOE delineated a series of policies prohibiting discrimination over the use of federal funds to support its vocational programs for defense. After this policy move, a series of other nondiscrimination initiatives were quickly formulated. On August 31, 1940, the NDAC formulated a statement to remove barriers that discriminated against workers based on age, sex, race, or color. On September 15, President Roosevelt endorsed the NDAC policy in a Congressional speech about the defense program. And then on October 12, Mr. Hillman released information about an agreement that the NDAC struck between the AFL and the CIO to stop discriminatory practices within these unions against Negro workers in defense industries.

These nondiscrimination agreements did represent victories. However, they failed to be influential in deterring either employers, government officials, or unions from discriminating against blacks. In *Negro Labor*, Weaver writes that the USOE had half heartedly adopted the nondiscrimination policy even though the negotiations had required six weeks of constant meetings on the part of the NDAC. Moreover, he contended that the policy was given short shrift. "It was interpreted in the

field as representing no departure from the existing practices of vocational education and had little practical value in widening Negro participation in defense training."[37]

As he had done in his previous federal positions, Weaver was unper-
turbed by the lack of compliance with the policies about training as well
as employment. In fact, he took on a more activist role. It was an uphill
journey that would require considerable ability as he worked to ensure
compliance with the negotiated cooperative agreements:

> I . . . assembled a staff of about 18 professionals, who covered the
> country and we, as everybody else in the labor division, tried to make
> bricks without straw. We had no authority but we did have the backing
> of, at least the titular backing, of the Administration, we could speak
> for the government, and we then proceeded to work in the field. [T]he
> first thing that faced us was the matter of employment on construction
> because there were a large number of camps that were being built and
> there was a question of getting Negro craftsmen employed . . . We
> went immediately to Hillman and worked out a (*sic*) arrangement with
> the internationals in the Building Trades for issuing work permits to
> non-white craftsmen . . . We then sent people into the areas: number
> one, to see that the unions lived up to their agreements and number
> two, to see that the non-white craftsmen were employed and this was a
> matter of negotiations. I'm afraid we implied we had a little more au-
> thority than we did, but as long as we had identifications which were
> very, very, formidable looking, in nice looking leather cases, like the
> FBI carries it impressed the contractors. With an appeal to patriotism
> and the fact that we had to get the labor real quickly and we could sup-
> ply the bodies and a little bit of bluff, we were able to make some
> progress.[38]

"Some" is the operative term. The NDAC, dependent on negotiations and cooperative agreements, was unable to fully confront the
thorny issue of labor discrimination. The agency was ineffective; it
lacked enforcement powers. To offset the inadequacies of the NDAC, the
Office of Production Management (OPM) was created in 1941. Its Labor
Division became responsible for employment and training issues. Sidney
Hillman was its codirector and head of the Labor Division. On April 11,
a major policy initiative was undertaken. Hillman issued a letter to defense contractors, "'to examine their employment and training policies at
once to determine whether or not these policies make ample provision

for full utilization of available and competent Negro workers."[39] The letter represented a more direct intervention approach and an attempt to do something different. In *Negro Labor*, Weaver contends that Hillman wrote the letter in response to great pressure from Negroes and the liberal press.[40] However, Weaver was much more actively involved in creating this initiative to eliminate discrimination. "Yes, I wrote the letter," Weaver told Frances Hardin in 1973. But then he changed his response as he continued to describe how he finessed situations to get blacks into training and jobs during the defense program:

> Dr. Will [Alexander] and I wrote the letter. Well, we were in the position of, as I say, building bricks without straw, and one of the things that we had to have was some documentation to say that this was national policy and so [we] concocted the notion (and how it was concocted, I don't remember) of a letter, and we sat down and drafted it and we finally got it approved and issued.[41]

About the same time, the Negro Employment and Training Branch (NETB) was established in the Labor Division of the OPM. Weaver became its chief and was responsible for a small field staff who were assigned to increase black participation in war production.

Despite the intent of these policy initiatives, the color line remained virtually fixed, according to Weaver. Only "a few defense contractors indicated their willingness to co-operate with government policy . . . the growing corps of business representatives, temporarily in government service with the OPM, had almost universally taken a hands-off attitude. Small wonder that industrialists outside the government paid little attention to the appeals of the OPM for full utilization of minorities."[42] As a result, despite the wartime buildup, black labor was unfairly treated—the blatant disregard was very evident. While white workers, male and female, were being absorbed rapidly into the increasingly tight labor markets, joblessness among Negroes was rising. In the few instances where blacks found jobs, they were in nondefense work.

Eventually "the Negro community became aroused," Weaver writes.[43] The OPM initially responded by slightly expanding the NETB's staff. Other branches of the Labor Division of the OPM expressed their concerns about the issue. However, the real problem was the policy of negotiation and persuasion, which agencies refused to change. To be sure, Weaver's office, the NETB, was able to get a few jobs for blacks in the aircraft, electrical machinery, ordnance, shipbuilding, and machine-tools industries. Unfortunately, this was not enough. The removal of the color-caste system during the wartime initiative was a national problem involving thousands of defense contractors. More had to be done if black labor was to benefit from the defense production industry.[44]

More would be done as blacks became increasingly discontent with the slow pace of government action. According to Weaver, black protests sprang up across the nation: "Conferences seemed to produce but small results and a plan was developed for more drastic action."[45] A part of this plan included A. Philip Randolph, president of the Brotherhood of Sleeping Car Porters and Maids, and his efforts to organize the March on Washington. The march was seen as the way to openly dramatize the plight of blacks who were being denied defense-related jobs. Organizers of the march planned to have fifty thousand black protestors descend on Washington, D.C., and walk down Pennsylvania Avenue. The image of thousands of blacks in the streets of the nation's capital was threatening. Despite entreaties from the administration, march organizers remained steadfast to their plans. The tenacity of the march's leadership made the administration realize how serious blacks were about taking their protests to the streets of Washington, D.C. The threat worked; it lead to two major policy initiatives.[46]

On June 12, 1941, President Roosevelt released a memo officially endorsing Hillman's earlier letter to defense contractors. The memo directly attacked employment discrimination and encouraged the use of all citizens, regardless of race and nationality, in the nation's war production industries. Unfortunately, the memo came too late. Blacks were suspicious of the government because it had continued to renege on its promise to dismantle the color-caste system. They wanted more direct intervention. President Roosevelt invited Randolph and other leaders of the march to the White House for a conference. This discussion led to the second policy initiative. On June 25, President Roosevelt issued Executive Order 8802, which reaffirmed the government's commitment to equal employment in the defense industries. It also established the Committee on Fair Employment Practices (later to be called the FEPC) to investigate discrimination complaints and to offer ways to redress accusations of discrimination if they were found to be valid.[47] Also, the FEPC had jurisdiction to make recommendations to specific government agencies and the president about ways to achieve the nondiscrimination goals that the order stipulated.[48] Weaver saw the threat of a March on Washington as singularly important; a display of political might that to led to the ground-breaking Executive Order and the FEPC. The march represented a groundswell of public will and action within the black community. Blacks were "united in pressing for training, employment, and up-grading in all war industries. . . . [This] was not the agitation of a few Negro radicals; it had become the will of the Negro people."[49] Weaver contends that the willingness of blacks to make demands had come from a sense of entitlement developed during the New Deal. During this earlier period, they became aware that they deserved to be treated fairly and to have equal access to jobs and training. Blacks' "growing political power enabled them, under the guidance of able and effective leadership, to make protest felt," Weaver writes.[50] He continues:

> Now I have no way of knowing this but my guess is that if they had a march, they would certainly not have had one hundred thousand Negroes, they might not have had ten thousand but Washington would have thought there were one hundred thousand. If they'd had a hundred, they'd had almost the same impact. There was no question that Randolph held a gun at the President's head and was successful in getting this through and it was only he, I think who could have done it. Certainly there was no idea in the Administration when the negotiations were begun, that there would be an executive order.[51]

The political might of the black community— an element of force— had pushed the cause for equal employment and training further than governmental policies had done before.

Despite this ground-breaking legislation and what it enabled black workers to accomplish, it did not go far enough. In a complicated series of relocations from one government agency to another, the FEPC attempted to hew to the letter of the executive order. From July 1941 to January 1942, the FEPC was in the Labor Division of the OPM. When the OPM was abolished, FEPC was transferred to the War Production Board (WPB) on January 26, 1942, where it would remain until July, when the War Manpower Commission (WMC) was created. In a similar way, Weaver's federal career was also marked by several relocations. After the OPM was dismantled, the NETB was transferred to the WPB in the Labor Division. Weaver remained the chief of the NETB. When the WMC took over the functions of the Labor Division of WPB, Weaver served as the chief of Negro Manpower Services from 1943 to 1944.

Despite the changes and relocations, Weaver remained close to the FEPC as it attempted to create full employment and remove the color-caste system. For example, the NETB staff of the OPM conducted systematic site visits to defense contractors to promote the utilization of minority workers and conducted initial review of complaints for the FEPC. Moreover, during this period the FEPC served as a board of appeals for the NETB.[52]

Weaver was convinced that the executive order and the FEPC had had a significant impact on black employment and upgrading black occupational status, especially within the federal government. "By the fall of 1942, there was dramatic evidence that the Executive Order was effective. . . . In agency after agency, the old barriers to Negro clerical workers were giving way, and colored women, in particular, were entering the government in increasing numbers."[53]

However, within the private sector and beyond the nation's capital, federal policy did little to change the color-caste system. This level of minimal impact was very clear from his description about the unwillingness of the USOE to revamp its procedures to comply with the federal nondiscrimination policies. First, USES (United States Employment Services) personnel had developed procedures and attitudes during the Great Depression that made federal policies ineffective. As Weaver saw it, "the most important of these [attitudes] was the desire to comply fully with employers' specifications."[54] Therefore, "it was natural, though unfortunate, that the USES would continue in wartime to seek the favor of employers."[55] At the state level, few Employment Services branches made vigorous efforts to get employers to utilize Negro workers. Even under the tight labor conditions that were prevalent during the early defense program, local branches "accepted 'white' specifications and imported white workers without calling employers' attention to the fact that qualified local Negroes were available."[56]

The problem of lax compliance within the USOE continued, despite the enactment of the executive order. The goal was to remain faithful to the tradition of never questioning an employer's hiring or labor practices. Even in those cases, when there was evidence of a violation of the executive order, "the chief of the USES was quick to observe that it was not the Employment Service that was discriminating but rather the employer." And he added, despite the president's statement, that this discrimination on the part of the employer was not illegal. In his opinion, it was an undesirable social and economic practice and, as such, could not be eliminated by the Employment Service."[57] At this juncture, the critical question, given the lackluster performance of federal policy, was how was Weaver able to write the following?

Between 1940 and 1944, significant changes occurred among Negro workers. Over a million Negroes entered civilian jobs. They moved from farm to factory. The number of Negroes employed at skilled jobs doubled, as did the number of single-skilled and semi-skilled colored workers. . . . Much of what happened . . . was contrary to the accepted pattern of Negro employment and is significant, largely, because of this departure from older practices. For the war gave many Negroes their first opportunity to demonstrate [their] ability to perform basic factory operations of skilled, single-skilled, and semi-skilled types in a wide range of industries and plants. . . . Most of the gains occurred after 1942. In the summer of that year, for example, it was estimated that only 3 per cent of those in war industries were colored; by September, 1944, the proportion was over 8 percent.[58]

Weaver's glowing description represents an understanding about the complexity of the issue. As a result, in most cases when Weaver discusses the benefits of wartime production, he mentions "economic conditions"; more precisely, manpower shortages and the need for trained workers was a key element that allowed Negroes to get jobs and enter new industries. The confluence of government pressure and economic need combined to advance the cause of black labor. As he stated, the impact of these twin forces was especially apparent after 1942. At this point, employment among blacks as well as their presence in nontraditional jobs in aircraft, communication equipment, and other defense-related industries started to show gradual yet marked increases.

Weaver goes further by suggesting that labor-market conditions were the critical agent in softening the color-caste system. In the article "Negro Employment in the Aircraft Industry," he admits that government intervention was a key policy element. However in Weaver's mind "the most important single factor in bringing about the employment and upgrading of minorities [was] the degree of tightness in the labor market."[59]

The special economic environment created by the war was a cause for joy and concern—joy for the jobs and opportunities that blacks acquired, concern over what would happen after the war's end, as the society converted from a defense to peace economy. In *Negro Labor*, Weaver describes a bleak future for black workers.

Any type of reconversion will present serious problems to the black worker. He will suffer from a much higher incidence of unemployment

than the white worker. The Negro worker will often be displaced from
the better jobs he held during the war, and Negro women will, for the
most part, leave industrial employment.[60]

This awful situation would be avoided if the federal government enacted
policies to maintain the full-employment environment that prevailed during the war. "Such a program is not one of government regulation and
control; it is a program of government part icipation. Its basic principles
are few: the state has a responsibility for assuring full employment. It is
not automatic," Weaver writes.[61] "In order to assure it, the government
must be in a position to measure the adequacy of the effective demand
and supplement it when necessary."[62] Full employment, Weaver contended, would preserve the gains that blacks had made during the
wartime expansion.

   Despite his doubts, in 1947 Weaver was optimistic about postwar reconversion and that black workers would continue to upgrade their job
status as they moved into new and better types of jobs. As he saw it, there
was no turning back. Those who benefited from wartime jobs were the
"beach head from which subsequent participation of additional members
of the group is projected in the next period."[63] In addition, his analysis of
labor statistics demonstrated that reconversion had not led to a major displacement of blacks. Consequently, "the Negro has . . . a chance to con-
solidate some of his wartime gains and in many industries and firms
where he had long been employed and was upgraded for the first time."[64]

   On February 1, 1944, Weaver resigned from his position as chief of
Negro Manpower Service in the War Manpower Commission. According
to Robert L. Gill, Weaver left "because of the government swing to the . . .
right,"[65] which he feared was intending to undo the liberal gains accomplished during the New Deal.[66] After his resignation, he accepted the position of executive director of the Mayor's (Hon. Edward J. Kelly)
Committee on Race Relations in Chicago.

   Although tight labor-market conditions were pivotal to the employment advances made during the war, this does not in any way diminish
the significance of Robert Weaver's role as a crusader in the struggle to
achieve employment equality. His virtues, as discussed in *Negro Labor*,
came from his capacity to use what was available—making bricks without straw—to push black labor forward into better employment opportunities. Throughout the period, he relentlessly struggled to eliminate the
color-caste system.

One cannot help but to be awestruck by the intelligence, confidence, and courage that it took for Robert Weaver and John Davis to participate in the Congressional hearings to ensure the interests of blacks would be considered as the National Recovery Act codes were being formulated. This was no mean feat. It took incredible temerity to face an all-white panel of congressmen and to discuss technical economic issues during a period when legalized segregation made black issues minor concerns.

Weaver's conviction and determination was apparent in each of his federal appointments. During the New Deal, he understood that his role as a black federal policymaker obligated him to work in the interest of blacks. Working tirelessly, he gave speeches and negotiated with unions to hire black construction workers to build the PWA's public housing projects. His brilliance and ingenuity were evident as he helped to implement the seminal 1936 national survey and create the nation's first affirmative action program.

He continued to be dedicated to the cause of full employment opportunity as World War II brought new challenges and opportunities. He knew that the wartime buildup was a propitious moment. Different from the World War I expansion, World War II was a chance to get blacks out of low-paying, "hot and heavy" positions into better jobs in factories as skilled and semiskilled workers. As he had done before, Weaver took on an activist role, recognizing the ineffectiveness of nondiscrimination policies that were being formulated. He assembled a staff, supplying them with official-looking identification, to monitor union compliance with agreements to hire Negro craftsmen to help build army encampments. It was his initiative and that of Dr. Will Alexander that produced the pivotal letter that become federal policy that required defense contractors to train and employ blacks as factory workers. Throughout the wartime buildup, in each federal position that he held Weaver continued the fight to end the color-caste system. He used staff to monitor compliance with FEPC regulations and make site visits to defense contractors as the war effort intensified.

While the economic conditions were pivotal, as was the political might of the black community that forced Roosevelt to issue Executive Order 8802, it was the unrelenting efforts of Robert Weaver that laid the groundwork for the employment advances during the New Deal and World War II. Weaver was able to take very little and to transform it into actual policy and programs. He was a pioneer and crusader, and blacks benefited from his valiant efforts.

## NOTES

1. Alba M. Edwards, "The Negro as a Factor in the Nation's Labor Force," *Journal of the American Statistical Association* 33. nos. 193–196 (1936): 533.

2. *Ibid.*, p. 540.

3. *Ibid.*, p. 533.

4. Alba M. Edwards, "The White Collar Workers," *Monthly Labor Review* 38 (March 1934): 508. Alba M. Edwards, "The Growth and Significance of the White-Collar Class," *American Federationist* 38 (January 1938): 32.

5. Robert C. Weaver, "Negro Labor since 1929," in Arnold M. Rose, ed., *Race-Prejudice and Discrimination: Readings in Intergroup Relations in the United States* (New York: Alfred A. Knopf, 1951), p. 117.

6. *Ibid.*, p. 118.

7. Department of the Interior, Office of the Advisor on Negro Affairs, *The Urban Negro Worker in the United States, 1925–36: An Analysis of the Training Types and Conditions of Employment and the Earnings of 200,000 Skilled and White Collar Negro Workers*, by Ira De A. Reid, Preston Valien, and Charles S. Johnson (Washington, D.C.: U.S. Department of the Interior, Office of the Advisor on Negro Affairs, 1937), p. 1.

8. *Ibid.*, pp. 1, 3.

9. *Ibid.*, p. 7.

10. *Ibid.*, p. 5.

11. Robert C. Weaver, *Negro Labor: A National Problem* (New York: Harcourt, Brace, and Company, 1946), p. 107.

12. Weaver, *Negro Labor*, p. 6 ; Robert C. Weaver, "Wither Northern Race Relations Committees," *Phylo* 5, no. 3 (1944): 206. In this *Phylo* article, Weaver eloquently adds to his discussion about the institutionalization of discrimination: "The older concepts stick because they are old and because they give convenient justification for the current patterns of racial segregation and discrimination. They become the basis for such absurd practices as segregation of Negro blood in the blood-bank. Our democracy escapes its full share of moral incident to its treatment of the Negro by rationalizing that the brown American is an inferior person for whom an inferior position is in accord with the laws of nature. This assumption of inferiority must be challenged if are to achieve effective racial cooperation in America," p. 207.

13. Weaver, "Whither Northern Race Relations Committees," p. 206.

14. Robert L. Gill, "The Crusading Spirit of Robert C. Weaver," *Negro Educational Review* 2 (July–October 1951): 121. In a 1978 interview with Judah Grabert, Weaver referred to the survey as the "the most significant" project undertaken while he was at the Department of Interior during the New Deal. The

sense of pride emanated from his belief that the survey goals had been achieved, which had everything to do with getting blacks employed and into well-paying and higher-level positions. The survey had two purposes, Weaver told Grabert: "First, we wanted to find out what happened to trained blacks in white-collar, skilled, and trained occupations [since the Depression]. Second, we wanted to re-solve the terrible problem we were having getting Negroes employment in re-search projects in the WPA. Even where they were employed, blacks were employed at the state level where they usually were paid lower wages than whites. So this was set up as federal project and I was the administrator of it. I was able to get equal pay and hire about 200 professional people, many of whom became quite prominent as time went on. And, all told, I employed about 1,500 people in about 31 states, and we got two volumes published from the research. So that was very interesting." Robert C. Weaver, interviewed by Judah L. Grabert, January 19, 1978. Robert Clifton Weaver Papers (Additions), 1930–1987, Oral History Transcripts, Schomburg Center for Research in Black Culture, New York: p. 4.

15. Robert C. Weaver, interview by Frances Hardin, November 30, 1973. Robert Clifton Weaver Papers (Additions), 1930–1987, Oral History Transcripts, Schomburg Center for Research in Black Culture, New York, p. 1. In a 1992 in-terview with Phoebe Roosevelt, Weaver provides more specifics about the Negro Industrial League and the hearings to discuss the NRA codes. "We [Weaver and Davis] were very much concerned because the NRA codes were setting up mini-mum wages for people in basic industries, and there were many industries of which blacks were a part, and we felt they should have some representation. So we set up the Negro Industrial League, of which I was the Industrial League and John [Davis] was the Negro. And we went before the hearing on the cotton indus-try. . . . I had written most of the testimony; John, a little short guy, sort of pompous, he liked to speak, well he read it." Robert C. Weaver, interviewed by Phoebe Roosevelt, February 18, 1992. Robert Clifton Weaver Papers (Addi-tions), 1930–1987, Oral History Transcripts, Schomburg Center for Research in Black Culture, New York, p. 15.

16. Interview by Phoebe Roosevelt, p. 15.

17. Robert C. Weaver, "The Black Cabinet," in Katie Louchheim, ed., *The Making of the New Deal: The Insiders Speak* (Cambridge: Harvard University Press, 1983), p. 261.

18. *Ibid.*, p. 262.

19. Interview by Judah L. Grabert, p. 1.

20. *Ibid.*

21. *Ibid.*

22. *Ibid.*, p. 3.

23. Interview by Frances Hardin, p. 2.

24. Weaver, *Negro Labor*, p. 11.

25. *Ibid.*, p. 10.

26. *Ibid.*, p. 11.

27. Interview by Judah L. Grabert, p. 3; Gill, "Crusading Spirit," p. 121. In the 1992 interview by Phoebe Roosevelt, Weaver described the innovative nature of this first affirmative action program: "No one had used figures before, and that went back to the Second Morrill Act [1890] . . . this was the only . . . federal educational program where there was equitable distribution of funds, and that was all on the basis of the census data. That was the basis of my proposal . . . for the public housing program" (p. 3).

28. Weaver, *Negro Labor*, p. 11.

29. Weaver, *Negro Labor,* p. 11; Interview by Judah L. Grabert, p. 3.

30. Interview by Judah L. Grabert, p. 4.

31. *Ibid.*

32. Weaver, *Negro Labor*, p. 13.

33. *Ibid.*, p. 15.

34. Robert C. Weaver, "Defense Industries and the Negro." In Thorsten Sellen and Donald Young, eds., *The Annals of the Academy of Political and Social Sciences: Minority People in a Nation at War* (Philadelphia: Academy of Political and Social Sciences, 1942), 60–61.

35. Weaver, *Negro Labor*, pp. 78–79.

36. Interview by Phoebe Roosevelt, p. 16.

37. Weaver, "Defense Industries," pp. 64–65.

38. Weaver, *Negro Labor*, pp. 57, 131; Weaver, "Defense Industries," p. 61.

39. Weaver, *Negro Labor*, pp. 57–58.

40. Interview by Frances Hardin, pp. 3–4. In this interview, Weaver says the following about the difficulty of getting blacks these construction jobs, "It was our job . . . to get the craftsmen and we worked through local organizations, through the Urban Leagues, through anybody we could work through to identify the craftsmen and ultimately later to also get them to move to the jobs because they were usually in remote areas."

41. Weaver, *Negro Labor*, p. 132.

42. *Ibid.*

43. Interview by Frances Hardin, p. 4.

44. Weaver, *Negro Labor*, p. 132.

45. *Ibid.*, p. 133.

46. *Ibid.*, p. 134.

47. *Ibid.*

48. Weaver, *Negro Labor*, p. 14. In particular, this sense of steadfastness was true of A. Philip Randolph, whom Weaver saw as "a man who had a iron will [and who] stood as firm as the Rock of Gibraltar." Interview by Frances Hardin, p. 6.

49. Eileen Boris discusses the FEPC in greater detail in the preceding chapter entitled, "Black Workers, Trade Unions, and Labor Standards: The Wartime FEPC."

50. Weaver, "Defense Industries," p. 62.

51. Weaver, *Negro Labor*, p. 17.

52. *Ibid.*, p. 237.

53. Interview by Frances Hardin, p. 6.

54. Weaver, *Negro Labor*, p. 135.

55. *Ibid.*, p. 137.

56. *Ibid.*, p. 145.

57. *Ibid.*

58. *Ibid.*, p. 147.

59. *Ibid.*, p. 147.

60. *Ibid.*, pp. 78–79.

61. *Ibid.*

62. Weaver, "Negro Employment in the Aircraft Industry," pp. 623–624.

63. Weaver, *Negro Labor*, p. 272.

64. *Ibid.*, p. 263.

65. Robert C. Weaver, *The Negro Ghetto* (New York: Harcourt, Brace, and Company, 1948), pp. 135–136.

66. *Ibid.*

67. Gill, *Crusading Spirit*, p. 125.

# CHAPTER 9

# Black Workers, Trade Unions, and Labor Standards
## The Wartime FEPC

EILEEN BORIS

After (Mrs.) Lillian M. Potts unsuccessfully applied for an operator's job at the Pacific Telephone and Telegraph Company in March 1944, she contacted the San Jose chapter of the National Association for the Advancement of Colored People (NAACP). The NAACP then filed a complaint on her behalf with the regional branch of the President's Committee on Fair Employment Practices (FEPC). Her conversation with Pacific Bell's personnel official illuminates the ways that race provided the key term through which citizenship and national identity remained differentially defined even during World War II, a conflict fought for democracy and against racial supremacy. And race was gendered, with exclusions and stereotypes derived from conceptions of black and white womanhood and manhood. "When the application called for *nationality*," Potts explained, "she said, 'just American won't do, you'll have to state race.' I said Negro. 'Negro!['] the lady exclaimed, then added, 'Well, I am sorry but we don't have any vacancies just now.' " But Potts "noticed they were hiring girls then, but not my color of skin."[1] Lillian Potts's experience was common. She found white-collar work in the private sector closed to a black woman. But she did not merely face discrimination; she sought restitution, turning to the state—by way of a race-advancement organization—to receive "the right to work"[2] denied by combinations of employers, workers, and trade unions.

Historians celebrate wartime industrial mobilization for "the most dramatic improvement in economic status of black people that has ever taken place in the urban industrial economy."[3] They argue that, "as a war for democracy and against racism," World War II advanced the "notion" of "equality for African-Americans."[4] But the World War II experience of African Americans wage laborers proved to be more complex than such pronouncements suggest. Wartime upgrading of black workers developed out of labor shortages; as one columnist in The *Chicago Defender* quipped, "[the] most powerful Black Cabineteer right now is War Time Emergency."[5] But black protest made it possible that such "emergency" would challenge the existing segmentation of the labor market. In defending "equality of work opportunity,"[6] the FEPC despite its institutional weakness, legitimatized the rights consciousness of black America and thus galvanized black protest.

African Americans, especially in the North, had won only limited gains through the New Deal. Some programs contained outright discriminations, expressed in regional or occupational terms, as with the wage differentials of National Recovery Act (NRA) codes and the exclusion of domestic and agricultural labor from Social Security and the Fair Labor Standards Act (FLSA). The efficacy of race-neutral relief programs depended on who administered them; implementation at the state and local level opened the door to differential treatment. Only the Public Works Administration experimented with racial proportionalism in determining its work force.[7] The expansion of the state during wartime, in contrast, offered spaces for political and personal challenges to existing structures of racial hierarchy and subordination, including the fear of "social equality," the white supremacist code word for integration.[8]

This chapter analyzes the African American struggle for fair employment during World War II by untangling two interrelated themes: the place of African American workers in employment policy and labor law, and the relationship of black workers to trade unionism. Central to these themes is the FEPC. But this is no simple story of betterment. Despite official pronouncements by the American Federation of Labor (AFL) as well as the more racially egalitarian and committed Congress of Industrial Organization (CIO), white racism remained a potent force, particularly within AFL unions. Among CIO unions, those with a strong Communist and left presence fought for black rights; the CIO itself established in 1942 the Committee Against Racial Discrimination (CARD) in response to demands by black unionists.[9] But race-neutral structures won by unions, like seniority, disadvantaged the last-hired black workers. Meanwhile employers proved even more willing to embrace discrimination for profit, even though shop-floor confrontations over inequality disrupted wartime centers of production and interfered with efficiency.[10]

Moreover, demobilization without federal commitment to full employment or fair employment enforcement would undermine wartime advances. The unsuccessful campaign for a permanent FEPC from 1945 into the 1950s brought together trade union leaders and the NAACP; the Leadership Conference on Civil Rights evolved out of this coalition.[11] Title VII of the Civil Rights Act of 1964 finally re-created the FEPC as the Equal Employment Opportunity Commission (EEOC).[12] This victory occurred twenty years too late; nondiscrimination became the law of the land when deindustrialization and the shift to white-collar work marked the decline of both blue-collar labor and industrial unionism. African American men won the right to industrial jobs when industrial jobs were becoming a scarce commodity; African American women, whose foothold in industry had been even less secure, could enter service, the increasingly proletarianized clerical sectors, or find themselves reduced to welfare, that is, to combining low-wage jobs with public assistance.[13]

## WARTIME "GAINS"

Certainly the war years witnessed rising income, upgraded occupations, and a shift from agriculture and service to industrial labor that came with urban migration, especially out of the South. But this shift was not immediate. In 1942, the National Urban League discovered "a disproportionate number" of urban blacks still on relief. In the North as well as the South, African Americans often found training programs, the first step to obtain a defense job, closed to them. Restrictive housing in crowded production areas also posed a barrier to war employment.[14]

Nor did black women benefit to the same extent as black men. About half of all American women found employment sometime during the war. As a result, the percentage of black women in the overall female labor force actually dropped from 13.8 to 12.5 percent. While the numbers of black women in clerical work quadrupled due to employment in government agencies, including the War and Navy departments, they still composed a mere 2 percent of this fastest-growing area for female labor. As the Brooklyn Urban League noted in September 1943, "Negro woman power is still the most greatly neglected segment of the Negro proletariat." Not only did they receive "the left-over and undesirable jobs in war industries," but also they had to have higher qualifications. Training alone did not always lead to positions. They suffered from barriers of "physical types . . . and intangibles not imposed on white female work-ers." African American women remained in the less-skilled and lower-paid sectors of the labor market.[15]

But manpower shortages opened jobs. By 1944, African Americans composed 8 percent of war workers, up from 2 percent in 1942. In No-vember of that year, approximately 107,000 "nonwhites" were in air-craft, 182,000 in shipyards, and 142,000 in ordnance—all areas of manufacturing that would witness steep a decline with V-J Day. African Americans entered government employment in record numbers, nearly 300,000 at the peak, though the vast majority labored at industrial jobs for the army and navy. 100,000 were in federal offices, but blacks worked in temporary classifications at the bottom of the civil-service lad-der and were employed predominantly in Washington as opposed to re-gional branches of federal agencies. The location and manner of black incorporation into these better jobs foreshadowed their massive layoffs with the end of the war.[16]

## THE FEPC AND ORGANIZED LABOR

Threatened by the black-only March on Washington Movement (MOWM) under A. Philip Randolph of the Brotherhood of Sleeping Car Porters (BSCP), President Franklin D. Roosevelt issued Executive Order 8802 in June 1941. In creating the FEPC, Roosevelt sought to end discrimination in employment related to the war effort. The FEPC covered employers, including government agencies, and unions. It targeted African Ameri-cans and other racial minorities, Jews and other religious minorities, and aliens or those of non–United States nationality. However, African Americans filed more than 90 percent of the complaints, which—along with the circumstances of its birth—led the general public to view the agency as one devoted exclusively to black rights. The FEPC did not in-clude women as a minority group, only as members of covered groups. Between July 1943 and December 1944, at the height of the agency's reach, they composed 30.8 percent of cases docketed, with black women composing 86.2 percent of the cases among women.[17]

A subsequent Executive Order, 9346, reconstituted the committee (known as the Second Committee) as an independent agency in May 1943 under the Office of Emergency Management; this occurred after an earlier transfer to the War Manpower Commission (WMC) in 1942. Dur-ing the year prior to the war's end, the FEPC reported to have "held 15 public hearings and docketed a total of 3,485 cases, settling 1,191." Dur-

ing its five years, it claimed settlement of "5,000 cases by peaceful negotiation, including 40 strikes caused by racial differences." It adjudicated
most of these cases through quiet negotiation, but high-profile cases in
which employers and unions rejected or ignored its directives (especially
involving railways and the West Coast shipyards) highlighted its limited
effectiveness.[18]

FEPC was to be an emergency measure to bring efficiency to war
production. It would be " 'sold' to the country as primarily designed to
prevent limitations of the use of all manpower rather than as a present
basis for the general advance of the Negro race," argued White House administrative assistant Jonathan Daniels. "Minority groups," however,
viewed fair employment as "a moral issue." Randolph explained: "If
American democracy will not give jobs to its toilers because of race or
color . . . it is a hollow mockery and belies the principles for which it is
supposed to stand." The FEPC was central to the Double V campaign,
victory against fascism and "empire over subject peoples" abroad and
against Jim Crow and "white supremacy" at home. White southerners
also saw the FEPC as a moral issue, an attempt to "saddle social equality
upon Dixie," as the African American *Pittsburgh Courier* explained. Fair
employment generated a conundrum for the Roosevelt administration,
which still depended on Southern Democrats in Congress, whose committee chairmanships—a product of a seniority derived from white
primaries and black disenfranchisement—had allowed them to block inclusion of African Americans in New Deal legislation.[19]

The FEPC appeared as the culmination of a series of labor laws, an
extension of the Wagner Act, Social Security, and the Fair Labor Standards Act. Just as "the right to organize is a natural right," Monsignor
Francis J. Hass, FEPC chairman in 1943, told the AFL National Convention, so fair employment represented "minority group members [right] to
obtain opportunity for economic security." It would promote participation in trade unions and thus ensure the right to earn a living.[20] Unlike the
National Labor Relations Board (NLRB), the FEPC lacked enforcement
powers. Working only by individual complaint, it had to proceed through
hearings, conferences, and ultimately the agreement of conflicted parties; it could not bring offenders to court or issue cease and desist orders
with any teeth. Its sole remedy—the withdrawal of a government contract—could only be recommended to the president, who choose to accommodate to those in the administration who held production too
important to disrupt for fair employment. No contracts ever were lost because of discriminatory practices.

The FEPC lacked power to counter political pressure. Paul McNutt of the WMC, for example, canceled hearings against southern railways and the railroad brotherhoods. After the FEPC finally proceeded in September 1943, Roosevelt responded with appointing another fact-finding committee rather than enforcing an FEPC directive to end discrimination and so risk a disruption of rail service.[21] These hearings, in turn, provided an excuse for Virginia Democrat Howard W. Smith to conduct a hostile Congressional hearing in which the railroad's attorney charged the FEPC with being "a 'doctrinaire and starry-eyed, bureaucratic agency.'" Other southern Congressmen claimed that the FEPC was "more concerned in tearing down the existing social order" than with fighting employment discrimination or winning the war.[22] Northern Republican conservatives joined the attack by associating its restrictions on employers with Communism. The FEPC would succumb to such conservative opposition, which defunded the wartime agency and refused to let bills for a permanent FEPC come up for Congressional passage. It nonetheless maintained pressure on the federal government to hire on merit, trained a cadre of future civil-rights leaders, and gave a green light to black protest.[23]

Sitting on the FEPC were representatives of trade unions, the AFL's Boris Shishkin, the brotherhood's Milton Webster, and the CIO's John Brophy.[24] At the war's start, ten AFL craft unions still had bars against black members, down from the twenty-four who had such exclusions before the breakaway CIO began organizing the black as well as white workforce in mass-production industry. But other AFL unions continued to exclude blacks through "tacit understanding," while some created "jim crow 'auxiliaries,' under rules which deny [blacks] any voice in union affairs or an opportunity to be promoted to better jobs."[25] Speaking the language of "equal rights," AFL leaders endorsed nondiscrimination, but the structure of their organization meant that the federation would not interfere with those constituent unions that acted otherwise. At its sixty-fourth annual meeting in 1944, for example, the federation endorsed a permanent FEPC but refused to condemn the dual unionism generated by Jim Crow auxiliaries. AFL unions feared blacks as low-skilled and low-paid workers whose entrance would undermine union power.[26]

The CIO, in contrast, argued that "segregation of any kind is discrimination" (the National Labor Relations Board finally agreed in 1945 in a case against Local 219 of the Tobacco Workers International Union, an AFL affiliate[27]). Many affiliates acted on this belief by insisting on nondiscrimination clauses in contract language. Those with Communist leadership proved to be particularly vigilant. Indeed, the CIO considered itself "the best and most reliable friend the Negro has in America today," as President Philip Murray explained in the June 1945 *Negro Digest*.[28] Secretary-Treasurer James Carey, head of the Committee Against Discrimination, pledged to "stand up and fight against discrimination." But this understanding suffered from an inability to think through the hidden structural features that turned race-neutral rules discriminatory. And, however progressive the leadership, officers could not threaten the security of members, who feared undercutting of wages by lower-paid African Americans. Thus Carey refused to modify seniority in a situation of job scarcity, believing that it "should be a means of eliminating special preferences, not creating them." The CIO would seek other means to advance racial equity.

A social democratic agenda would advance such goals. Full employment, as during the war, became the key to fair employment. Walter Reuther, president of the United Automobile Workers and the last head of the CIO before its merger with the AFL in 1955, contended that "the price of brotherhood is the creation of a society of abundance and freedom for all, in which only the peddlers of bigotry will be unemployed." The CIO would "Take . . . Care of the Negro Whether He Is Mentioned or Not," one black newspaper columnist explained, because it "proposes to help the workers, as citizens, to help themselves" through universal health insurance, school lunches, full education, and other social welfare measures. The black veteran would benefit as much as the white one from veteran's benefits. The problem with this program derived, not from intent to discriminate, but from the prewar absence of African Americans from the industrial labor force, their continuing presence at lower ends of the job ladder, and their subsequent lesser seniority. Such structural features suggest antidiscrimination alone, without a challenge to race and sex-segmented labor markets, would leave the right to work vulnerable to reconversion layoffs.[29]

CIO leadership was crucial to the postwar liberal coalition. But trade unionism and black rights were not always compatible when unions failed to gain larger social benefits through politics and had to be content with winning benefits only for members through collective bargaining. Concentrated in unorganized sectors, African Americans, particularly black women, stood outside of unions. Nondiscrimination clauses in union contracts meant nothing to such workers; they needed jobs that paid a living wage.[30]

Ultimately employers, as Robert Weaver of the War Production Board understood, held "the primary responsibility for ending racial discrimination in war industry . . . If there are union objections to hiring . . . industry can handle that situation," with appeals to the FEPC.[31] Much evidence exists that employers were reluctant to hire African Americans, claiming concern over worker protest to justify their own prejudices. Such employers long had used black workers to break strikes and reduce labor costs.[32] Such economic rationales for discrimination became sexualized in the holds of shipyards and the crowded streetcars where physical proximity prefigured equality. But it wasn't necessarily working people who recoiled from integration. One steel executive drew upon such a subtext when he complained, "The CIO fools them with parties and social gatherings so that they get the idea they're as good as white people." Shipyard ethnographer Bernice Anita Reed concluded, "Management accommodated to integration of Negro employees less readily than non-supervisory employees." A black packinghouse worker similarly explained the absence of black women from "the cleanest department in the whole plant" by explaining that management argued "that the public objects to black hands touching the bacon."[33]

## THE TANGLED WEB OF CONFRONTATION

When we move from national policy and pronouncements to shop floor interaction, the tangled web of labor laws, union representation, employer and worker resistance, and race discrimination becomes apparent. The FEPC had to fight against structural as well as ideological restraints, against a labor market segmented by race and sex as well as outright racist practices. But the relationship between sex and race in the labor market could be complex because both manhood and womanhood were racialized. Whiteness could count more than manhood.[34]

The case against Capital Transit illuminates these factors. Capital Transit filed "white-only" job orders with the U.S. Employment Service; even after agreeing to comply with the FEPC in December 1942, it still rejected black applicants. The FEPC reorganization delayed action until mid-1943, but this case dragged on until the end of the war—and, for all intents and purposes, the demise of the FEPC.[35]

Employers often replaced white men with white women instead of drawing upon black men. Although some southern trade unionists called for the use of black men before white women out of the belief that women did not belong in heavy industry, employers from Mobile to Detroit hired or upgraded white women before turning to black men to meet "manpower" needs.[36] Capital Transit was such an employer. It attempted to hire white women when faced with a shortage of workers to meet the strains on Washington, D.C.'s transportation system. Five full-time women in April 1943 grew to slightly over fifty-five by October 1944. (There were nearly three thousand workers overall.) No standard qualifications existed for women operators; the company admitted bypassing the criteria by which it judged men. The *Chicago Defender* viewed this employment of white women as an attempt "to avoid compliance with the FEPC."[37]

Rather than hire African Americans, the company also advertised outside of the D.C. area. It petitioned other government agencies to cut non rush hour service, obtain more cars, and even increase the pay of its predominantly white male workforce. Its request for wage adjustments before the National War Labor Board (NWLB) appeared an attempted buy-off of white male workers, who had to give up the 12 to 4 P.M. and 4 to 8 P.M. shifts (or "runs") so the company could deploy women and still comply with labor laws that "prohibited women from working on any job in which they must stand continually for more than six hours at a time." In August 1943, the Amalgamated Association of Street, Electric, and Motor Coach Employees (AFL) reportedly "worked out the agreement" with the company for vacation allowance, time-and-a-half overtime and preparatory pay, more lunch time, and a "general wage increase of five-cents an hour" that then went to the NWLB. *The Defender* charged the wage hike necessary "to clinch the deal and make the 'bumping' concession sufficiently attractive." In essence, the company was rewarding men for foregoing seniority rights "that the women might have the more desirable runs," an FEPC investigator explained.[38]

The NWLB postponed ruling on the general wage increase, but approved vacations, other fringe benefits, and wage adjustments for jobs in the transportation department, shops, garage, carhouse, track, and roadway—places dominated by white men. Wartime agencies, other than the FEPC, often choose to reward "efficiency" rather than punish "discrimination."[39]

The company had turned to white women after white men protested against the upgrading of black men to platform workers. When the company introduced one carefully selected black man as an operator in February 1943, the white training operator refused to take him out and walked off the job, followed by sixteen others. The company did nothing to forestall this stoppage nor did it discipline those who tied up the tracks. Neither did it introduce a critical mass of black workers at one time. Under pressure from the FEPC, it hired an industrial relations sociologist to survey the attitudes of white workers, but it developed no educational program on the basis of this report.[40]

The report documented the unwillingness of white men, 80 percent of whom were from the South, to work with African Americans. But foremost in their minds was their role as breadwinners. "Quite frequently we would get the man moving over to a point of saying, 'Well now, I have got a wife and child. I have got this house to pay for,' " admitted the industrial relations consultant Paul S. Lunt. This understanding cut more than one way. White men could think twice before striking; they feared black male replacements undermining pay or seniority. Only 14.2 percent of the interviewed men claimed they were financially able to easily walk off the job; another 34.3 percent believed they could without undue hardship. Reinterviewed a year later, many recognized that striking would make them subject to the draft since it took sixty days to obtain a release from a war-designated position. Following the government takeover of the Philadelphia Transit Company, which had also tried to recruit white women rather than hire black men,[41] the Capital Transit workers thought that they could not get away with striking. Most admitted they would soon return. Lunt hypothesized that group cohesion, "fear of bodily harm or account of pressure from other operators," led about 20 percent of the men to say they would not train black workers. Certainly that was the case in Philadelphia, where a grand jury reported that employees held a "curiously weak social attitude which makes the right thinking man hesitate to stand right when he sees his fellows act wrongly." But what these commentators called "fear of the term 'scab' " measured a working-class brotherhood that had been nurtured on racial distinction and white supremacy.[42]

The AFL transit union was a segregated one, with separate meetings for black and white workers (not male and female ones, for race was the salient signifier). The International Union of Operating Engineers opposed discrimination, but leaders of the local refused to take a strong stand. At the next election, the victorious challenger William F. Sims defeated the incumbent president, whom he accused of "intermingling with Negroes." Sims objected to the use of black workers on platforms or even as "shifters" who drove buses or streetcars to another location after cleaning them. Racism mixed with working-class masculinity, as the "drunks" among the operators were "literally anxious to fight with Negroes" and reportedly carried "large knives." Almost a year later, in

December 1945 the head of the NAACP Legal Defense Fund Charles Hamilton Houston resigned from the FEPC to protest Truman's failure to end discriminatory practices when the army seized Capital Transit from striking workers. The company had hired few black men and no black women.[43] Capital Transit illustrates the weakness of the FEPC against employer intransigence, revealing how pockets of working-class racism offered an excuse for employer discrimination. It also suggests how employers manipulated gender as well as racial divisions of labor, preferring to add women than expand the racial diversity of the workforce.

The case against the International Brotherhood of Boilermakers, Iron Ship Builders, and Helpers of America (AFL) further reveals the gap between complaint, findings, and compliance. But here the self-activity of black workers generated a court case that reaffirmed the right to earn a living as fundamental to the Fourteenth Amendment.

The Boilermakers Union had exclusive jurisdiction over the West Coast shipyards, a closed-shop Master Agreement, which meant that all hires had to join the union to maintain their employment. But the international excluded African Americans from membership until 1937, when it decided to create segregated and unequal auxiliary lodges. Wartime shipyard locals allowed blacks to work without any kind of membership until early 1943, when rising numbers of black workers led the union to establish auxiliaries. Though blacks had to pay the same dues, they gained few services and those that they did—like insurance—were unequal. They alone received discipline for "intoxication." As historian Merle Reed, who provides the fullest account of the case, notes, the auxiliaries "lacked such basic union functions as membership in the international, the right to have independent business agents and grievance committees, the universal transfer of members seeking employment in other cities, and the right to advance in status."[44] Threatened by prefabrication, the union sought to maintain control over crafts skills; this need meshed with its refusal to admit black members, seen as lower-skilled, lower-paid workers.[45]

With "no voice in the affairs of the main body," with officers "subject" to the white local, black workers complained of "taxation without representation," as Joseph James of the San Francisco Committee Against Segregation and Discrimination protested in June 1943. Others called the union a "racket" into which one had to pay "to keep my job."[46]

James and his group were closely linked with the NAACP. An East Bay Shipyard Workers' Committee was close to the Communist Party; it attempted to take over an auxiliary but came up against the white power structure of the presiding local, which negated auxiliary election returns.

The NAACP group proved more militant, refusing to join segregated locals.[47] Like the March on Washington Movement, the shipyard dissidents drew upon the American creed in proclaiming their patriotism. They argued:

> We are Americans and we are at war. There is no time for discrimination and segregation in defense work. We are all trying to win this war and we must win. Then will a thousand or more Negroes be thrown out of work because they want their rights as Americans. We will have no part of an auxiliary. And to our white friends who are members of this Local this is a fight that concerns you.

They associated the union's "Jim Crow set-up" with Hitler's "master race" theories and drew upon the FEPC Executive Order to legitimatize their claims.[48] The union, as one plaintiff charged, "has denied to him the right to become a member of the Union whereby he may gain the means to support himself and family and to elevate himself and family in the social scale of the community." The very definition of manhood was at stake. These would-be boilermakers shared the sentiments of other angry black laborers who talked back to an official of Portland's Local 72. When "asked who the hell we thought we were," they "told him, men, the same as he or any other man."[49]

The union believed it had "a social problem," rather than an economic one. During the fall of 1942, Local 72 President Tom Ray had refused to establish auxiliaries, fearing them as the first step toward mixing African Americans with white women. Employer and union both rejected placement of black women in the higher grades, contending that they were too fat or illiterate. One man mocked these discriminatory practices by asking if "my wife [should] turn white for a job."[50] But Frances Albrier, the first black woman welder at Kaiser's Richmond, California, yards, got a temporary work permit by knowing her rights under the President's order—she was legislative chair of the State Association of Colored Women's Clubs—and by refusing to go away. She claimed that her letter to Roosevelt pushed the WMC to force establishment of auxiliaries in the Bay Area to get around the manpower shortage without undermining collective bargaining. These militant black shipworkers demanded inclusion in the union, not the end of the union contract as the Boilermakers countered. They argued that discrimination "weakens unions and the war effort," claiming that "the MEN and WOMEN who build the ships are the unions," that "true unionism" demanded "an end to discrimination." Before the Superior Court of California, they contended that "the demand . . . for equal membership . . . is an entirely different thing from an attack on the closed shop."[51]

The question before the courts became "whether a closed union coupled with a closed shop is a legitimate objective of organized labor." The union argued that it was a "private, voluntary association" and in that regard had the "right to limit membership to persons mutually acceptable." In *James v. Marinship Corporation*, the Supreme Court of California decided in December 1944 that "where a union has . . . attained a monopoly of the supply of labor," whether from a closed shop or any other kind of collective action, "such a union occupies a quasi public position similar to that of a public service business and it has certain corresponding obligations." A trade union, thus, was not like a golf club or fraternity: "Its asserted right to choose its own members does not merely relate to social relations; it affects the fundamental right to work for a living."[52] Moreover, employers could not hide behind such a contract to justify refusal to hire or their dismissal of black workers.

This ruling reinforced a Supreme Court decision earlier that year, *Wallace v. NLRB*, that employers could not rely on a closed-shop contract to discriminate. It went beyond the "fair representation" Tunstall and Steele cases decided against the railroad brotherhoods and Louisville and Nashville railroad, which merely said that union members treated unfairly could seek redress; a union chosen to represent all workers must treat each one the same.[53] Despite legal reinforcement, the FEPC found it difficult to gain adherence to its directives; its chair Malcolm Ross recounted that the union and management both felt "that it had no authority and could go jump in the lake."[54] The employers resisted acknowledging their role, but stopped firing black workers who refused to join the auxiliaries. The FEPC debated whether it could tackle segregation under its nondiscrimination mandate and in the end fudged the issue by deciding that the union had partially corrected its behavior, though the auxiliaries remained subordinate. The Boilermakers replaced the auxiliaries with separate black locals that retained many of the original disadvantages, such as transfer rights only to other "Negro lodges." The FEPC found that such a dual system "is inconsistent with the principle of majority rule." The long drawn out nature of this contestation meant that the end of the war and subsequent curtailment of shipbuilding left the case unresolved. Yet during the battle, individual black workers retained their jobs and the federal government joined with militants to assert African American rights at work.[55]

The legal victory in *Marinship* was pyrrhic. Local 6's 36,000 members, 3,000 of whom were black in 1944, dwindled to 1,800 by 1948, 150 of whom were black in an integrated local. Two-thirds of black San Francisco households were "skilled" in wartime tabulations because of the preponderance of shipyard jobs. Three years later, those numbers had dropped to one-third, with service workers and the unskilled composing more than half the black workforce. African Americans maintained their small gains in government and clerical work, but suffered disproportionately from unemployment.[56]

## CONCLUSION: THE STRUCTURAL DILEMMA

If the enemies earned by a government agency marked the extent of its effectiveness, then the FEPC successfully exposed union and management complicity with the structures of discrimination built into the "free" market. The Seafarers International Union (AFL) complained that the FEPC was forcing its members into unwelcome "physical proximity" by requiring work groups consisting of blacks and whites; so did the International Brotherhood of Teamsters (AFL). Telephone companies rejected directives to hire black women as operators "because of the intimate nature of the work, the close cooperation necessitated by the crews on the switch boards." St. Louis businessmen similarly justified discriminatory quotas by "citing a 'social pattern.' "[57] By puncturing the mythologies of race—that blacks were lazy, dirty, diseased, and poor workers; that you couldn't "mix" the races; that black men would rape and black women contaminate white women—the FEPC further earned the animus of powerful congressmen. National postwar politics dampened African American economic progress.

The fight for a permanent FEPC occurred in the context of economic reconversion. The UAW recognized:

> This issue isn't only one of fairness to our Negro brothers. The plot to destroy fair employment policy is part of a much bigger thing, an overall campaign to destroy the unity of workers. . . . They're planning scarcity, top profits, and a dog-eat-dog fight among the unemployed for the few available jobs.

During this retreat from full employment, "the destruction of FEPC protection," like "super-seniority" for veterans, belonged to a larger strategy of pitting workers against each other. The NAACP similarly recognized the importance of full employment for the fair employment campaign. It believed "it will be that much easier to enforce the rights under [FEPC], if there are jobs for all." The proposed Full Employment Act of 1945 had made it a federal obligation to provide jobs when private industry failed. But the act that actually passed in 1946 merely called for "maximum employment, production, and purchasing power" without anything more than authorizing a presidential annual report on the economy.[58]

Congress also returned the U.S. Employment Service to the states. Without a FEPC watchdog, those terminated from wartime labor as well as returning veterans faced Southern regimes, which had promoted employment discrimination in the past. As the *Pittsburgh Courier* accurately noted, "It is not as likely that unemployment compensation benefits will be administered equitably in States where the standard of living of colored people is depressed and State policy is to discriminate against them in the denial to them of political and civil rights."[59]

Victory ended war-related industry, canceling contracts in ordinance, shipbuilding, aircraft, and munitions, where 90 percent of black war workers labored. Nonwhite employment in manufacturing in Detroit, for example, dropped from 13.2 percent to 10.7 percent; black women lost whatever gains they had made.[60] With labor shortages ending, black workers faced the old foes of joblessness and low wages. During the war, cotton pickers received $3.90 per hundred pounds, but by September 1945, it was "back to starvation wage" at $2.10 per hundred, a move approved by the secretary of agriculture. Mechanization of agriculture depressed rural conditions, encouraging further migration to cities and thus increasing job competition at the bottom of the industrial and service markets.[61]

But in meatpacking, steel, and automobiles, industries with strong CIO unions, black male workers retained a foothold, even if they remained plagued by lesser seniority and disproportionately stood at the low end of job ladders. Employers, after all, retained their ultimate right to hire, despite union insistence on nondiscrimination and efforts to upgrade black workers.[62] Where the civil rights movement was also strong, as in Detroit, black men still held on to semiskilled jobs, rising to over a quarter of the automobile labor force by 1960. National averages, however, reflected the maintenance of racial bars in the South: from 1940 to 1960, African Americans in automobile work grew only from 4 to 9 percent.[63]

The failure to sustain federal protection of "the right to work" would reverberate throughout the succeeding decades. In the absence of government-generated jobs during the subsequent era of deindustrialization, the black working class could turn mainly to public assistance from states that denied jobs and discriminated against welfare eligibility. The

1964 Civil Rights Act came too late. We suffer from these developments still.

## NOTES

Research for this chapter depended on grants from Howard University, Office of the Academic Vice-President.

1. "Summary of the Complaint: 12-BR-276," in "Request for Further Action," memo to Mr. Will Maslow, Director of Field Operations, from Harry L. Kingman, Regional Director, December 6, 1944, in Papers of the President's Committee on Fair Employment Practice (FEPC), microfilm edition of Record Group 228, National Archives, Roll 106F (field offices), hereafter referred to as FEPC Papers.

2. FEPC officials and their progressive supporters deployed this term, not to be confused with the anti-union "right to work" that the Taft-Hartley Act of 1947 promulgated. For one example, "The Right to Work," radio script, Office Files of Max Berking, FEPC Papers, Roll 3H. I discuss this concept in " 'Right to Work is the Right to Live!': Fair Employment and the Quest for Social Citizenship," in Manfred Berg and Martin Geyer, eds., *The Culture of Rights* (New York: Cambridge University Press with the German Historical Institute, forthcoming).

3. Harold M. Baron, "The Demand for Black Labor: Historical Notes on the Political Economy of Racism," in James Green, ed., *Workers' Struggles, Past and Present: A "Radical America" Reader* (Philadelphia: Temple Univiversity Press, 1971), p. 47. See also Thomas J. Sugrue, *The Origins of the Urban Crisis: Race and Inequality in Postwar Detroit* (Princeton: Princeton University Press, 1996), p. 92.

4. Michael Goldfield, *The Color of Politics: Race and the Mainsprings of American Politics* (New York: The New Press, 1997), pp. 265–266.

5. Charley Cherokee, "National Grapevine: May It Rest in Peace," *The Chicago Defender*, February 12, 1944, p. 13.

6. "Testimony of Malcolm Ross, Chairman, President's Committee on Fair Employment Practice, Before the House Labor Committee in Hearings on HR 3986—78th Congress, Second Session," in file: "Office Files—Max Berking," Reel 3H, FEPC papers, 1. For an analysis that parallels my own, Nelson Lichtenstein, "Rights Consciousness and the Social Market Economy," in Pauli Kettunen and Hanna Eskola, eds., *Models, Modernity and the Myrdals*, (Helsinki: Renvall Institute for Area and Cultural Studies, 1997), pp. 40–41.

7. Dona Cooper Hamilton and Charles V. Hamilton, *The Dual Agenda: The African-American Struggle for Civil and Economic Equality* (New York: Columbia University Press, 1997), pp. 8–42; Paul D. Moreno, *From Direct Action to Affirmative Action: Fair Employment Law and Policy in America, 1933–1972*

(Baton Rouge: Louisiana State University Press, 1997), pp. 54–65; see also Eileen Boris, "The Racialized Gendered State: Constructions of Citizenship in the United States," *Social Politics* 2 (Summer 1995): pp. 170–172.

8. I've discussed the sexualizing of economic demands through the cry of "social equality" in " 'You Wouldn't Want One of 'Em Dancing with Your Wife': Racialized Bodies on the Job in WWII," *American Quarterly* 50 (March 1998): 77–108.

9. Robert H. Zieger, *The CIO: 1933–1955* (Chapel Hill: University of North Carolina Press, 1995), pp. 152–163; Kevin Boyle, " 'There Are No Union Sorrows That the Union Can't Heal': The Struggle for Racial Equality in the United Automobile Workers, 1940–1960," *Labor History* 36 (Winter 1995): pp. 5–23; Michael Goldfield, "Race and the CIO: The Possibilities for Racial Egalitarianism During the 1930s and 1940s," *International Labor and Working Class History* 44 (Fall 1993): 1-32; Robert Korstad and Nelson Lichtenstein, "Opportunities Found and Lost: Labor, Radicals, and the Early Civil Rights Movement," *Journal of American History* 75 (December 1988), 786–811. Marshall F. Stevenson, Jr., however, suggests whatever progress existed came from the demands of black trade unionists; see "Beyond Theoretical Models: The Limited Possibilities of Racial Egalitarianism," *International Labor and Working-Class History* 44 (Fall 1993): 45–52. For another more negative assessment, Bruce Nelson, "Class, Race and Democracy in the CIO: The 'New' Labor History Meets the 'Wages of Whiteness,' " *International Review of Social History* 41 (1996): 351–374.

10. For discussion of such conflict, see below, and Earl Lewis, *In Their Own Interests: Race, Class, and Power in Twentieth-Century Norfolk, Virginia* (Berkeley: University of California Press, 1991), pp. 167–198; Joe William Trotter, Jr., *Black Milwaukee: The Making of an Industrial Proletariat, 1915–45* (Urbana: University of Illinois Press, 1985), pp. 147–195; August Meier and Elliott Rudwick, *Black Detroit and the Rise of the UAW* (New York: Oxford University Press, 1979); Michael K. Honey, *Southern Labor and Black Civil Rights: Organizing Memphis Workers* (Urbana: University of Illinois Press, 1993), pp. 177–213; Richard W. Thomas, *Life for Us Is What We Make It: Building Black Community in Detroit, 1915–1945* (Bloomington: University of Indiana Press, 1992), pp. 143–173; Marilynn S. Johnson, *The Second Gold Rush: Oakland and the East Bay in World War II* (Berkeley: University of California Press, 1993), pp. 60–82.

11. Kevin Boyle, *The UAW and the Heyday of American Liberalism, 1945–1968* (Ithaca: Cornell University Press, 1995), pp. 108–113.

12. Hugh Davis Graham, *The Civil Rights Era: Origins and Development of National Policy* (New York: Oxford University Press, 1990); Paul Burstein, *Discrimination, Jobs, and Politics: The Struggle for Equal Employment Opportunity*

*in the United States since the New Deal* (Chicago: University of Chicago Press, 1985).

13. For a brilliant tracing of this process, Thomas J. Sugrue, "The Structures of Urban Poverty: The Reorganization of Space and Work in Three Periods of American History," in Michael B. Katz, ed., *The "Underclass" Debate: Views from History* (Princeton: Princeton University Press, 1993), pp. 85–117; for black women's work patterns, Jacqueline Jones, *Labor of Love, Labor of Sorrow: Black Women, Work, and the Family* (New York: Basic Books, 1986).

14. E. Franklin Frazier, "Ethnic and Minority Groups in Wartime, with Special Reference to the Negro," *American Journal of Sociology* 48 (November 1942): 373–374.

15. Lorenzo F. Davis, "Negro War Worker—Asset or Liability? America Must Decide Now," *Semi-Annual Report*, Brooklyn Urban League Industrial Department, pp. 6–7, attached to letter to Jonathan Daniels from Francis J. Haas, September 2, 1943, Box 4, File: "Aug.–Sept. 43," Office Files 4245-G, Roosevelt Library, Hyde Park (FEPC-FDR); for statistics, D'Ann Campbell, *Women at War with America: Private Lives in a Patriotic Era* (Cambridge: Harvard University Press, 1984), pp. 74–76, 107; Susan Hartmann, *The Home Front and Beyond: American Women in the 1940s* (Boston: Twayne, 1982), pp. 77–82.

16. George Lipsitz, *Rainbow at Midnight: Labor and Culture in the 1940s* (Urbana: University of Illinois Press, 1994), p. 73; *Final Report: Fair Employment Practice Committee*, June 28, 1946 (Washington D.C.: U.S. Government Printing Office, 1947), p. 3; Desmond King, *Separate and Unequal: Black Americans and the US Federal Government* (Oxford: Oxford University Press, 1995), pp. 72–108; for massive layoffs, "Statement of the United Electrical, Radio and Machine Workers of America (UE) to Sub-Committee on Labor and Labor Management Relations of the Senate Labor and Public Welfare Committee Urging Immediate Adoption of Federal FEPC Legislation," May 6, 1952, Pt. 13, Ser. B, Reel 13, "FEPC-General, 1951–54," Papers of the NAACP, microfilm edition.

17. Merl E. Reed, *Seedtime for the Modern Civil Rights Movement: The President's Committee on Fair Employment Practice, 1941–1946* (Baton Rouge: Louisiana State University Press, 1991); Herbert Hill, *Black Labor and the American Legal System: Race, Work, and the Law* (Madison: University of Wisconsin Press, 1985), pp. 173–381; Paula F. Pfeffer, *A. Philip Randolph, Pioneer of the Civil Rights Movement* (Baton Rouge: Louisiana State University Press, 1990); for percentage of cases, Table 9, "Comparison of docketings with closings . . . involving total and Negro women complainants by region," *First Report: Fair Employment Practice Committee*, July 1943–December 1944 (Washington, D.C.: U.S. Government Printing Office, 1945), p. 133.

18. In addition to sources in note 17, see also *Final Report*, VIII, pp. 8–23.

19. Executive Office of the President, Bureau of the Budget, Memorandum for Mr. Marvin McIntyre from Jonathan Daniels, January 26, 1943, attached to Memorandum for Honorable Francis Biddle, February 1, 1943, Box 3, File "Jan.-April 43," FEPC-FDR; *Call to Negro America*, n.d., in Charles Dellums Papers, Carton 21, Folder "March on Washington," Bancroft Library, University of California, Berkeley; A. Philip Randolph, "Why Should We March?" *Survey Graphic* (November 1942): 488; "What About the FEPC?" *Pittsburgh Courier*, April 17, 1943; Jill Quadagno, *The Color of Welfare: How Racism Undermined the War on Poverty* (New York: Oxford University Press, 1994), pp. 17–25.

20. Monsignor Francis J. Haas, "Address to the Sixty-Third Convention of the American Federation of Labor," in Reel 75H, Folder "Press Releases," FEPC papers.

21. For a version of these events, see FEPC's last chair, Malcolm Ross, *All Manner of Men* (New York: Reynal and Hitchcock, 1948), pp. 118–141; Eric Arnesen, "The Failure of Protest: Black Labor, the FEPC, and the Railroad Industry," paper presented at the Tenth Southern Labor Studies Conference, Williamsburg, Virginia, September 1997.

22. Quoted in Ross, *All Manner of Men*, pp. 134, 114.

23. For an overall assessment, Reed, *Seedtime*, pp. 345–357.

24. For the membership of the FEPC, see Reed, *Seedtime*.

25. Stanley High, "How the Negro Fights for Freedom," *The Reader's Digest* 41 (July 1942): 117; "30 Unions Bar Negroes," *Pittsburgh Courier*, July 7, 1945, p. 18.

26. Office of War Information, Press Release, N-294, "Southern War Labor Conference," n.d., 1945, in Ser. A., Reel 12, "Cutbacks"; pamphlet, *A.F. of L. Wants F.E.P.C.*, Ser. B, Reel 13, "FEPC, General, 51–54," both in Pt. 13, NAACP Papers; "AFL to Keep Dual Unions," *Pittsburgh Courier*, December 9, 1944, pp. 1, 4.

27. "Separate Union Plan Attacked," *Pittsburgh Courier*, January 13, 1945, p. 4; "Outlaw Separate Locals for Workers," *Pittsburgh Courier*, March 3, 1945, pp. 1, 5.

28. For a summary of the CP, see Goldfield, *The Color of Politics*, pp. 190–198; "Murray Says: CIO Is Negro's Best Friend," *Pittsburgh Courier*, June 9, 1945, p. 17.

29. P. L. Prattis, "CIO Pledges Equality at Labor Meet," *Pittsburgh Courier*, October 13, 1945, p. 15; "One Policy for North, South, CIO Pledge," *Pittsburgh Courier*, December 23, 1944; Walter P. Reuther, "You Can't Buy Brotherhood," *A Labor Reports Reprint* (New York: Atran Center, n.d.), Pt. 13, Ser. B, Reel 13, "FEPC-General, 1951–54," NAACP Papers; P. L. Prattis, "The Horizon," *Pittsburgh Courier*, December 2, 1944, p. 7.

30. Nelson Lichtenstein, "From Corporatism to Collective Bargaining: Organized Labor and the Eclipse of Social Democracy in the Postwar Era," in Steve Fraser and Gary Gerstle, eds., *The Rise and Fall of the New Deal Order, 1930–1980* (Princeton: Princeton University Press, 1989), pp. 122–252.

31. Weaver in "Labor: Equality Campaign," *Business Week*, May 9, 1942, p. 71.

32. St. Clair Drake and Horace R. Cayton, *Black Metropolis: A Study of Negro Life in a Northern City*, I (1945: New York: Harper and Row, 1962, revised edition), pp. 214–262, 287–341; Margaret Brown, "Race at Work: A Comparison of the Employment Policies of Three Industrial Firms During World War II," unpublished paper, Social Science History Association, Fall 1995; Bernice Anita Reed, "Accommodation Between Negro and White Employees in a West Coast Aircraft Industry, 1942–1944," *Social Forces* 26 (1947).

33. Bernice Anita Reed, "Accommodation Between Negro and White Employees," *Social Forces* 26 (1947): 83–84; other quotations from Drake and Cayton, *Black Metropolis*, pp. 336, 334; see also Robin D. G. Kelley, "Contested Terrain: Resistance on Public Transportation," in *Race Rebels: Culture, Politics, and the Black Working Class* (New York: Free Press, 1994), pp. 55–75; Boris, " 'You Wouldn't Want One of 'Em Dancing.' " For the racial militancy of the United Packinghouse Workers of America (CIO), Rick Halpern and Roger Horowitz, *Meatpackers: An Oral History of Black Packinghouse Workers and Their Struggle for Racial and Economic Equality* (New York: Twayne, 1996).

34. For another example, Bruce Nelson, "Organized Labor and the Struggle for Black Equality in Mobile during World War II," *Journal of American History* 80 (December 1993): 952–988.

35. The most complete discussion of the case is in Hill, *Black Labor*, pp. 322–331; see also, Ross, *All Manner of Men*, pp. 156–162.

36. "Summary Sent to FEPC," n.d., p.170, and "Information For Committee On Seven (7) To Be Discussed In Connection With Atlas Powder Company, As Set Forth In Our Letter Of May 29, 1943," p. 113, both in St. Louis Scrapbook, Brotherhood of Sleeping Car Porters, Chicago Historical Society; "Racial Employment Problems," p. 1, Box 5, File "Catledge," FEPC-FDR Library; testimony of William Mitch, United Mine Workers of America, at Birmingham Hearings of FEPC, June 18, 1943, Vol. I, 95, Reel 17H; "Report on Conditions at the Dodge Plant as Told by Francis Glenn, Dodge Local #3 to G. James Fleming," January 29, 1943, Reel 59F, Folder "Chrysler, Dodge Division," both in FEPC papers; see also Bruce Nelson, "Organized Labor and the Struggle for Black Equality in Mobile during World War II," *Journal of American History* 80 (December 1993): 952–988.

37. Hill, *Black Labor*, pp. 322–330. Ernest E. Johnson, "FEPC Maneuvers To Get Race Men On D.C. Busses," *The Chicago Defender*, August 14, 1943; for number of women hired, statement of Edward A. Roberts, Director of Passenger Operations, Highway Transport Dept., Office of Defense Transport, p. 71; statement of Samuel E. Emmons, Transportation Manager, Capital Transit, p. 102; "In the Matter of: Capital Transit Company Respondent, Washington, D.C., Jan. 15, 1945," Alderson Reporting Co., Case No. 70, Reel 22H, "Capital Transit," FEPC Papers.

38. Johnson, "FEPC Maneuvers To Get Race Men On D.C. Busses"; "NAACP Washington Branch," *Evening Star*, April 21, 1945; "Negroes Fight Plan to Cut Service," *Washington Tribune*, March 24, 1945; "Plan to Cut Transit," *Evening Star*, March 21, 1945; "Group Protest Plan to Reduce Street Car Trips," *Washington Post*, March 28, 1945; for a summary of company maneuvers, see statement of Mrs. Evelyn Cooper (for FEPC), pp. 10–18, January 15, 1945, Hearing.

39. "In Capital Transit Company and Amalgamated Association of Street, Electric Railway and Motor Coach Employees of America, Division no. 689 (AFL)," Case No. 13-264, August 7, 1943, p. 10, *War Labor Board Reports* 783 [*War Labor Board Reports: Wage and Salary Stabilization*, Vol. 10 (Washington, D.C.: Bureau of National Affairs, 1944)]. Eventually the NWLB refused the across-the-board raise, but approved a bonus plan. "In the Matter of Capital Transit Company," QQ-12, Case No. 13-264, March 29, 1944, in United States Department of Labor, *The Termination Report of the National War Labor Board*, Vol. 3: *Industrial Disputes and War Stabilization in Wartime*, January 12, 1942–December 31, 1945 (Washington, D.C.: U.S. Government Printing Office, 1947), pp. 1005–1007.

40. Statement of Evelyn Cooper, January 15, 1945, Hearing, pp. 12–15; "Opening Statement of Edmund L. Jones, Counsel of Capital Transit Company," Press Release, Box 7, File: "NWLB," FEPC-FDR Library, pp. 4–5.

41. Lipsitz, *Rainbow at Midnight*, p. 79.

42. Statement of Paul S. Lunt, January 15, 1945, Hearing, pp. 108–131; Federal Grand Jury for June in the District Court of the United States for the Eastern District of Pennsylvania, "In Re: Investigation of the Philadelphia Transportation Co. Strike," pp. 6–7, attached to letter to Philleo Nash from Gerald A. Glesson, October 6, 1944, Box 8, File: "Philadelphia," FEPC-FDR Library. For working-class racism, David R. Roediger, *The Wages of Whiteness: Race and the Making of the American Working Class* (New York: Verso, 1991).

43. "Racial Conditions in the District of Columbia," December 7, 1944, pp. 1–3, attached to letter to Jonathan Daniels from J. Edgar Hoover, December 9,

1944, Box 7, "NWLB," FEPC-FDR Library; but for confirmation on racism of the union and its new president, "Minutes," Citizens Committee on Race Relations, January 23, 1945, Discussion on FEPC hearing, Charles Hamilton Houston Papers, pp. 163–219, Folder 1, Moorland-Spingarn Research Center, Howard University; "Houston Tells Why He Resigned," *Chicago Defender*, December 1945, Clipping in Box 163-17, folder 35, Houston Papers; for Truman's seizure and Houston's resignation, see Reed, *Seedtime*, pp. 333–337.

44. Reed, *Seedtime*, pp. 267–317, quote at p. 268; see also, Hill, *Black Labor*, pp. 185–206; Ross, *All Manner of Men*, pp. 142–152; Charles Wollenberg, "James v. Marinship: Trouble on the New Black Frontier," in Daniel Cornford, ed. *Working People of California* (Berkeley: University of California Press, 1995), pp. 159–179; William H. Harris, "Federal Intervention in Union Discrimination: FEPC and West Coast Shipyards During World War II," *Labor History* 22 (Summer 1981): 325–347.

45. See the discussion in Johnson, *The Second Gold Rush*, pp. 67–76.

46. Joseph James, *Against the Setting Up of Auxiliary Unions for Negroes*, Case 1E-UR-70, Boilermakers' Local 6, San Francisco; to FEPC from W. A. Stiles, February 15, 1943; to Mrs. Roosevelt from Amazel Gordon, January 24, 1944, both in Case 12-UR-32, Boilermakers Local 513, Richmond, all in Reel 108F, FEPC Papers.

47. Johnson, *The Second Gold Rush*, pp. 72–73. The actions of the San Francisco committee come through in FEPC records on the Boilermakers, Reel 108F.

48. James, *Against the Setting Up of Auxiliary Unions*; flyer, *Attention Boilermakers*, May 22, 1943, Reel 108F, Case 1E-UR-70, Boilermakers' Local 6, San Francisco, FEPC Papers.

49. In the Circuit Court of the State of Oregon for Multnomah County, *Lee Anderson v. Mr. Hood*, Local 72 et al., *Complaint in Equity*, 5; see also, letter from Robert L. Rhone Jr. to Msgr. F. J. Haas, September 3, 1943, both in Reel 108F, Case 12-UR-57, Boilermakers' Union Local 72, Portland, and complaint, R. H. Mitchell, October 16, 1943, Reel 108F, Case 12-UR-37, Boilermakers Local 401, Vancouver, both in FEPC papers.

50. R.T. White to Kind Sir, President, March 23, 1943, in Reel 112F, Boilermakers Auxiliary Union, Issue August 20, 1943, Exhibit C, FEPC Papers.

51. Hill, *Black Labor*, pp. 199, 193–195; Reed, *Seedtime*, pp. 280, 306; Shipyard Workers Committee Against Discrimination, " 'Put a Man in a Ditch . . . ,' " undated pamphlet; in the Superior Court of the State of California, *Joseph James vs. Marinship*, No. 15371, "Plaintiff's Memorandum in Support of Order for Issuance of Injunction," 2, both in Reel 108F, Boilermakers', FEPC Papers.

52. *James v. Marinship Corporation*, [25 Cal. 2d] 155 P.2d (1944) at pp. 334-335.

53. *Steele v. Louisville & Nashville Railroad*, 323 U.S. 192 (1944); *Tunstall v. Brotherhood of Locomotive Firemen and Enginemen*. 323 U.S. 210 (1944); Marjorie McKenzie, "Pursuit of Democracy: NLRB Case and Not Rail Brotherhood Goes to Hear of Issue Facing Negroes," *Pittsburgh Courier*, December 30, 1944, p. 6; "Firemen Win Railroad Fight," *Pittsburgh Courier*, December 23, 1944, pp. 1, 5; see also, Eric Arnesen, "The Death Knell of Jim Crow Unionism? Race, Law, and Railroad Labor in Mid-Twentieth Century America," unpublished paper in author's possession.

54. Ross quoted in Wollenberg, "James v. Marinship," p. 173.

55. Hill, *Black Labor*, pp. 204–206; Reed, *Seedtime*, pp. 298–317.

56. Wollenberg, "James v. Marinship," pp. 174–175.

57. *Final Report*, pp. 18–22; Ross, *All Manner of Men*, pp. 108–117; Harry Kingman to Clarence Mitchell on Status of Telephone Cases, November 28, 1944, p. 2, Case No. 12-BR-276, Folder "Pacific Telephone and Telegraph Co., Palto Alto," Reel 106F, FEPC Papers.

58. "Planning Recess Despite Critical Needs," *United Automobile Worker* 9 (July 15, 1945), 8; Hamilton and Hamilton, *The Dual Agenda*, pp. 62, 70; NAACP, "Jobs for All," draft of a leaflet on full employment, August 1945, in Pr. 13, Ser. B, Reel 12, "FEPC—General, 1935," NAACP Papers.

59. Louis Lautier, "Senate Passes States Rights Jobless Pay Bill; Ends USES," *Pittsburgh Courier*, September 29, 1945.

60. For reconversion figures, see *Final Report*, pp. 48–83, esp. p. 62

61. "Dixie Cotton Pickers Helpless To Protest $2.10 Wage Scale," *Pittsburgh Courier*, September 29, 1945; *Final Report*, pp. 94–95. Nicholas Lemann, *The Promised Land*, provides one portrait of this process.

62. John H. Young III, "Job Famine May Sweep Nation," *Pittsburgh Courier*, August 25, 1945, pp. 1, 4; Boyle, *The UAW and the Heyday of American Liberalism*; Halpern and Horowitz, *Meatpackers*.

63. Women workers as women made even less progress; see Ruth Milkman, *Gender at Work: The Dynamics of Job Segregation by Sex During World War II* (Urbana: University of Illinois Press, 1987), p.126.

# Epilogue
## African Americans and the Dawning
## of the Postindustrial Era

### HENRY LOUIS TAYLOR, JR., AND MARK NAISON

This volume about African Americans is one that emphasizes agency, community building, and the struggle to shape federal labor and New Deal policies. Michael B. Katz, in *The Underclass Debate: Views from History*, defines two elements of agency that concerns us. His first meaning of agency refers to action directed toward individual goals such as the maintenance of home and family, or the pursuit of rewarding work. In its second sense, agency means collective action directed toward group goals, including politics, protest, and community building.[1]

Agency, then, stands at the center of this volume. Black people faced hostile racism and structural inequality throughout the industrial era. In this setting, their ability to advance and make progress was dependent in part on the internal strength of the black community. Between 1900 and 1950, African Americans both individually and collectively fought against racism and searched for a good place to live and raise their families, build communities, secure work, and advance occupationally. However, in the industrial city such simple pursuits brought them up against racism, the status quo, and those who wanted to maintain the color occupational system, with its castelike features.[2]

During the period from 1900–1950, there was a widening recognition that black advancement not only required a transformation of racist attitudes but also a dismantling of those structural elements that reinforced the place of African Americans in the existing social order. So in the industrial era, in many ways the struggles of African Americans were as much against the structures of inequality as they were against the hostile, racist attitudes of whites. The legacy of the industrial era is that it bequeathed a postindustrial era in which there was a new set of structural inequalities that continued to create havoc in the lives of African Americans. Consequently, blacks remained at the bottom of the economic ladder during the postindustrial era, even though they made great strides on the Civil Rights front.

The black industrial city experience consisted of two interactive dimensions. One dimension dealt with *agency* and the internal strength of the black community. From the high ground of retrospection, blacks in the industrial era—despite setbacks—built strong communities and won important victories in their struggles against racism and the structures of inequality. Community building combined with these victories to set the stage for the emergence of the modern civil rights movement and tearing down of the color bar. [3]

Four factors explain the success of blacks during this period. First, black communities were continually infused with new residents from the countryside. This meant that black urban communities were not only growing in the industrial city, but they also were constantly being renewed with energetic, hopeful residents. Second, the movement of blacks from farm to the city led to a social transformation of the urban population that greatly strengthened the black community.[4] Steady migration to the industrial city led to much greater social and economic differentiation in the black community, which spawned the emergence of an industrial proletariat and cultural middle class that fortified and led the black community during this complex period. Third, the African American working- and middle classes grew more prosperous during the 1940s and 1950s. This gave them the financial ability to buy new homes, move into white neighborhoods dominated by owner-occupied housing, and expand the ranks of the college-educated elites.[5] Finally, African Americans stressed unity throughout the period, which allowed them to remain a cohesive group despite class and gender divisions.

Of these four factors, black unity was the key ingredient. Solidarity, more than any other factor, explains why blacks were able to advance during the industrial era. The African American community was no monolith. Class and gender-based divisions spawned chronic tensions. For example, in Atlanta, some working class blacks sought to defend their dignity and expand their incomes in ways that offended the city's black middle-class leaders. They gravitated to the junk joints and clubs of Decatur Street, held turbulent rent parties, stole from employees, and engaged in individual outbursts against segregation practices in public transportation.[6]

These patterns of resistance co-existed with a vibrant black working-class church culture where poor African Americans, especially black women, could express themselves freely.[7] Expressive and hedonistic elements found in popular religious movements such as the Nation of Islam and Father Divine's Movement, Pentacostal and Holiness churches and political movements such as the Universal Negro Improvement Association and Communist Party appealed to working class African Americans.[8] These cultural differences combined with differences in work and everyday life were sources of constant tension within the African American community.[9]

The confrontation of blacks with overt racism, white supremacy, and racial violence explains why these class dissimilarities did not split apart the black community. When African Americans moved to urban centers, they faced both racially segmented labor markets and severe limits on their access to housing, health care, education, consumer purchasing and public recreation. U.S. cities, in the industrial era, resembled a minefield where physical assault, insult, or public humiliation threatened blacks in most residential neighborhoods, in parks, playgrounds, and beaches, and in portions of downtown business districts and public transportation systems. Blacks had their access to public space severely limited not only in Washington, Baltimore, and St. Louis, but also in New York and Chicago, where police practices and white harassment made blacks unable to freely shop, stroll, or use public recreation space outside of black neighborhoods.[10] In this volatile setting, unity and collective action were essential to racial advancement and this led to the development of a culture of protest among African Americans.

Together, continual renewal of the black community with energetic new residents, the rise of the industrial proletariat and cultural middle class, the growth of individual and community wealth, the ideology of racial pride, self-help, solidarity, and group advancement combined with the development of a culture of protest to greatly strengthen the black community and supercharge agency in the black community.[11]

Community building and agency reflected the internal dimensions of black advancement and community development. These internal forces demonstrated the ways in which African Americans responded to their circumstances through the building of families and communities, struggling against the varied forms of racism, and fighting to advance occupationally.[12] However, during the industrial era, black agency was constrained by powerful *external* forces, which formed the second dimension that shaped the development of black life in the industrial city.

Consequently, despite the internal strength of the African American community and their victories against racism, the legacy of the industrial city still left them in a weakened state.

First, while blacks won many important battles, the color occupational structure remained intact. For example, Robert C. Weaver believed that while programs such as the PWA, the NRA, and the Fair Labor Standards Act ended the era of racial wage differentials, they did not dismantle the color occupational structure. It remained intact throughout the industrial era and continued into the postindustrial era. The color occupational system was characterized by a dual labor market that kept blacks from competing with whites for jobs and opportunities and that channeled them into the most technologically backward and obsolete occupational categories.[13] Thus, despite the occupational advancements, black not only remained trapped in the occupational basement but also found themselves locked in the most technologically obsolete industrial jobs. The continued automation of those industries where African Americans were concentrated made scholars and policymakers deeply concerned about the plight of black workers. Unless blacks were able to get jobs in the newer, more technologically advanced industries on a nondiscriminatory basis, the future was bleak. Earlier, in 1936 Alba Edwards of the Census Bureau had the threat of automation in mind when he spoke in dire, but prophetic terms about the future of black workers:

> For many decades large numbers of Negroes have engaged in gainful occupations in the United States. They have helped produce its wealth, and they have had an important part in its social and economic life. . . . What has the future in store for Negro workers? As the years pass, will a larger or a smaller proportion of them engage in gainful labor, and will they become a more or a less important factor in the labor force of the nation? What changes will take place in their occupational and industrial distribution, and what changes in their socioeconomic status? If, with the further mechanization of industry, the machine takes over much of the unskilled work they are now doing, will they be able to rise to higher pursuits, or will they replace white workers in the remaining unskilled pursuits, or, finally, will they largely fall into that permanently unemployed class certain writers have prophesied that we shall have in the future?. . . . *Indeed, may it possibly come to pass that a century after a war was fought largely to free the Negro slaves, the descendants of the slave owners, along with other white persons, will be working to support on a permanent dole, large numbers of the descendants of the former slaves* [emphasis added].[14]

Robert Weaver probably had these rhetorical questions in mind when he offered a set of recommendations that would keep Edwards's prophesy from coming true. In these recommendations, he called for a national policy of "full employment," which was designed both as an alternative to welfare and as a mechanism for guaranteeing a job to all blacks who wanted to work.[15]

Specifically, Weaver supported passage of the Murray-Wagner Full Employment Bill, which would give government and private industry joint responsibility for creating full employment. In other words, when the private sector failed to produce enough jobs, the government would be responsible for generating work for those who could not find it. Second, he called for measures that would keep black war workers from losing their jobs during economic downturns. Third, he called for a reevaluation and assessment of seniority, and finally, he called for the continuation of the FEPC in postwar years (1) as evidence that the United States is committed to encouraging fair employment, (2) to prevent a resurgence of prejudiced labor union practices, and (3) to oversee the continual movement of blacks into new industrial jobs on a nondiscriminatory basis. These measures, if enacted, would make sure that black workers did not become members of "that permanently unemployed class certain writers have prophesied.[16]

These policies were embedded in Weaver's conviction that the problems facing African Americans could not be solved without dismantling the color occupational system and giving African Americans the "right to work" in a nondiscriminatory environment. But that did not happen. The proposed Full Employment Act of 1945, intended to initiate a federal obligation to provide jobs when private industry could not, was dramatically changed. When the act passed in 1946, it merely called for "maximum employment, production, and purchasing power" without anything more than authorizing a presidential annual report on the economy.[17] Moreover, the FEPC was defunded, which meant that there would be no watchdog agency to fight against employment discrimination. At a time when the economy was being converted from a war to peacetime one, whites believed there was no place for such a watchdog agency, even if it had no enforcement powers.[18]

Concurrently with the defeat of the Full Employment Act of 1945 and defunding of the FEPC came the introduction of a machine that ended the era of agriculture as a prominent part of black life and culture.[19] On October 2, 1944, an event took place in the Mississippi Delta that forever changed the lives of African Americans. On that day about three thousand blacks gathered in a cotton field on the outskirts of Clarksdale, Mississippi, to watch the first successful demonstration of the mechanical cotton picker. The crowd was overwhelmed by what they saw. In an hour, a top manual laborer could pick twenty pounds of cotton. The mechanical cotton picker could pick a thousand pounds of cotton in the same length of time. In 1949, about 6 percent of southern cotton was harvested by machine; by 1964, it was 78 percent, and by 1972, 100 percent of southern cotton was harvested mechanically.[20] The black agricultural worker had been displaced. Planters evicted millions of tenants from the land. Homeless and without work, they moved to southern, northern, and western cities in search of jobs and opportunities.

As they started the Second Great Migration, African Americans were unaware that a second technological revolution had already begun to eliminate jobs in the manufacturing industries of Chicago, Detroit, Cleveland, New York, and elsewhere. Initially blacks found limited access to unskilled jobs in the auto, steel, rubber, chemical, and meatpacking industries. However, as they advanced into the technologically obsolete industrial jobs, automation began taking its toll in the mid-1950s, especially in the unskilled jobs where African Americans were most heavily concentrated. For example, between 1953 and 1962, 1.6 million blue-collar jobs were lost in the manufacturing sector.[21] By the mid-1960s, not only were blacks experiencing double-digit unemployment but also declining participation in the labor force. For the first time, discouraged black workers were dropping out of the labor force.[22]

Earlier, the technological displacement of black workers took place in an expanding industrial economy that continually produced new, unskilled, low-paying jobs, which rapidly absorbed them. "This time," as the economist Jeremy Rifkin points out, "the economic displacement created in its wake a new and permanent underclass in the inner cities and the conditions for widespread social unrest and violence for the remainder of the century."[23] Commenting on the economic plight of black workers in the 1960s, the Civil Rights activist Tom Kahn lamented, "It is as if racism, having put the Negro in his economic place, stepped aside to watch technology destroy that place."[24] to summarize: when the industrial era started, a color occupational system kept blacks locked in low-paying jobs at the bottom of the economic ladder and concentrated them in technologically obsolete positions. When the period ended, the color occupational system still kept blacks locked in low-paying dead-end jobs at the bottom of the economic ladder and concentrated in technologically obsolete jobs. This time, however, the condition of black workers was different. The postindustrial economy was not producing enough jobs to absorb new and displaced black workers. For the first time in history, the place of

African Americans in the labor force was truly jeopardized. Sidney Wilhelm reflected on the significance of this development in his book *Who Needs the Negro?*: "With the onset of automation the Negro moves out of his historical state of oppression into one of uselessness. Increasingly, he is not so much economically exploited as he is irrelevant."[25]

A new, metropolitan-wide, urban form, characterized by a residential environment anchored by home ownership and neighborhoods stratified on the basis on housing cost and type, emerged in tandem with these economic developments.[26] In this urban setting, blacks were increasingly concentrated in central cities, while the white middle- and higher-income workers were increasingly concentrated in the suburban region. Building codes, zoning laws, subdivision regulations, and the discriminatory practices of the FHA and VA intensified the race and class stratification of the urban environment by fueling a race-based suburbanization movement in the 1950s and 1960s.[27] The suburbanization movement not only deepened residential segregation but also, as historian Thomas J. Segrue points out, it accelerated the outmigration of business and industry to the suburban region, which worsened the already fragile plight of black workers.[28] Thus by 1950 there had been a reorganization of urban residential space and places of work that increasingly concentrated blacks in the most marginal and dilapidated residential areas of the urban metropolis and spatially separated them from the most dynamic sectors of employment. In this new urban setting, increasingly blacks and whites lived in very different sections of the metropolitan region.

This *unprecedented* segregation of blacks took place at a time of unprecedented black migration to the cities. Remember, that when the industrial era started in 1900, about 83 percent of blacks lived and worked in rural areas. Fifty years later, when the industrial era came to a close and agricultural workers were displaced, over 60 percent of blacks lived in cities, and by 1970, the overwhelming majority of African Americans resided in urban areas. The central city was now the territory of African Americans.[29]

Ironically, as the Civil Rights movement tore down the color bar, the cultural middle class was able to realize its dream of residential separation from working-class and poor blacks.[30] So as blacks were being concentrated in the ghetto-slum, the cultural middle class started moving to the middle-class suburbs and into predominantly white neighborhoods. This led to the growing concentration of poverty in black neighborhoods and triggered the development of territorially based socioeconomic problems.[31]

This social transformation and reorganization of black residential life was fueled in part by the supplanting of the ideology of cultural pluralism—with its emphasis on the development of black communal life—with the ideology of integration and its emphasis on individual advancement.[32] These developments weakened agency among African Americans and made the struggle against racism and structural inequality in the post-industrial era more difficult. So, then, at the dawning of the postindustrial era, despite great victories on the Civil Rights front and a greatly expanded middle-class, African Americans were in deep trouble. In essence, then, during the rise of the postindustrial era, *agency* seemed to have weakened among African Americans at the very moment that the external forces were spawning unmatched socioeconomic challenges.[33]

Beginning in the mid-1960s, U.S. urban centers were rocked with a series of riots or urban rebellions. In retrospect, these riots were both an epilogue and prologue of the black experience in the United States. The industrial era had been a time of hope among African Americans: hope that was bolstered during the high tide of the Civil Rights movement. In the early 1960s, as the Civil Rights movement slowed and the socioeconomic problems of the northern ghettos gained prominence, it became increasingly clear that the hopes of yesterday were being dashed on rocks of the reality of postindustrial society.[34]

Looking backward in time, it seems that the epoch of long hot summers rocked by urban riots summarized decades of having dreams deferred and of living in a world where things seemed immutable, fixed in time and space; at the same time, the riots introduced the dawning of a new era when unemployment, underemployment, declining participation in the labor force, poverty, the rise of the underclass, and catastrophic social problems would replace Civil Rights as the dominant issues on the black agenda for advancement.[35] Against this backdrop economic displacement, growing unemployment, and declining labor force participation, Alba Edwards's prophesy seemed to be coming true.

> Indeed, may it possibly come to pass that a century after a war was fought largely to free the Negro slaves the descendants of the slave owners, along with other white persons, will be working to support on a permanent dole large numbers of descendants of the former slaves.[36]

Yet as the contemporary urban crisis deepened, one wondered if blacks would be able to meet the challenge of the new era by overcoming obstacles and gaining inspiration from that old Civil Rights song, "I know one thing we did right was the day we started to fight. Keep your eyes on the prize, hold on, hold on, hold on."[37]

## NOTES

1. Michael B. Katz, "Reframing the 'Underclass' Debate," in Michael B. Katz, ed., *The Underclass Debate: Views from History* (Princeton: Princeton University Press, 1993), pp. 440–477.

2. Robert C. Weaver, *Negro Labor: A National Problem* (New York: Harcourt, Brace and Company, 1946), p. 4.

3. See, for example, Chapter 2, Henry Louis Taylor, Jr., "Creating the Metropolis in Black and White" and Chapter 6, Liesl Miller Orenic and Joe W. Trotter, "African Americans in the U.S. Economy."

4. Darlene Clark Hine, "Black Migration to the Urban Midwest: The Gender Dimension, 1915–1945," in Kenneth W. Goings and Raymond A. Mohl, eds., *The New African American Urban History* (Thousand Oaks: Sage Publications, 1996), pp. 240–265.

5. See, for example, Thomas J. Sugrue, *The Origins of the Urban Crisis: Race and Inequality in Postwar Detroit* (Princeton: Princeton University Press, 1996), pp. 181–207.

6. Chapter 4, Georgina Hickey, "From Auburn Avenue to Buttermilk Bottom."

7. C. Eric Lincoln and Lawrence H. Mamiya, *The Black Church in the African American Experience* (Durham and London: Duke University Press, 1990), pp. 274–308.

8. Lincoln and Mamiya, *The Black Church*, pp. 20–46, 76–91, 115–163; Cheryl Lynn Greenberg, *"Or Does It Explode?" Black Harlem in the Great Depression* (New York and oxford: Oxford University Press, 1991): pp. 93–113.

9. Chapter 4, Hickey, "From Auburn Avenue to Buttermilk Bottom."

10. Taylor, "Prologue"; Chapter 1, Taylor and Ha, "A Unity of Opposites."

11. Chapter 4, Hickey, "From Auburn Avenue to Buttermilk Bottom," and Chapter 3, Andrea Tuttle Kornbluh, "Municipal Harmony: Cultural Pluralism, Public Recreation, and Race Relations."

12. Kenneth L. Kusmer, "The Black Urban Experience in American History," in Darlene Clark Hine, ed., *The State of Afro-American History: Past, Present, and Future* (Baton Rouge and London: Louisiana State University Press, 1986), pp. 91–122, 105.

13. Chapter 6, Orenic and Trotter, "African Americans and the U.S. Economy"; Chapter 9, Eileen Boris, "Black Workers, Trade Unions, and Labor Standards: The Wartime FEPC;" Weaver, *Negro Labor*, pp. 3–40.

14. Alba M. Edwards, "The Negro as a Factor in the Nation's Labor Force," *Journal of the American Statistical Association* 193-196 (1936): 529–540, 540.

15. Chapter 6, Orenic and Trotter, "African Americans in the U.S. Economy"; Chapter 8, Sigmund Shipp, "Building Bricks without Straw."

16. Chapter 6, Orenic and Trotter, "African Americans in the U.S. Economy"; Chapter 8: Shipp, "Building Bricks without Straw."

17. Chapter 8, Shipp, "Building Bricks without Straw."

18. Chapter 9, Boris, "Black Workers, Trade Unions, and Labor Standards."

19. Jeremy Rifkin, *The End of Work: The Decline of the Global Labor Force and the Dawn of the Post-Market Era* (New York: G. P. Putnam's Sons, 1995): p. 70.

20. Rifkin, *The End of Work*, p. 70.

21. Rifkin, *The End of Work,* pp. 73–80.

22. Arthur Butler, Henry Louis Taylor, Jr., and Doo-Ha Ryu, "Work and Black Neighborhood Life in Buffalo, 1930–1980," in Henry Louis Taylor, Jr., ed., *African Americans* and *the Rise of Buffalo's Post-Industrial City, 1940 to Present* (Buffalo: Buffalo Urban League, 1990), pp. 112–156.

23.. Rifkin, *The End of Work*, p. 73.

24. Tom Kahn, "The Problems of the Negro," *Dissent* (Winter 1964:) p. 115, cited in Rifkin, *The End of Work*, p. 74.

25. Sidney Willhelm, *Who Needs the Negro?* (Cambridge, Mass.: Schenkman, 1970), pp. 156–157, cited in Rifkin, *The End of Work*, p. 79.

26. See Chapter 2, Henry Louis Taylor, Jr., "Creating the Metropolis in Black and White."

27. Gail Radford, *Modern housing for America: Policy Struggles in the New Deal Era* (Chicago and London: University of Chicago Press, 1996), pp. 1–27, 29–57, 177–187, 199–209; Douglas S. Massey and Nancy A. Denton, *American Apartheid: Segregation and the Making of the Underclass* (Cambridge: Harvard University Press, 1993), pp. 1–16, 17–59, 60–82.

28. Thomas J. Sugrue, "The Structures of Urban Poverty: The Reorganization of Space and Work in Three Periods of American History" in Katz, ed., *The Underclass Debate,* pp. 85–117; Richard Harris, *Unplanned Suburbs: Toronto's American Tragedy, 1900 to 1950* (Baltimore and London: Johns Hopkins University Press, 1996), pp. 51–85.

29. Henry Louis Taylor, Jr., and Walter Hill, "Prologue"; Massey and Denton, *American Apartheid*, pp. 60–82.

30. E. Franklin Frazier, "Negro Harlem: An Ecological Study," *American Journal of Sociology* 43 (1937–1938): 72–88.

31. William Julius Wilson, *The Truly Disadvantaged: The Inner City, the Underclass, and Public Policy* (Chicago and London: University of Chicago

Press, 1987), p. 143; William Julius Wilson, *When Work Disappears: The World of the New Urban Poor* (New York: Alfred A. Knopf, 1996), pp. 3–24, 25–50, 51–86; Kenneth B. Clark, *Dark Ghetto: Dilemmas of Social Power* (New York: Harper and Row, 1965), pp. 21–62.

32. Andrea Tuttle Kornbluh, "From Culture to Cuisine: Twentieth-Century Views of Race and Ethnicity in the City," in Howard Gillette, Jr., and Zane L. Miller, eds., *American Urbanism: A Historiographical Review* (New York and Westport, Conn.: Greenwood Press, 1987), pp. 49–71.

33. For example, during the industrial era, black teachers, preachers, entrepreneurs, and workers were the driving forces behind black community development. In the postindustrial era, schools were greatly weakened as the black school teacher became an endangered species. Black neighborhood businesses were also greatly weakened, workers were deproletariatized, and churches lost their fabled positions in the black community. Kenneth L. Kusmer, "African Americans in the City since World War II: From the Industrial to the Postindustrial Era," in Goings and Mohl, eds., *The New African American Urban History*, pp. 320–368; Robin D. G. Kelley, *Race Rebels: Culture, Politics, and the Black Working Class* (New York: The Free Press, 1994), pp. 183–227; Paul A. Jargowsky, *Poverty and Place: Ghettos, Barrios, and the American City* (New York: Russell Sage Foundation), pp. 89–115; Scott Cummings, *Left Behind in Rosedale: Race Relations and the Collapse of Community Institutions* (Boulder: Westview Press, 1998), pp. 28–47.

34. Kenneth B. Clark, *Dark Ghetto: Dilemmas of Social Power* (New York: Harper and Row, 1965), pp. 21–62.

35. Henry Louis Taylor, Jr., "Introduction: Race and the City, 1920–1970," in Taylor, ed., *Race and the City*, pp. 20–21.

36. Edwards, "The Negro as a Factor in the Nation's Labor Force," *Journal of the American Statistical Association* 31(1936): 540.

37. Juan Williams, *Eyes on the Prize: America's Civil Rights Years, 1954–1965* (New York: Penguin Books, 1988), p. viii.

# Contributors

**Eileen Boris,** after teaching for fourteen years at Howard University, became professor of Studies in Women and Gender at the University of Virginia in the fall of 1998. Among her books is *Home to Work: Motherhood and the Politics of Industrial Homework in the United States* (1994), winner of the 1995 Philip Taft Prize in Labor History. She is currently writing a history of employment and welfare policy since World War II that highlights the rights of mothers and other working people.

**Vicky Dula,** former director of research at the Center for Urban Studies, School of Architecture and Planning, State University of New York at Buffalo, is an employment counselor at the University of Cincinnati. She coauthored with Henry Louis Taylor, Jr., "The Black Residential Experience and Community Formation in Antebellum Cincinnati," in Henry Louis Taylor, Jr., ed., *Race and the City: Work, Community and Protest in Cincinnati, 1820–1970* (1993).

**Song-Ho Ha** is a Ph.D. candidate in the History Department at the State University of New York at Buffalo. He is finishing a dissertation that analyzes the political aspects of U.S. government economic policies between 1801 and 1929. He has received numerous fellowships and grants, including a Fulbright Fellowship.

**Georgina Hickey** received her Ph.D. from the University of Michigan in 1995. She is an assistant professor of History at Georgia Southern University, where she teaches urban and labor history. She is currently completing a book on working-class women in Atlanta at the turn of the century.

**Andrea Tuttle Kornbluh** is an associate professor of History at the Raymond Walters College of the University of Cincinnati. She has published essays on urban history, race relations, and women's activism. She is currently working on a history of public recreation in Cincinnati during the industrial era, which examines the practice and ideology of tax-supported public recreation. She has also served as research director on various video documentaries.

**Liesl Miller Orenic** is a Ph.D. student in the Department of History at Carnegie Mellon University. Her research interest is in U.S. labor history.

**Mark Naison** is a professor of African-American Studies and History at Fordham University and directs its Urban Studies Program. He is the author of *Communists in Harlem During the Depression* (1993), is coauthor of the *Tenants Movement in New York City, 1904–1984* (1987), and is currently working on a memoir for Temple University Press entitled *Whiteboy: Reflections of a Life between Racial Boundaries.*

**Sigmund Shipp** is an associate professor in the Department of Urban Affairs and Planning at Hunter College in New York City. His research focuses on black business development.

**Henry Louis Taylor, Jr.,** is an associate professor in the Department of Planning at the State University of New York at Buffalo and is founder and director of the Center for Urban Studies. Taylor is the editor of two books, *African Americans and the Rise of Buffalo's Post-Industrial City, 1940 to the Present* (1990) and *Race and the City: Work, Community and Protest in Cincinnati, 1820–1970* (1993). He is currently completing a book entitled, *Menace to the City: Black Suburbanization and the Planning Movement in Cincinnati, 1900 to 1950.* Taylor is a historian, urban planner, and social commentator. He has written numerous essays and technical reports and has received several awards for his planning activities. In 1998, *Business First*, western New York's leading business newspaper, named him one of the one hundred most influential people in western New York. Taylor was the only scholar named to this list.

**Joe W. Trotter** is a professor of history at Carnegie Mellon University and is author of numerous books and articles on labor history and the black urban experience. Trotter is best known for his groundbreaking book, *Black Milwaukee: The Making of an Industrial Proletariat, 1915–1945* (1987).

**Andrew Wiese** is an associate professor of U.S. History at San Diego State University. His scholarly interests focus on the development of U.S. cities and suburbs in the 20th century, especially African American suburbanization, working-class home building, and the impact of race in the housing market. He has published essays in the *Journal of American History*, the *Journal of Urban History* and the *Journal of Social History*. He is currently completing a book on black suburbanization since 1916.

**Walter Hill** is a senior archivist/subject area specialist for African American History, Textual Reference Division, National Archives and Records Administration. He has published articles on the black experience in various journals, including the *Journal of Blacks in Higher Education*. He is also vice-president of the Association for the Study of Afro-American Life and History.

# Index